美

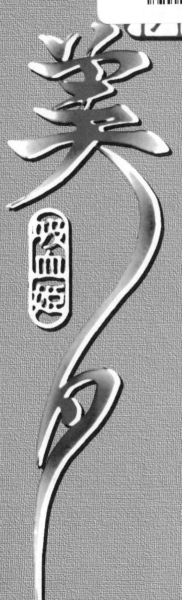

Studio Ironcat Presents:

NEW VAMPIRE MIYU
EPISODE V:
THE WRATH OF MIYU

STORY AND ART BY TOSHIHIRO HIRANO & NARUMI KAKINOUCHI

MANAGER & EDITOR: Kevin Bennett
ART DIRECTOR: Steven R. Bennett IV
TRANSLATOR: Sachiko Uchida
COVER DESIGN: Doug Smith
COPY EDITING: Stephanie Brown
ASSISTANT: Elaine Turner

This volume contains New Vampire Miyu Volume V in its entirety.

NEW VAMPIRE MIYU™ Graphi Novel Volume V. June 2001. ©1994 Naru Kakinouchi. Originally published by Akita Pub. Co.; Tokyo, Japan. English translation rights arranged between Akita Pub. Co. Ltd. and Studio Ironcat L.L.C. All rights reserved. Nothing from this book may be reproduced witho written consent from the right holders. Violators will be published to the full extent of the laws of the United States of America. All persons, places, and events depicted in this volume are ficticious. Any resmblence toactual pers places, or events is entirely coincidental. **PRINTED IN CANADA.**

Studio Ironcat L.L.C.
607 William Street, Suite #213
Fredericksburg, VA 22401

新

美

吸血姫

五

しん　ヴァンパイアミュ

平野俊弘
ひらの　としひろ
原案
げんあん

垣野内成美
かきのうちなるみ
構成
こうせい

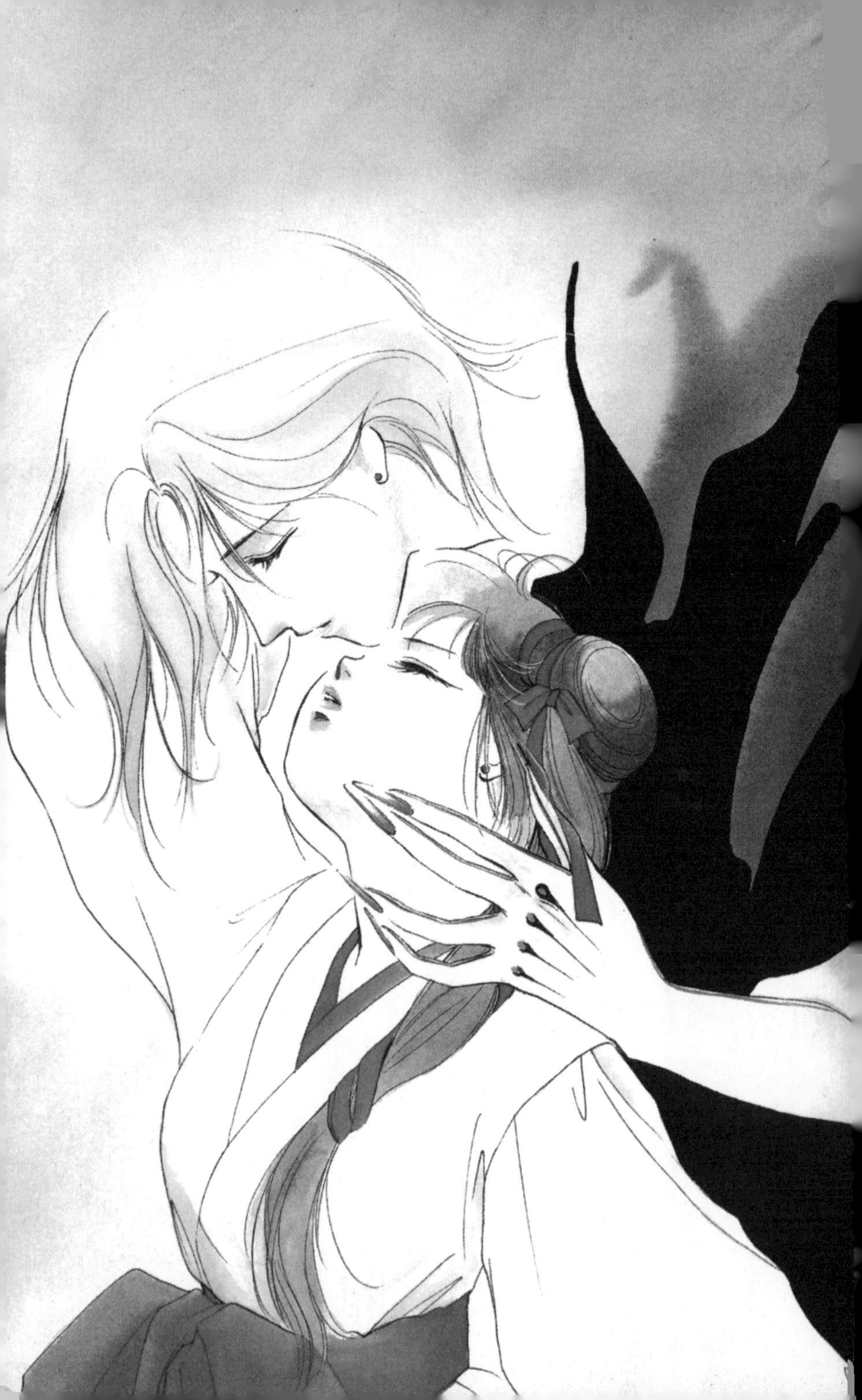

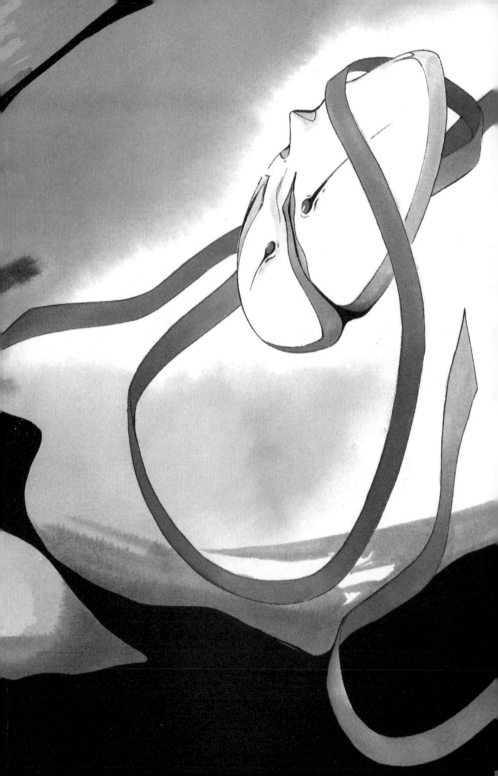

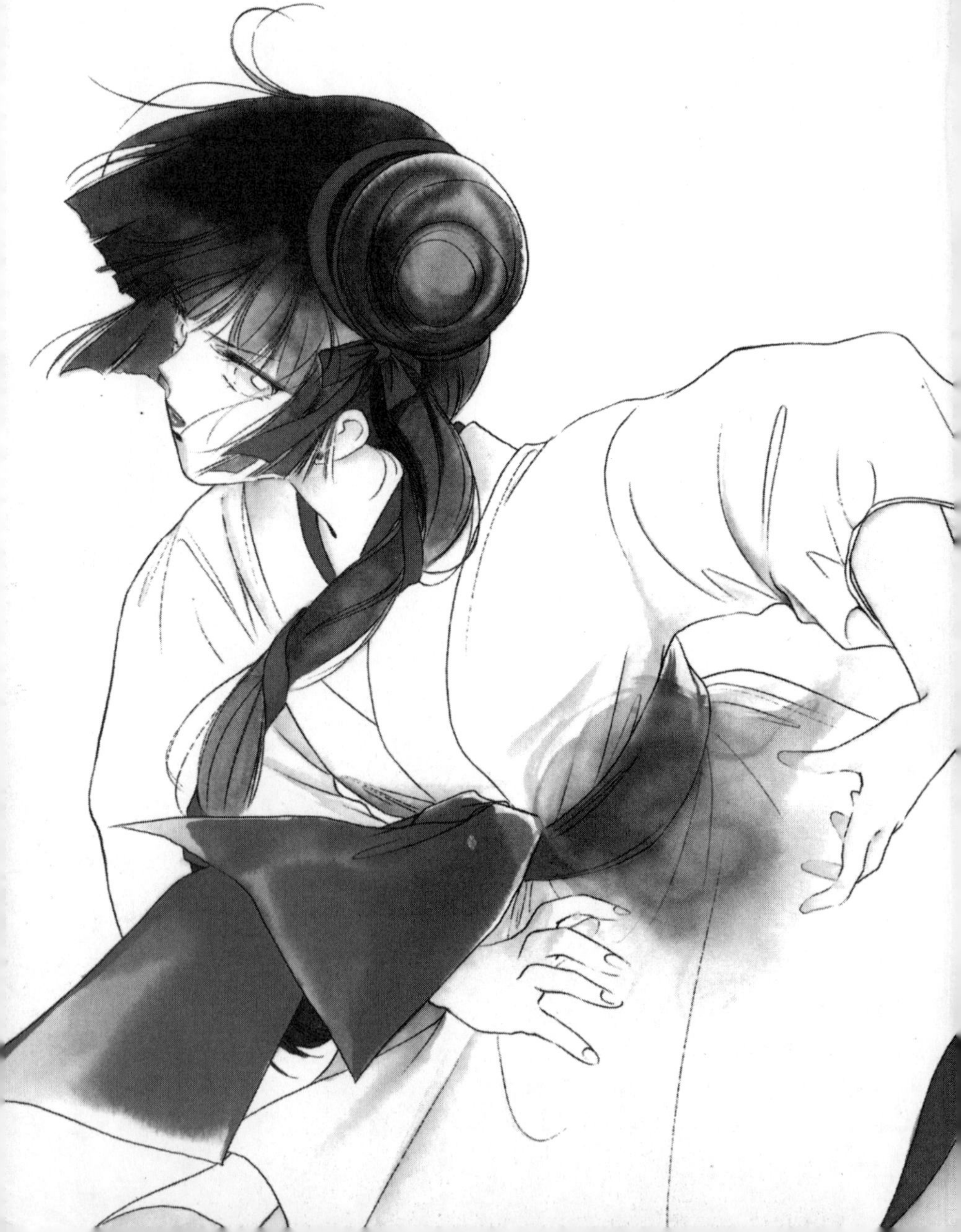

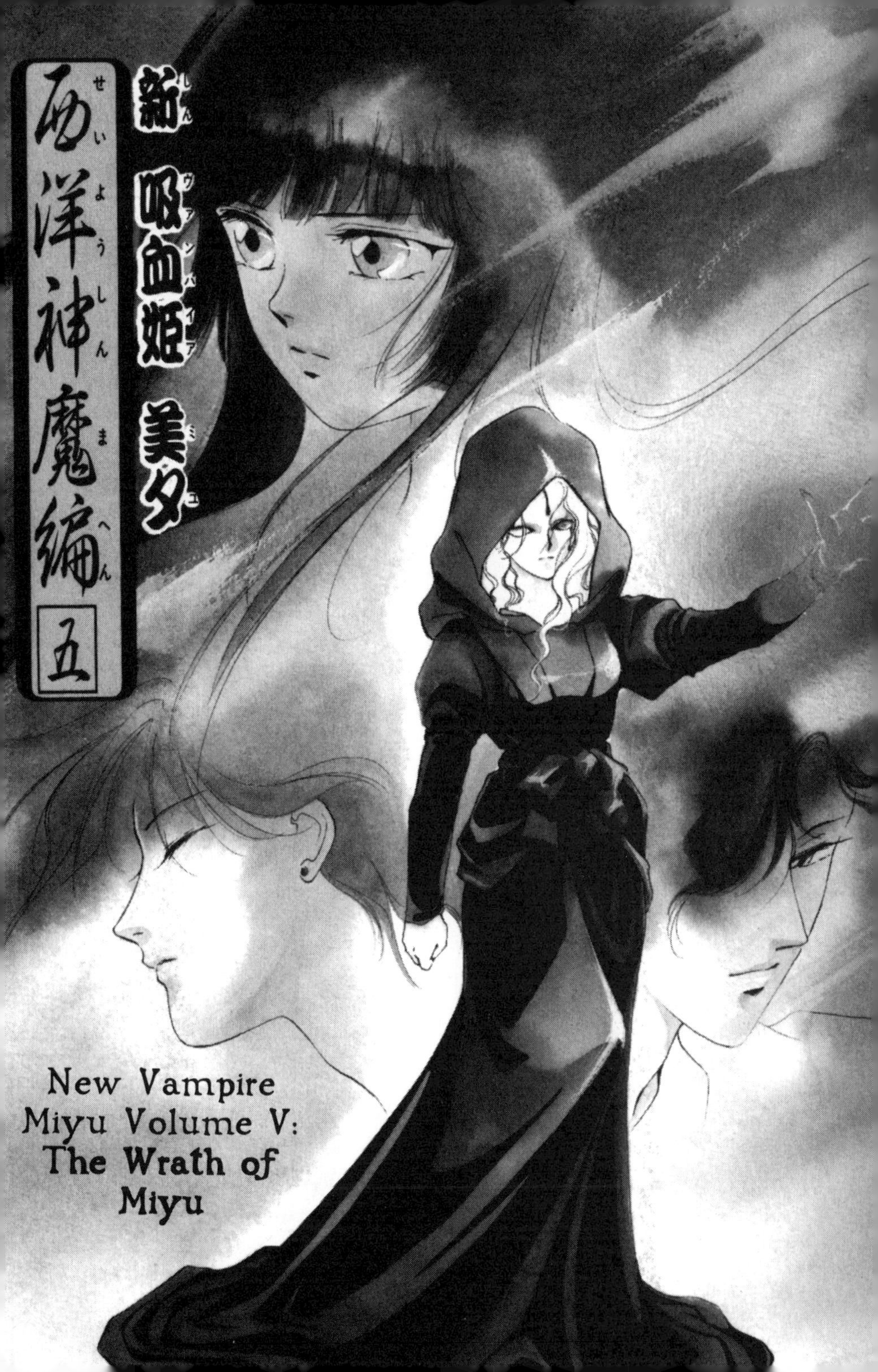
新吸血姫 美夕
西洋神魔編
五
New Vampire Miyu Volume V: The Wrath of Miyu

Japanese Shinma (Second Tier)

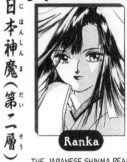

日本神魔（第二層）

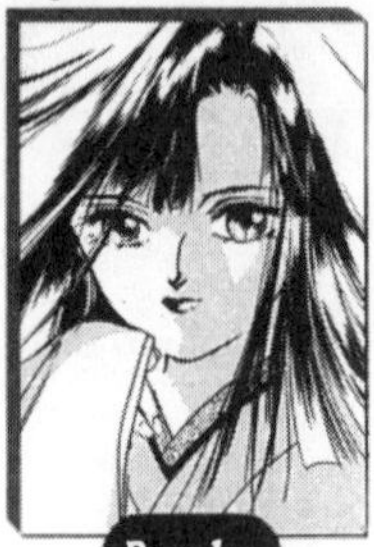

Ranka

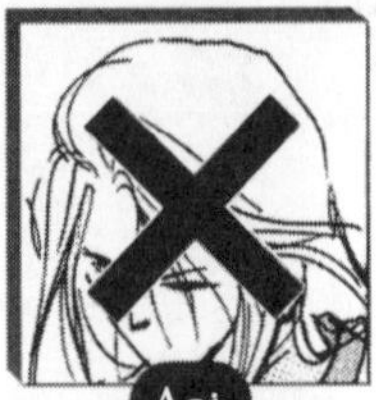

Aoi

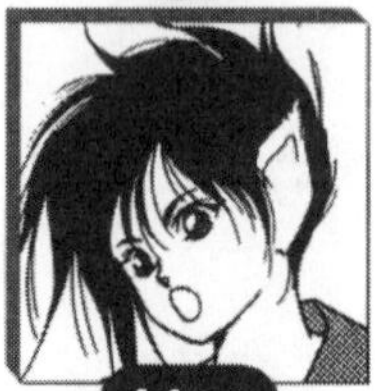

Ichiro

THE JAPANESE SHINMA REALM IS DIVIDED INTO FIVE TIERS. RANKA IS THE OVERSEER OF THE 2ND CLASS. AOI AND ICHIRO WORK UNDER HER.

The Shi Clan

鬼一族

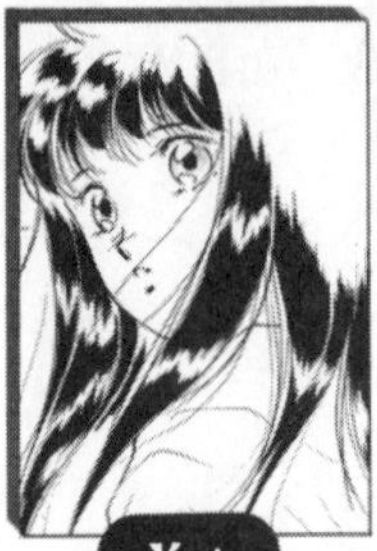

Yui

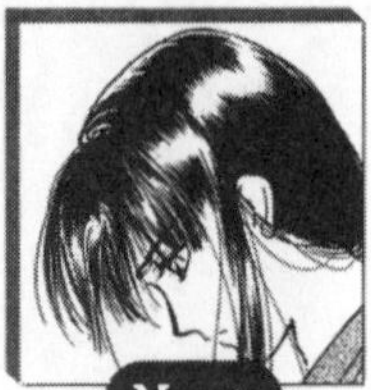

Nagi

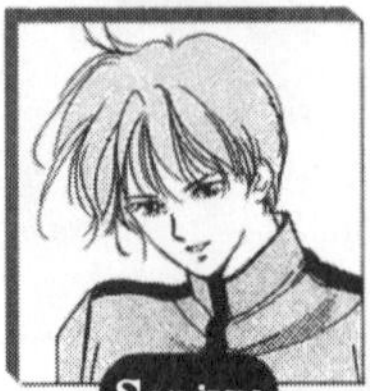

Senjyu

THE SHI IS THE OPPOSITE CLAN OF THE JAPANESE SHINMA. YUI IS THE PRINCESS OF THIS CLAN AND WAS BAPTIZED WITH MIYU'S BLOOD.

The Western Shinma

西洋神魔

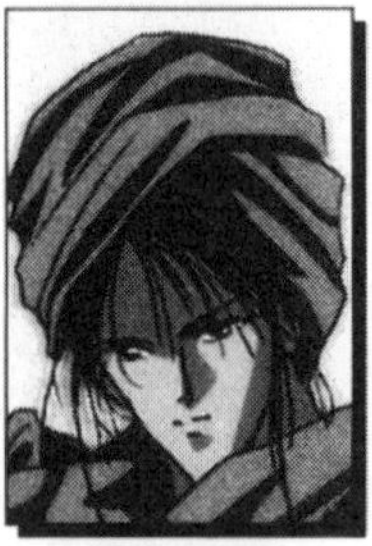

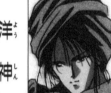

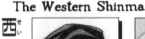

Pazusu

THE ELDEST OF THE WESTERN SHINMA. HE WAS LIKE A FATHER TO BOTH LARVA AND CARLUA, HAVING TAUGHT LARVA ALL HIS TRICKS.

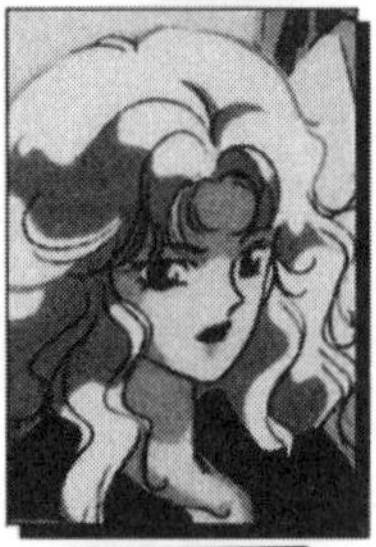

Carlua

SHE WAS RAISED ALMOST LIKE A SISTER TO LARVA AND HAS A STRONG ATTACHMENT TO HIM.

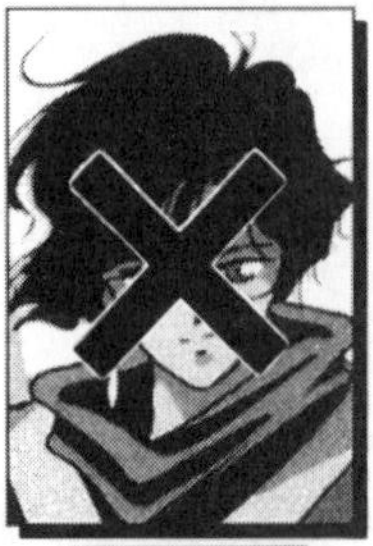

Lemunia

LEMULE'S BROTHER WHO CAME TO THE JAPANESE SHINMA REALM WITH LARVA BUT WAS KILLED BY THE FOUR QUARLS.

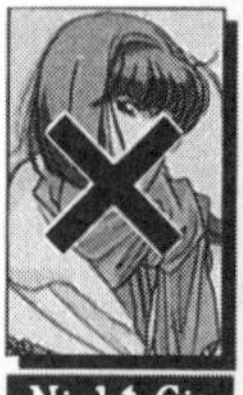

Night Gia

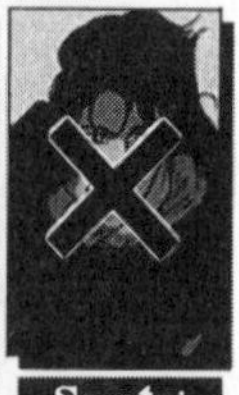

Spartoi

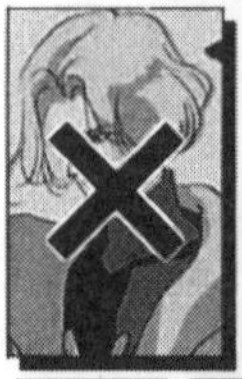

Amy

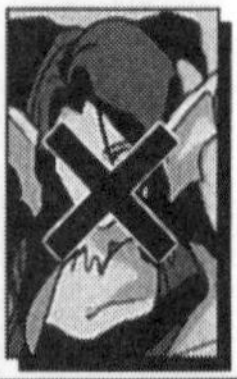

Water Lipper

The Quarls

ケアル一族

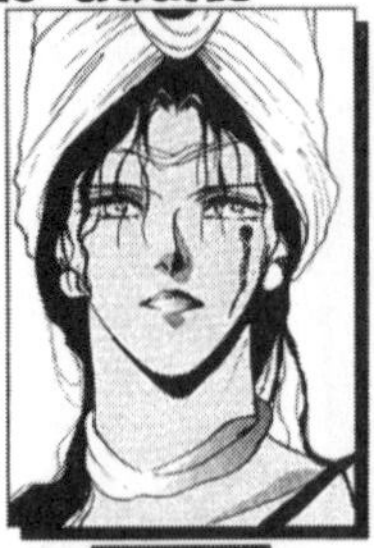

Quarl

THE QUEEN OF THE QUARLS. LONG AGO, SHE ATTACKED THE JAPANESE SHINMA AND WAS DEFEATED BY MIYU'S GRANDPARENT.

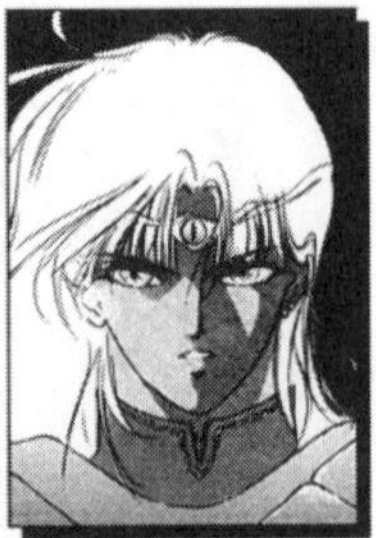

Cait Sith

THE PRINCE OF THE WESTERN SHINMA AND QUARLS. HE'S BEEN ON A QUEST TO FREE HIS MOTHER, QUARL, FROM HER TOMB.

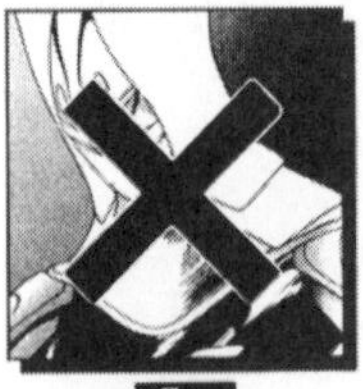

Gia

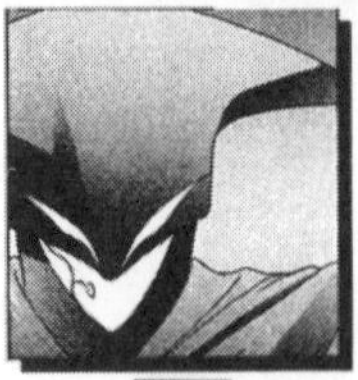

Gigi

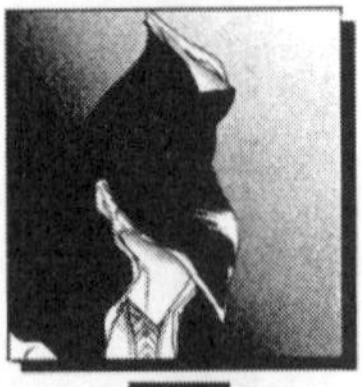

Gio

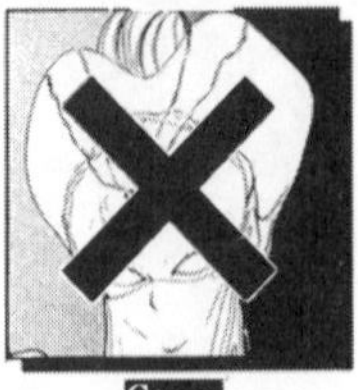

Gima

★

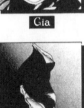

The story through the previous volume, in brief:

A group of Western Shinma have invaded the Japanese Shinma world, led by Cait-Sith of the Quarl Clan! The first opponent they encountered was Miyu, the watcher, and after a series of battles, Miyu is killed. The fatal blow came from Larva, her servant. He once again became allied with his Western Shinma brethren by a mysterious spell.

Miyu was the Japanese Shinma's only hope to fight against these foreign invaders. While Ranka and Aoi fought against Larva and Spartoi, Yui and Ichiro hurried to the realm where Miyu's soul was sleeping so they could revive her.

Cait-Sith had one other thing on his agenda: the revival of his lost mother, the Queen Quarl! For this task, he enlisted the help of the Four Quarls. Gia, Gigi and Gio were sent to find Yui and stop her from resurrecting Miyu, while Gima and Cait-Sith journeyed to a place protected by the Japanese Shinma Aoi. There rested the key to his mother's resurrection. Aoi staunchly refused to hand over the key, but in a treacherous exchange of Gima's life, Cait-Sith got what he wanted.

A severely wounded Yui, enduring attacks from both the Quarls and the enigmatic Shiki Clan, finally reached Miyu and revived her. This was the first step in the Japanese Shinmas' revenge. However, the Queen Quarl had also awakened from her long slumber. An unsuspecting Aoi, who had been pursuing Cait-Sith, encountered the Queen and lost his life as a result.

Up until now, both sides have suffered heavy casualties. the survivors are gearing up for a battle to avenge their fallen comrades! Who will come out victorious, the Japanese Shinma or the Western invaders?

The final showdown is set to begin...

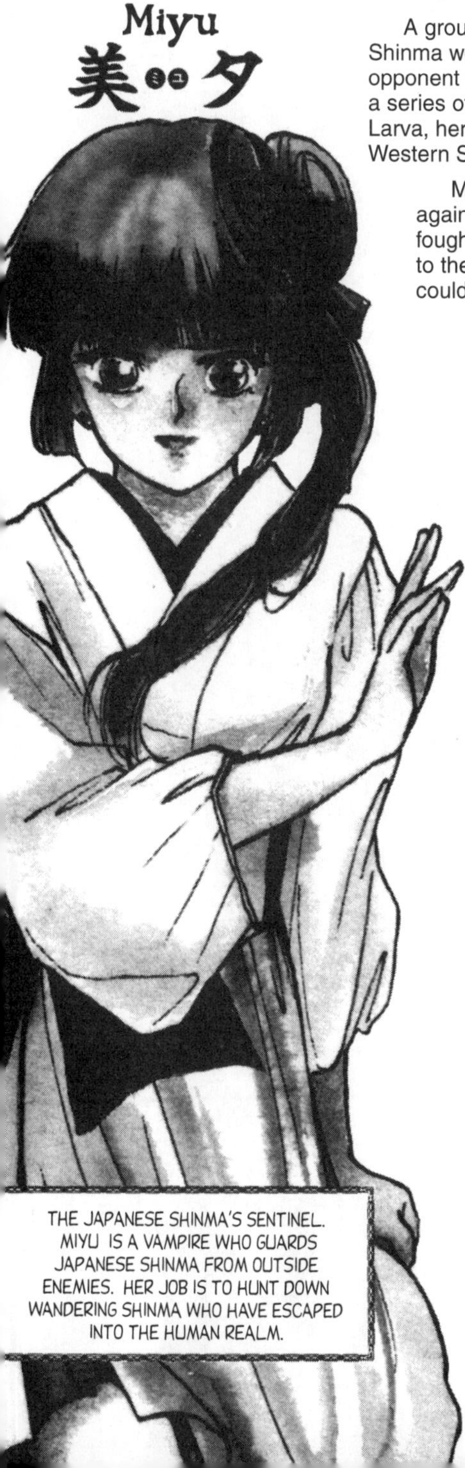
Miyu
美夕
THE JAPANESE SHINMA'S SENTINEL. MIYU IS A VAMPIRE WHO GUARDS JAPANESE SHINMA FROM OUTSIDE ENEMIES. HER JOB IS TO HUNT DOWN WANDERING SHINMA WHO HAVE ESCAPED INTO THE HUMAN REALM.

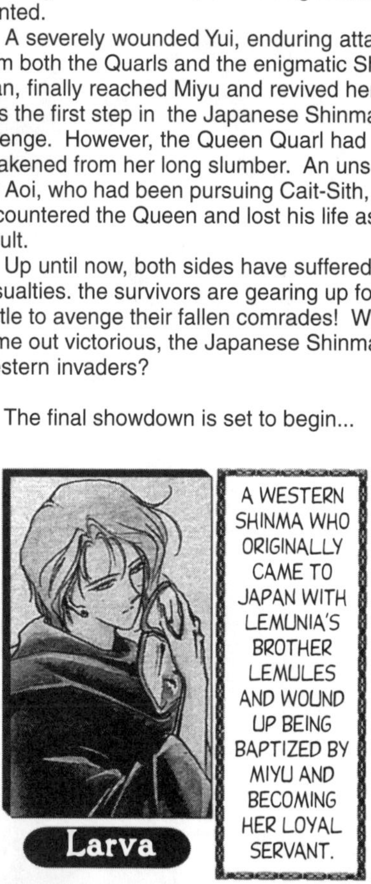
Larva
A WESTERN SHINMA WHO ORIGINALLY CAME TO JAPAN WITH LEMUNIA'S BROTHER LEMULES AND WOUND UP BEING BAPTIZED BY MIYU AND BECOMING HER LOYAL SERVANT.

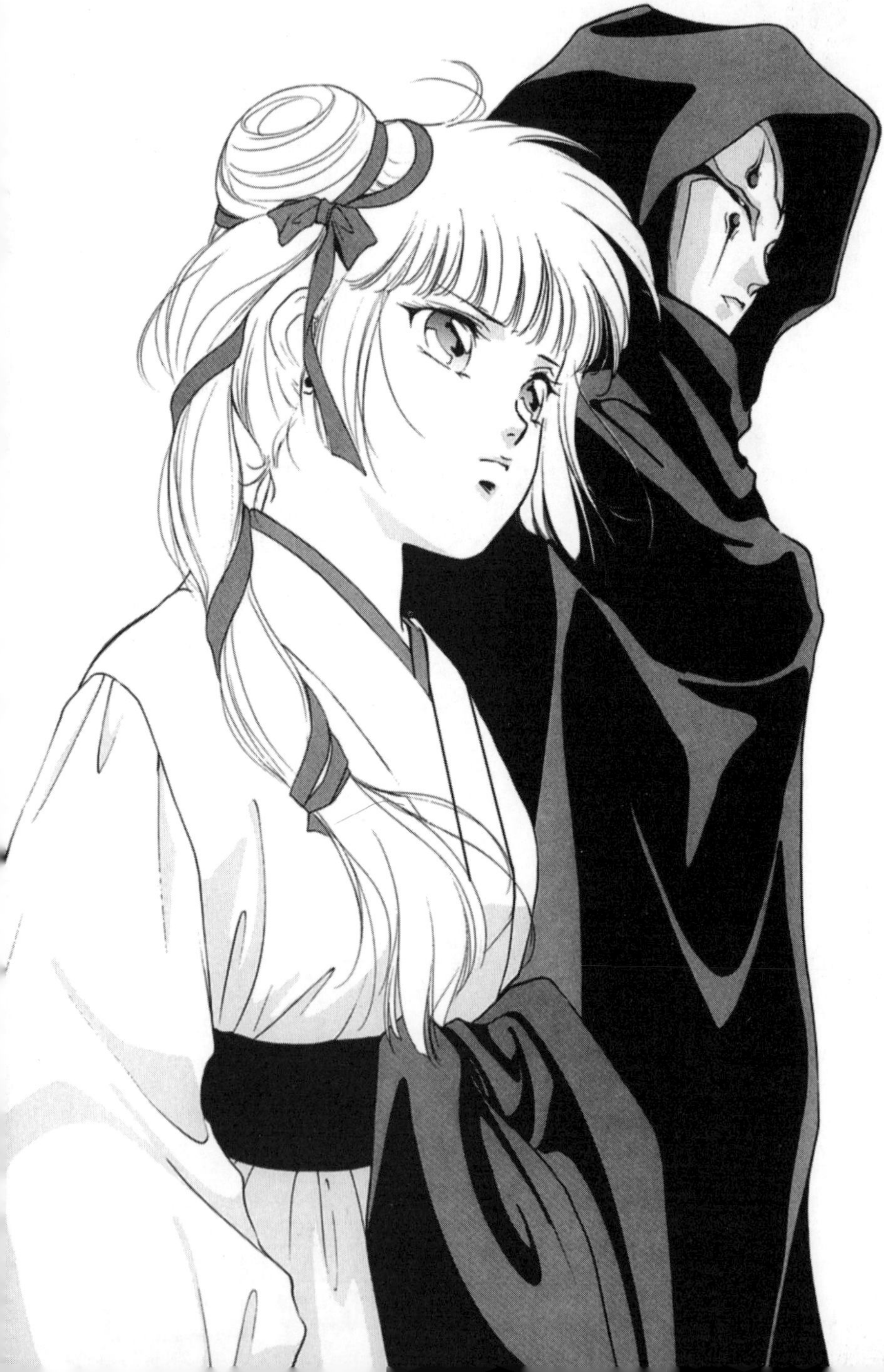

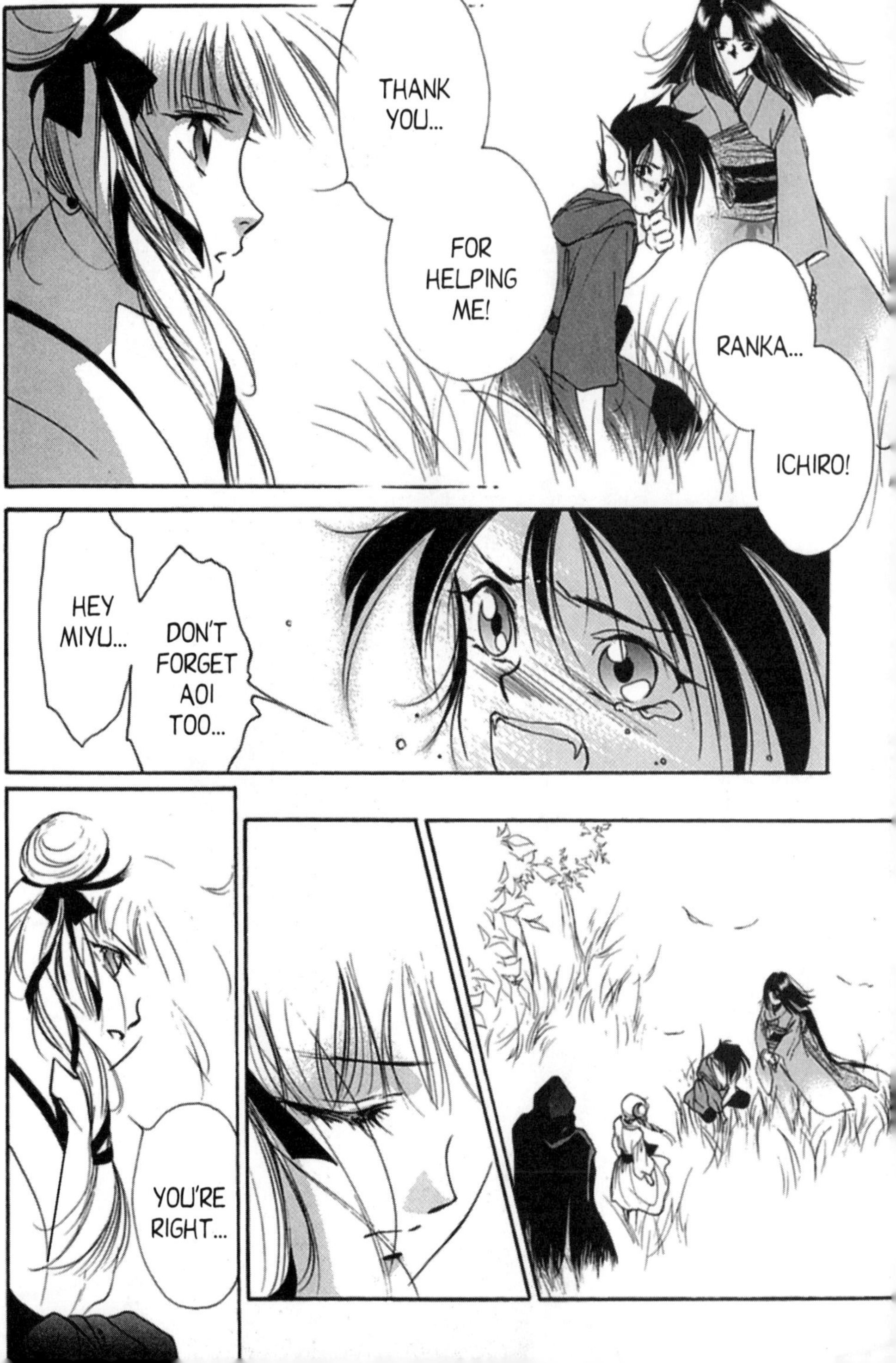
THANK YOU...
FOR HELPING ME!
RANKA...
ICHIRO!
HEY MIYU...
DON'T FORGET AOI TOO...
YOU'RE RIGHT...

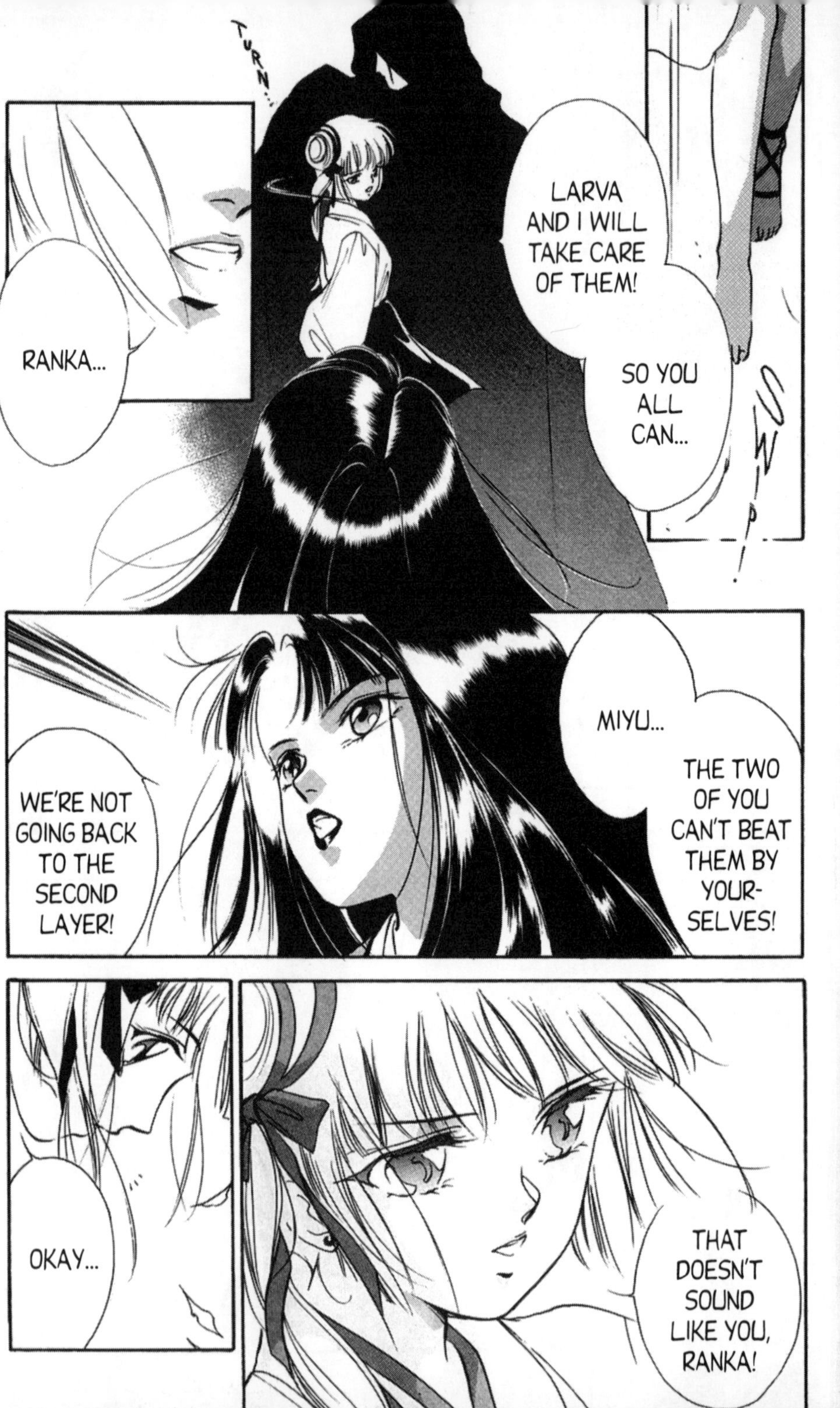

TURN...
LARVA AND I WILL TAKE CARE OF THEM!
SO YOU ALL CAN...
SWIP!
RANKA...
MIYU...
THE TWO OF YOU CAN'T BEAT THEM BY YOUR-SELVES!
WE'RE NOT GOING BACK TO THE SECOND LAYER!
THAT DOESN'T SOUND LIKE YOU, RANKA!
OKAY...

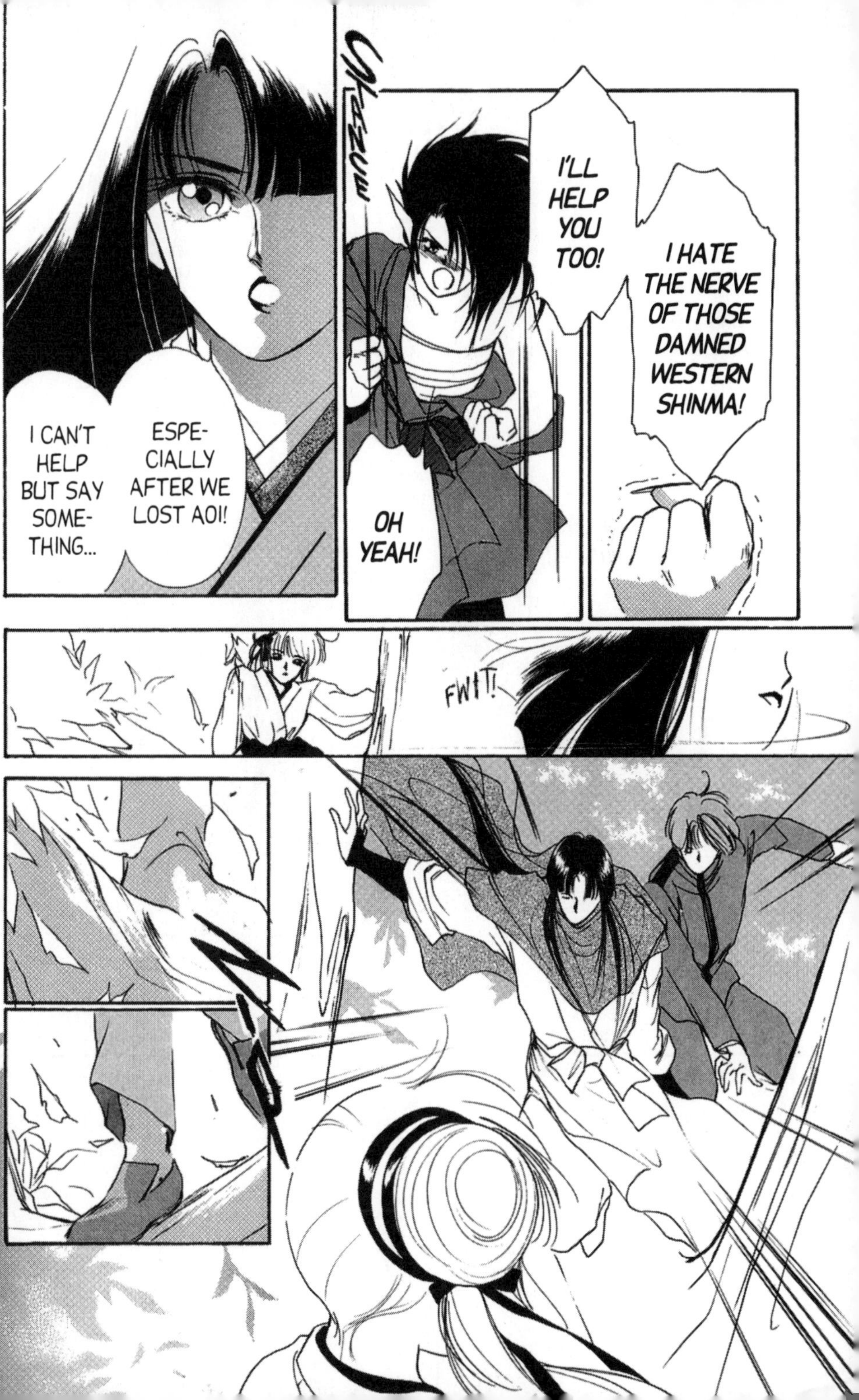
I CAN'T HELP BUT SAY SOME-THING...
ESPE-CIALLY AFTER WE LOST AOI!
OH YEAH!
I'LL HELP YOU TOO!
I HATE THE NERVE OF THOSE DAMNED WESTERN SHINMA!
FWIT!

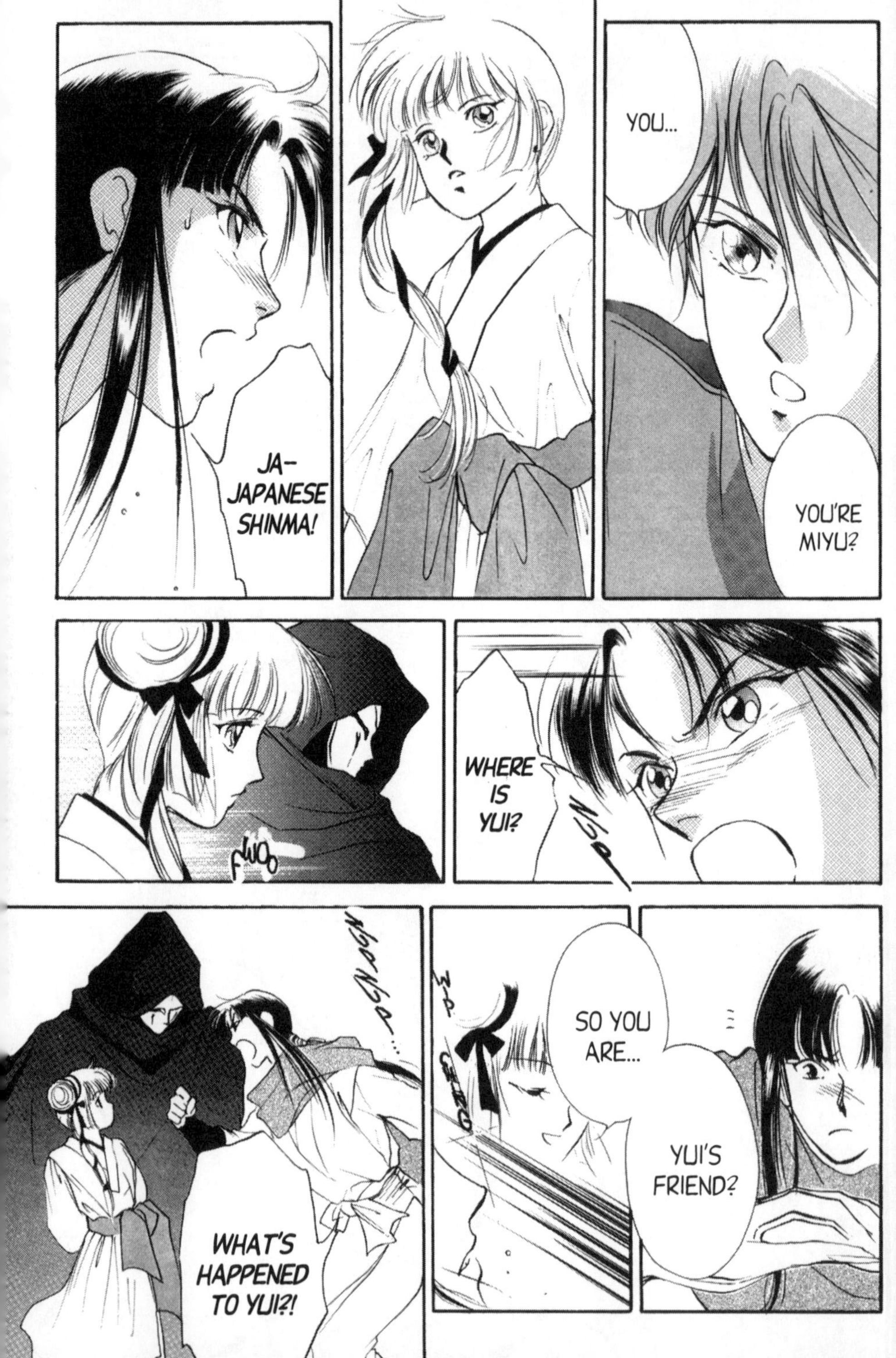
YOU...
YOU'RE MIYU?
JA- JAPANESE SHINMA!
WHERE IS YUI?
FWOO
SO YOU ARE...
YUI'S FRIEND?
WHAT'S HAPPENED TO YUI?!

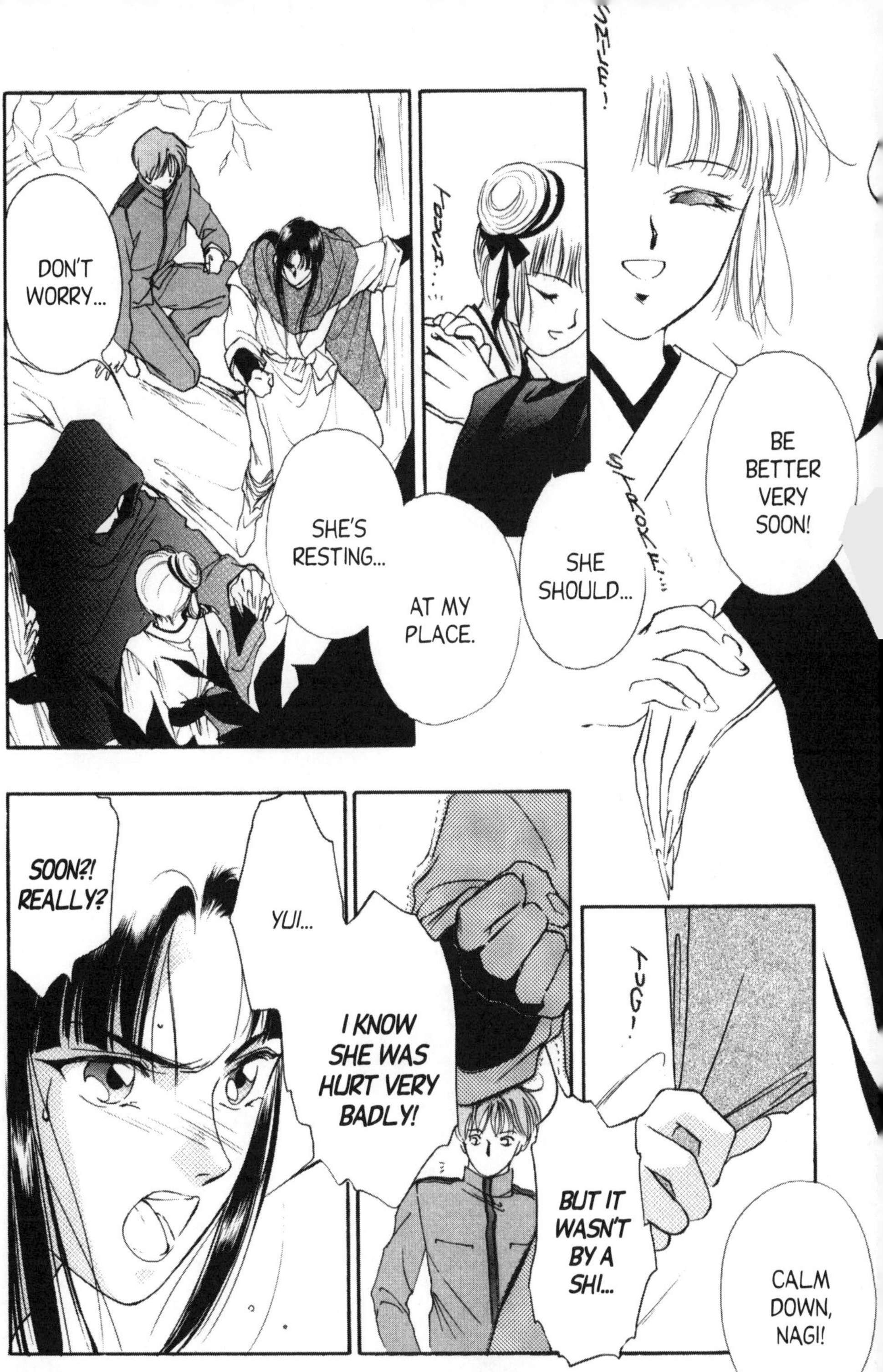
SMILE!
DON'T WORRY...
SHE'S RESTING...
AT MY PLACE.
STROKE!...
SHE SHOULD...
BE BETTER VERY SOON!
SOON?! REALLY?
YUI...
I KNOW SHE WAS HURT VERY BADLY!
TUG!
BUT IT WASN'T BY A SHI...
CALM DOWN, NAGI!

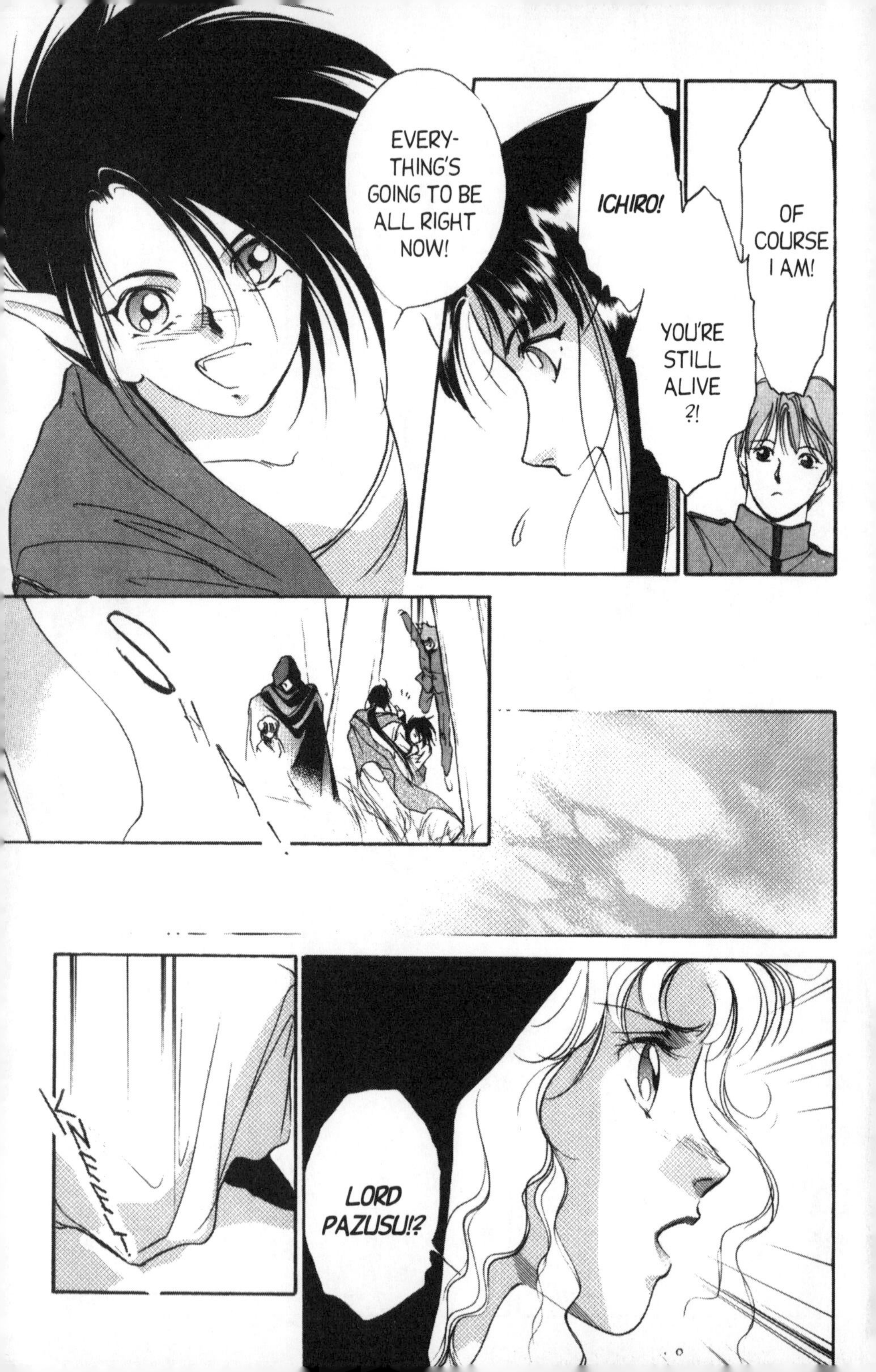
ICHIRO!
YOU'RE STILL ALIVE ?!
OF COURSE I AM!
EVERY-THING'S GOING TO BE ALL RIGHT NOW!
LORD PAZUSU!?

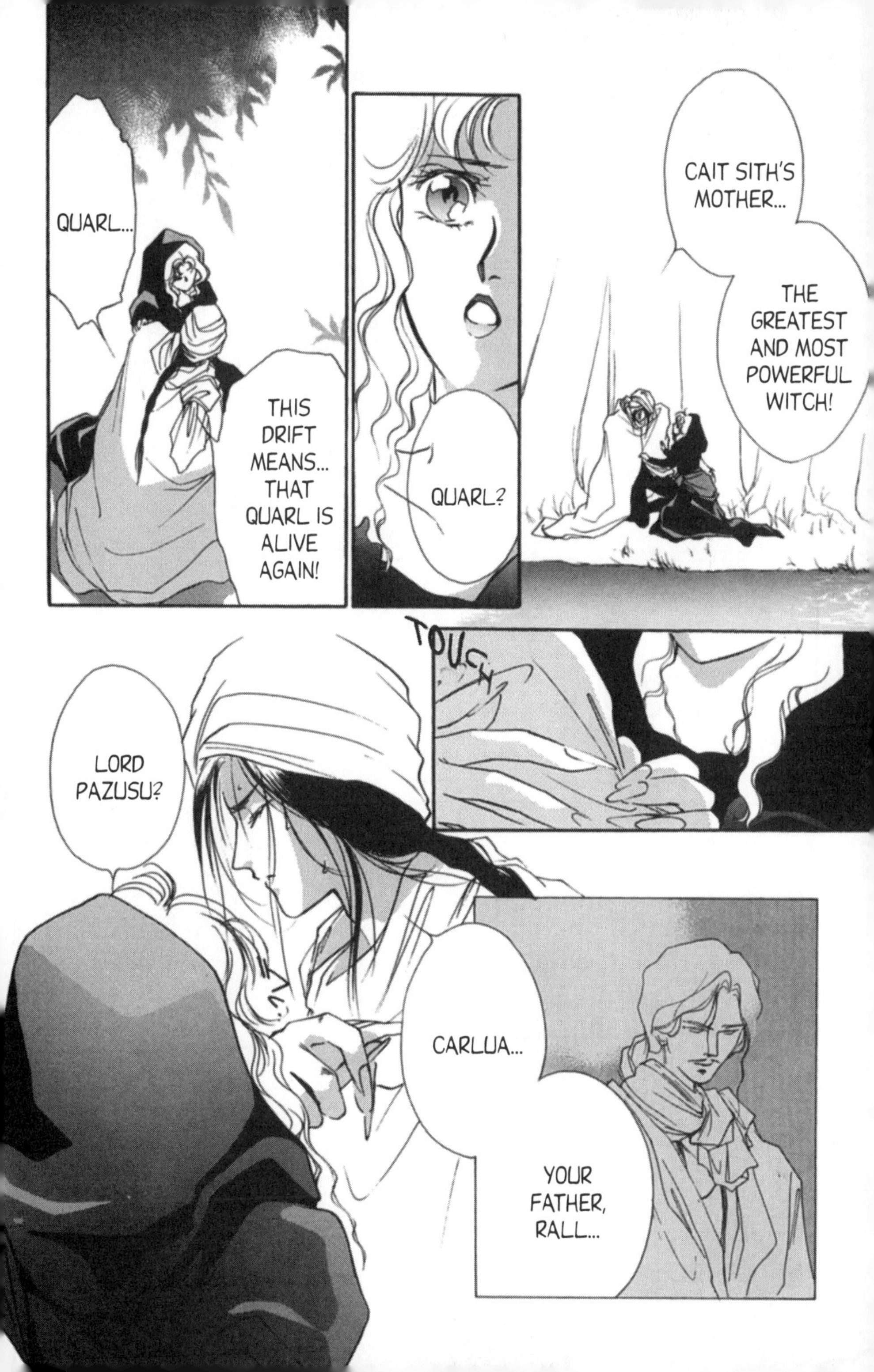
QUARL...
THIS DRIFT MEANS... THAT QUARL IS ALIVE AGAIN!
QUARL?
CAIT SITH'S MOTHER...
THE GREATEST AND MOST POWERFUL WITCH!
TOUCH
LORD PAZUSU?
CARLUA...
YOUR FATHER, RALL...

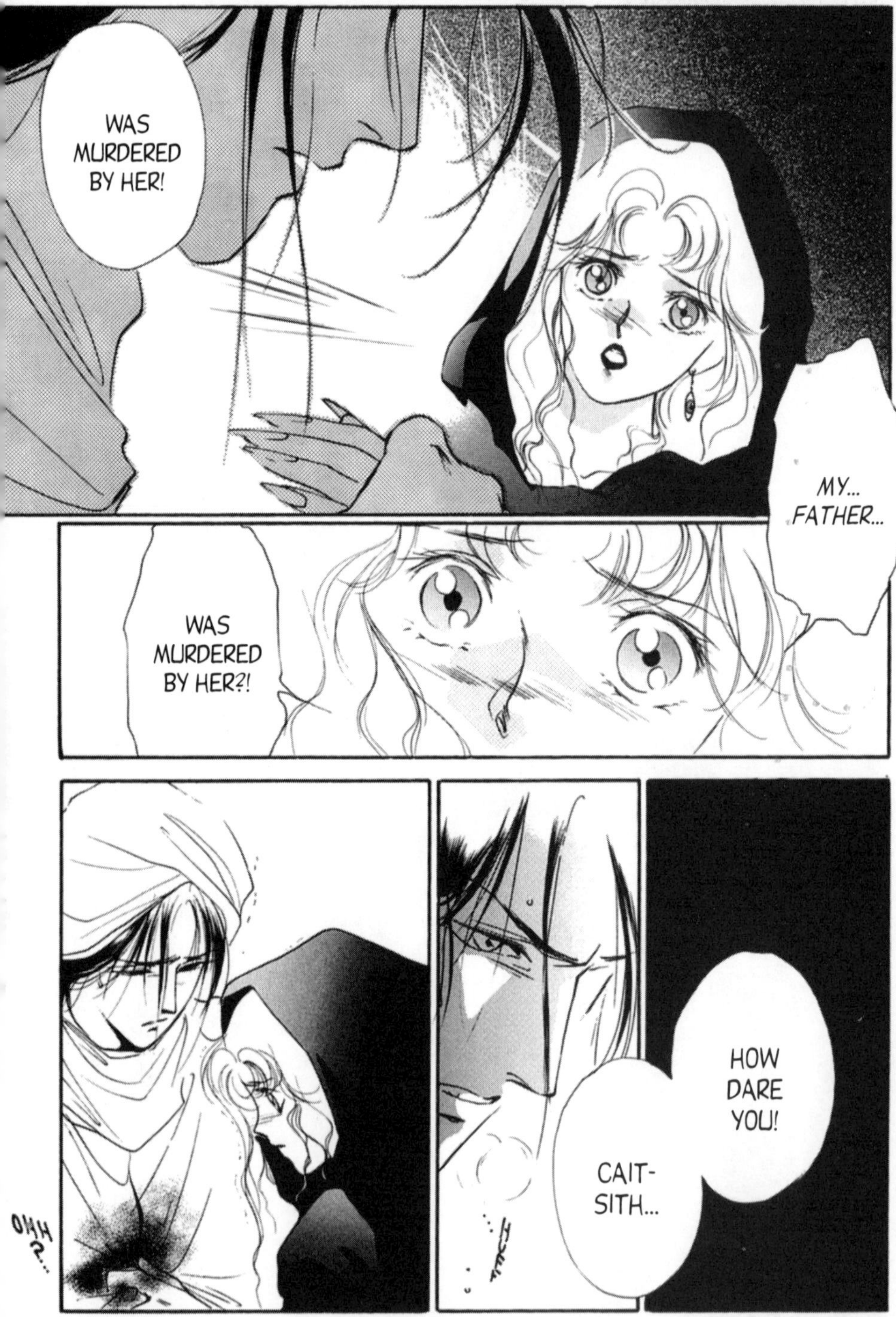
WAS MURDERED BY HER!
MY... FATHER...
WAS MURDERED BY HER?!
HOW DARE YOU!
CAIT-SITH...

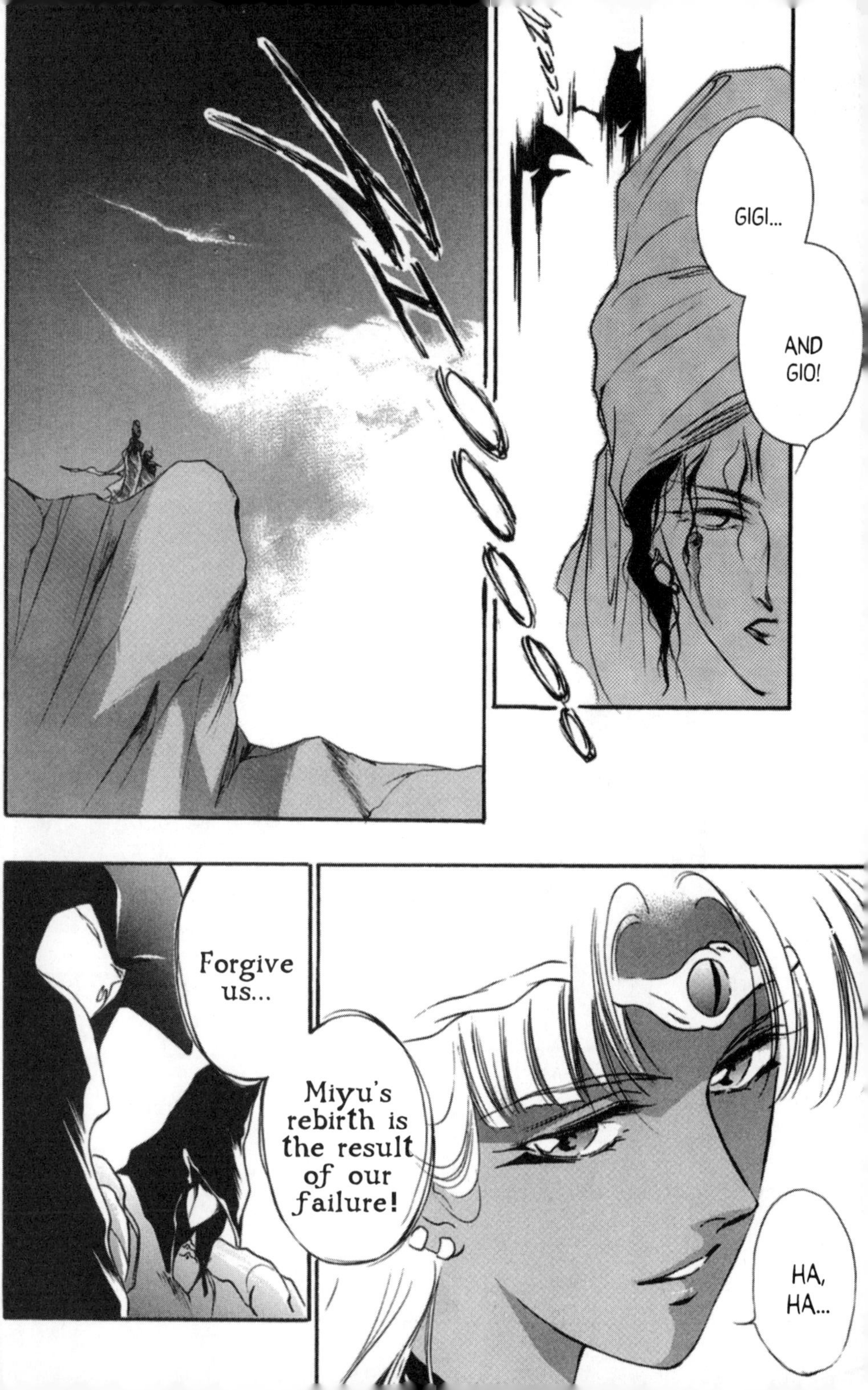
GIGI...
AND GIO!
HA, HA...
Forgive us...
Miyu's rebirth is the result of our failure!

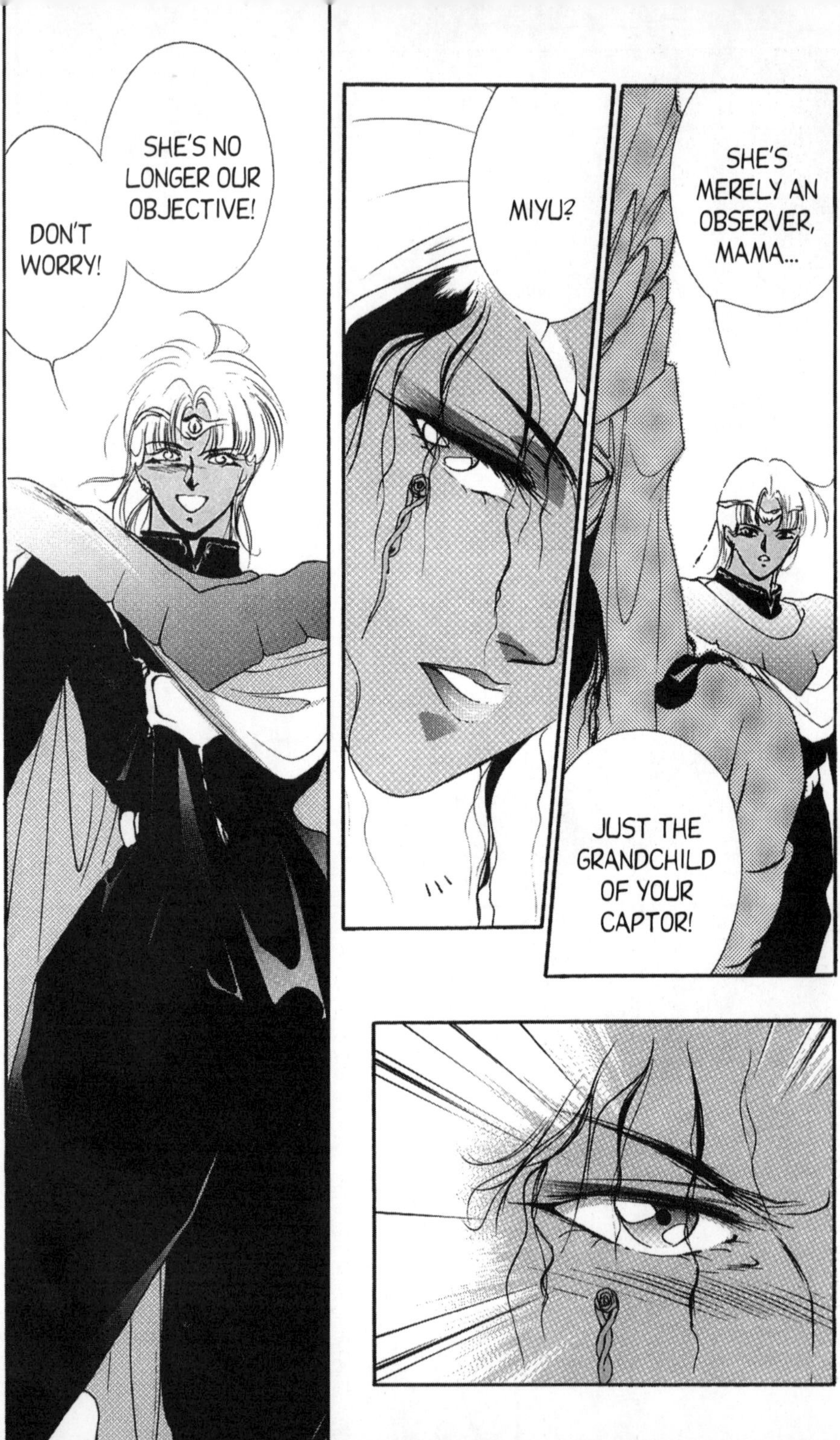
DON'T WORRY!
SHE'S NO LONGER OUR OBJECTIVE!
MIYU?
SHE'S MERELY AN OBSERVER, MAMA...
JUST THE GRANDCHILD OF YOUR CAPTOR!

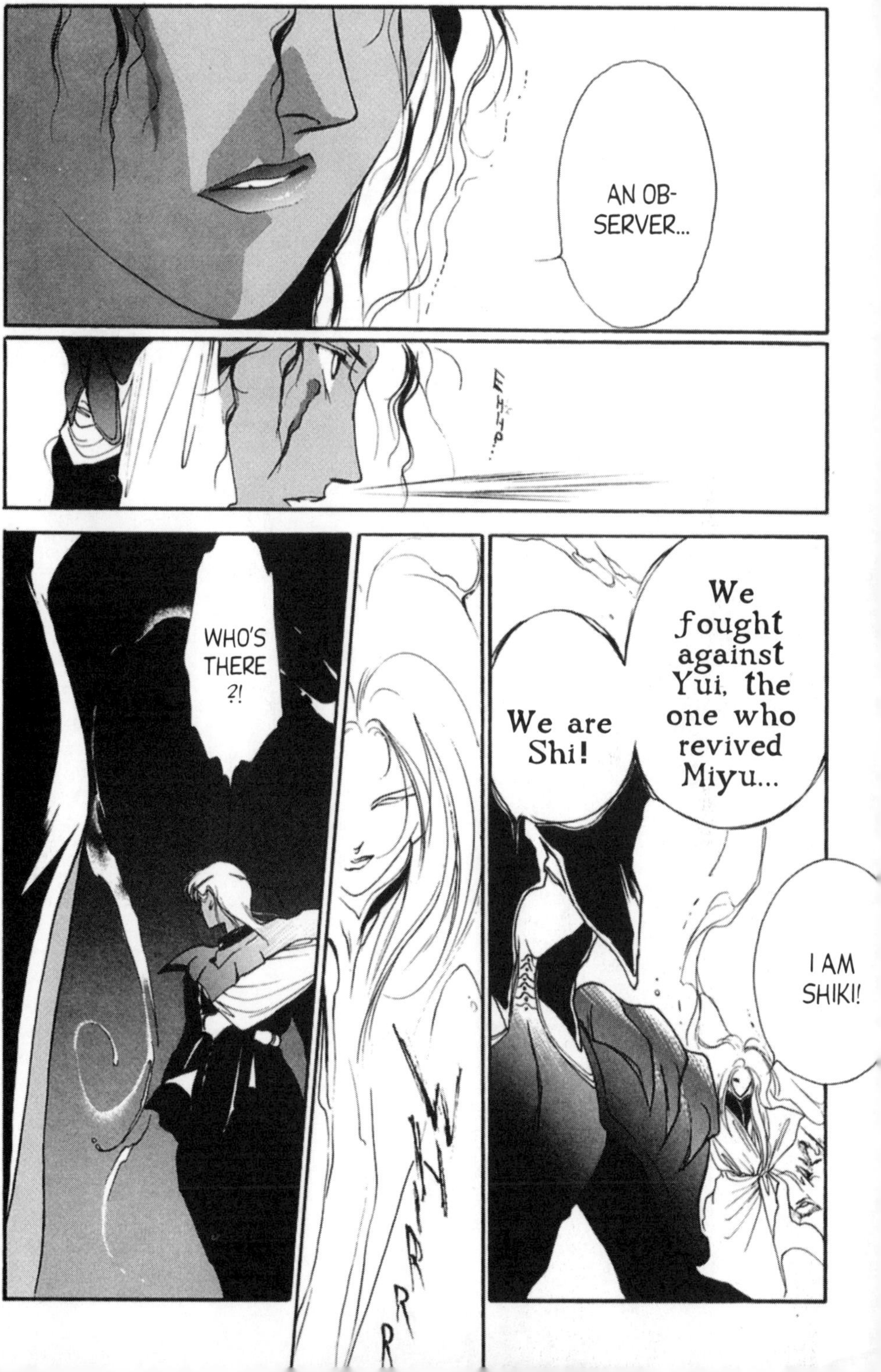
AN OB-SERVER...
WHO'S THERE ?!
We fought against Yui, the one who revived Miyu...
We are Shi!
I AM SHIKI!

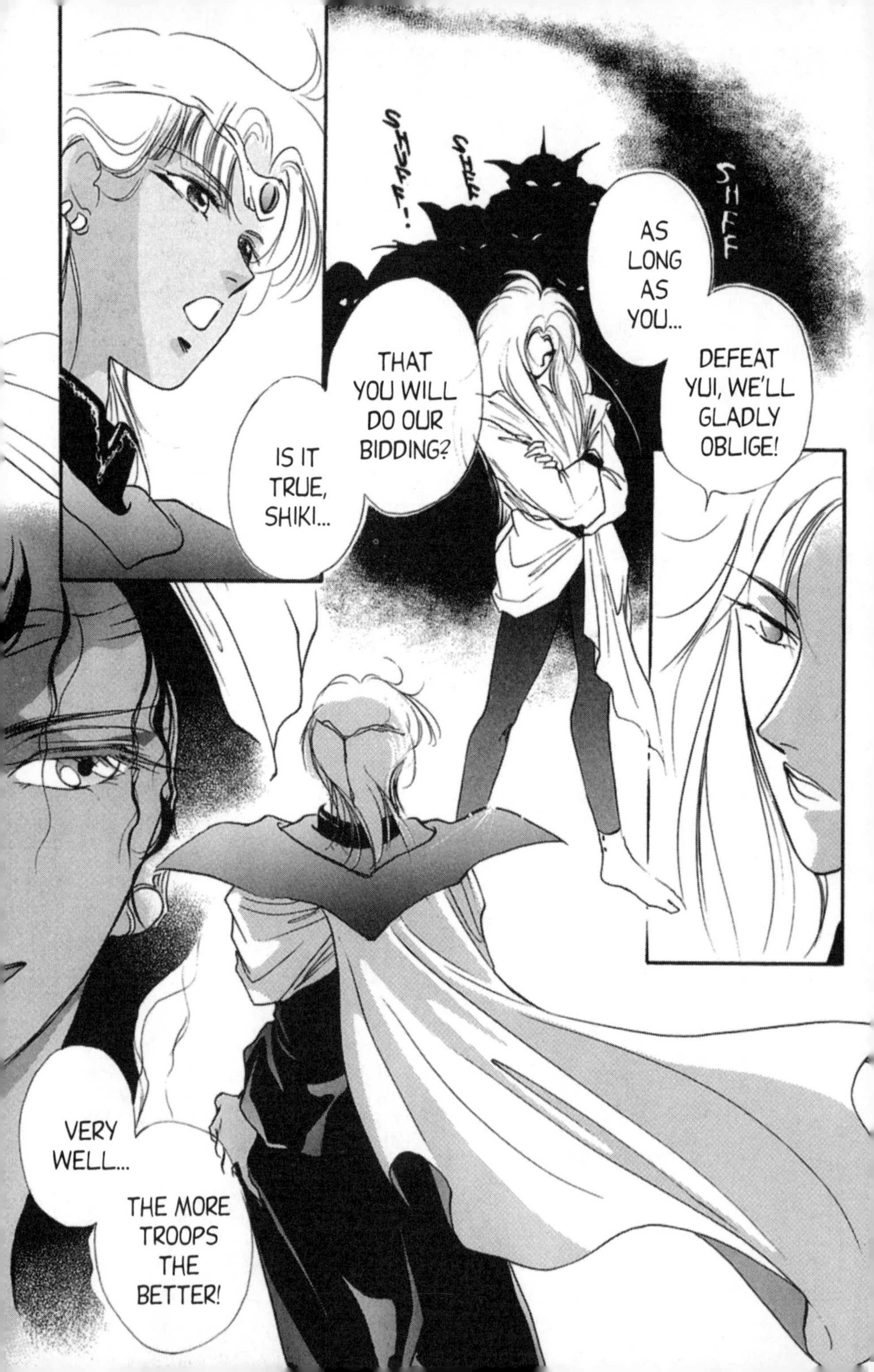
SHFF
AS LONG AS YOU...
DEFEAT YUI, WE'LL GLADLY OBLIGE!
IS IT TRUE, SHIKI...
THAT YOU WILL DO OUR BIDDING?
VERY WELL...
THE MORE TROOPS THE BETTER!

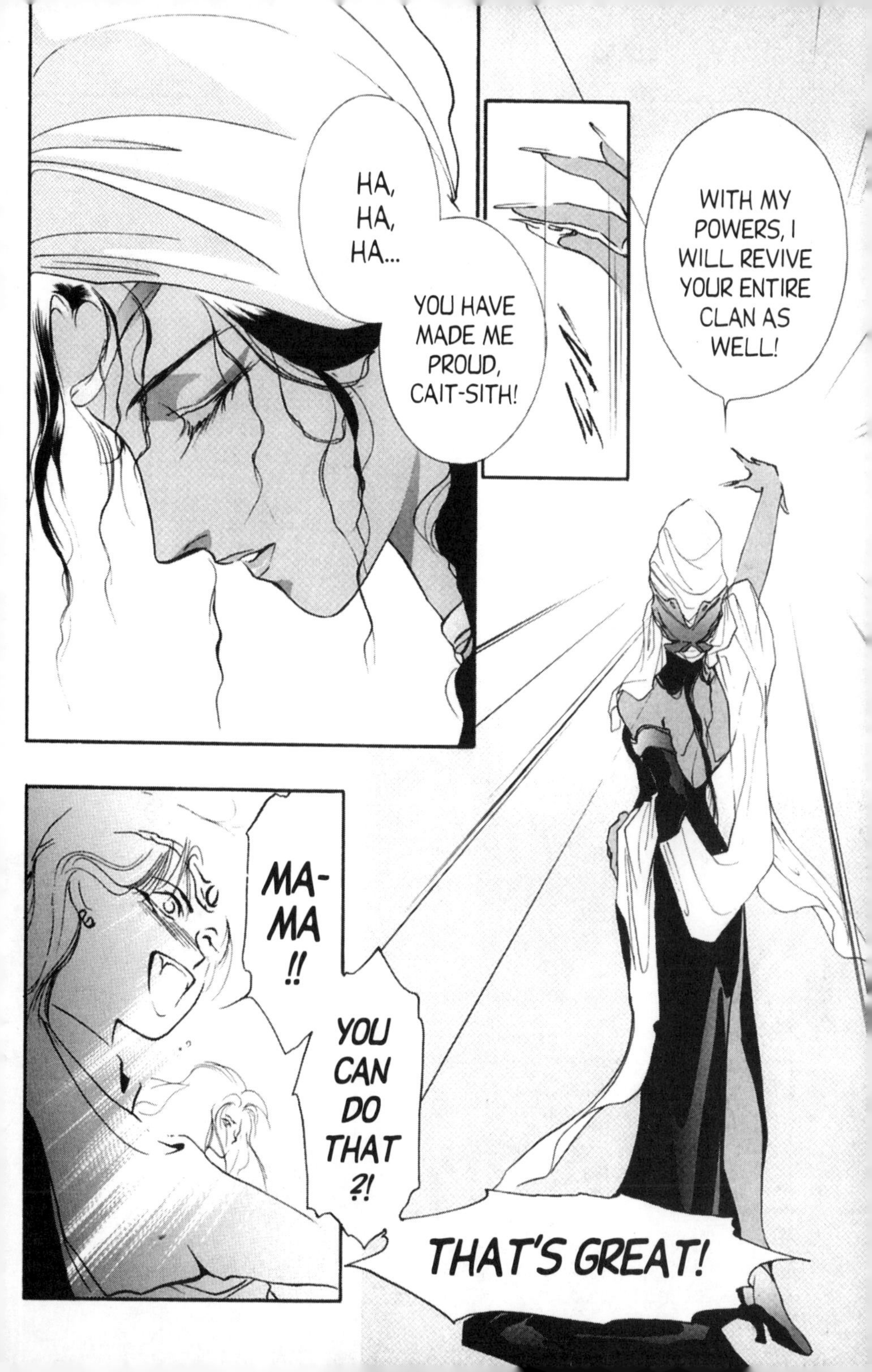
WITH MY POWERS, I WILL REVIVE YOUR ENTIRE CLAN AS WELL!
HA, HA, HA...
YOU HAVE MADE ME PROUD, CAIT-SITH!
MA-MA!!
YOU CAN DO THAT?!
THAT'S GREAT!

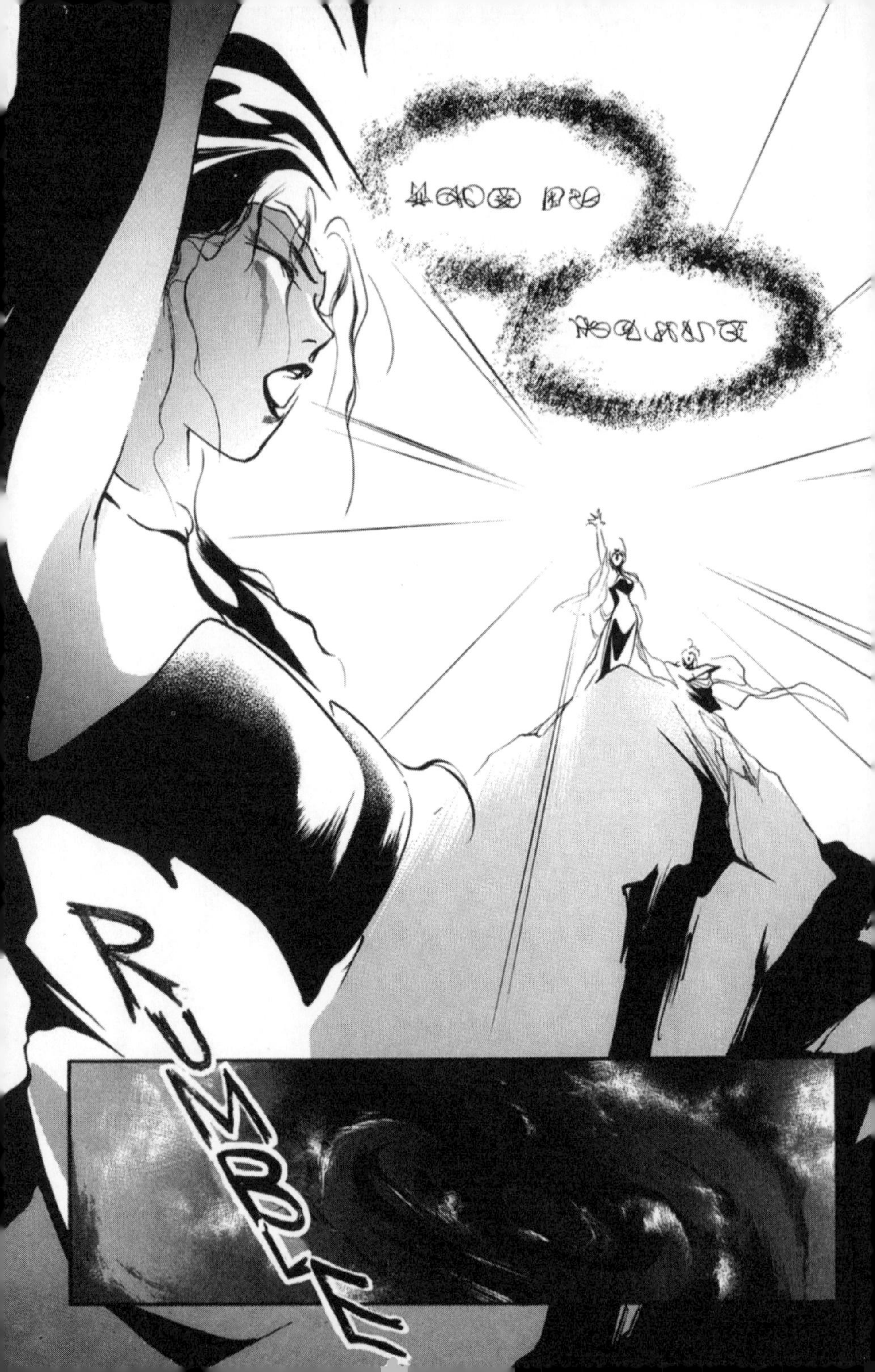
RUMBLE

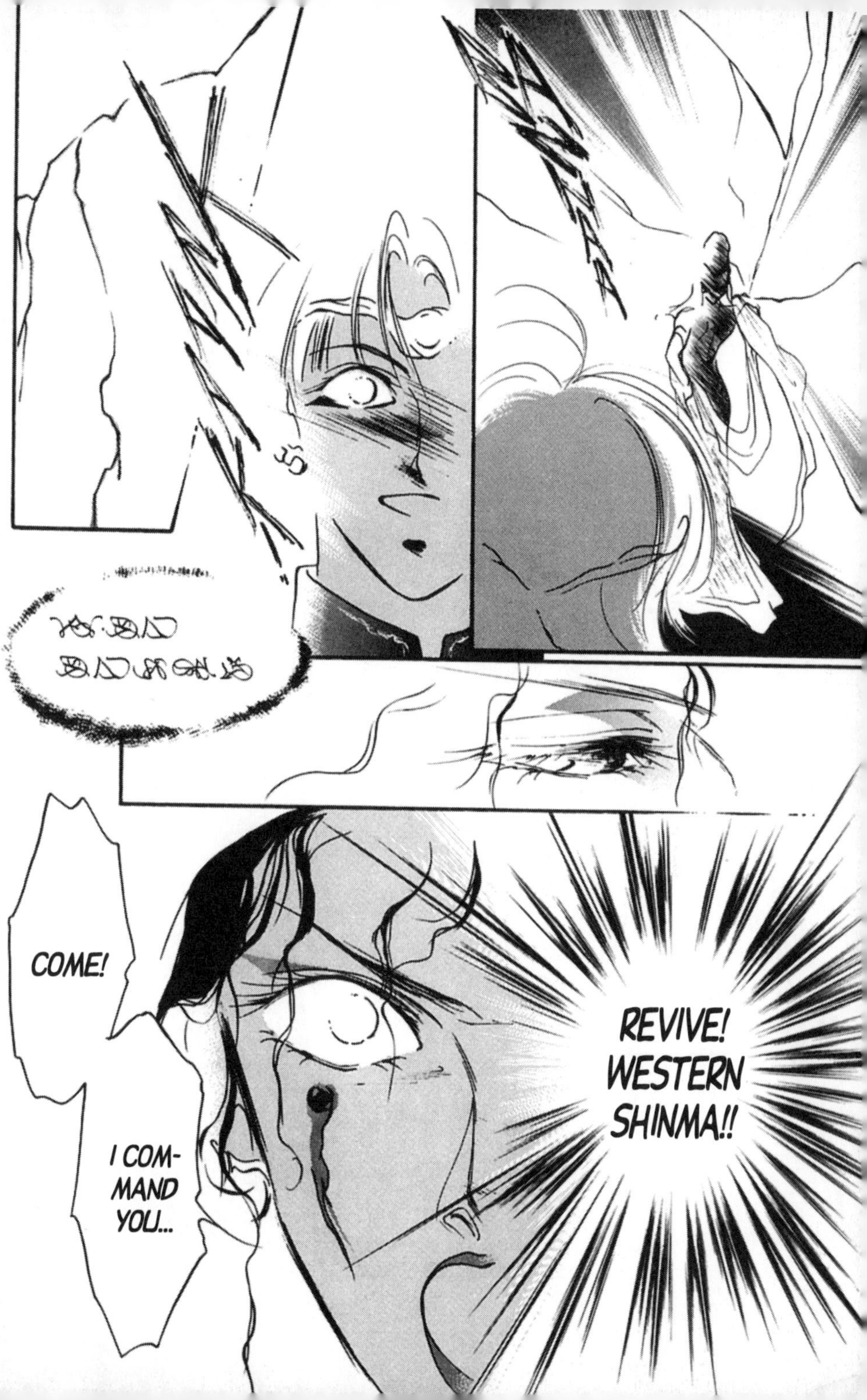
REVIVE! WESTERN SHINMA!!
COME!
I COM-MAND YOU...

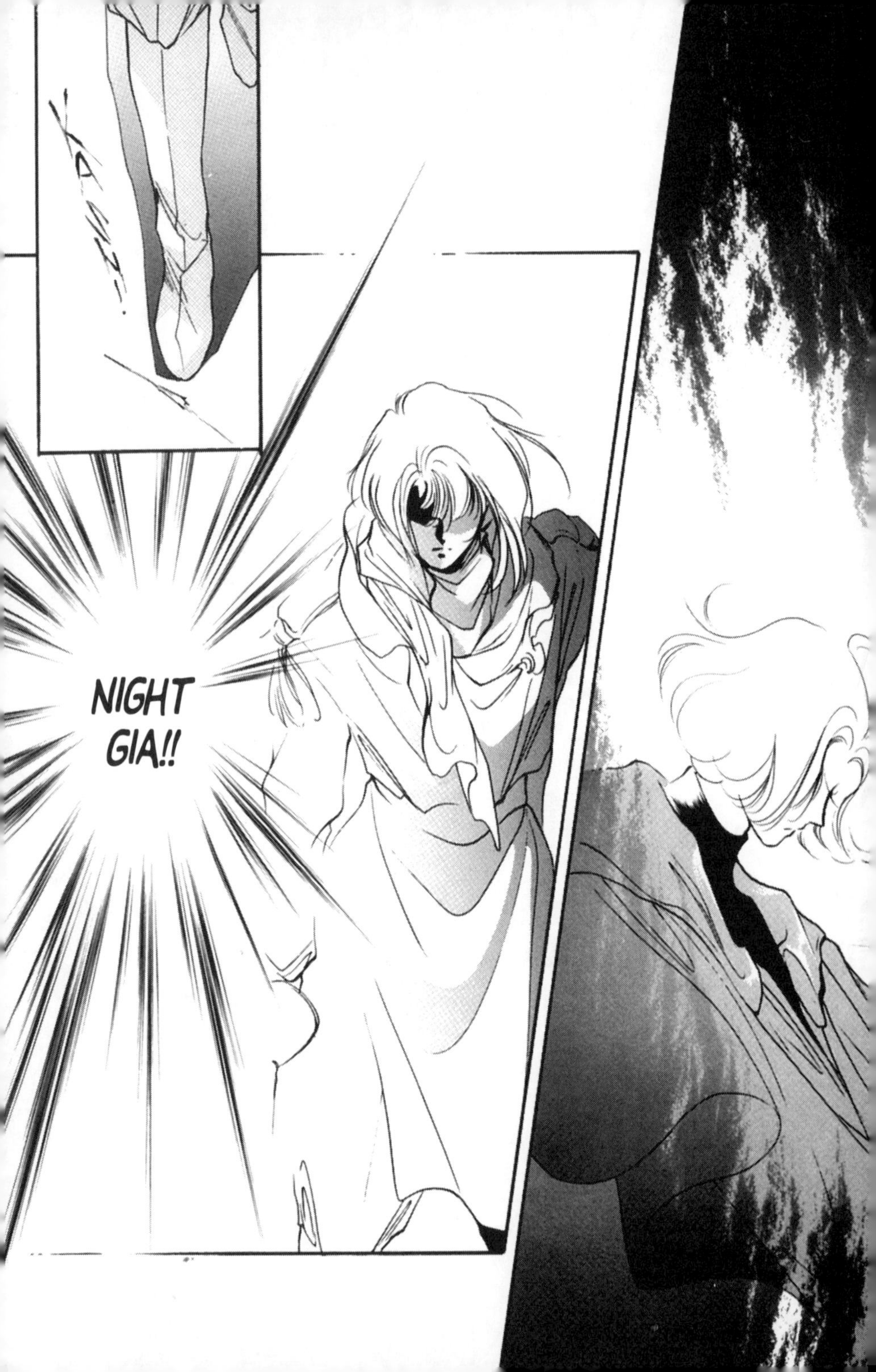
NIGHT GIA!!

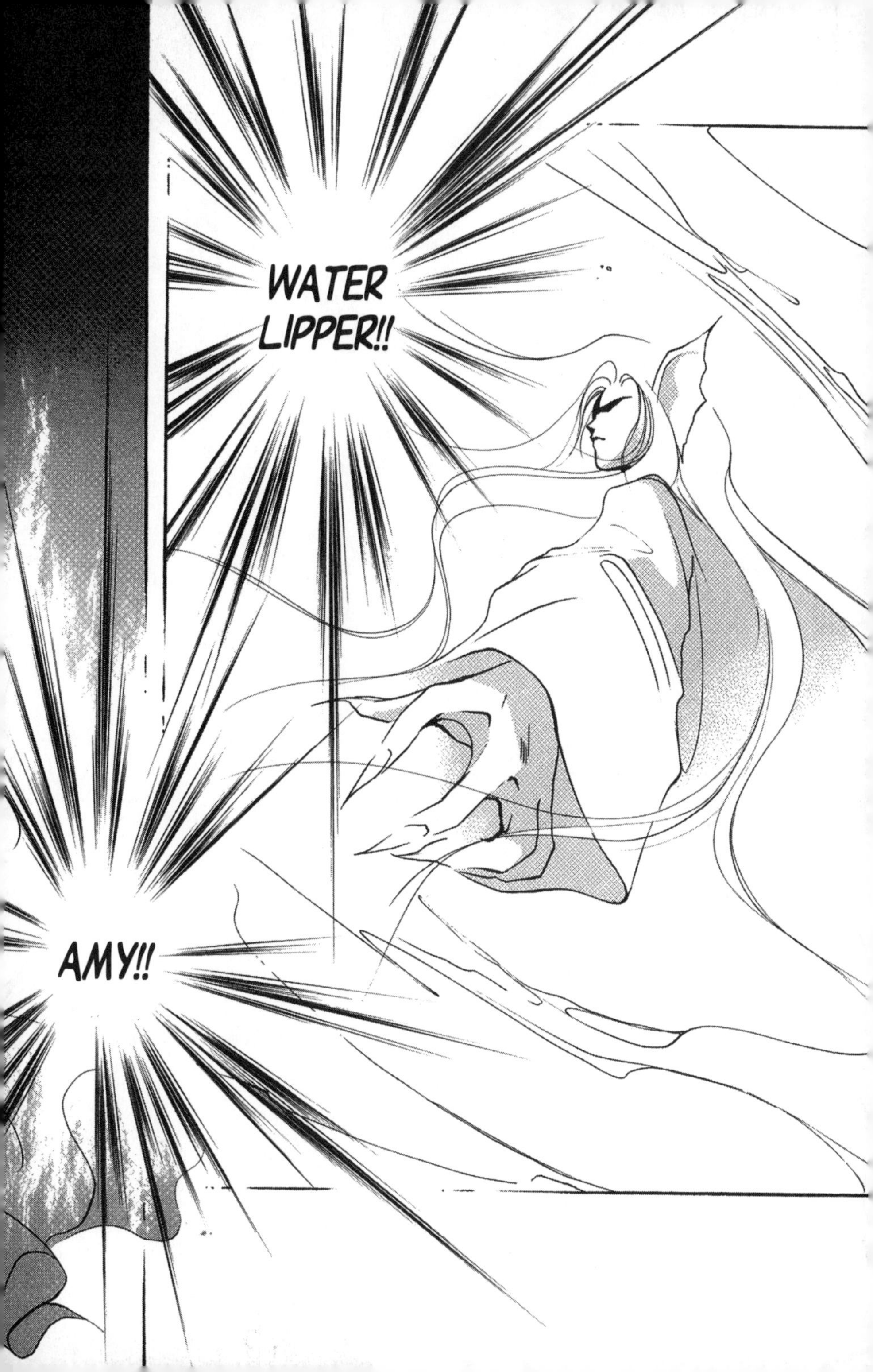
WATER LIPPER!!
AMY!!

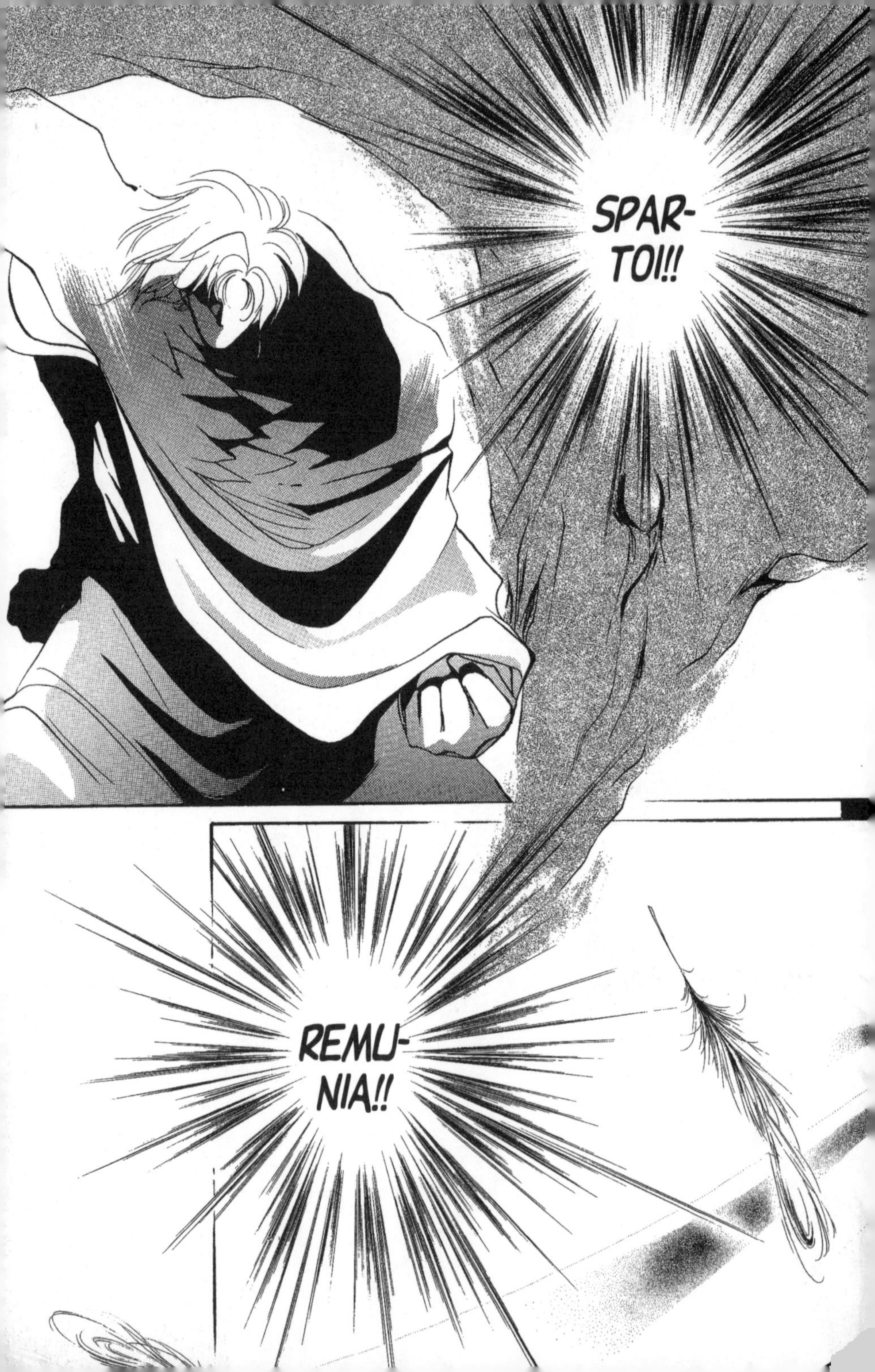
SPAR-
TOI!!
REMU-
NIA!!

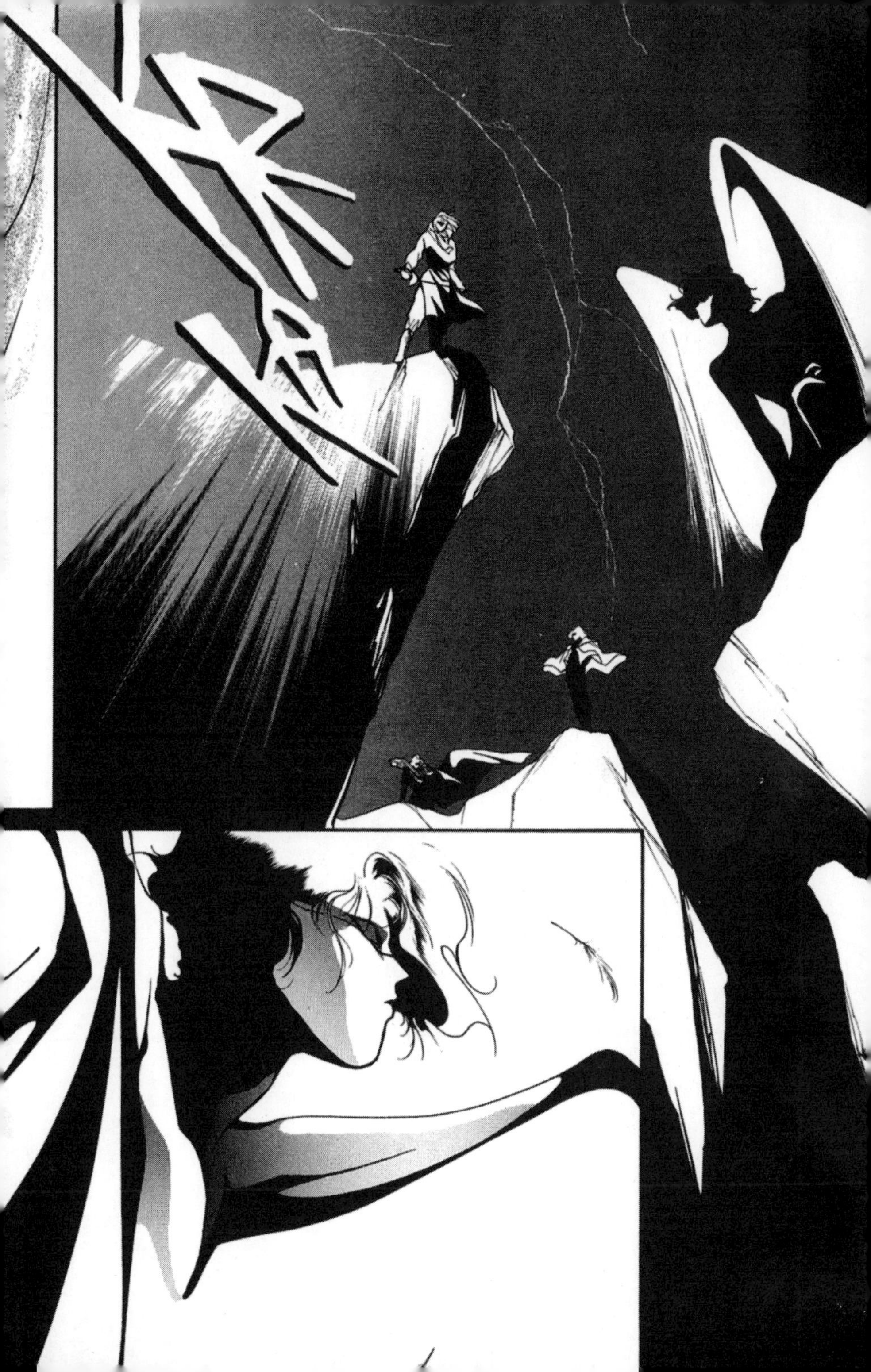

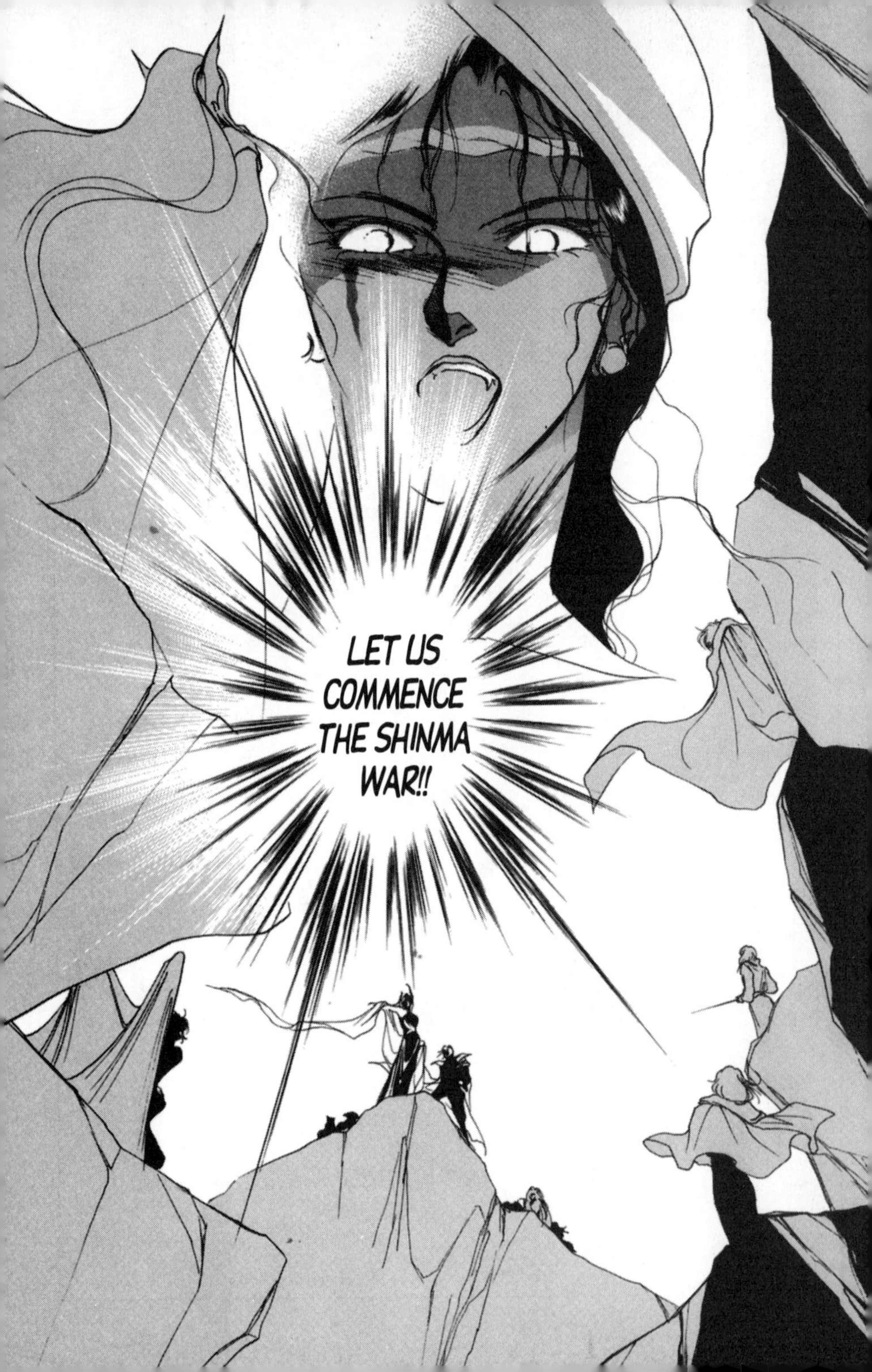
LET US COMMENCE THE SHINMA WAR!!

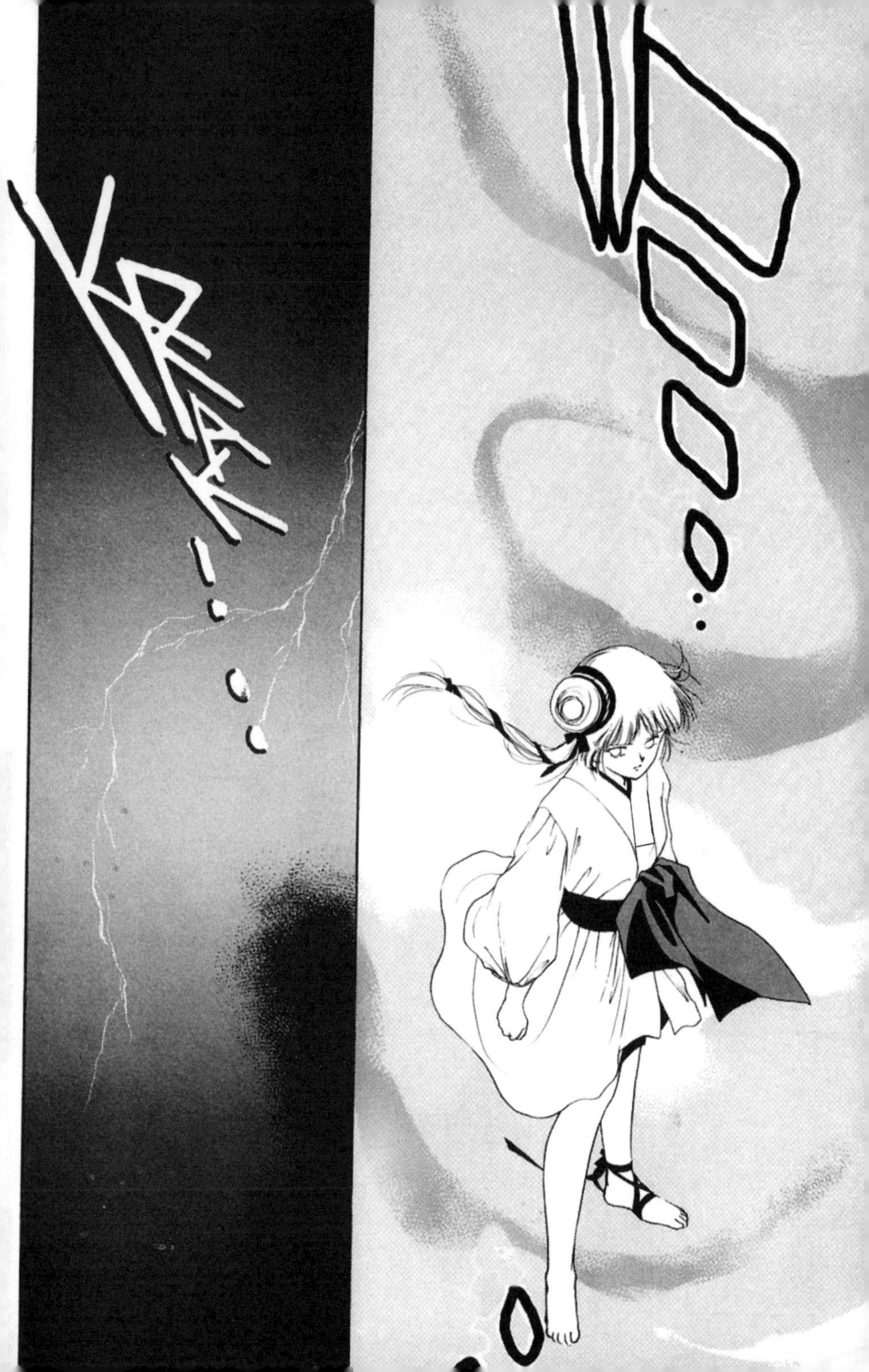

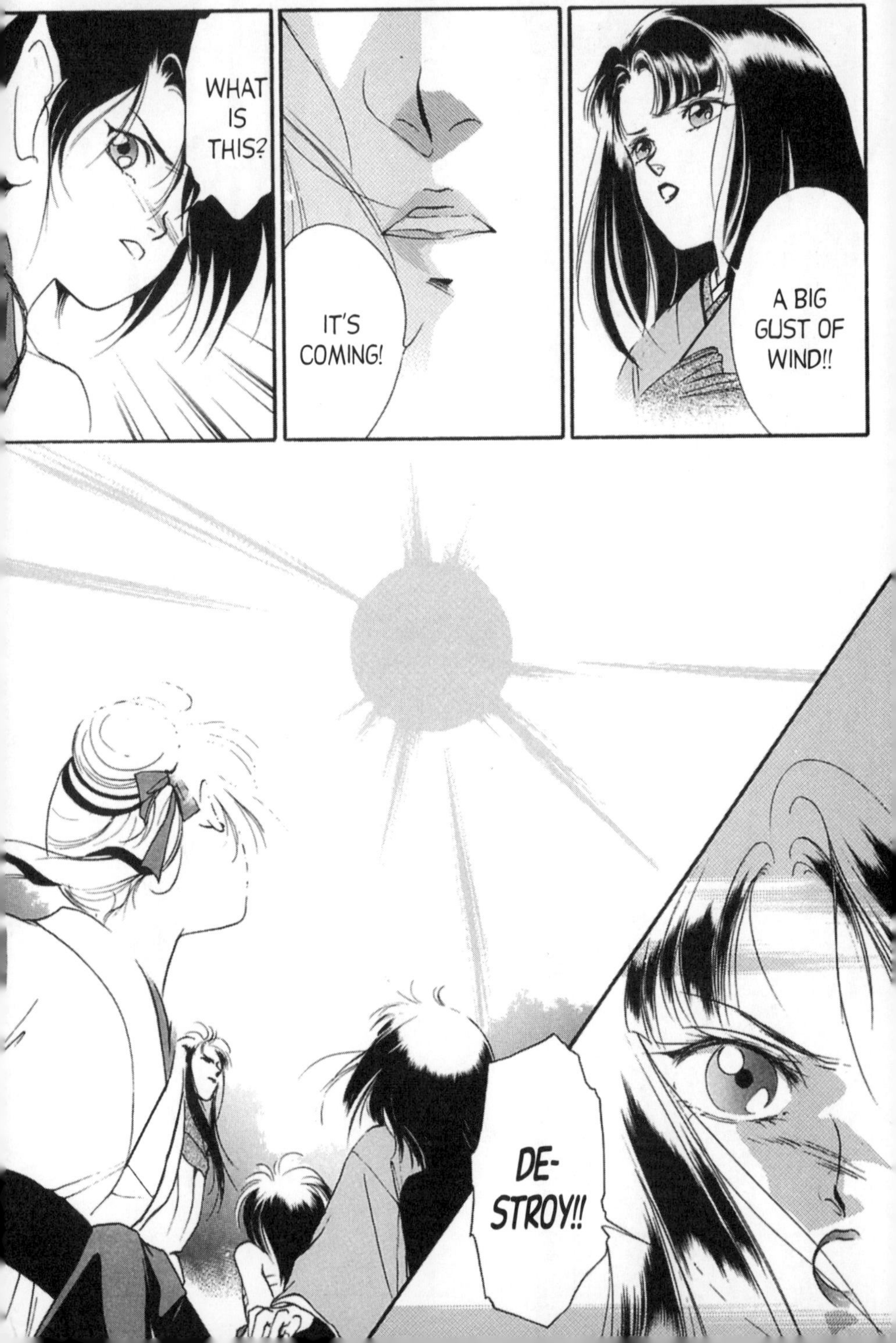
WHAT IS THIS?
IT'S COMING!
A BIG GUST OF WIND!!
DE-STROY!!

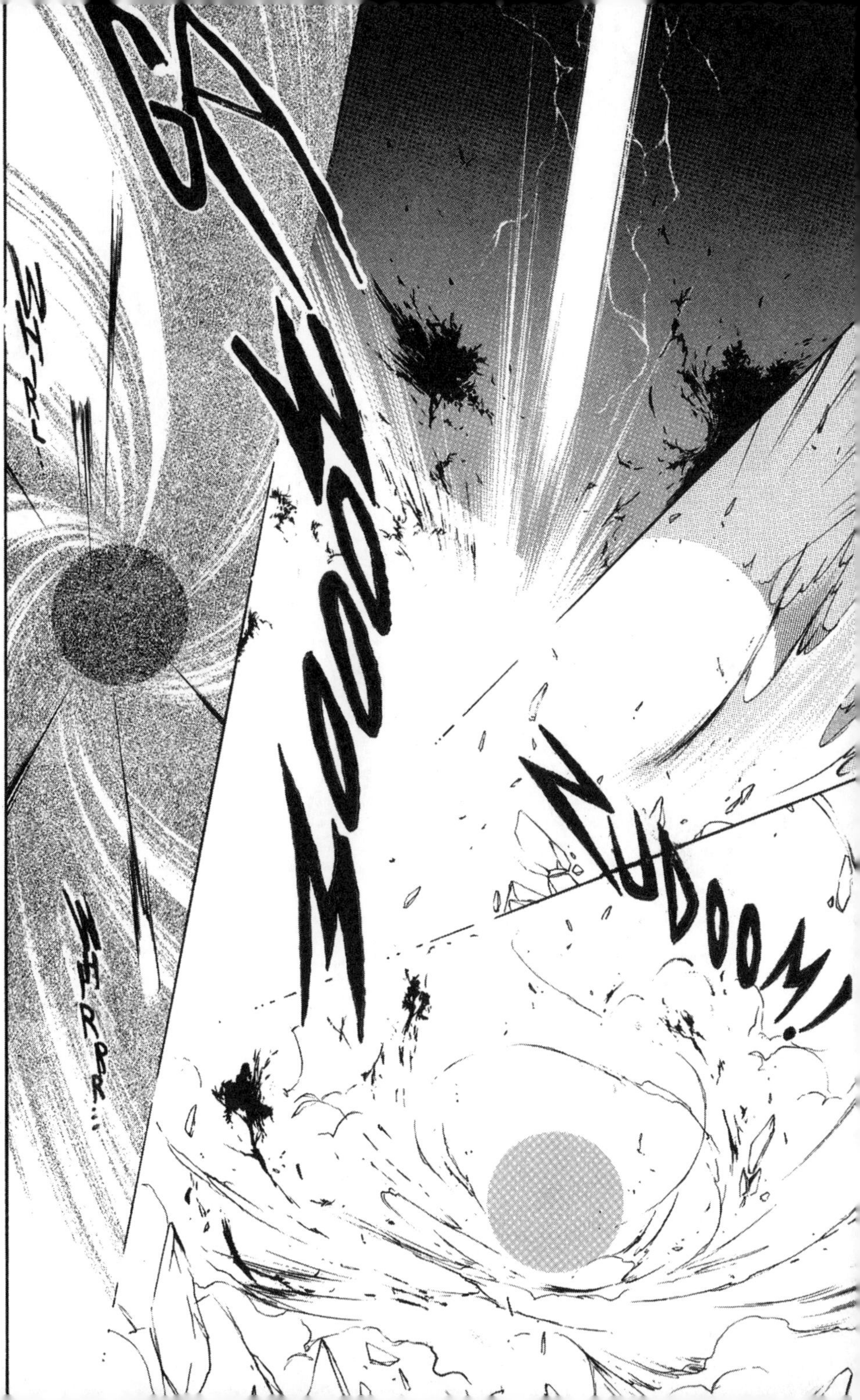
ZUDOOM!
GAHOOOM
WHIRL...
WHIRRR...

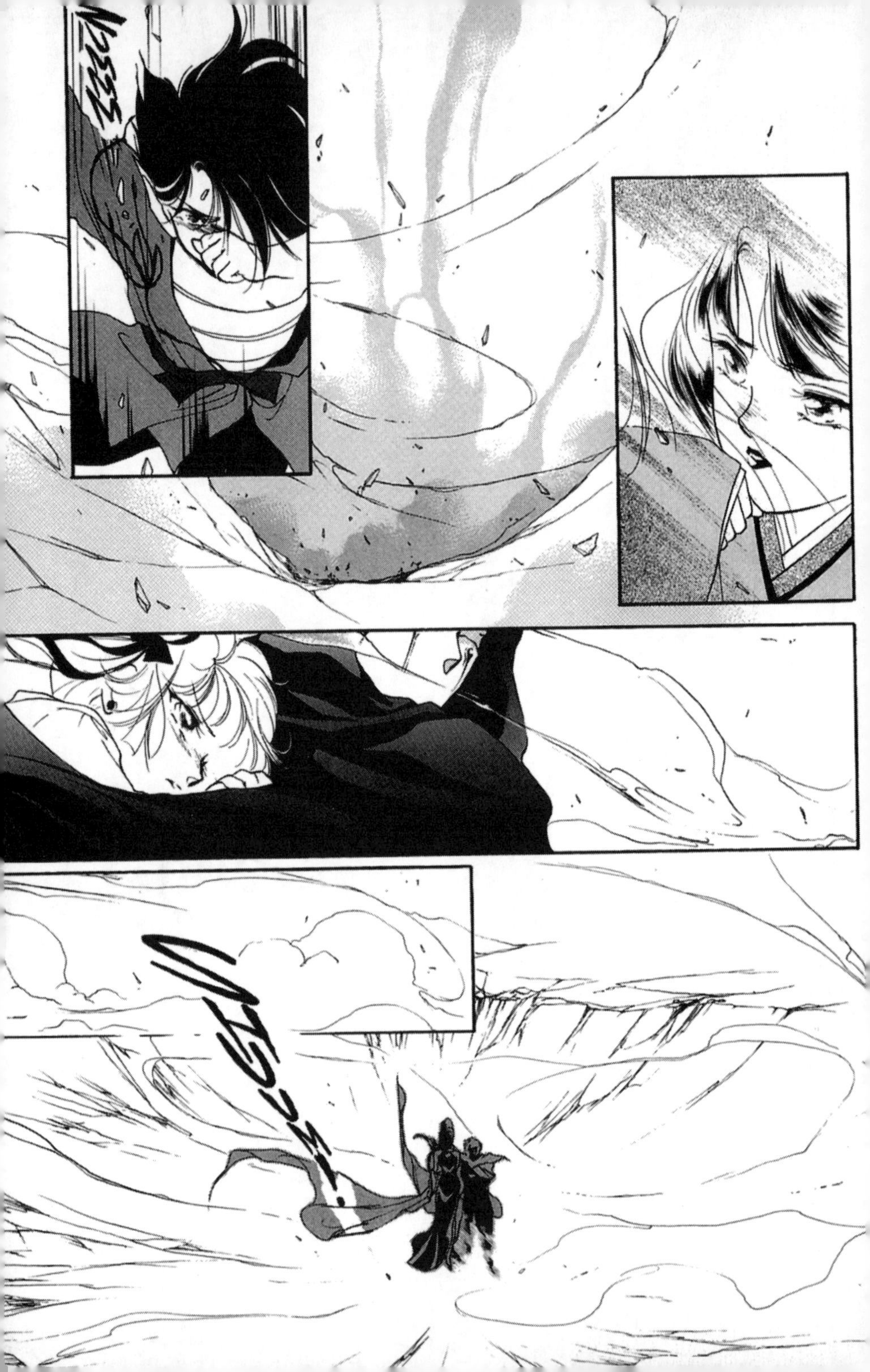

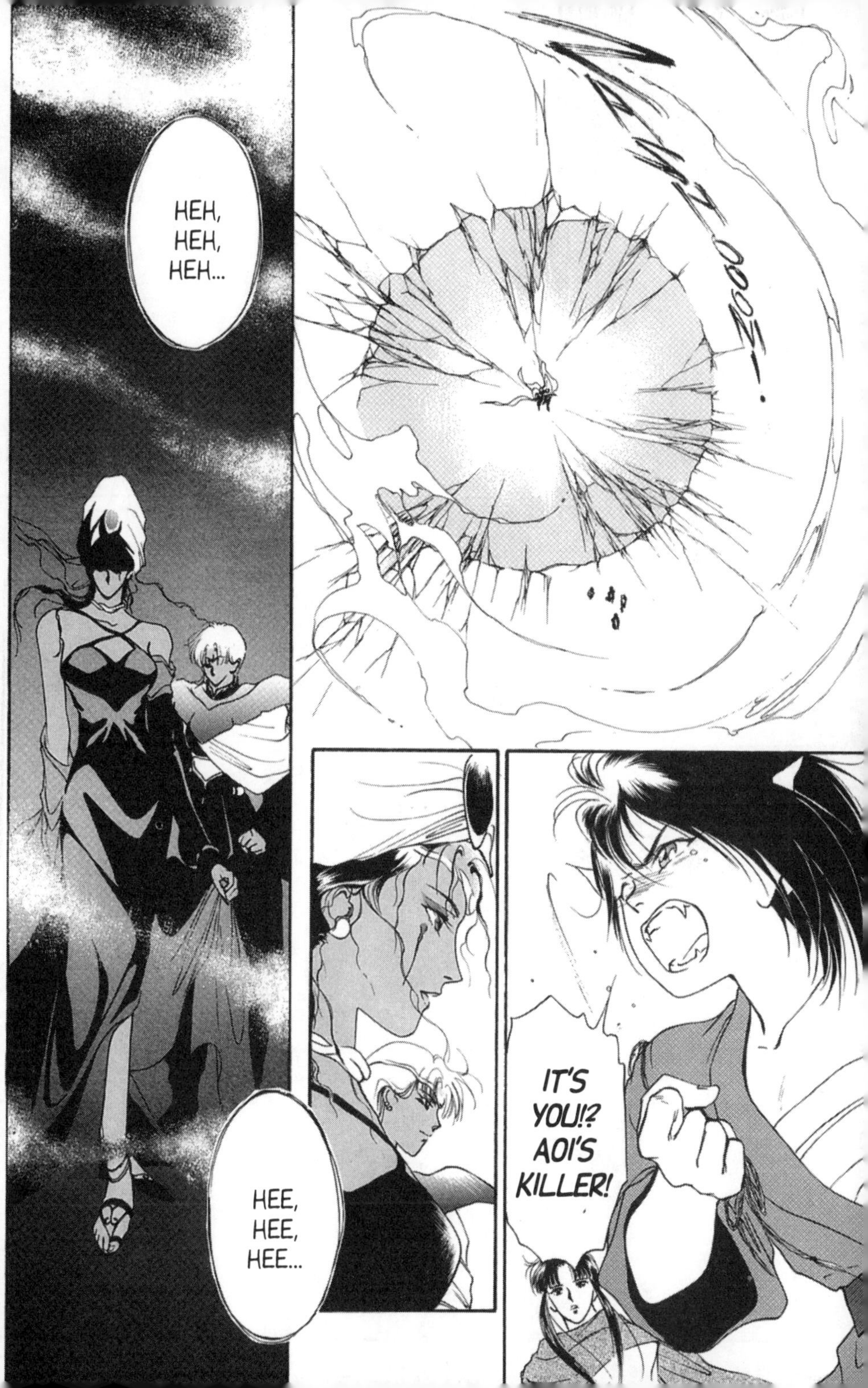

IT'S YOU!? AOI'S KILLER!
HEE, HEE, HEE...
HEH, HEH, HEH...

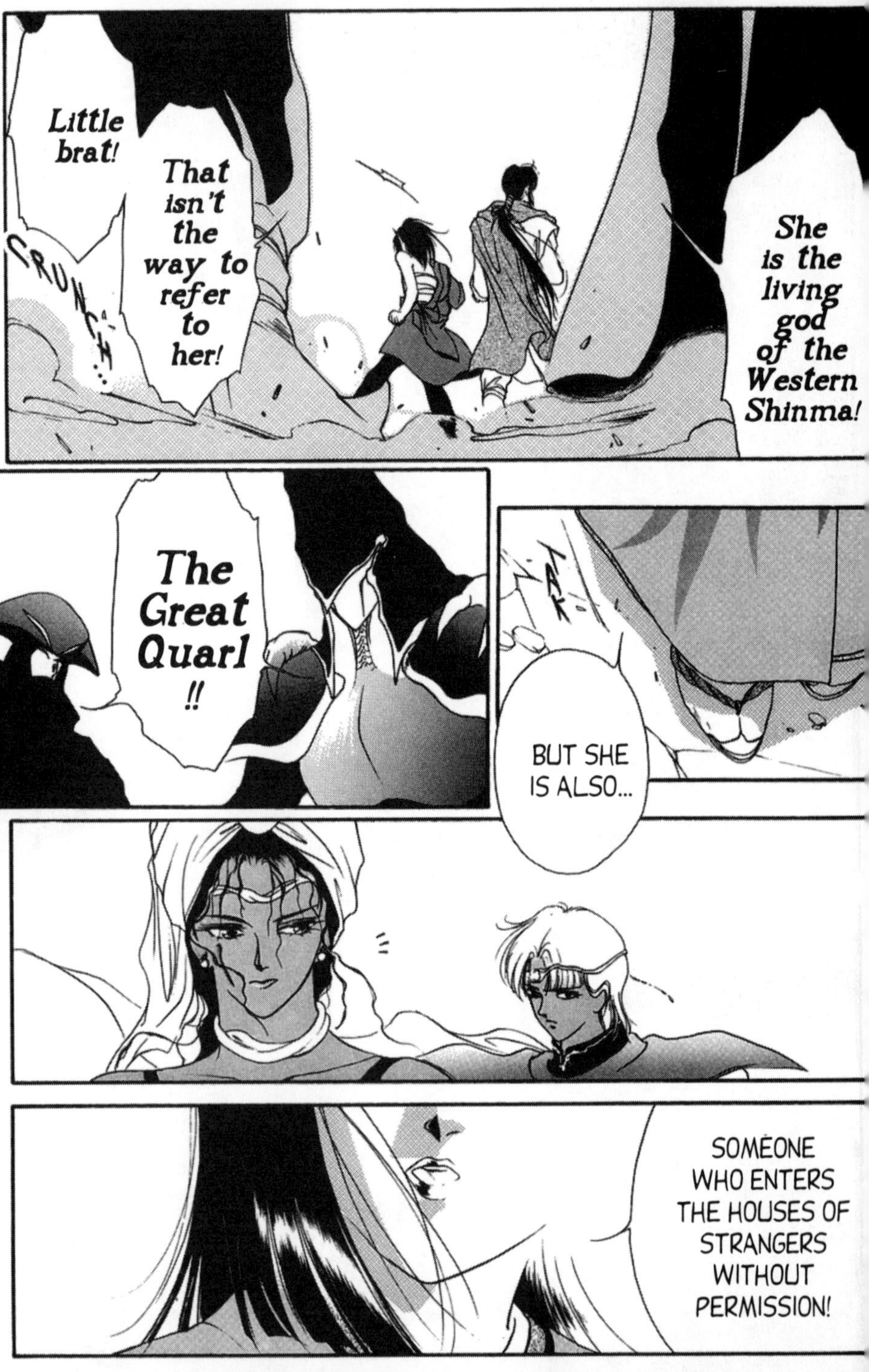

Little brat!
CRUNCH
That isn't the way to refer to her!
She is the living god of the Western Shinma!
The Great Quarl !!
BUT SHE IS ALSO...
SOMEONE WHO ENTERS THE HOUSES OF STRANGERS WITHOUT PERMISSION!

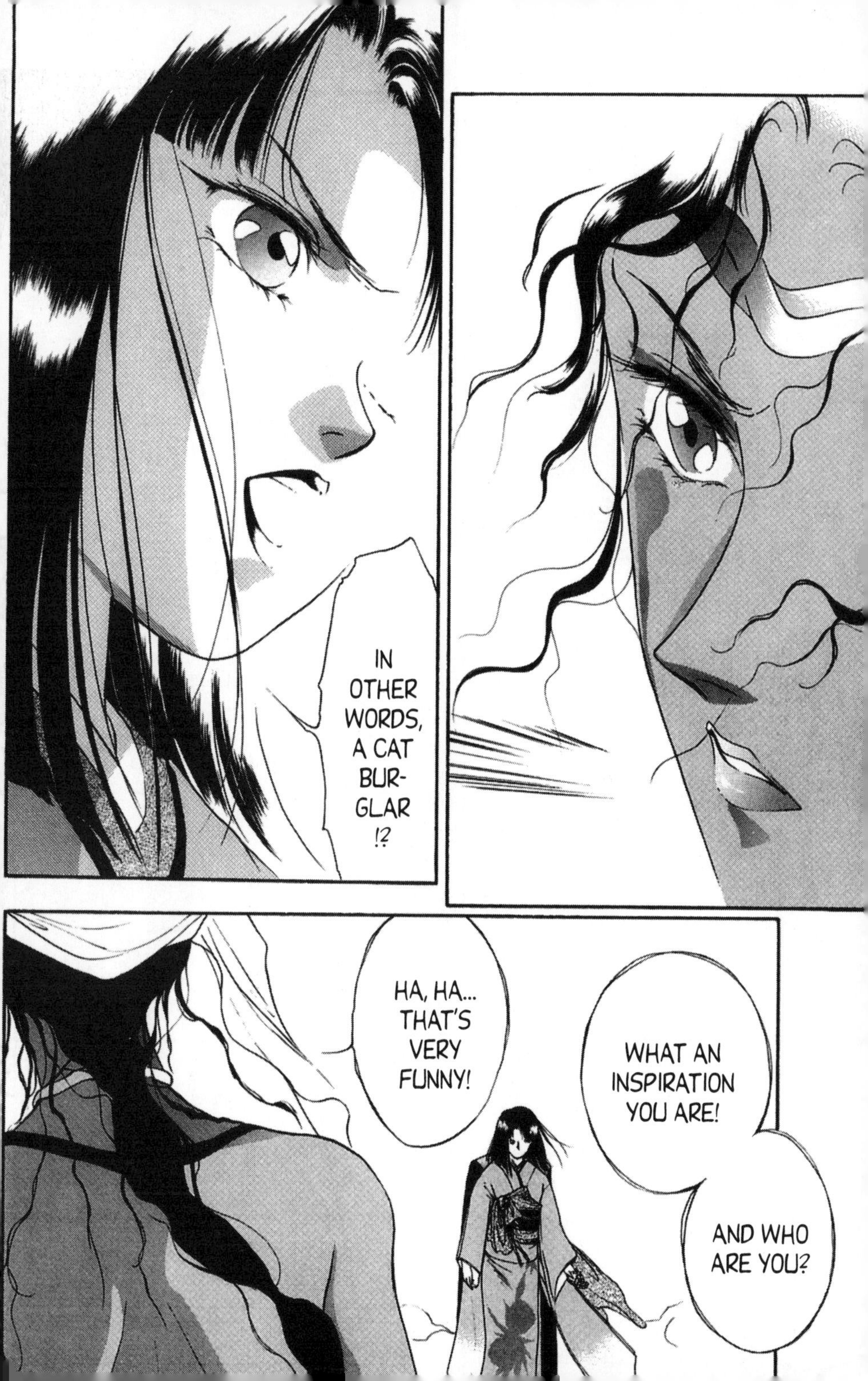
IN OTHER WORDS, A CAT BUR-GLAR !?
HA, HA... THAT'S VERY FUNNY!
WHAT AN INSPIRATION YOU ARE!
AND WHO ARE YOU?

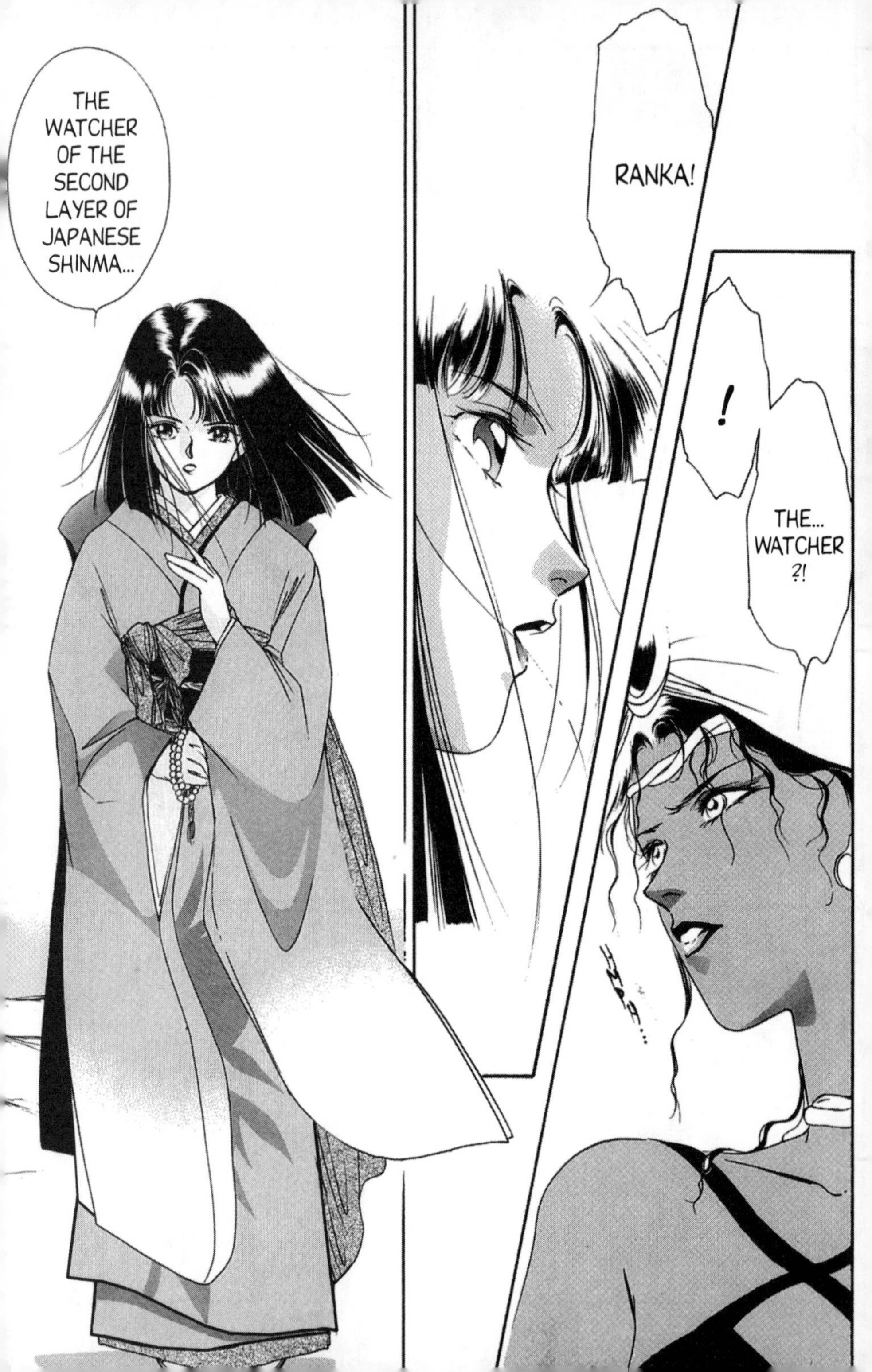
THE WATCHER OF THE SECOND LAYER OF JAPANESE SHINMA...
RANKA!
!
THE... WATCHER ?!

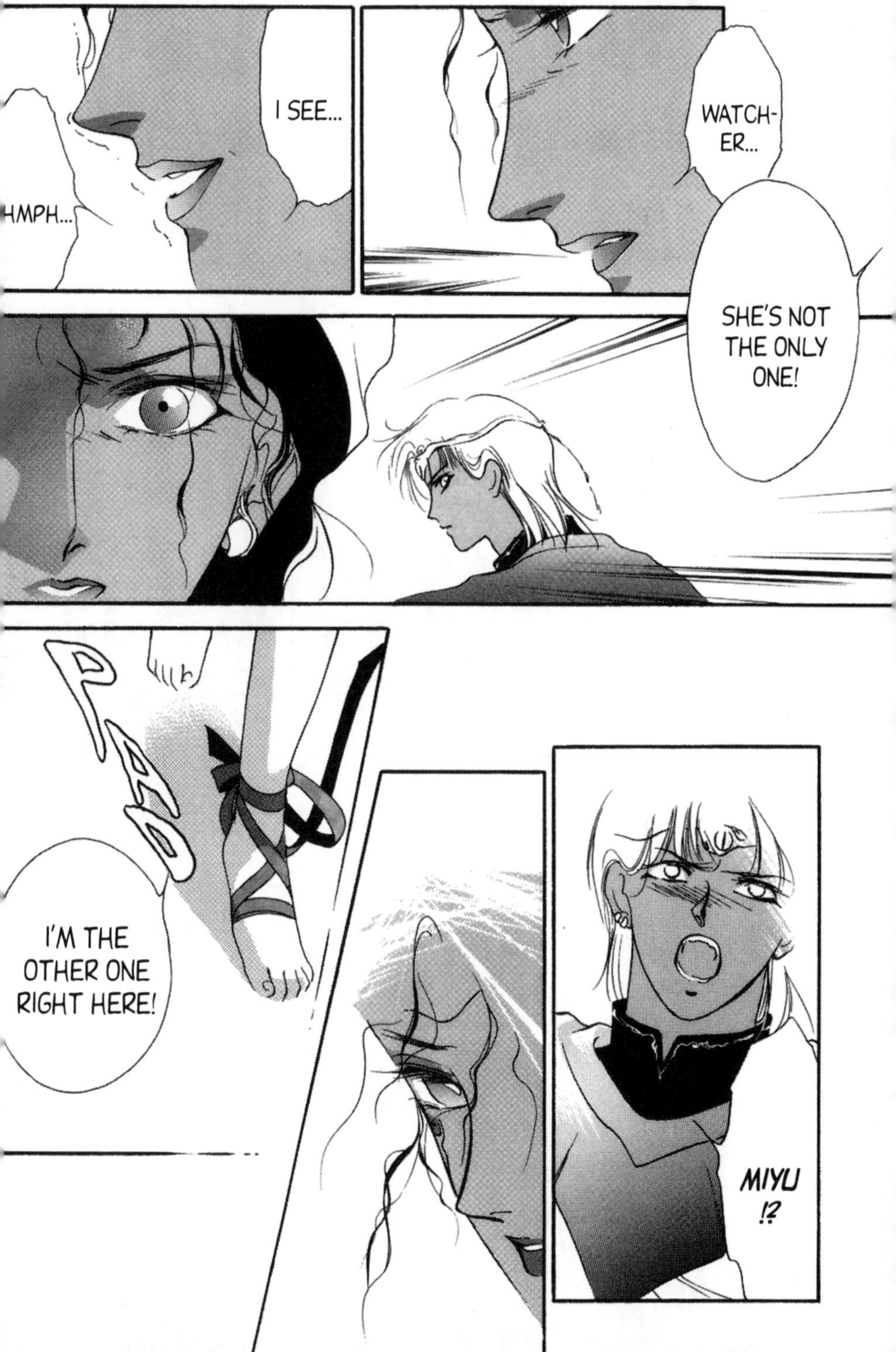
HMPH...
I SEE...
WATCH-ER...
SHE'S NOT THE ONLY ONE!
PAD
I'M THE OTHER ONE RIGHT HERE!
MIYU !?

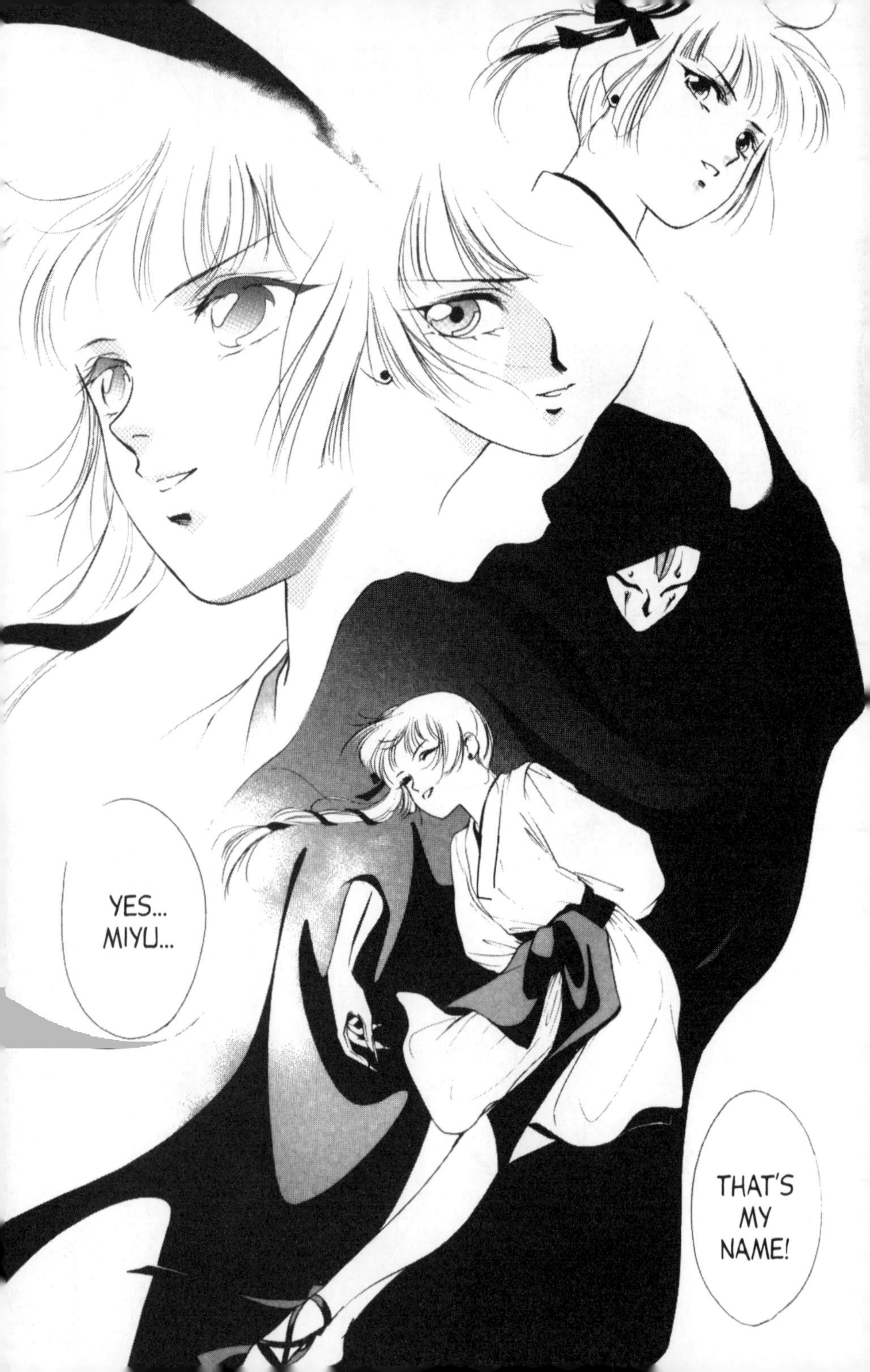

YES... MIYU...
THAT'S MY NAME!

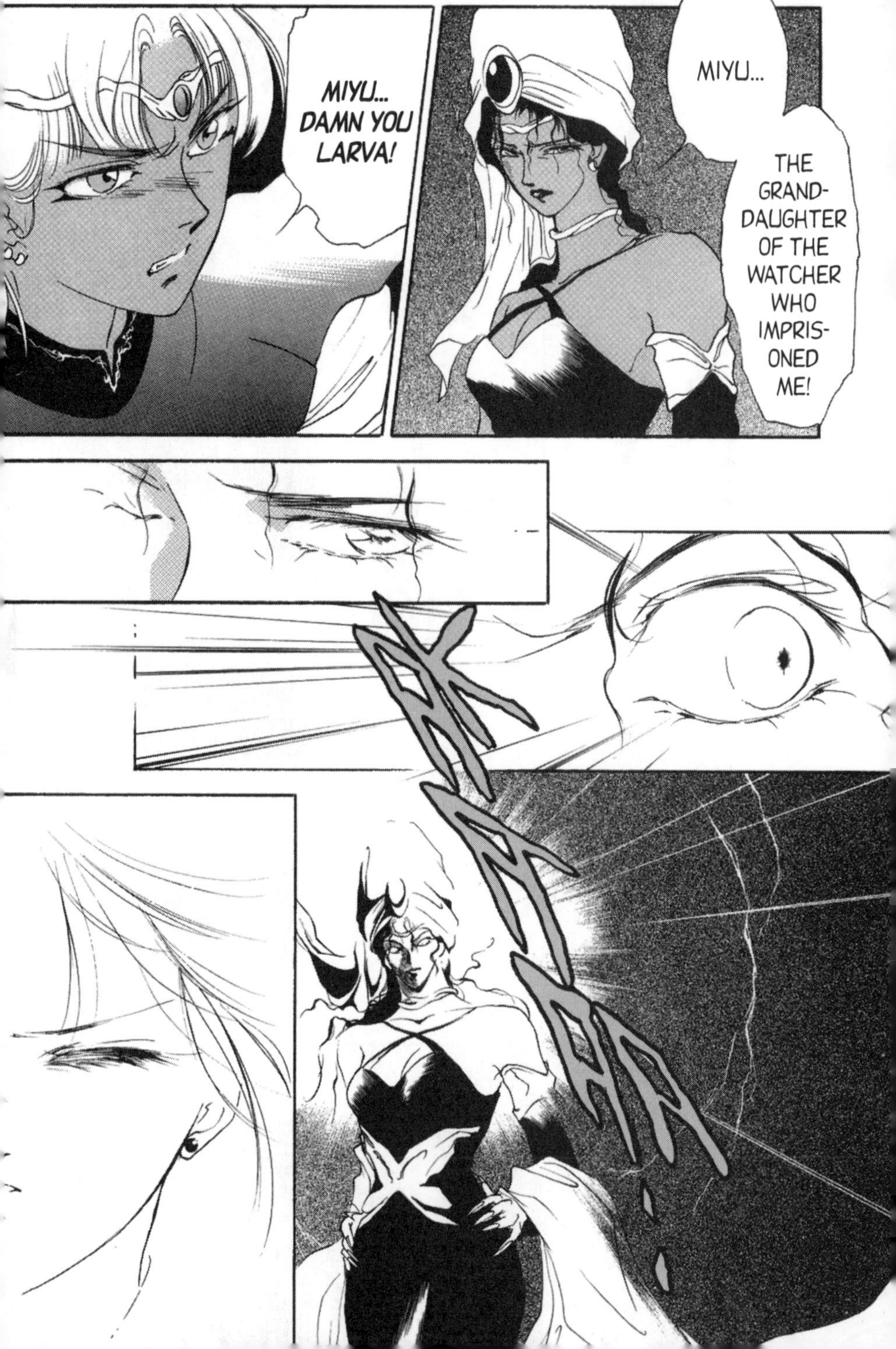
MIYU...
THE GRAND-DAUGHTER OF THE WATCHER WHO IMPRIS-ONED ME!
MIYU... DAMN YOU LARVA!

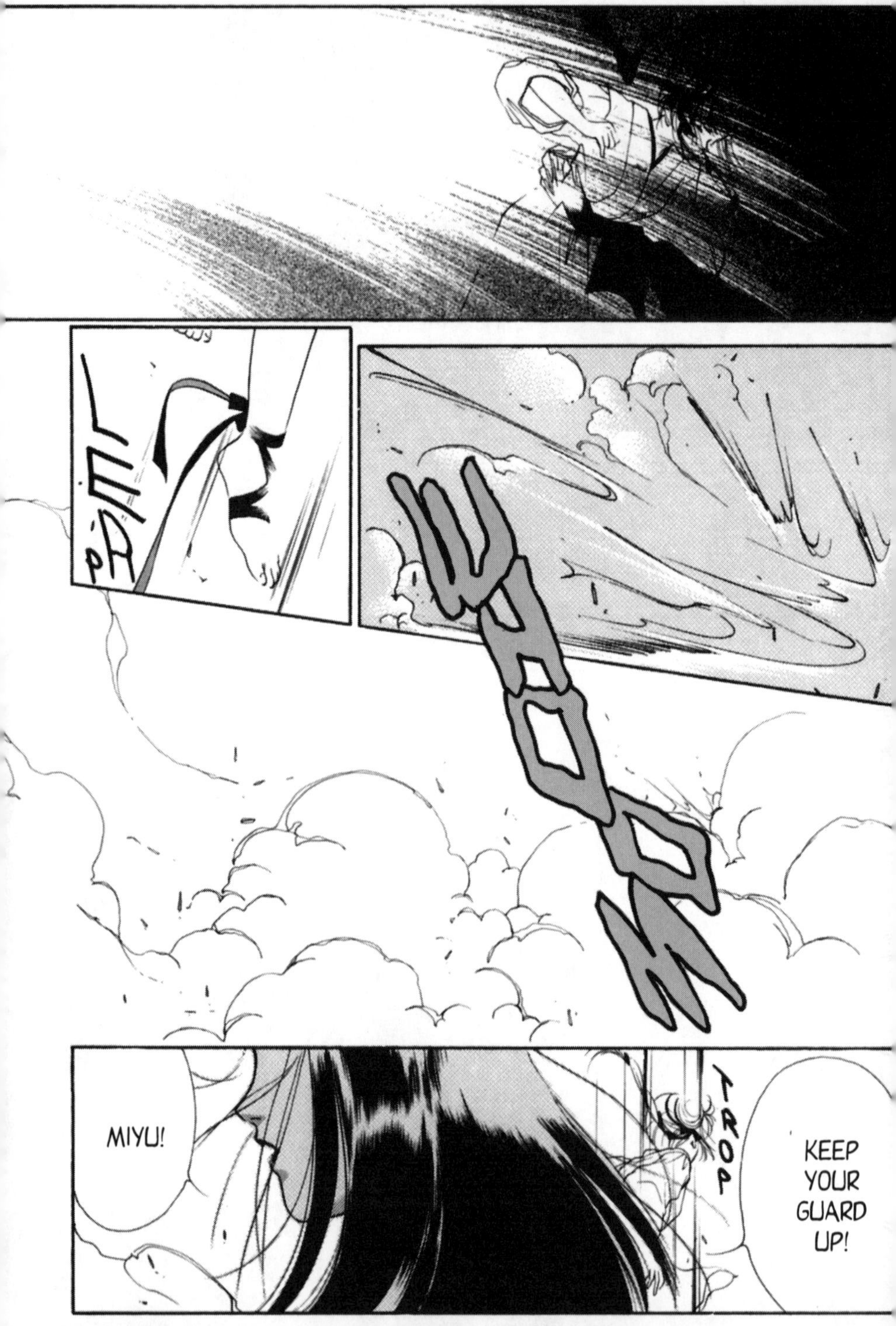
WHOOM
LEAP
KEEP YOUR GUARD UP!
TROP
MIYU!

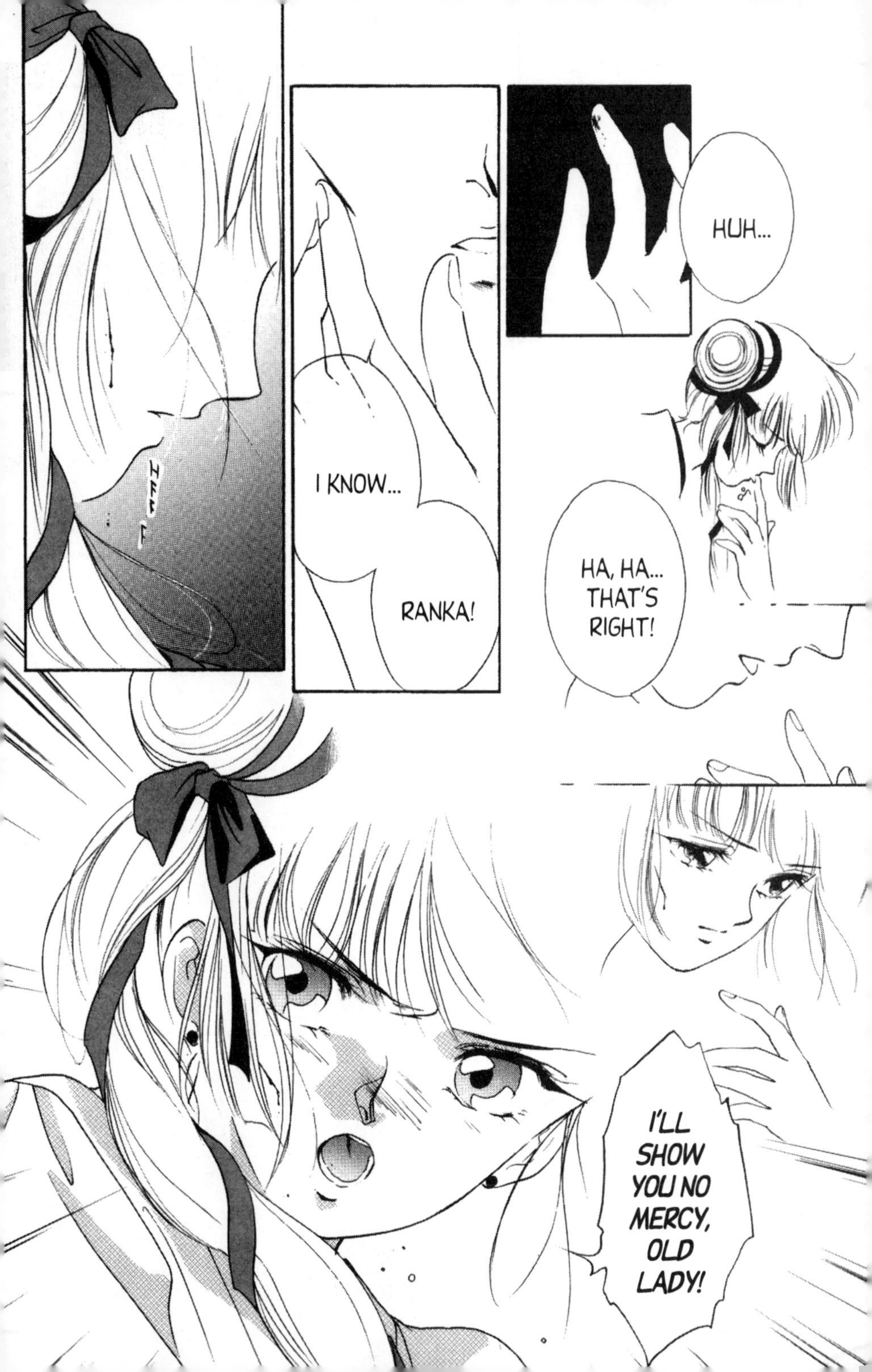
HUH...
HA, HA... THAT'S RIGHT!
I KNOW...
RANKA!
I'LL SHOW YOU NO MERCY, OLD LADY!

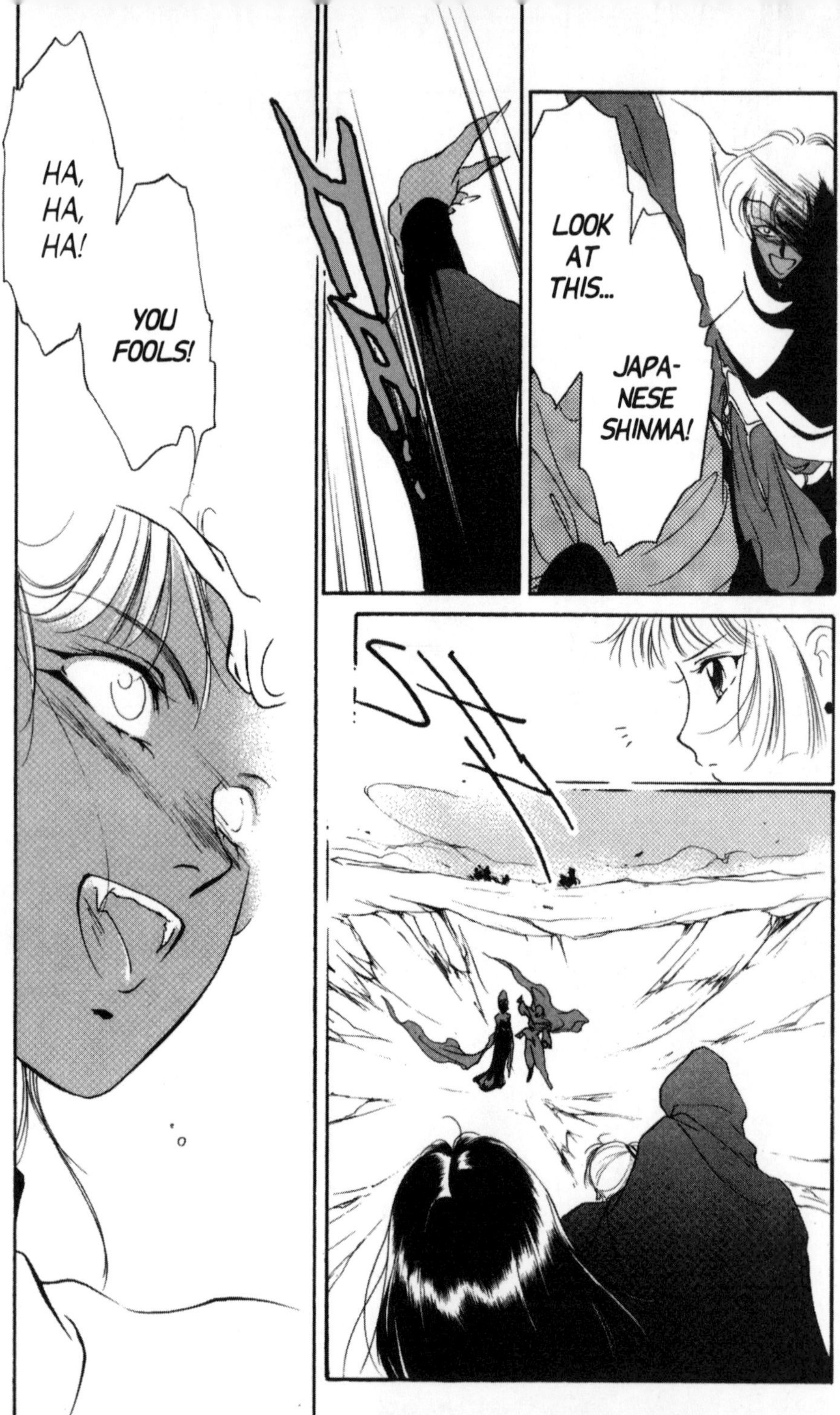
LOOK AT THIS...
JAPA-NESE SHINMA!
HA, HA, HA!
YOU FOOLS!

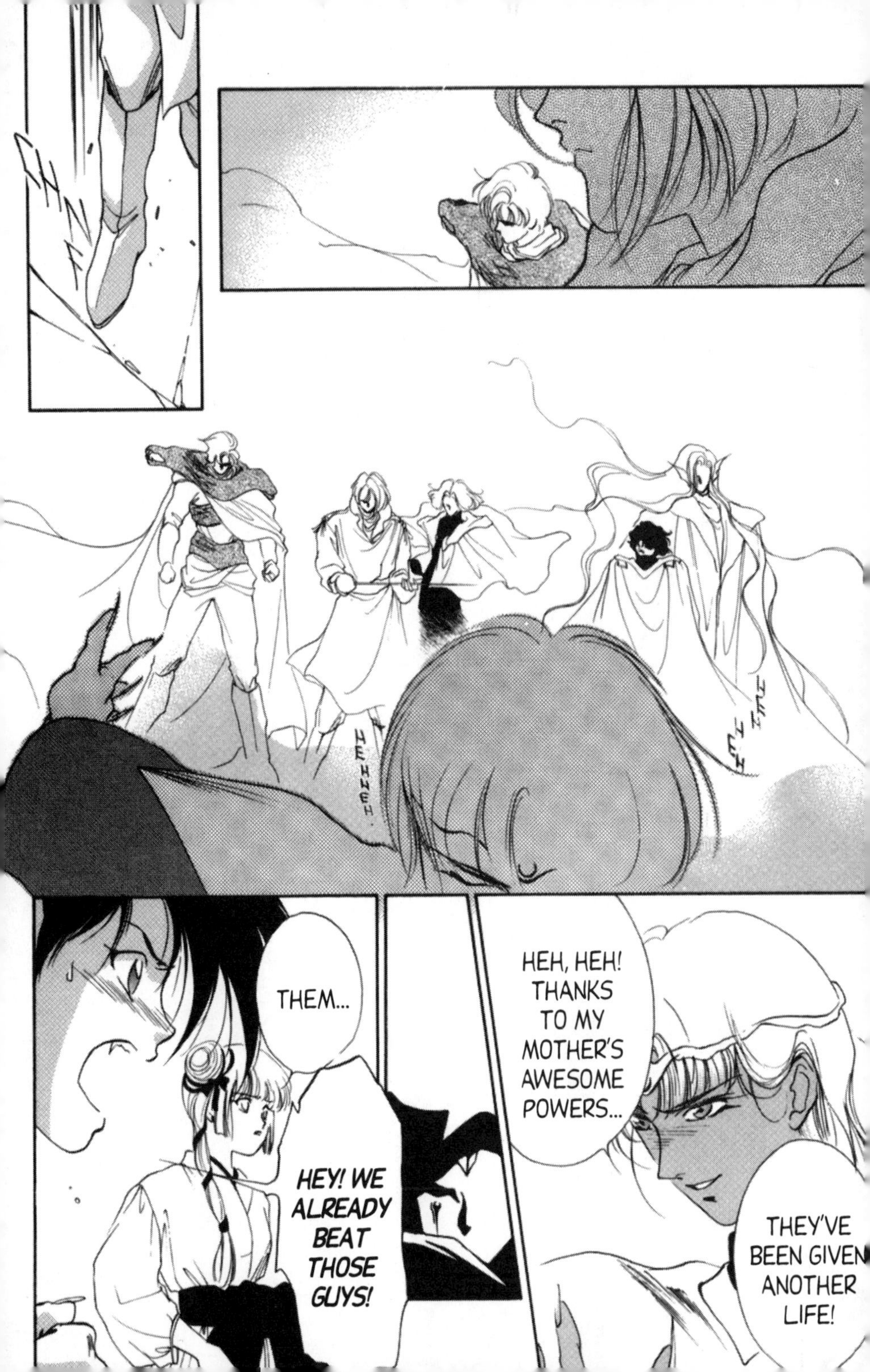

THEM...
HEH, HEH! THANKS TO MY MOTHER'S AWESOME POWERS...
THEY'VE BEEN GIVEN ANOTHER LIFE!
HEY! WE ALREADY BEAT THOSE GUYS!

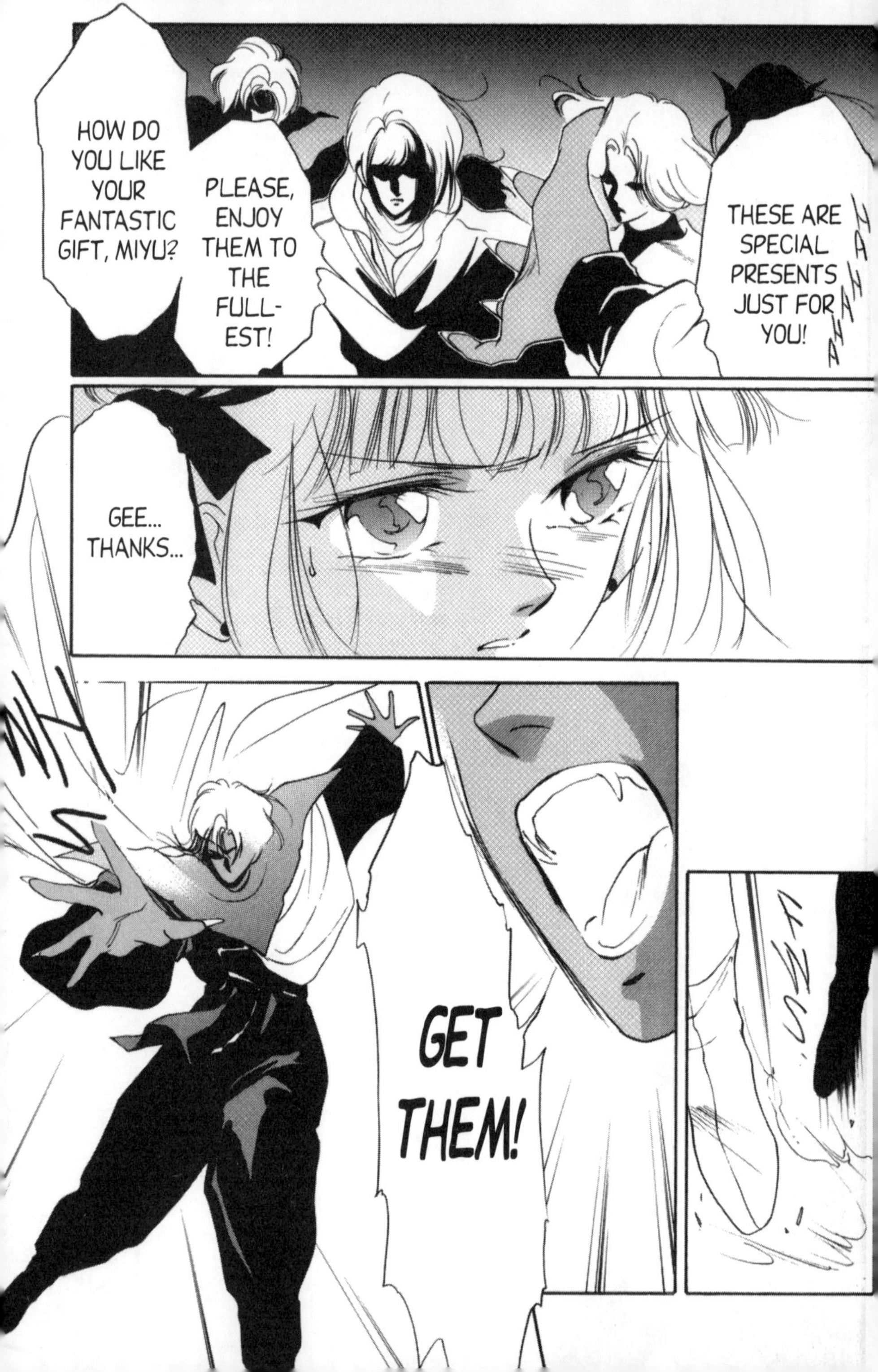
THESE ARE SPECIAL PRESENTS JUST FOR YOU!
PLEASE, ENJOY THEM TO THE FULL-EST!
HOW DO YOU LIKE YOUR FANTASTIC GIFT, MIYU?
GEE... THANKS...
GET THEM!

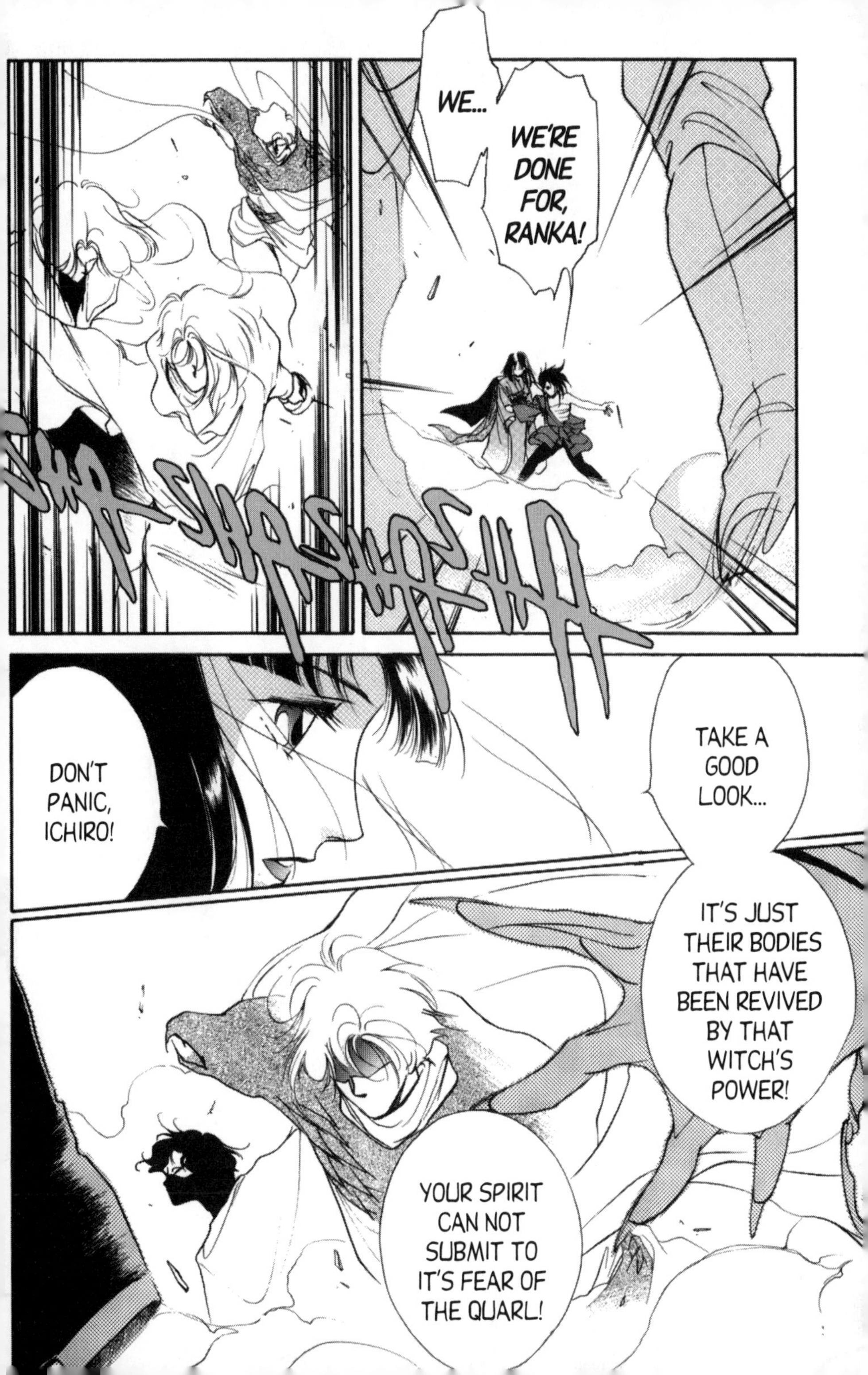

WE...
WE'RE DONE FOR, RANKA!
DON'T PANIC, ICHIRO!
TAKE A GOOD LOOK...
IT'S JUST THEIR BODIES THAT HAVE BEEN REVIVED BY THAT WITCH'S POWER!
YOUR SPIRIT CAN NOT SUBMIT TO IT'S FEAR OF THE QUARL!

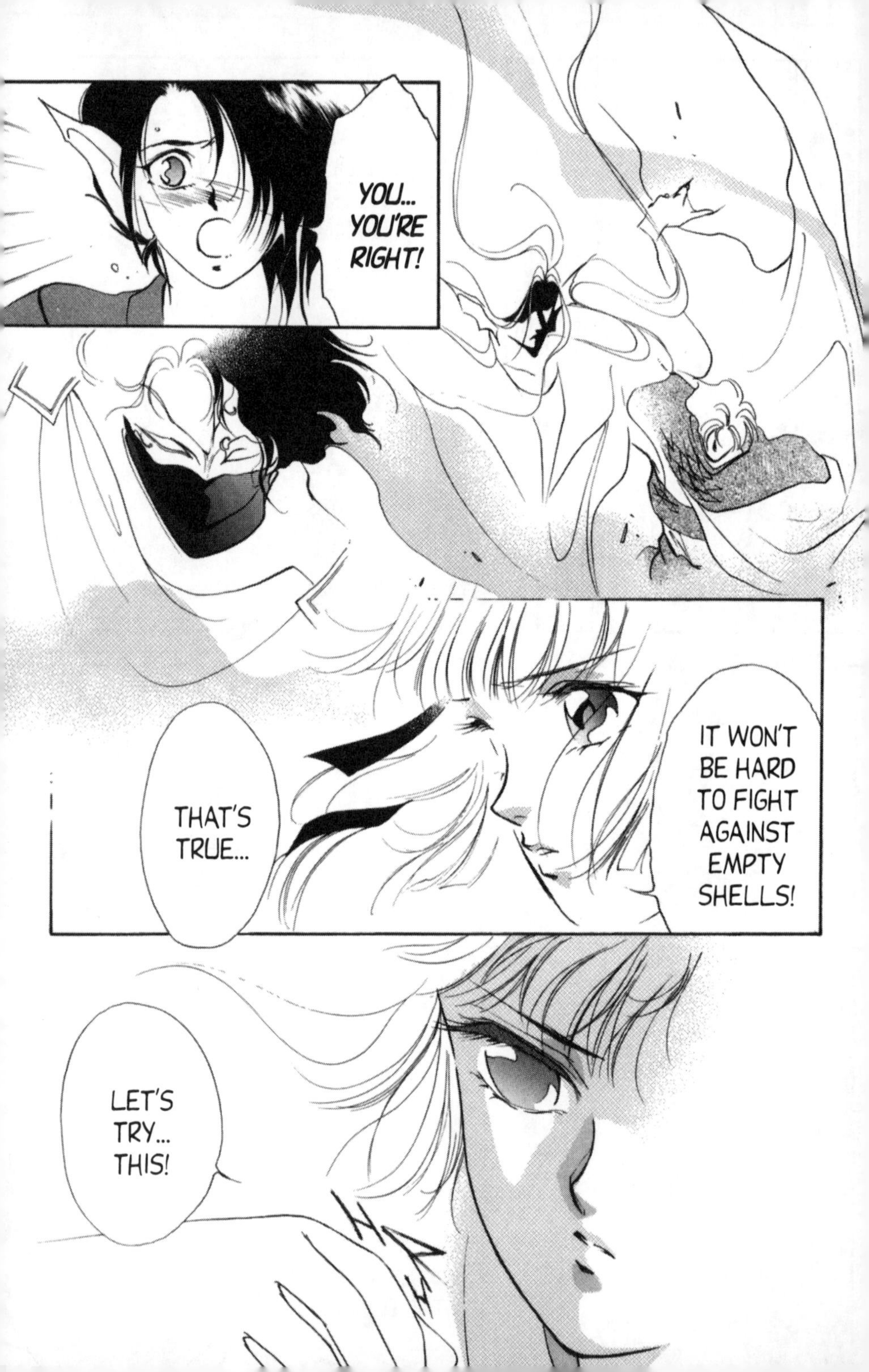
YOU... YOU'RE RIGHT!
IT WON'T BE HARD TO FIGHT AGAINST EMPTY SHELLS!
THAT'S TRUE...
LET'S TRY... THIS!

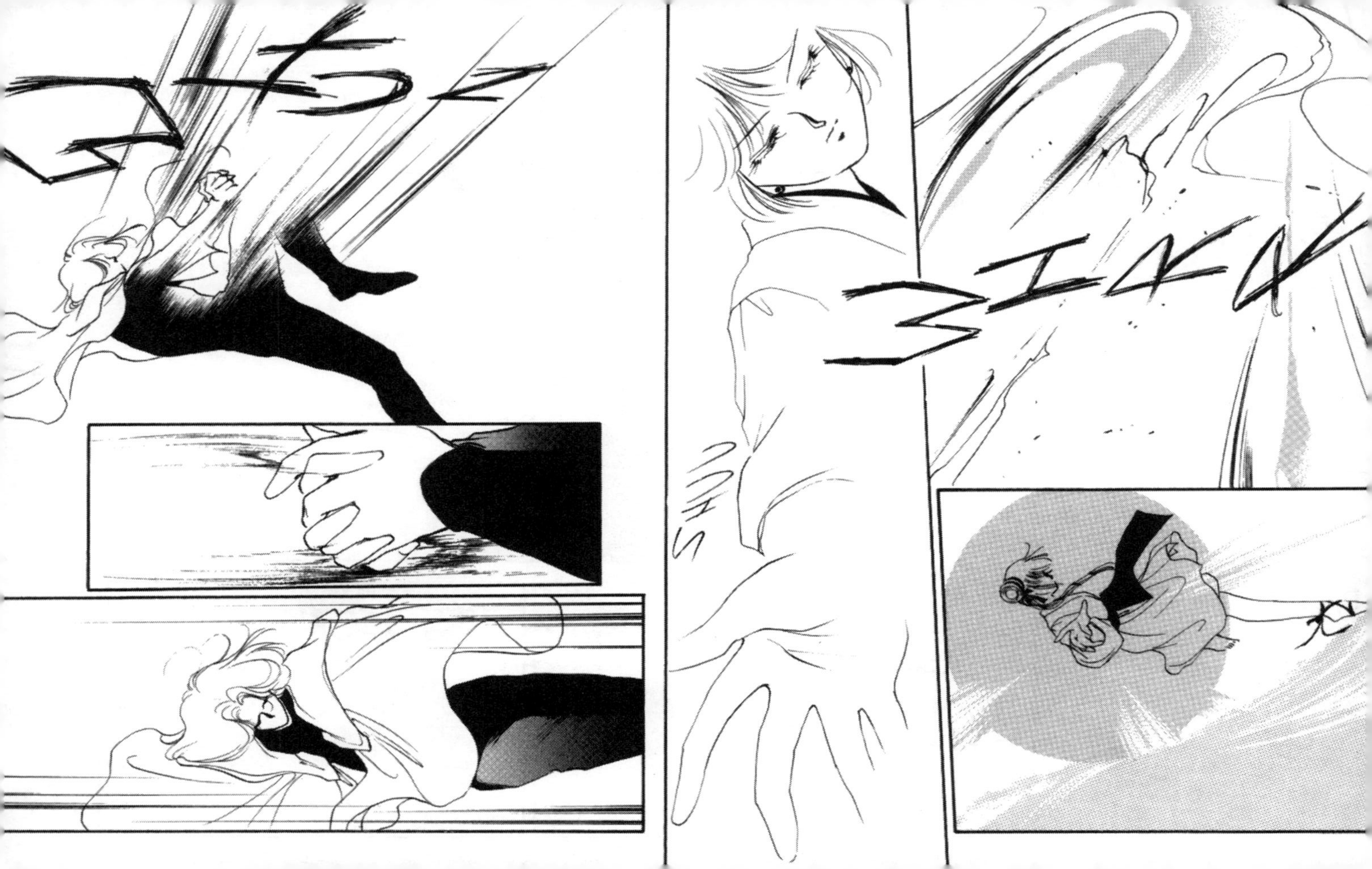
SHUU

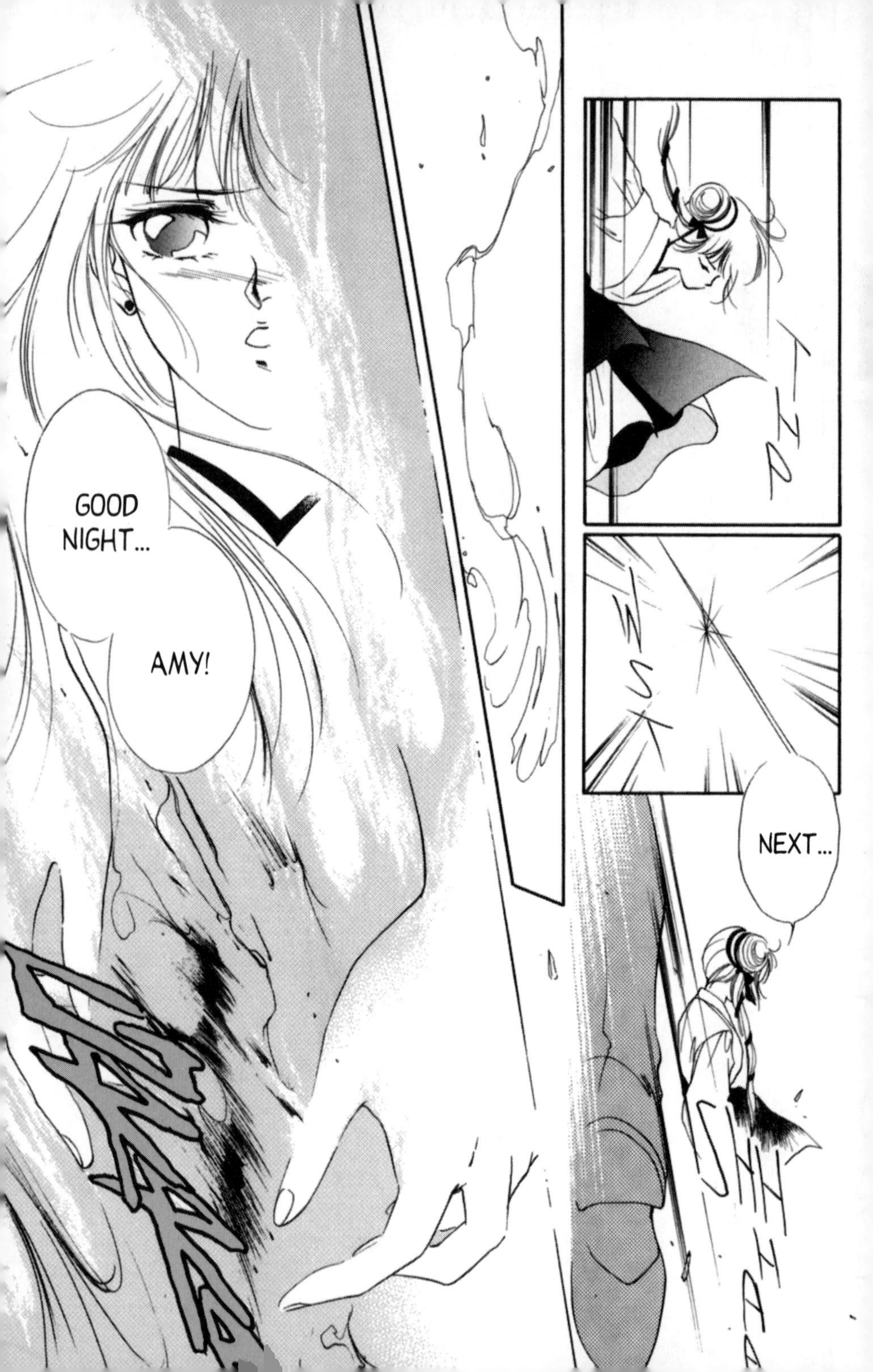
GOOD NIGHT...
AMY!
NEXT...

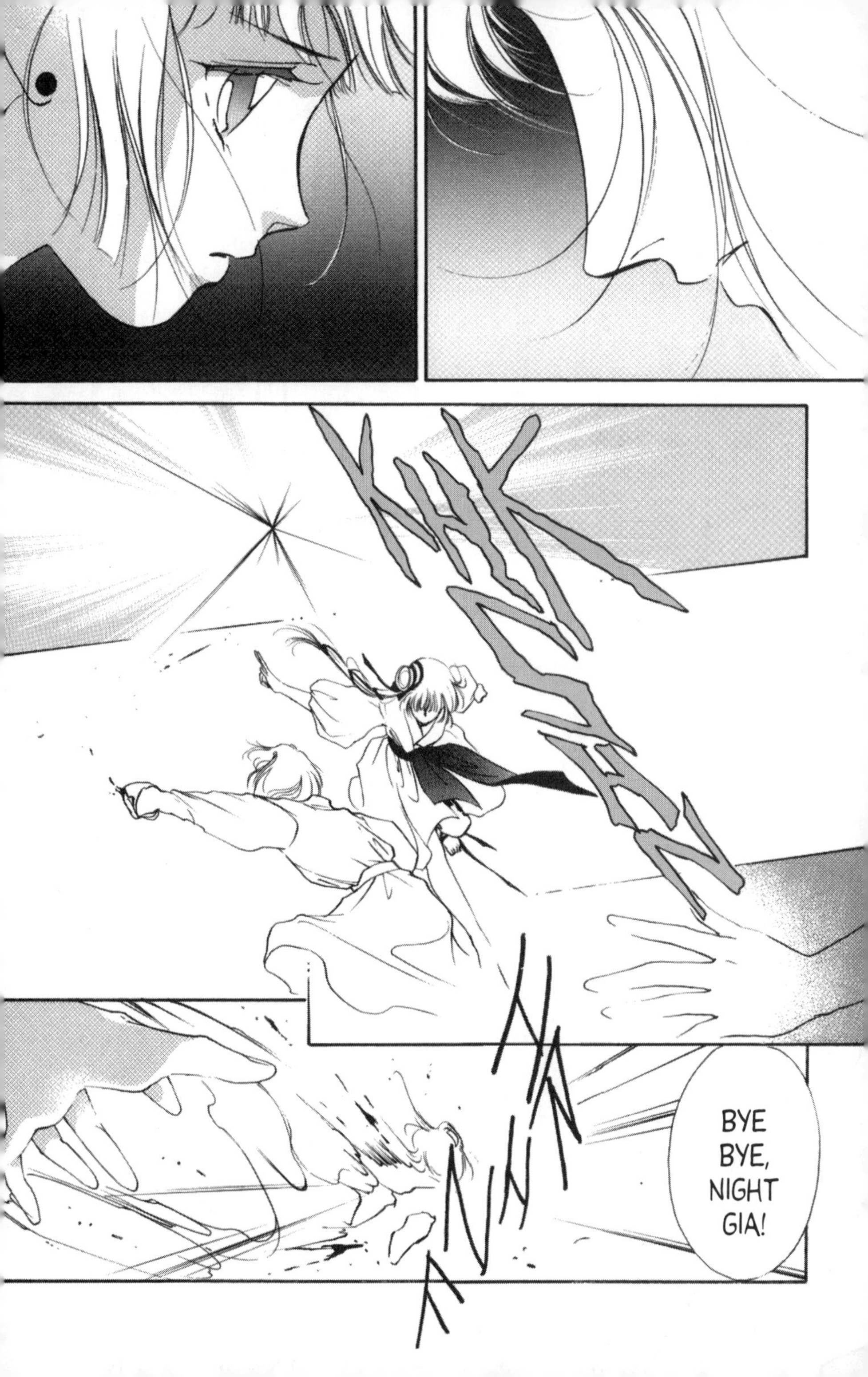
BYE
BYE,
NIGHT
GIA!

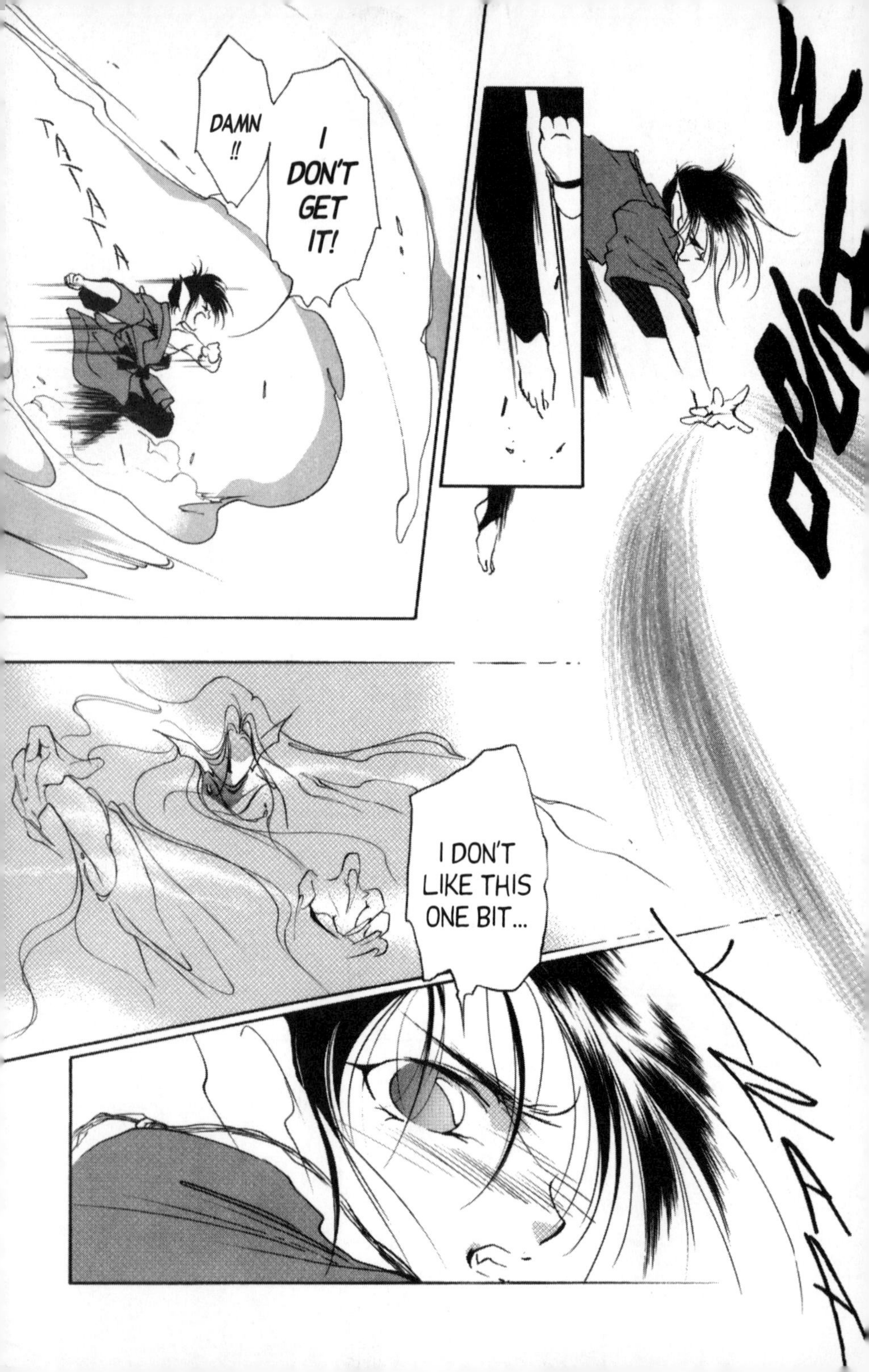
I DON'T GET IT!
DAMN!!
I DON'T LIKE THIS ONE BIT...

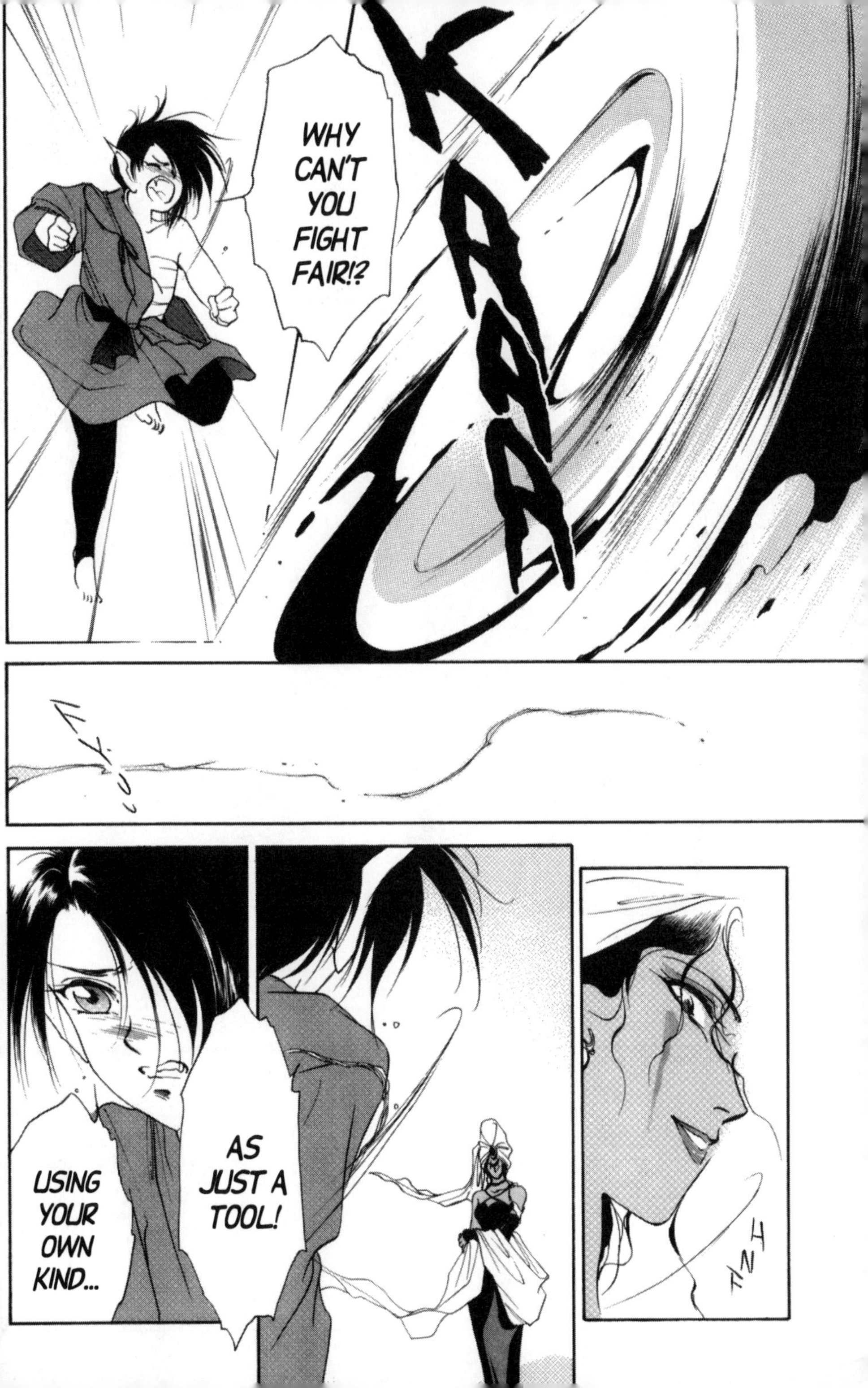
WHY CAN'T YOU FIGHT FAIR!?
USING YOUR OWN KIND...
AS JUST A TOOL!

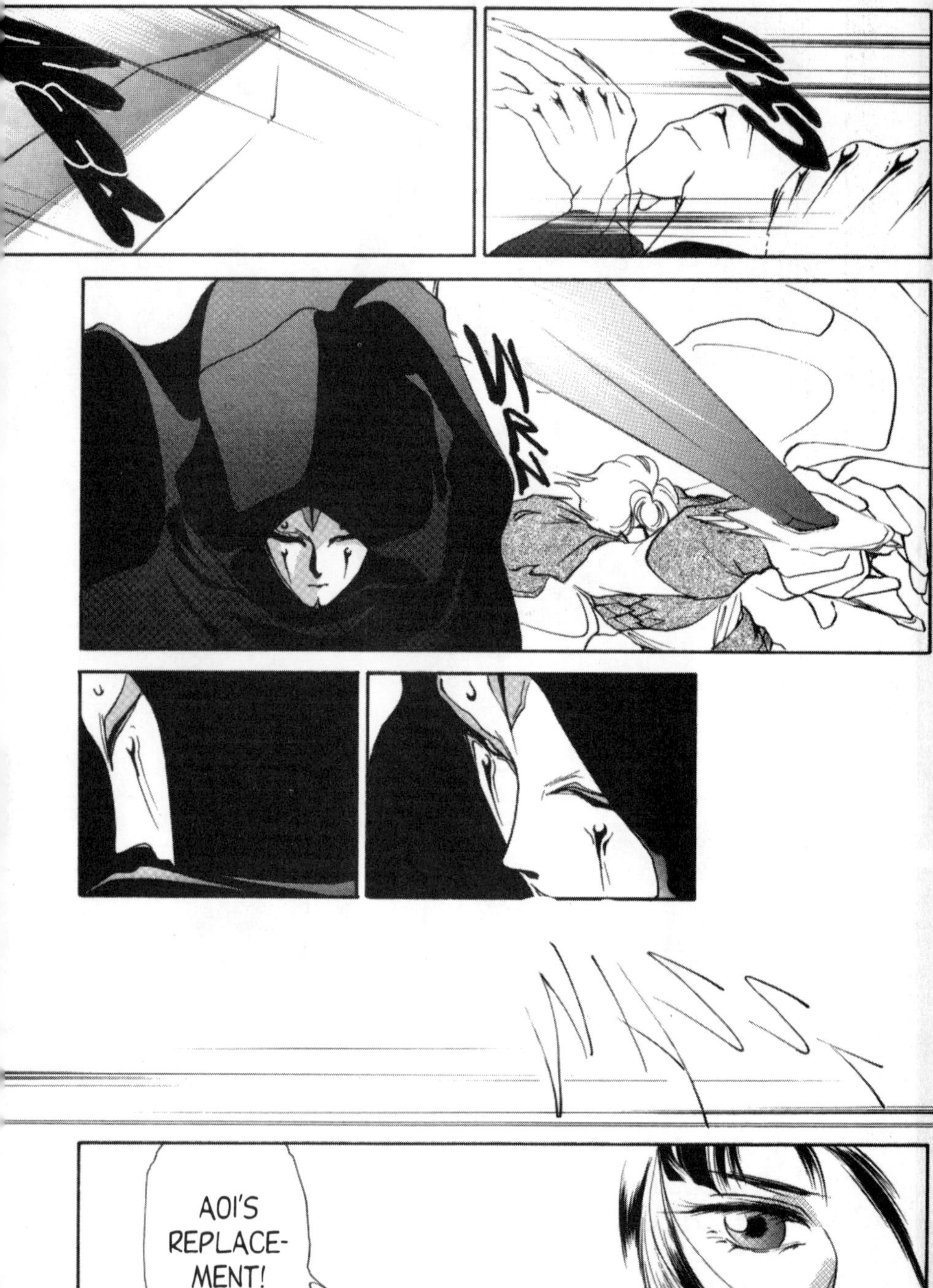
AOI'S REPLACE-MENT!

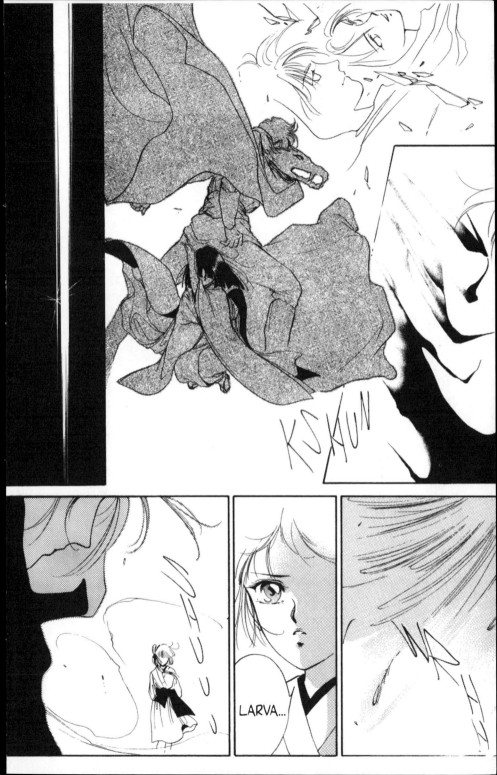

KSHUN

LARVA...

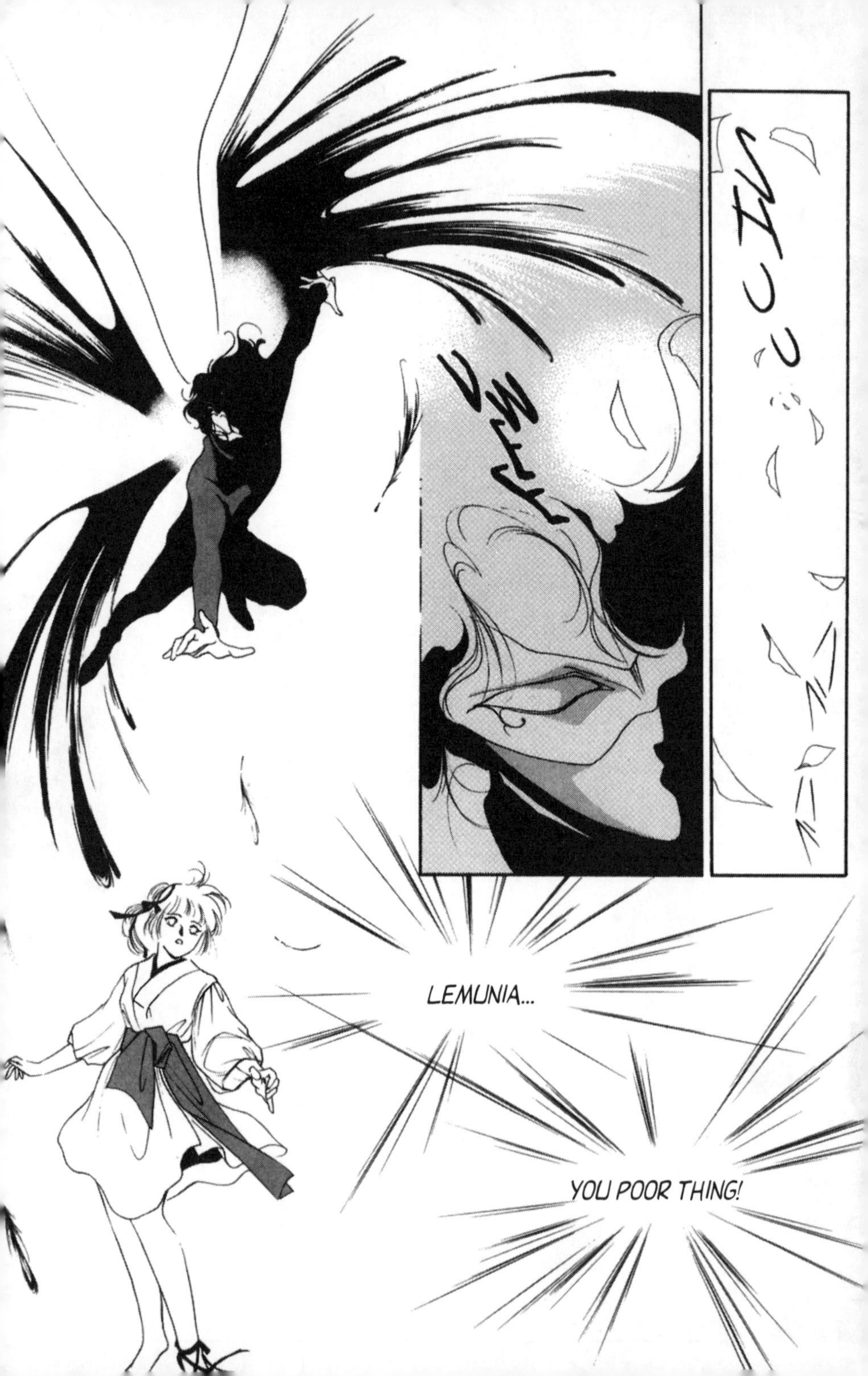
LEMUNIA...
YOU POOR THING!

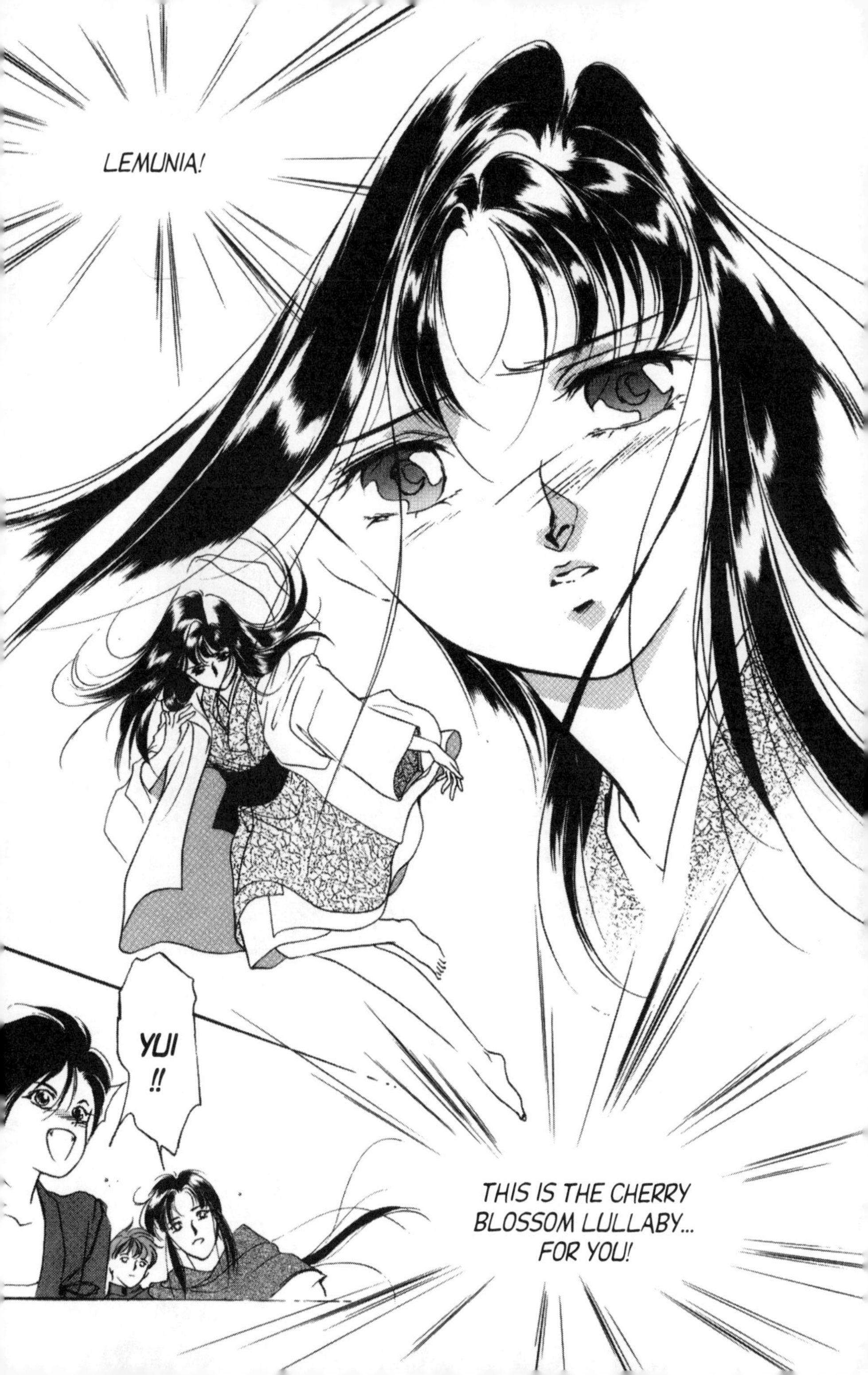
LEMUNIA!
YUI !!
THIS IS THE CHERRY BLOSSOM LULLABY... FOR YOU!

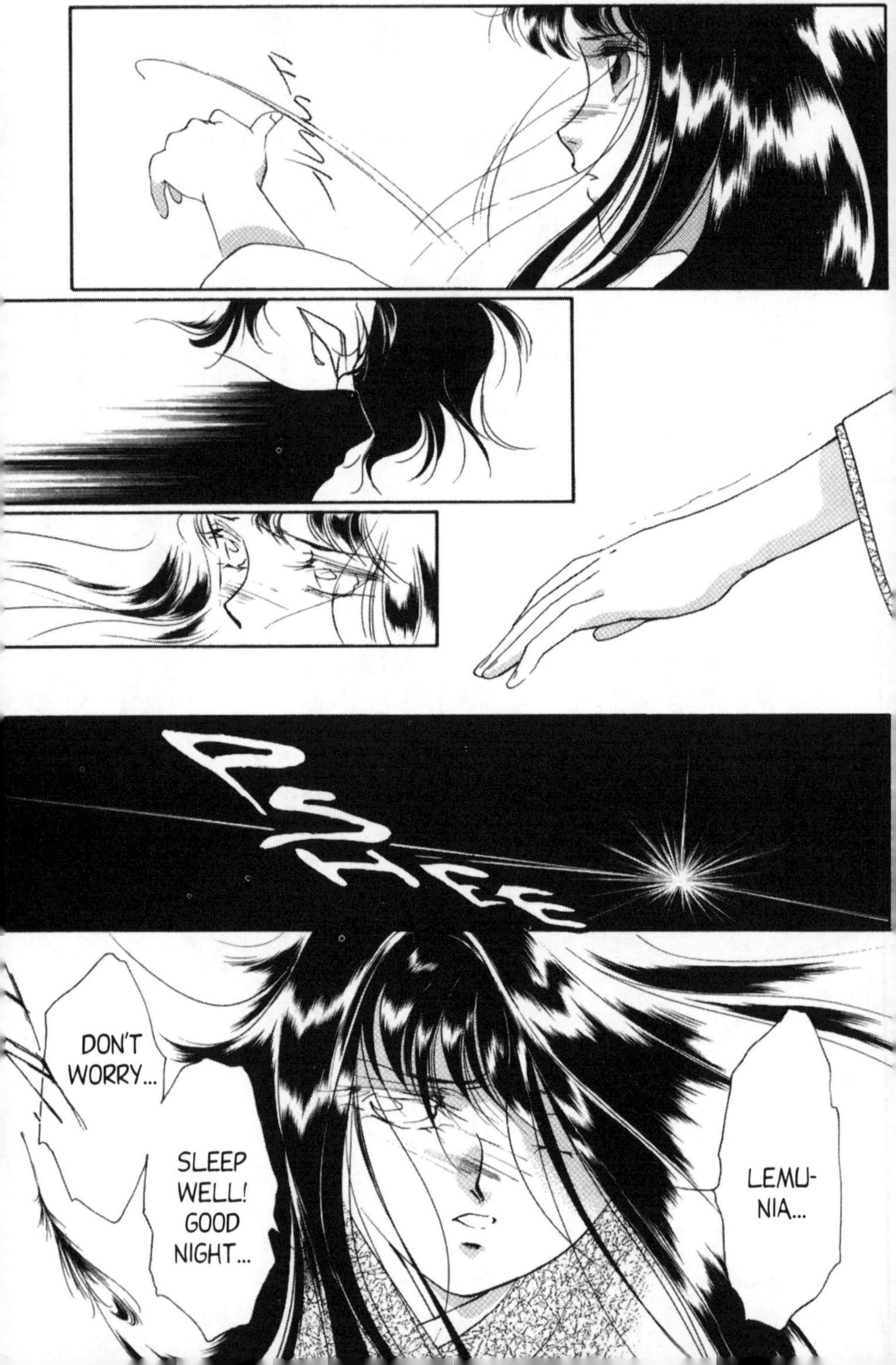
FSSS
PSHEEE
DON'T WORRY...
SLEEP WELL! GOOD NIGHT...
LEMU-NIA...

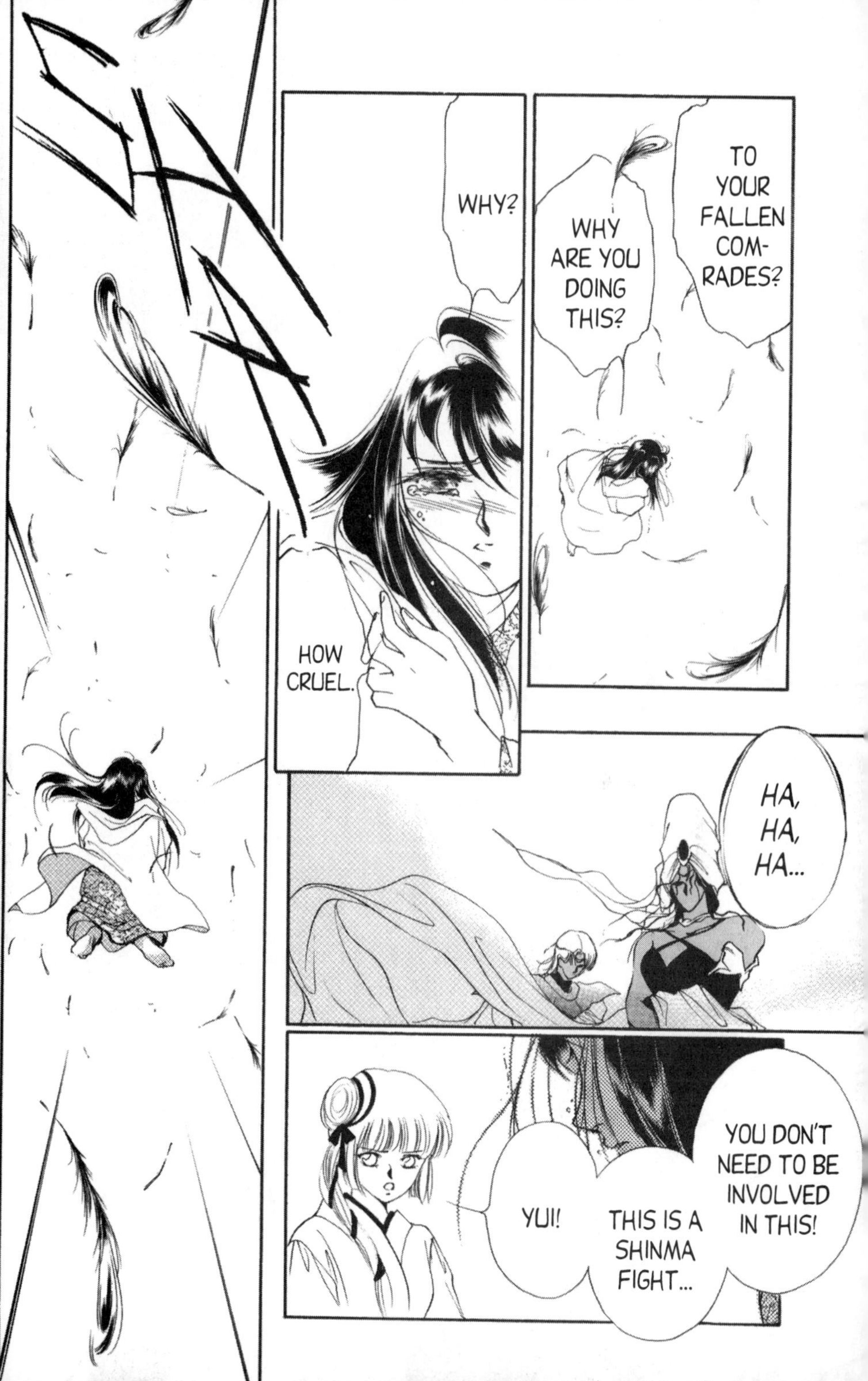
TO YOUR FALLEN COM- RADES?
WHY ARE YOU DOING THIS?
WHY?
HOW CRUEL.
HA, HA, HA...
YOU DON'T NEED TO BE INVOLVED IN THIS!
THIS IS A SHINMA FIGHT...
YUI!

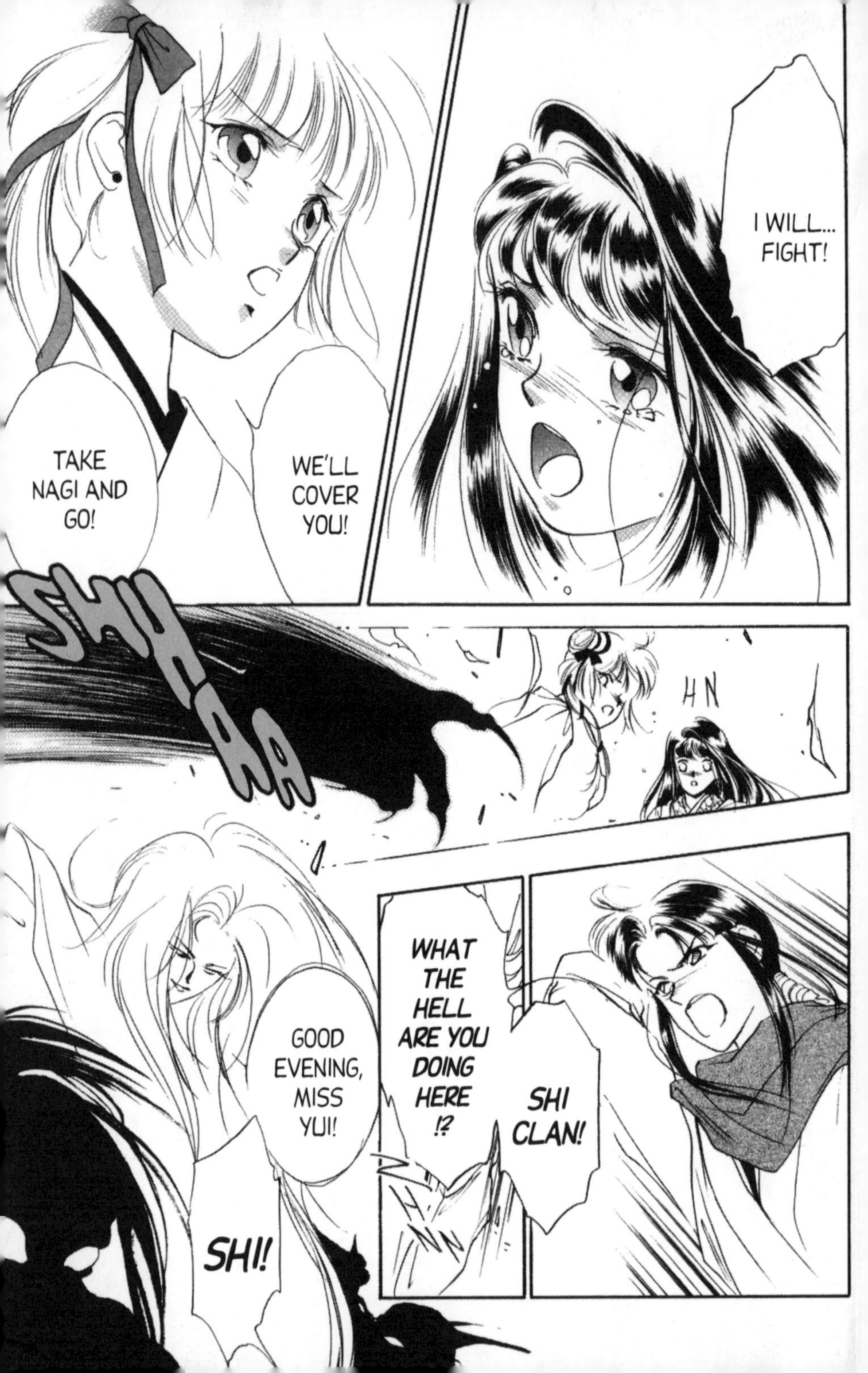
I WILL... FIGHT!
WE'LL COVER YOU!
TAKE NAGI AND GO!
HN
SHI CLAN!
WHAT THE HELL ARE YOU DOING HERE !?
GOOD EVENING, MISS YUI!
SHI!

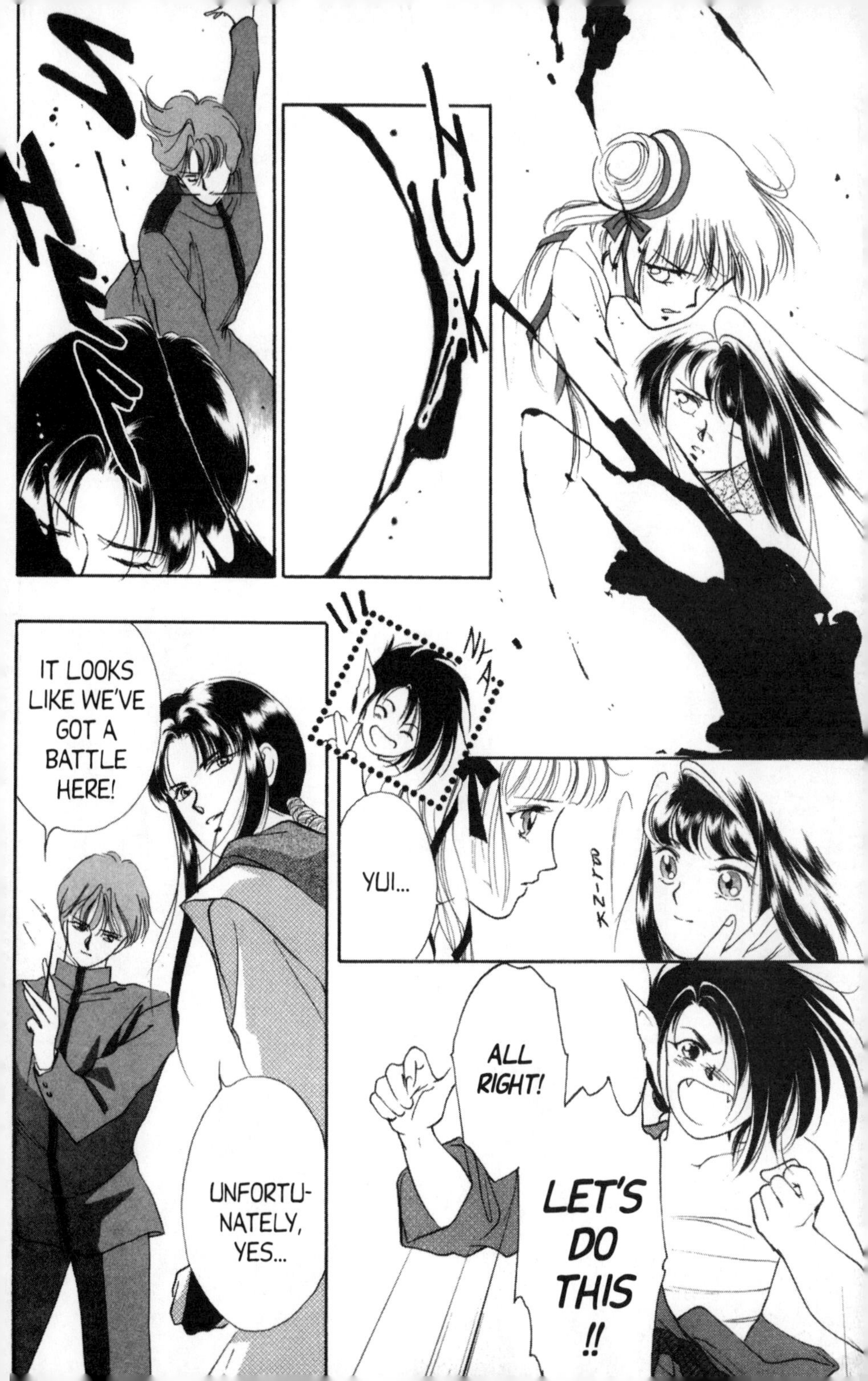

SHWA
HUK
IT LOOKS LIKE WE'VE GOT A BATTLE HERE!
UNFORTU-NATELY, YES...
NYA
YUI...
B-L-I-N-K
ALL RIGHT!
LET'S DO THIS!!

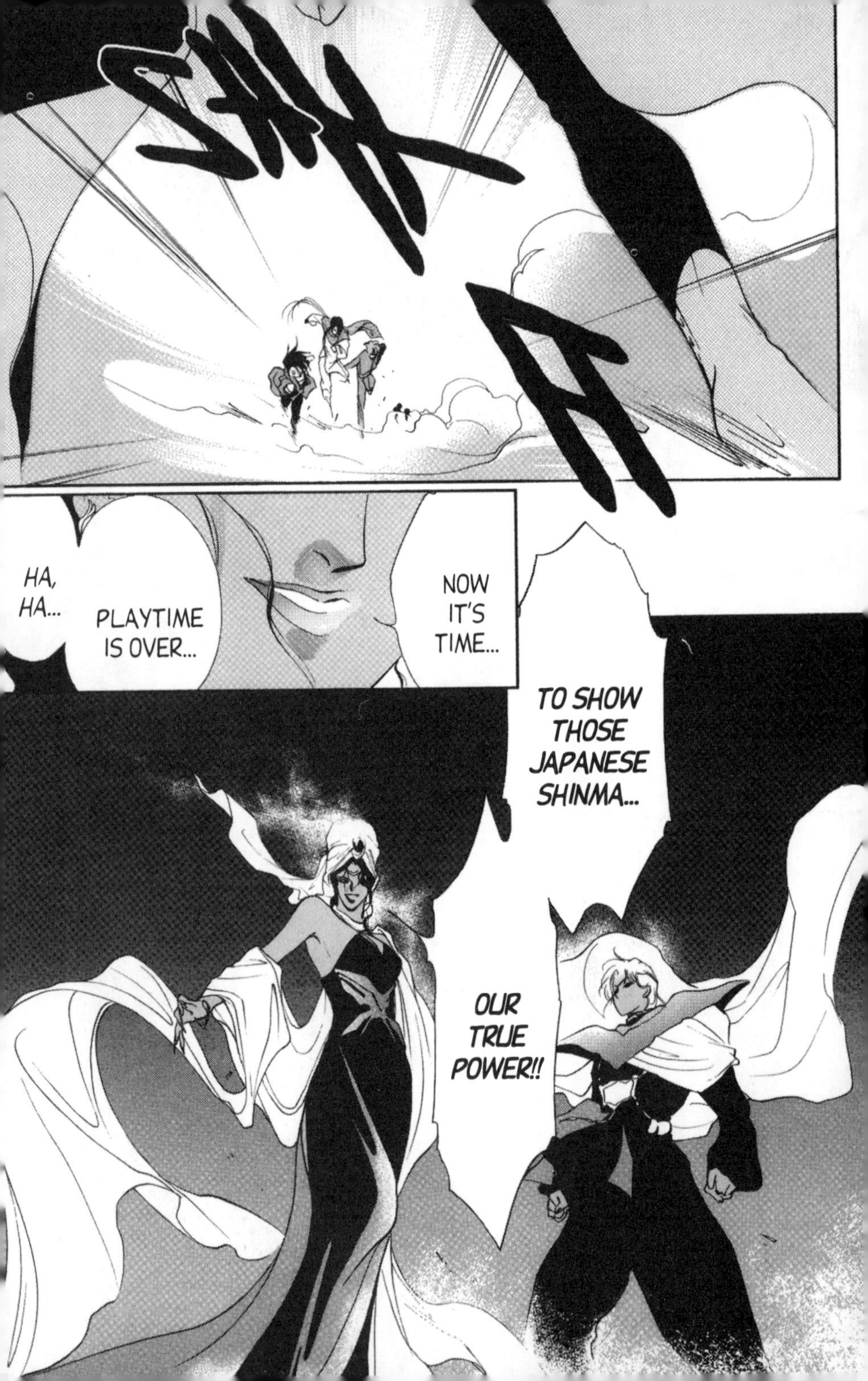
HA, HA...
PLAYTIME IS OVER...
NOW IT'S TIME...
TO SHOW THOSE JAPANESE SHINMA...
OUR TRUE POWER!!

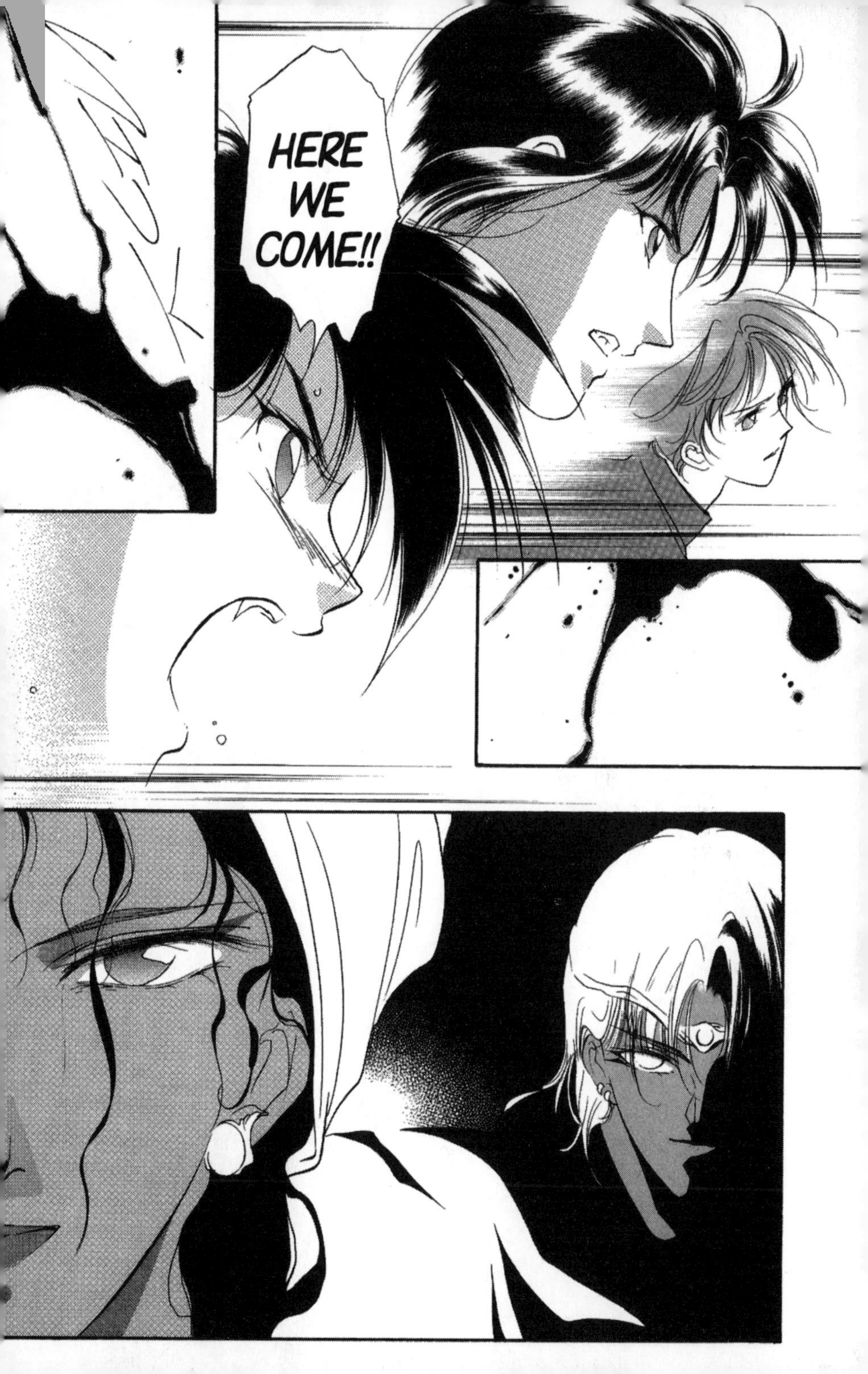
HERE WE COME!!

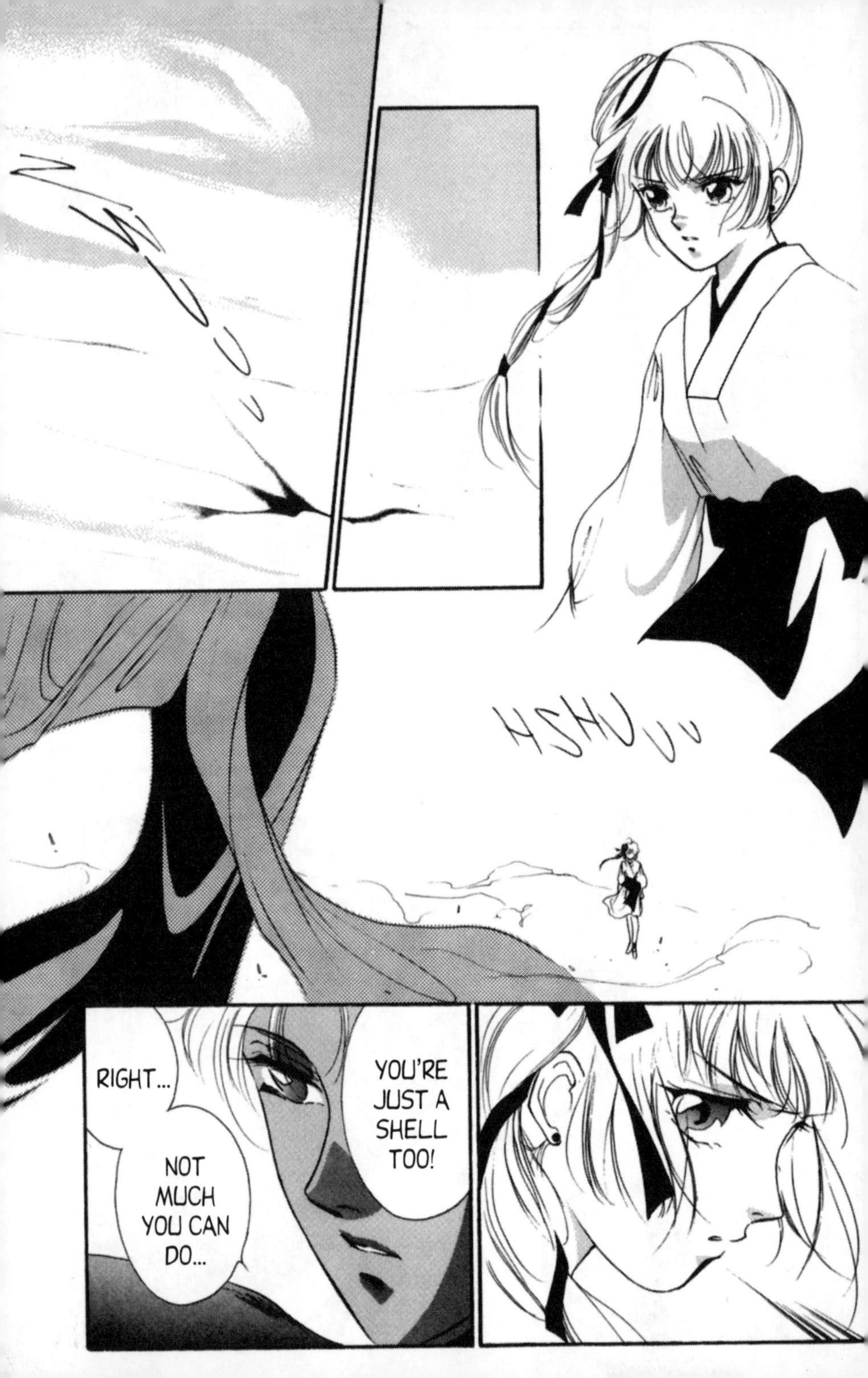
YOU'RE JUST A SHELL TOO!
RIGHT...
NOT MUCH YOU CAN DO...

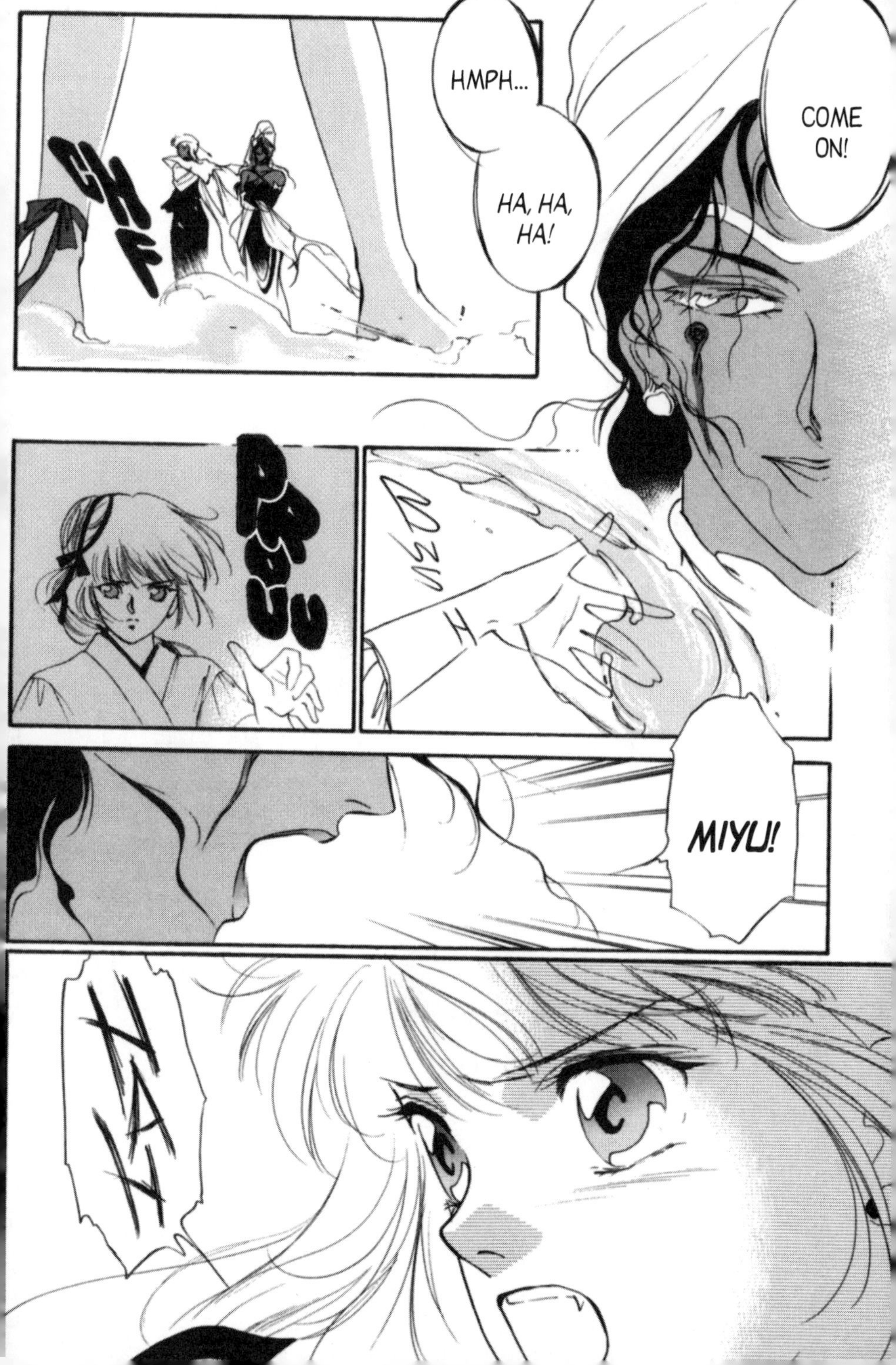
COME ON!
HMPH...
HA, HA, HA!
MIYU!

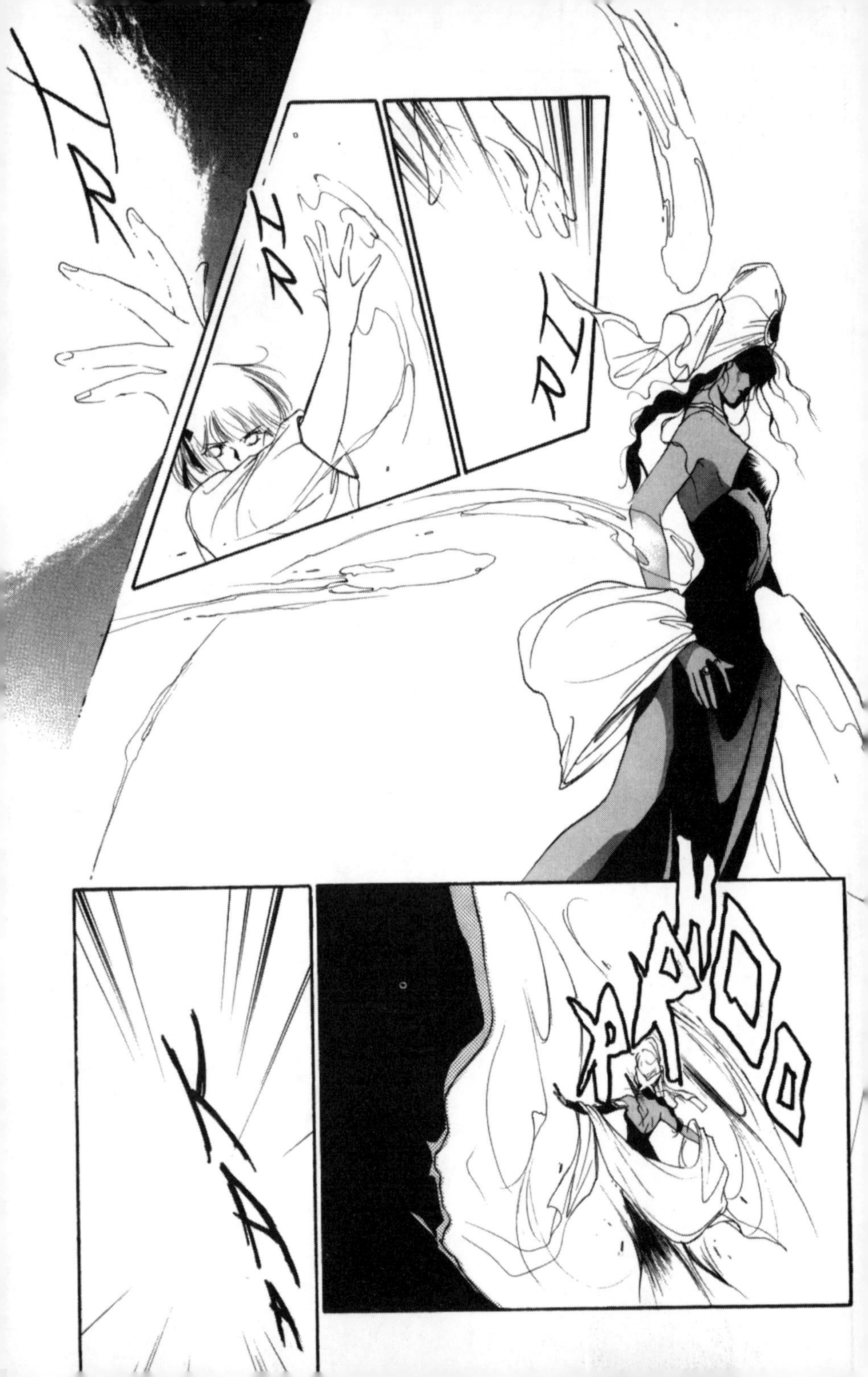
TRR
TRR
TRR
KAAA

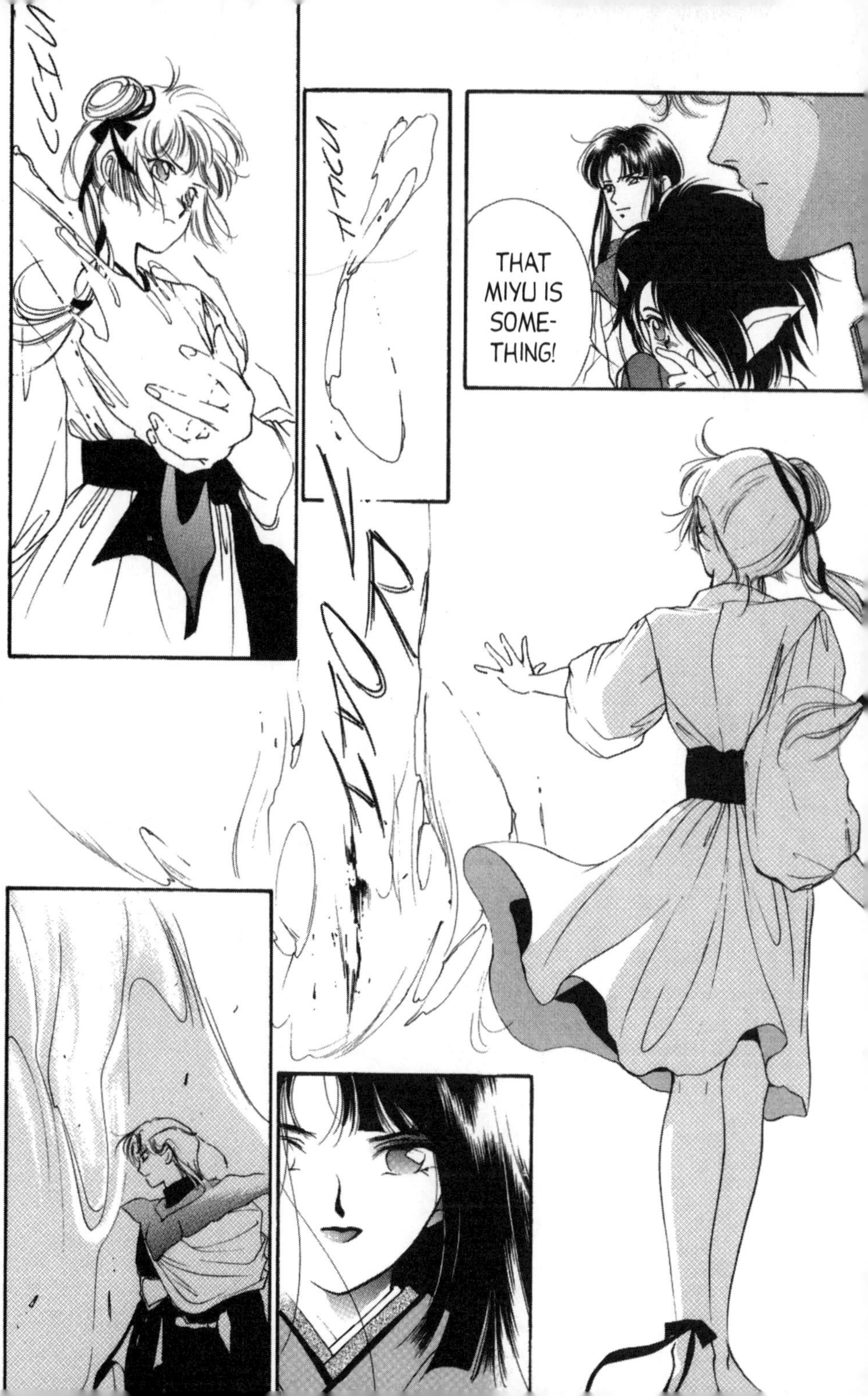
THAT MIYU IS SOME-THING!

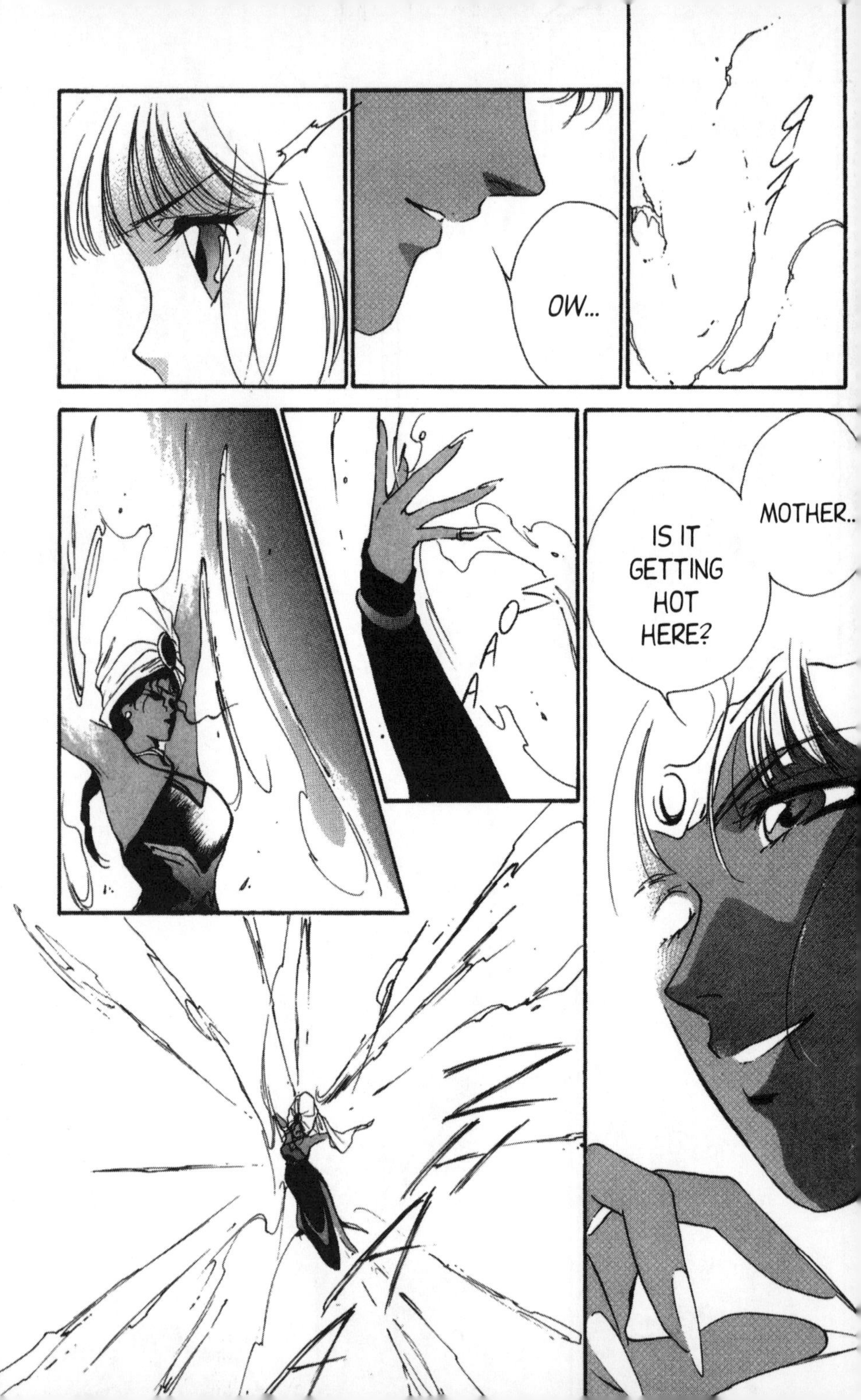
OW...
MOTHER..
IS IT GETTING HOT HERE?

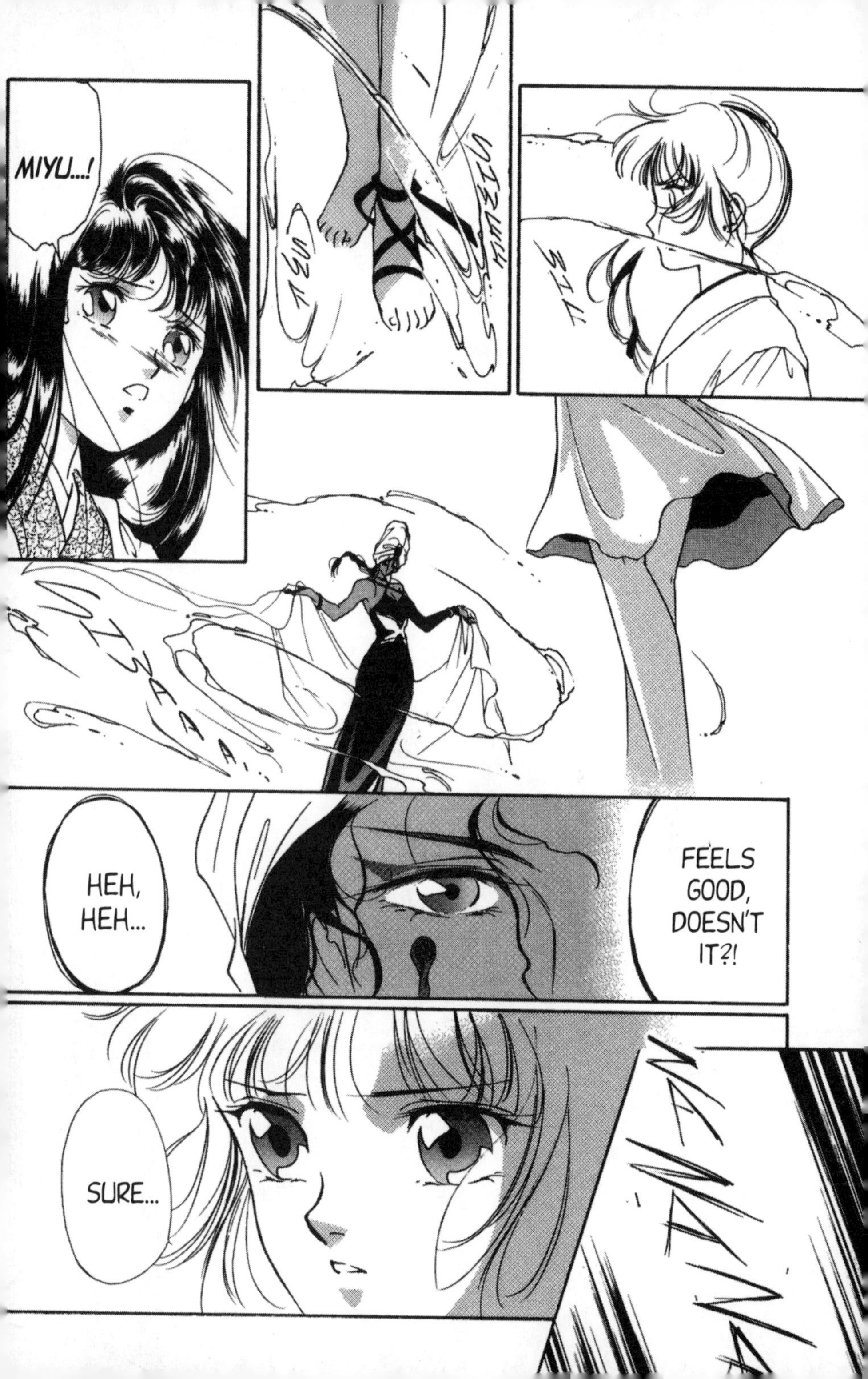
MIYU...!
FEELS GOOD, DOESN'T IT?!
HEH, HEH...
SURE...

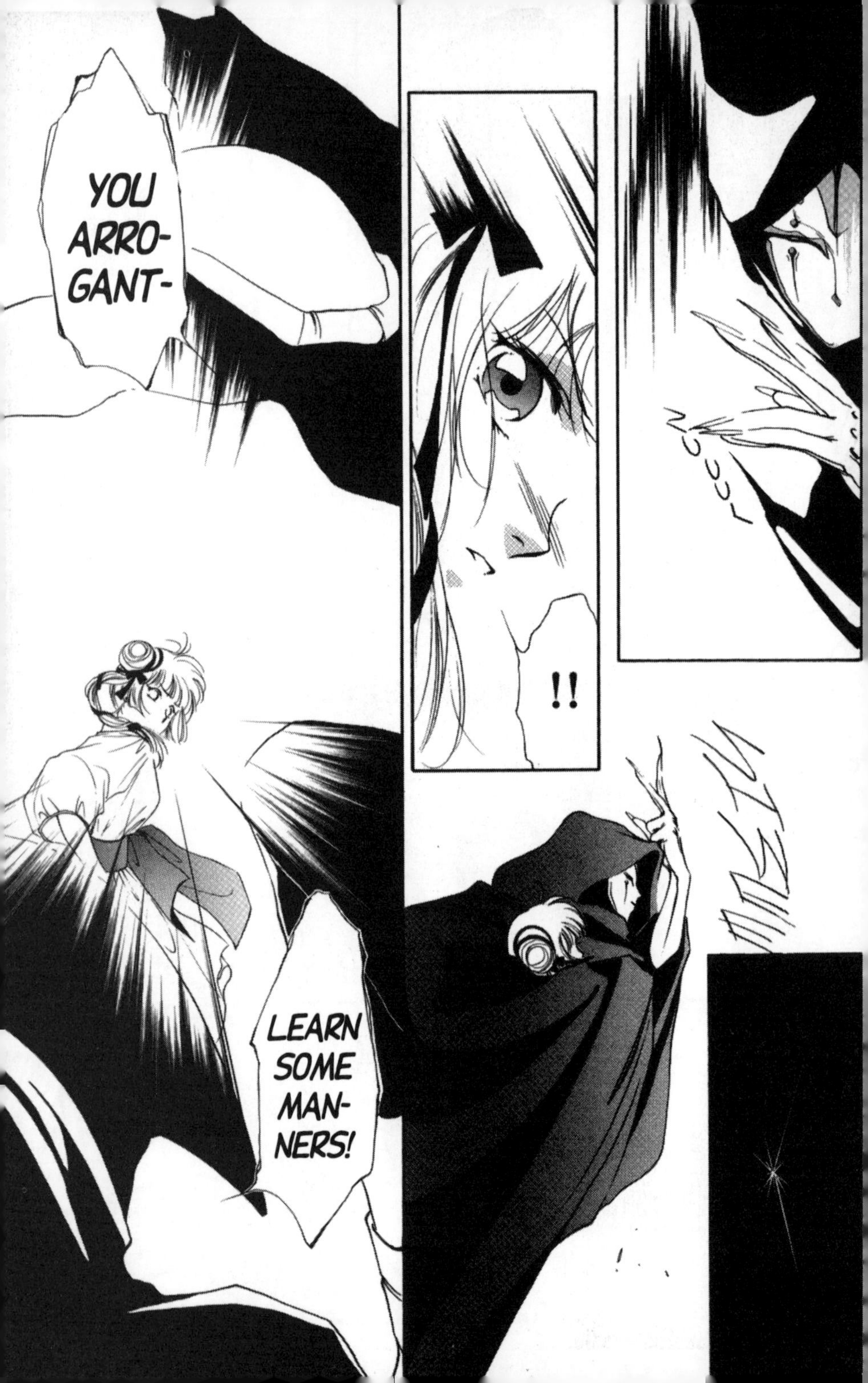

!!
YOU ARRO-GANT-
LEARN SOME MAN-NERS!

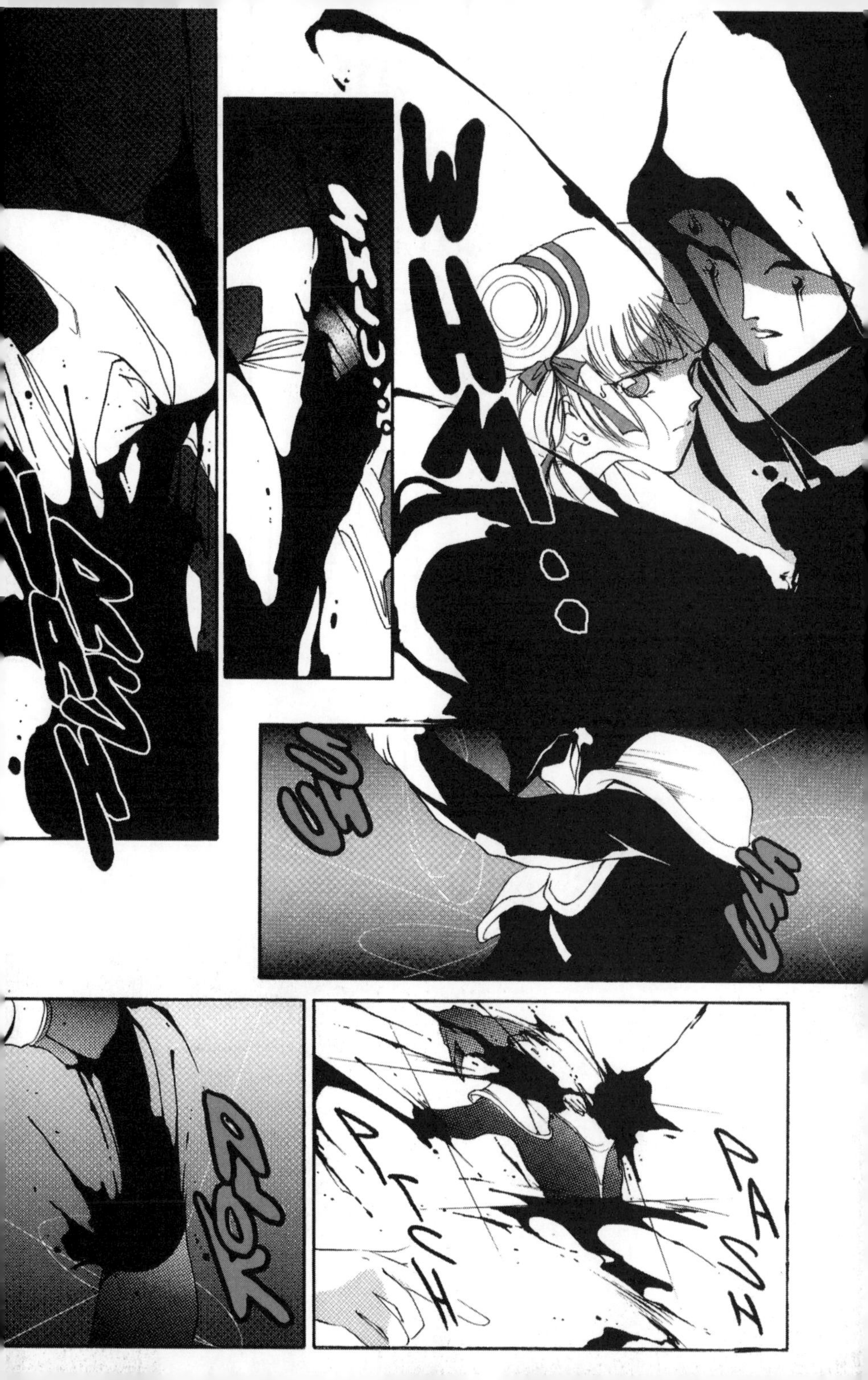

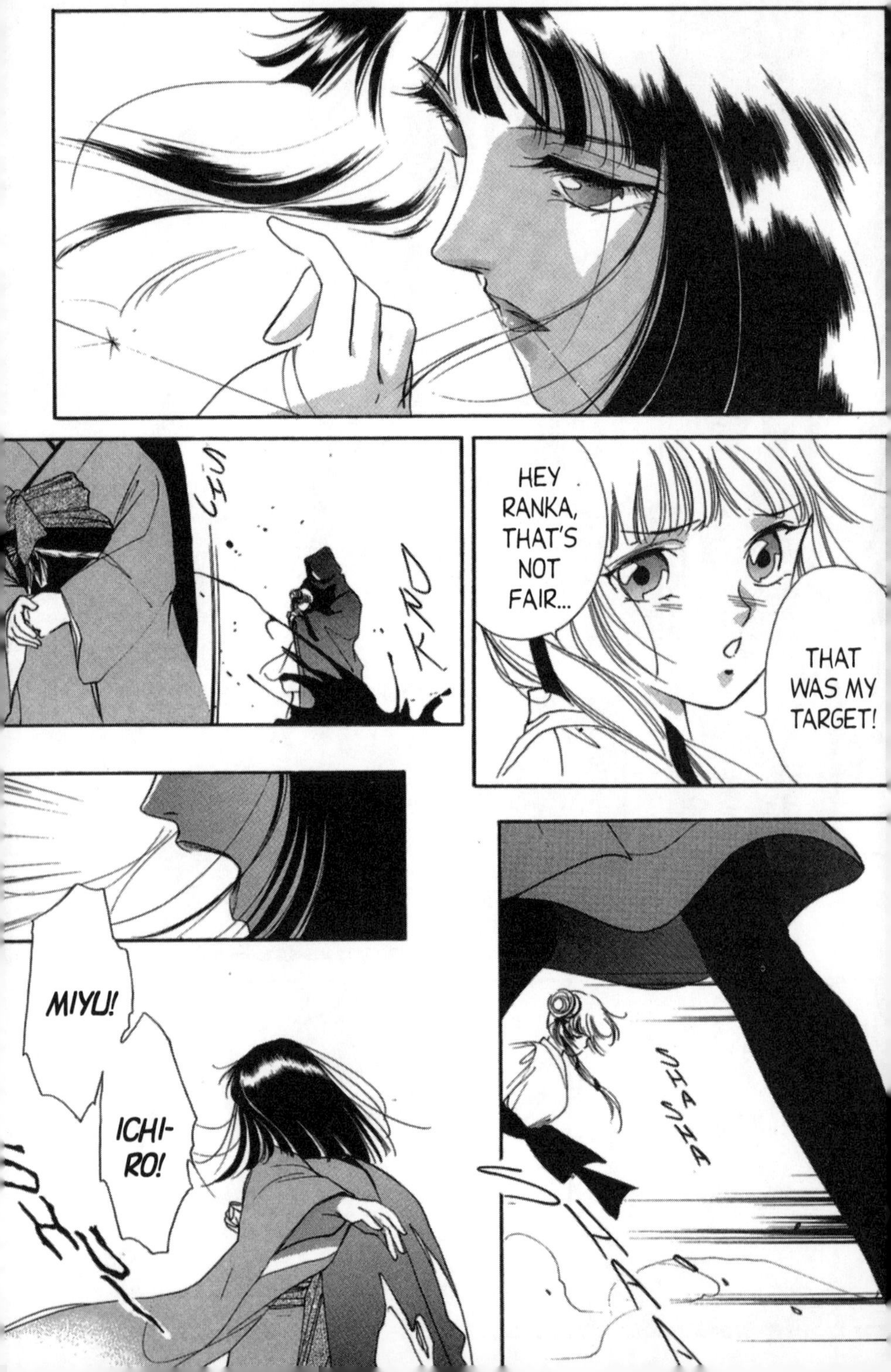
THAT WAS MY TARGET!
HEY RANKA, THAT'S NOT FAIR...
MIYU!
ICHI-RO!

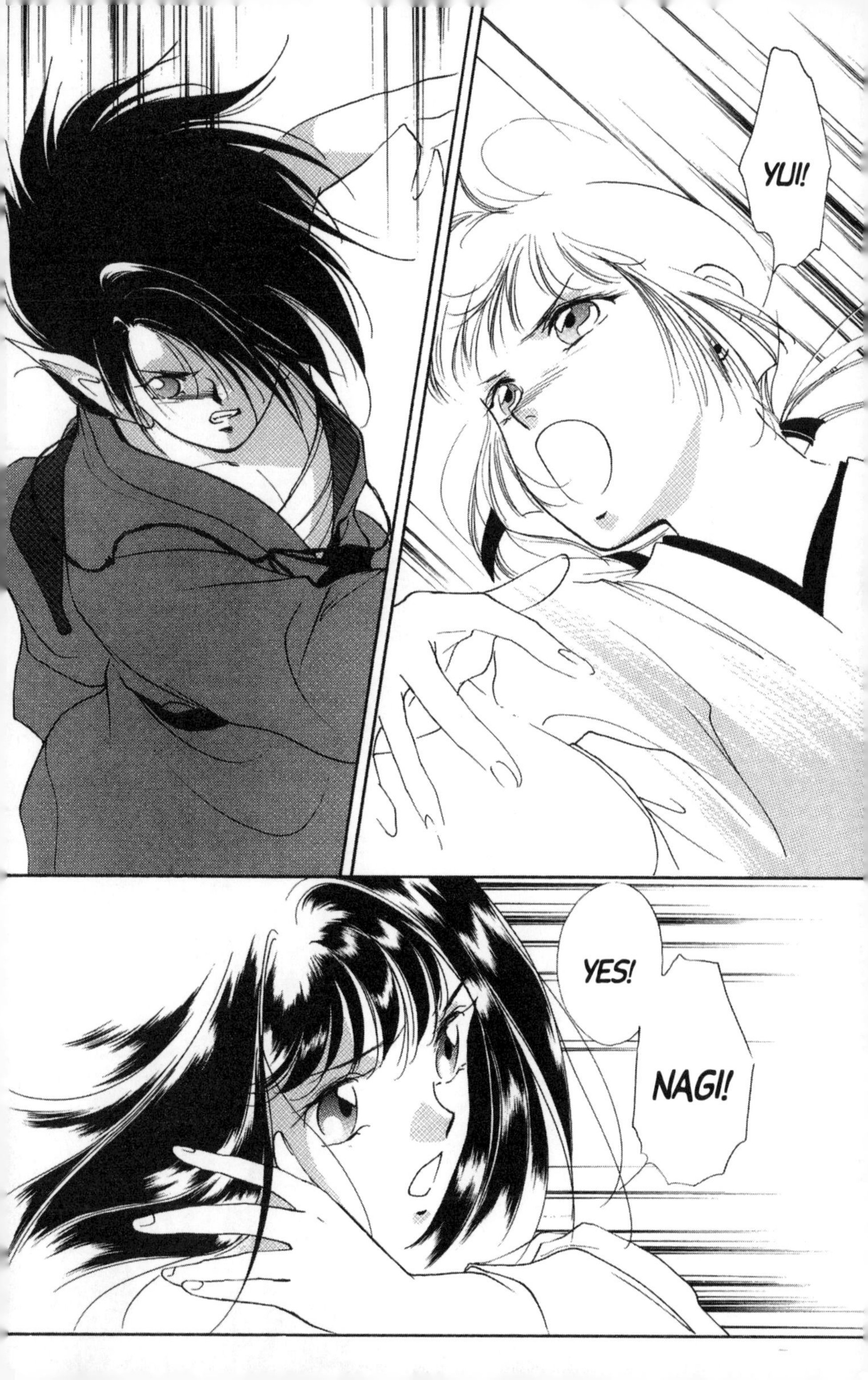
YUI!
YES!
NAGI!

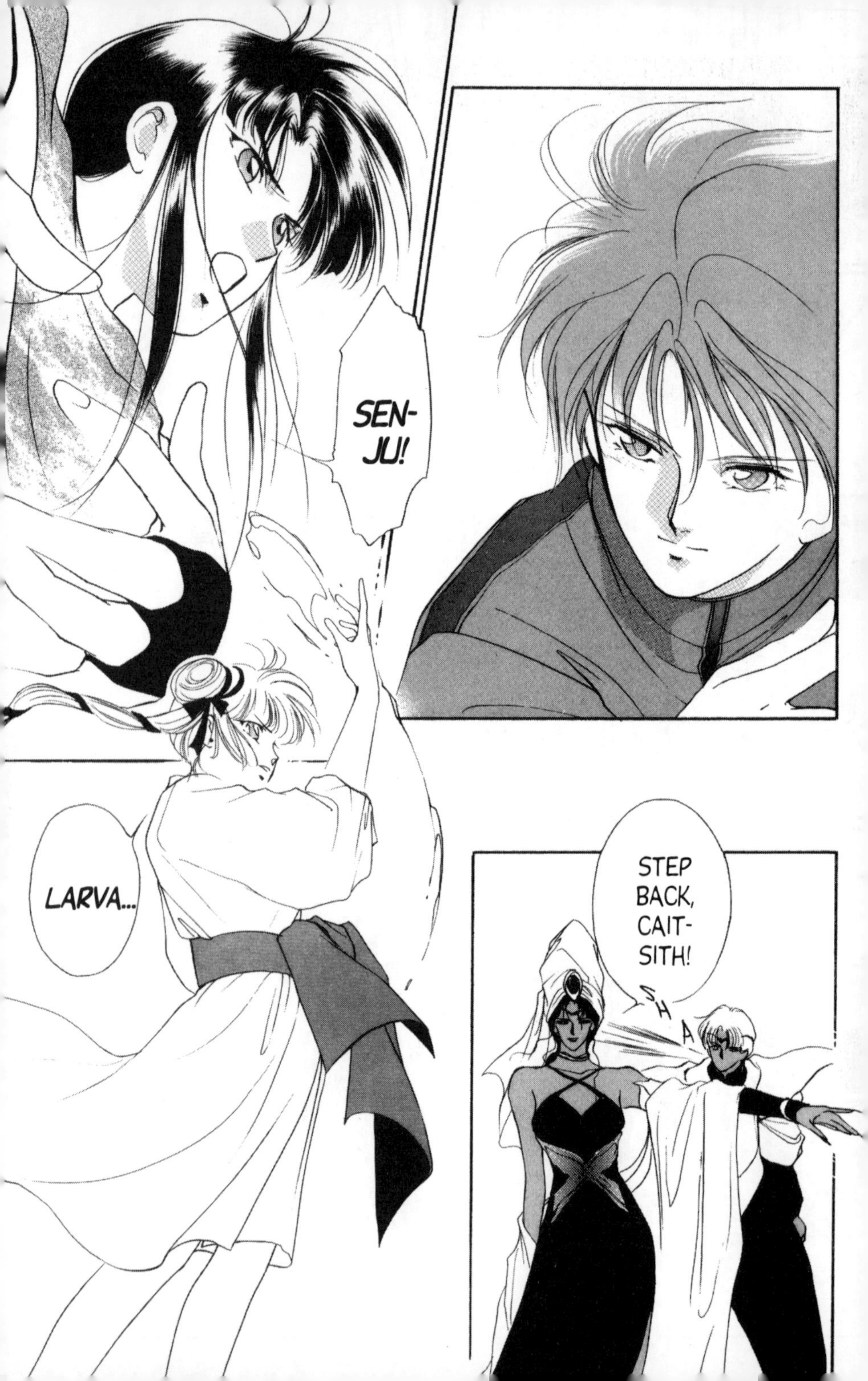
SEN-JU!
LARVA...
STEP BACK, CAIT-SITH!
SHA

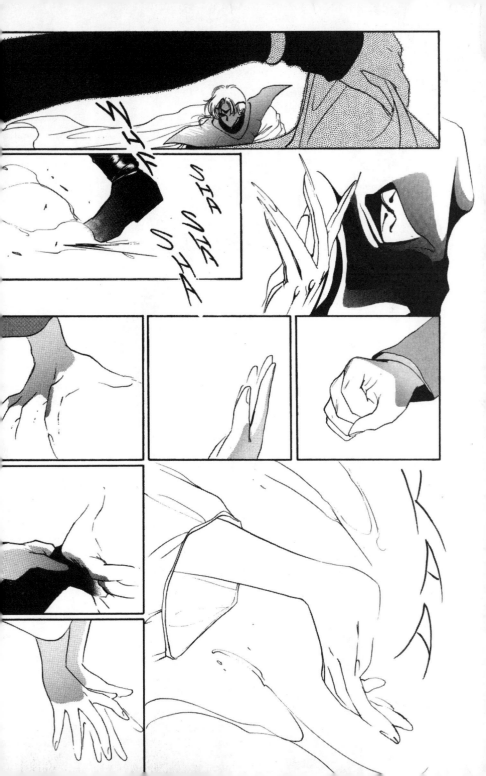

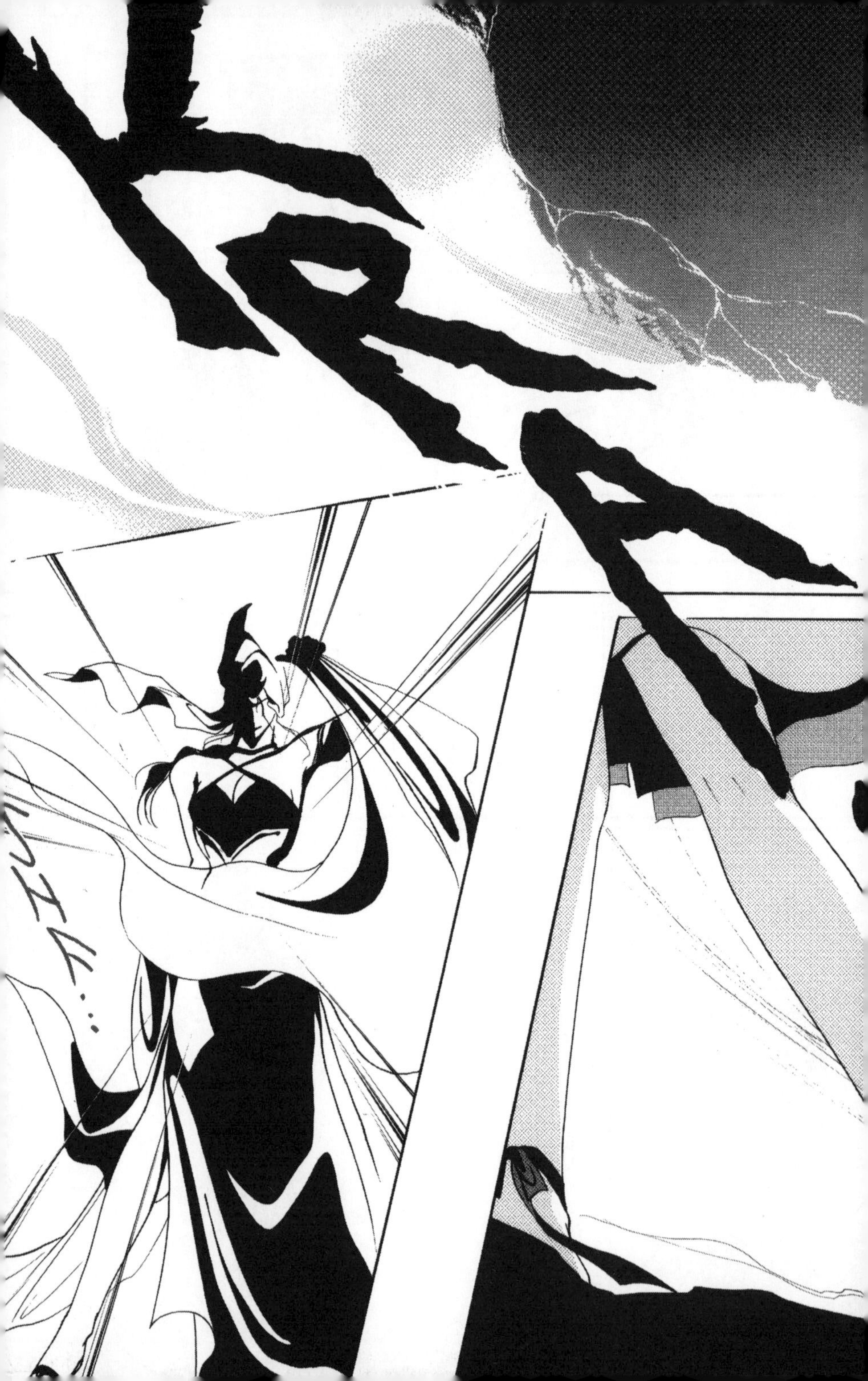
KRA

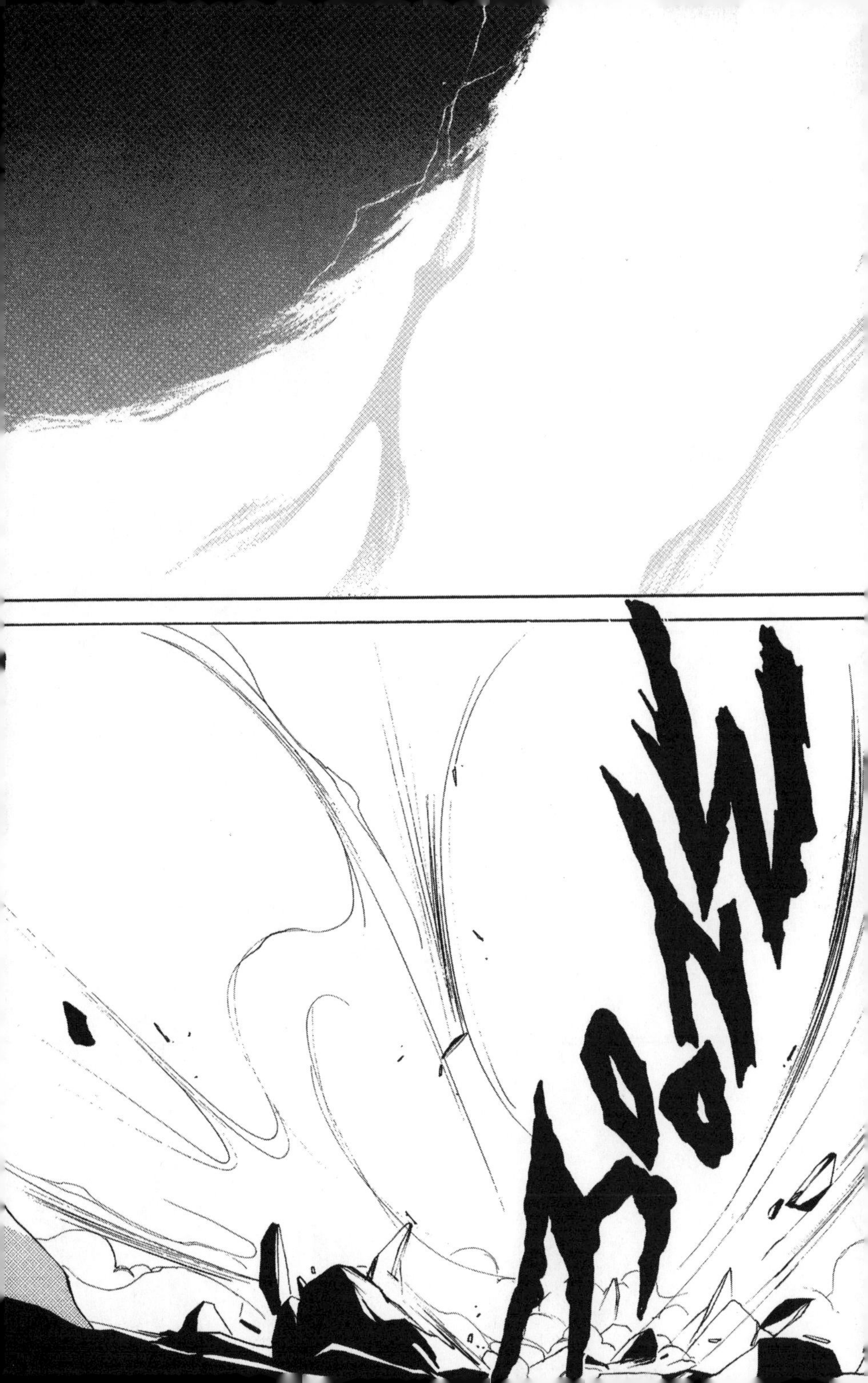

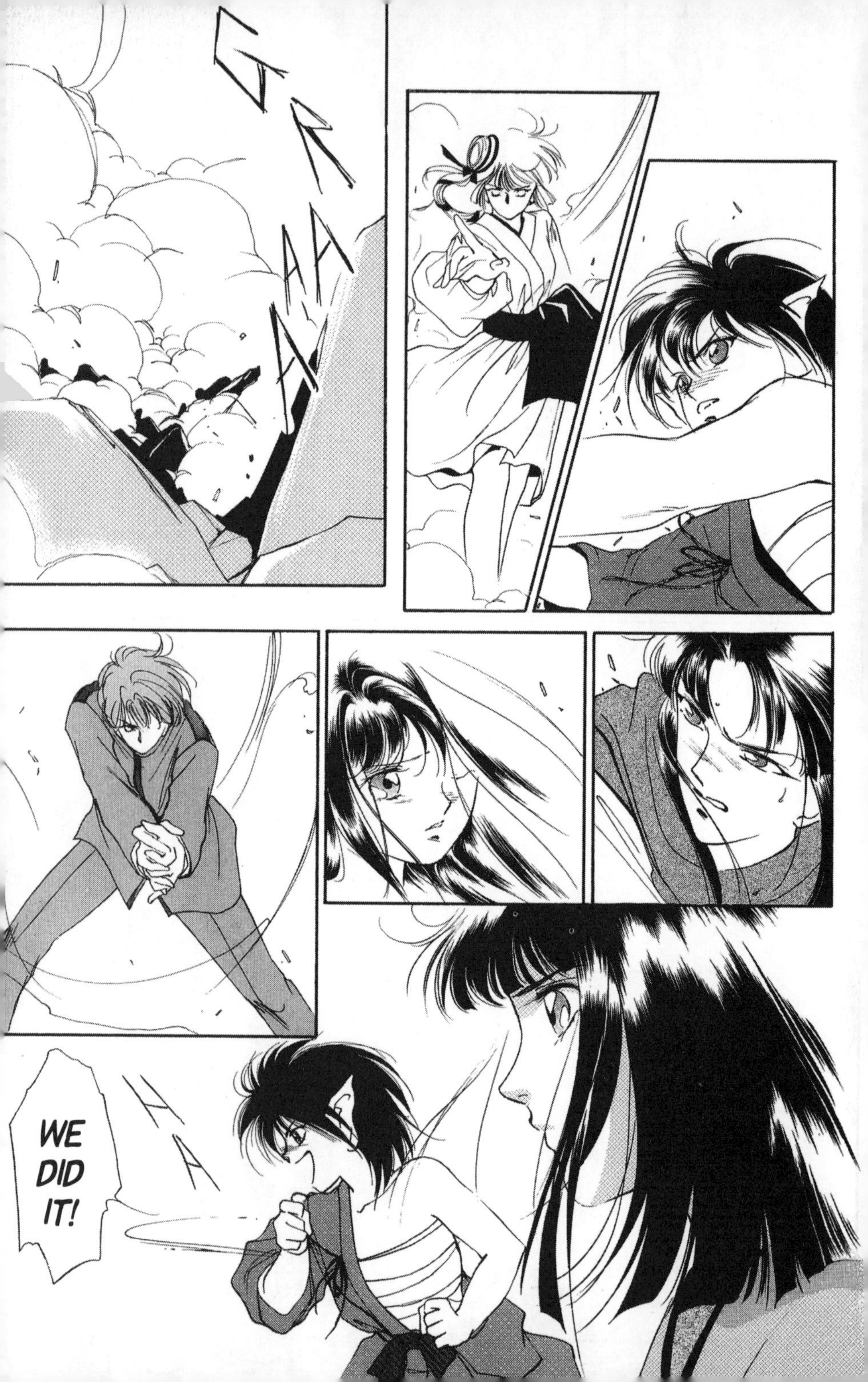
GRAAA
WE DID IT!

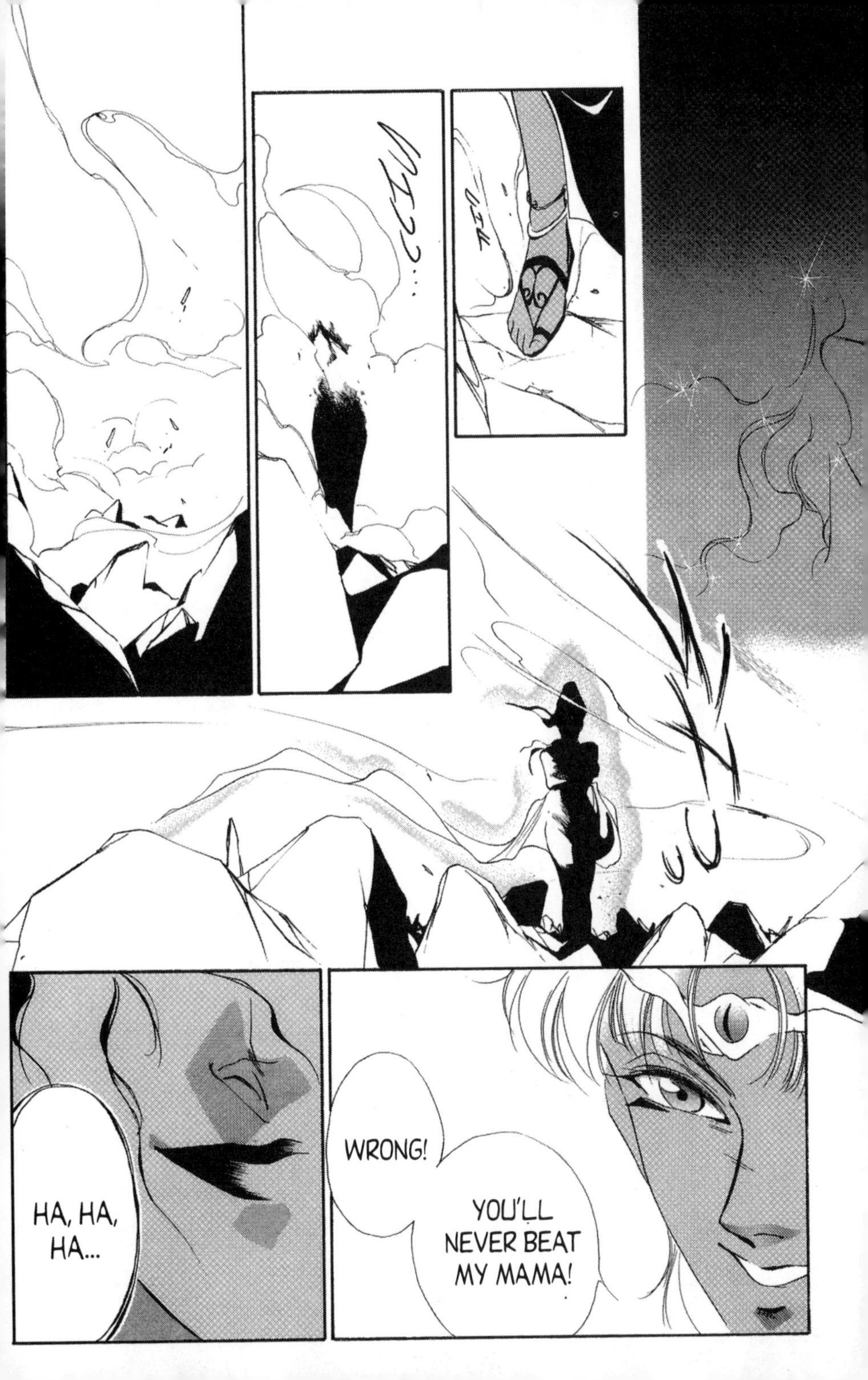
HA, HA, HA...
WRONG!
YOU'LL NEVER BEAT MY MAMA!

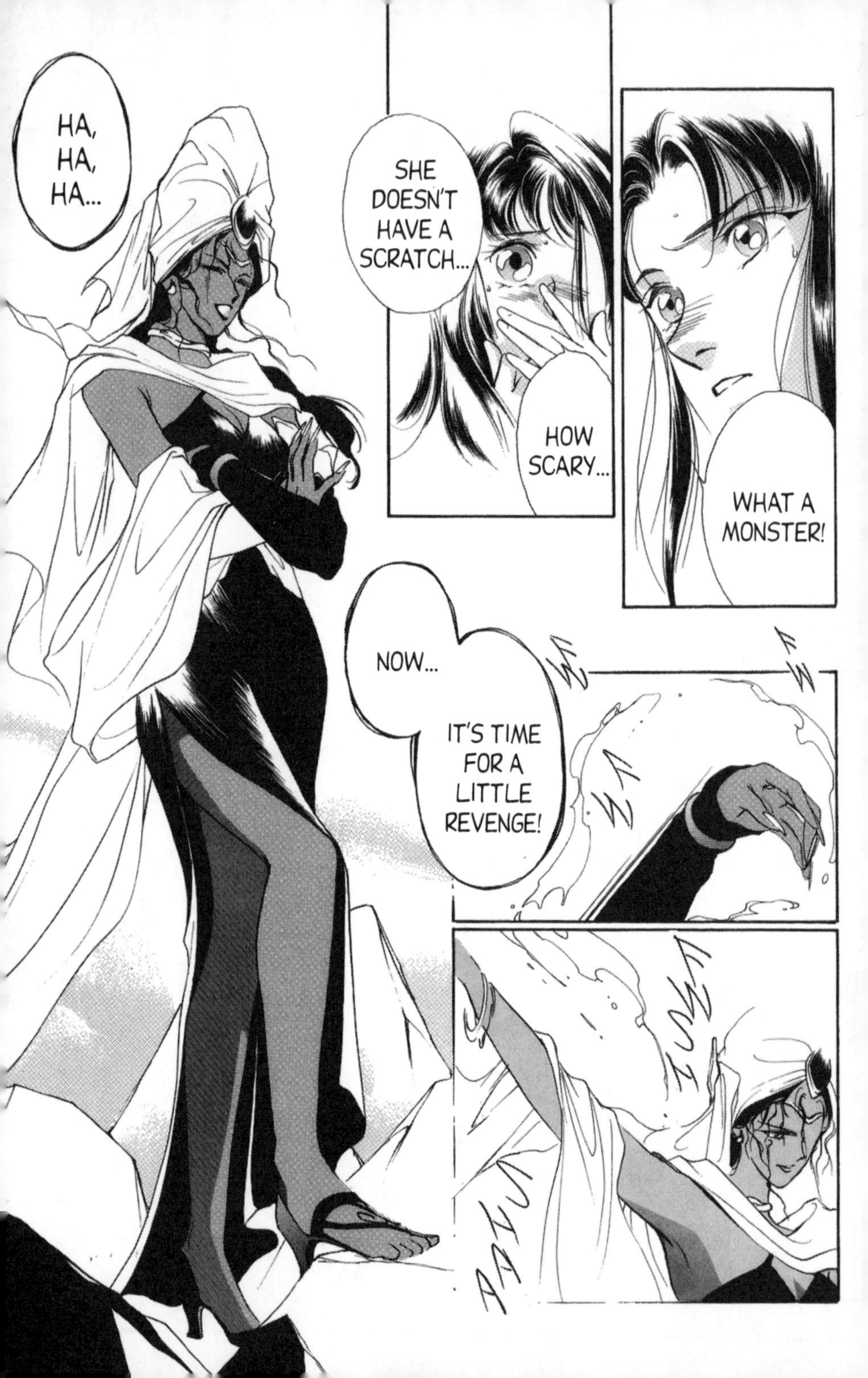
HA, HA, HA...
SHE DOESN'T HAVE A SCRATCH...
HOW SCARY...
WHAT A MONSTER!
NOW...
IT'S TIME FOR A LITTLE REVENGE!

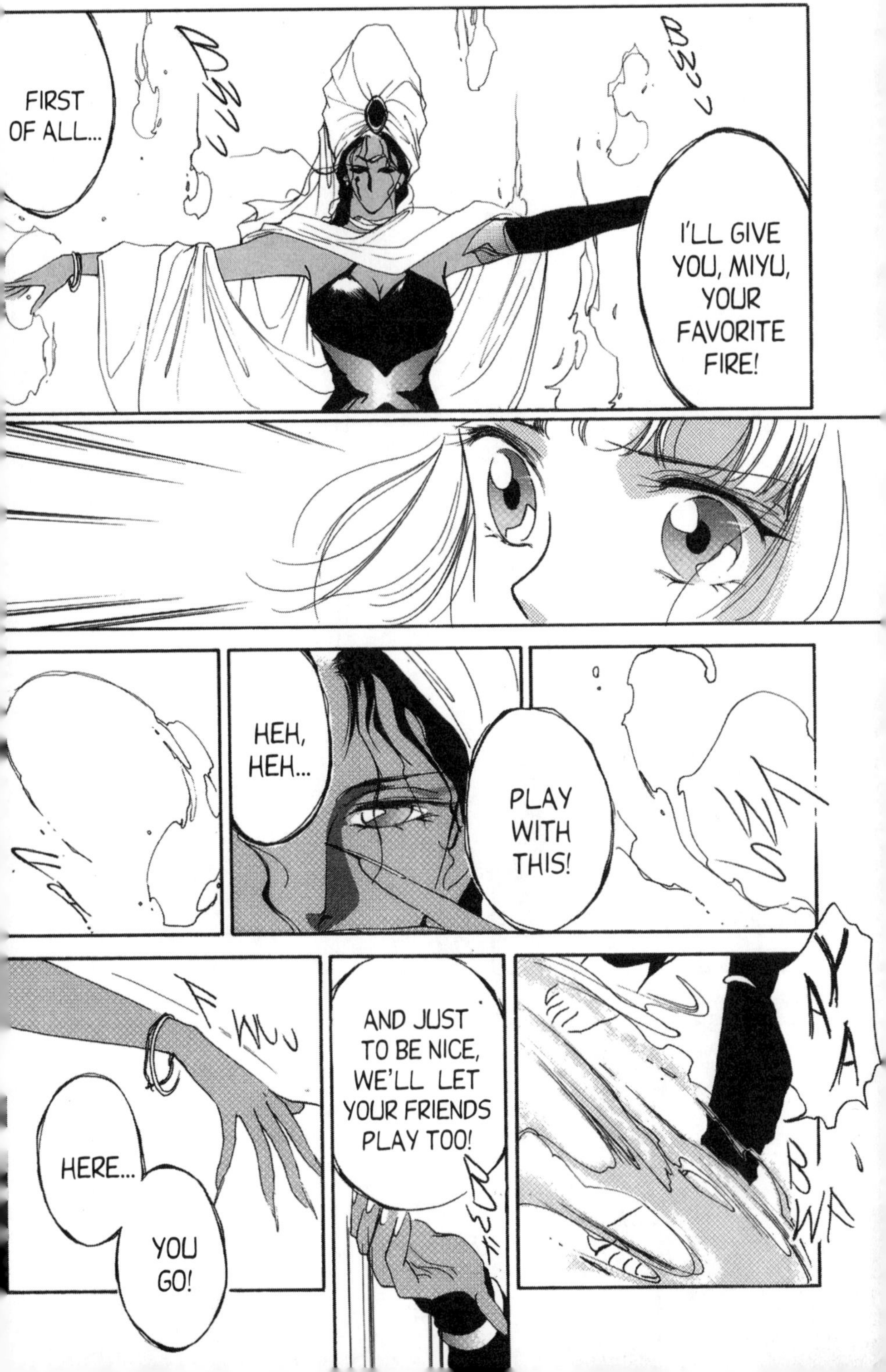
FIRST OF ALL...
I'LL GIVE YOU, MIYU, YOUR FAVORITE FIRE!
HEH, HEH...
PLAY WITH THIS!
HERE...
YOU GO!
AND JUST TO BE NICE, WE'LL LET YOUR FRIENDS PLAY TOO!

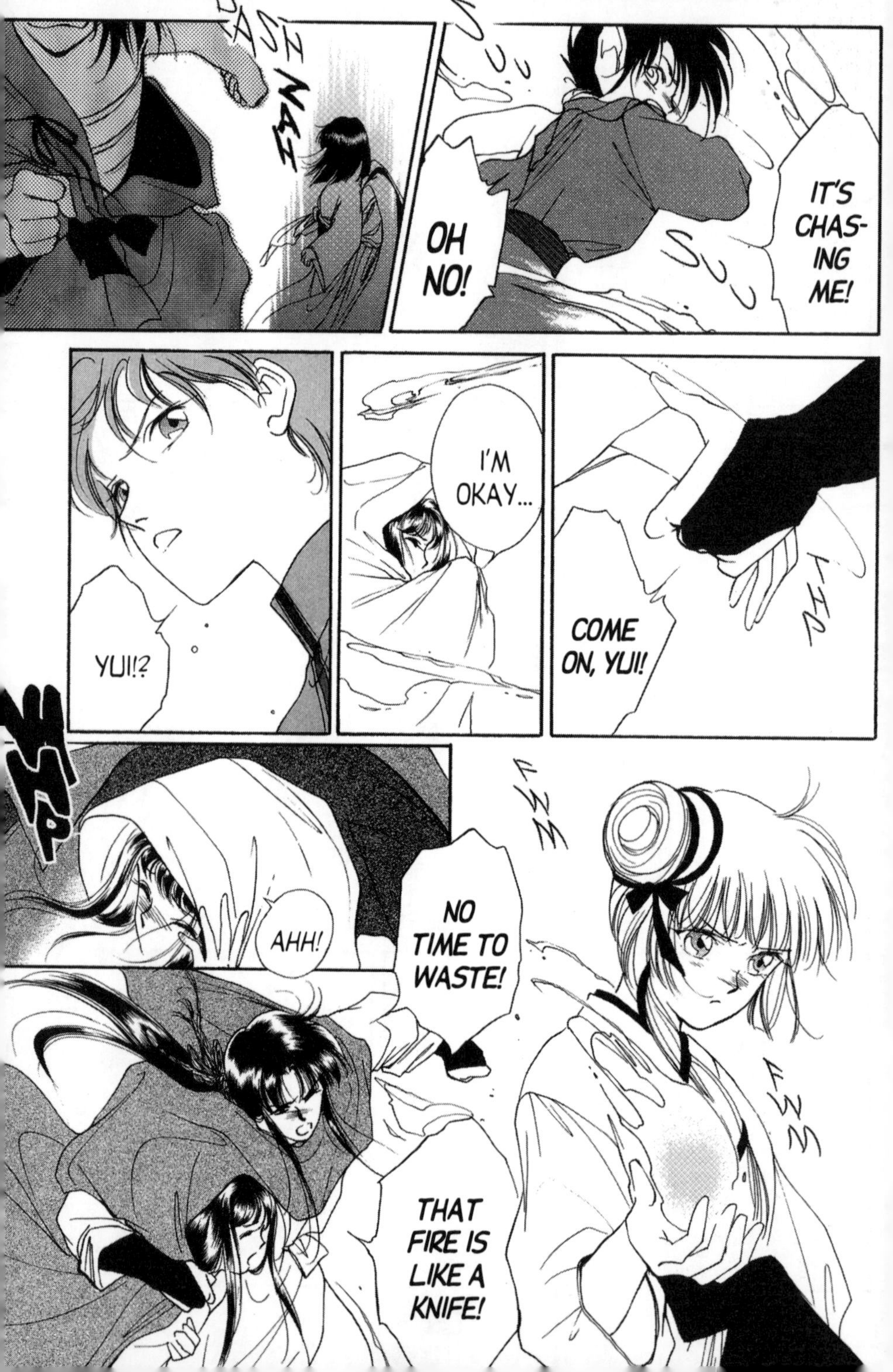
IT'S CHASING ME!
OH NO!
DASH
COME ON, YUJI!
I'M OKAY...
YUJI!?
NO TIME TO WASTE!
THAT FIRE IS LIKE A KNIFE!
AHH!

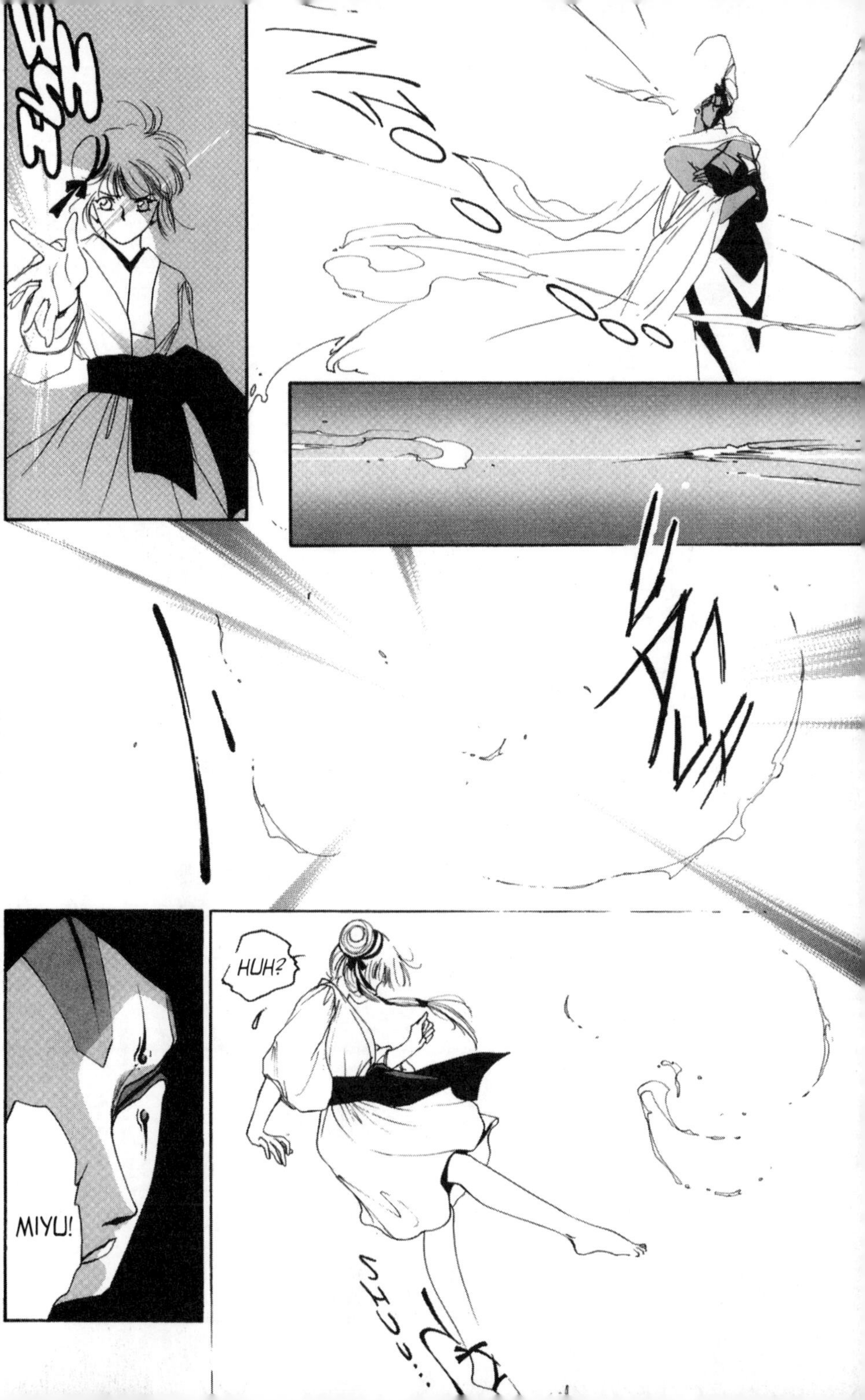
HUH?
SHUU...
MIYU!

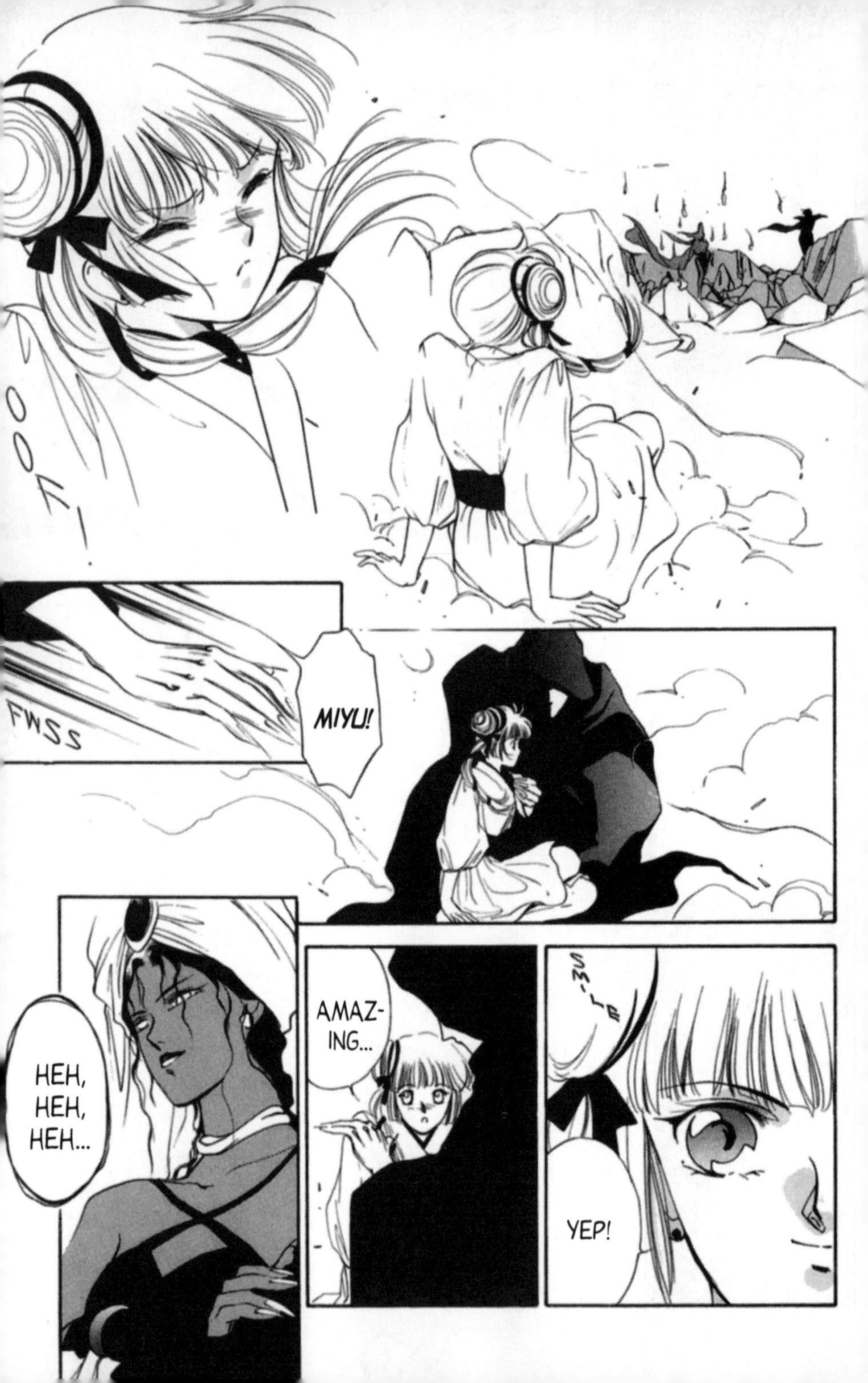
POOF!
FWSS
MIYU!
HEH, HEH, HEH...
AMAZ-ING...
SMILE
YEP!

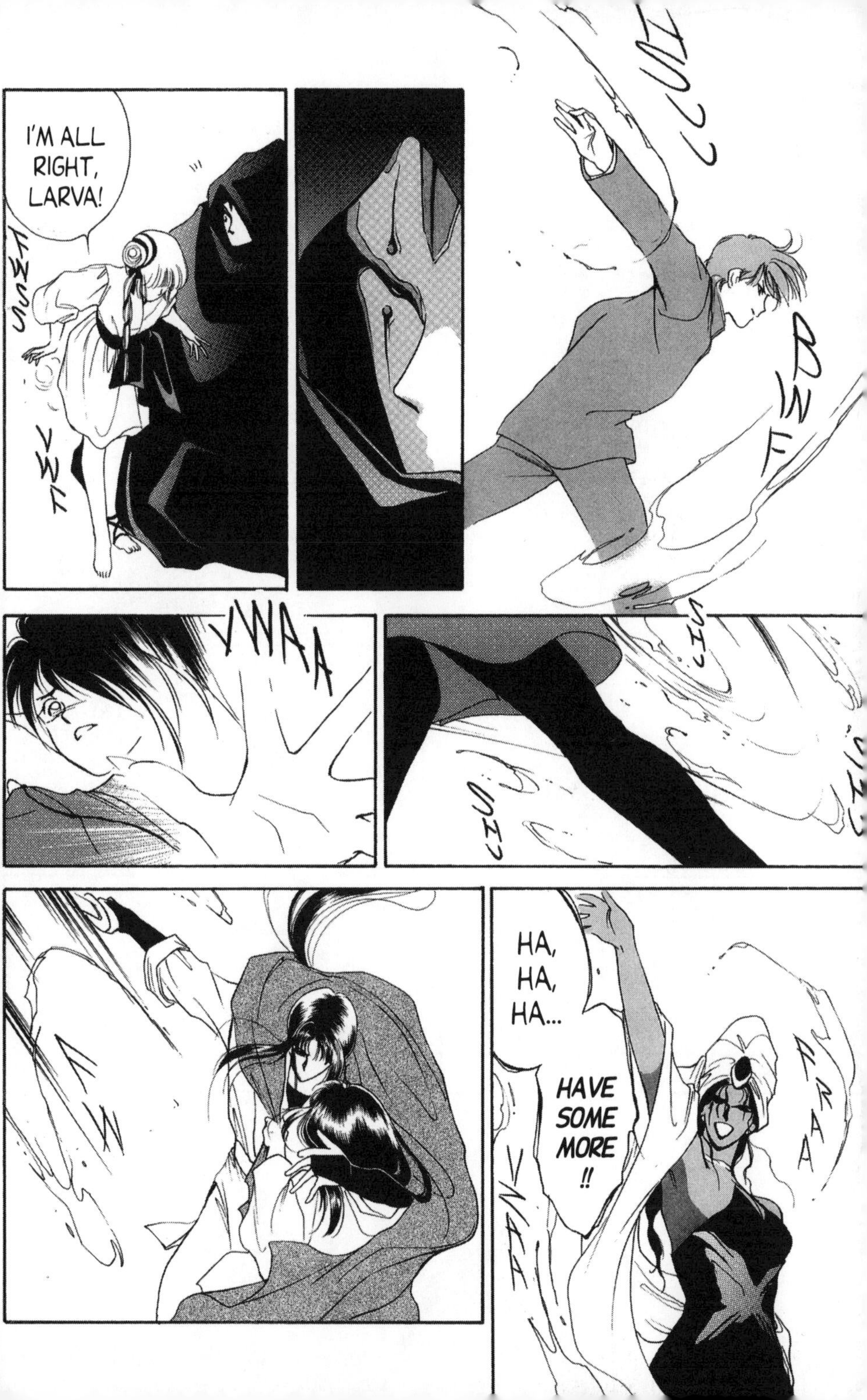
I'M ALL RIGHT, LARVA!
VWAA
HA, HA, HA...
HAVE SOME MORE !!

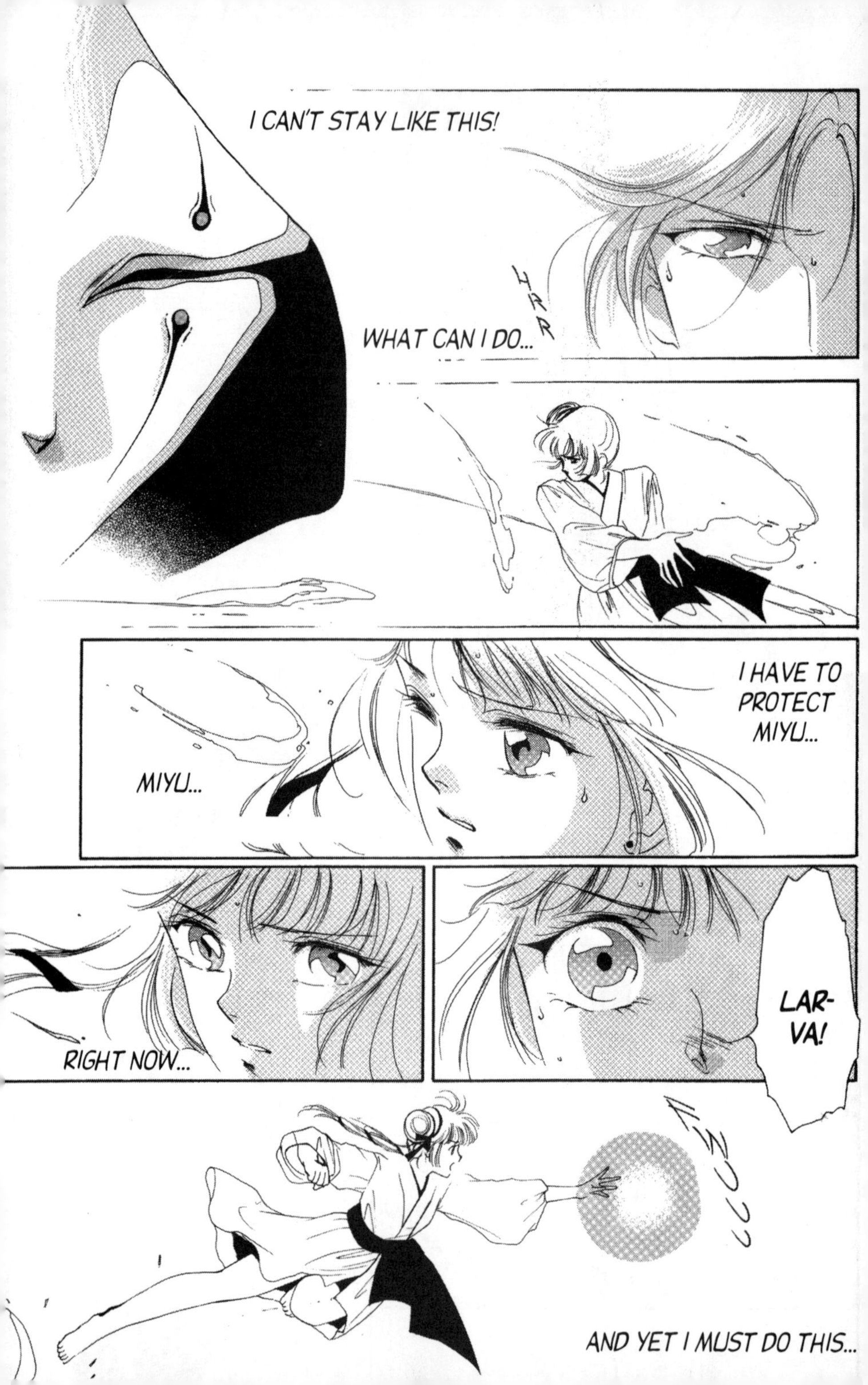
I CAN'T STAY LIKE THIS!
HRR
WHAT CAN I DO...
MIYU...
I HAVE TO PROTECT MIYU...
RIGHT NOW...
LAR-VA!
AND YET I MUST DO THIS...

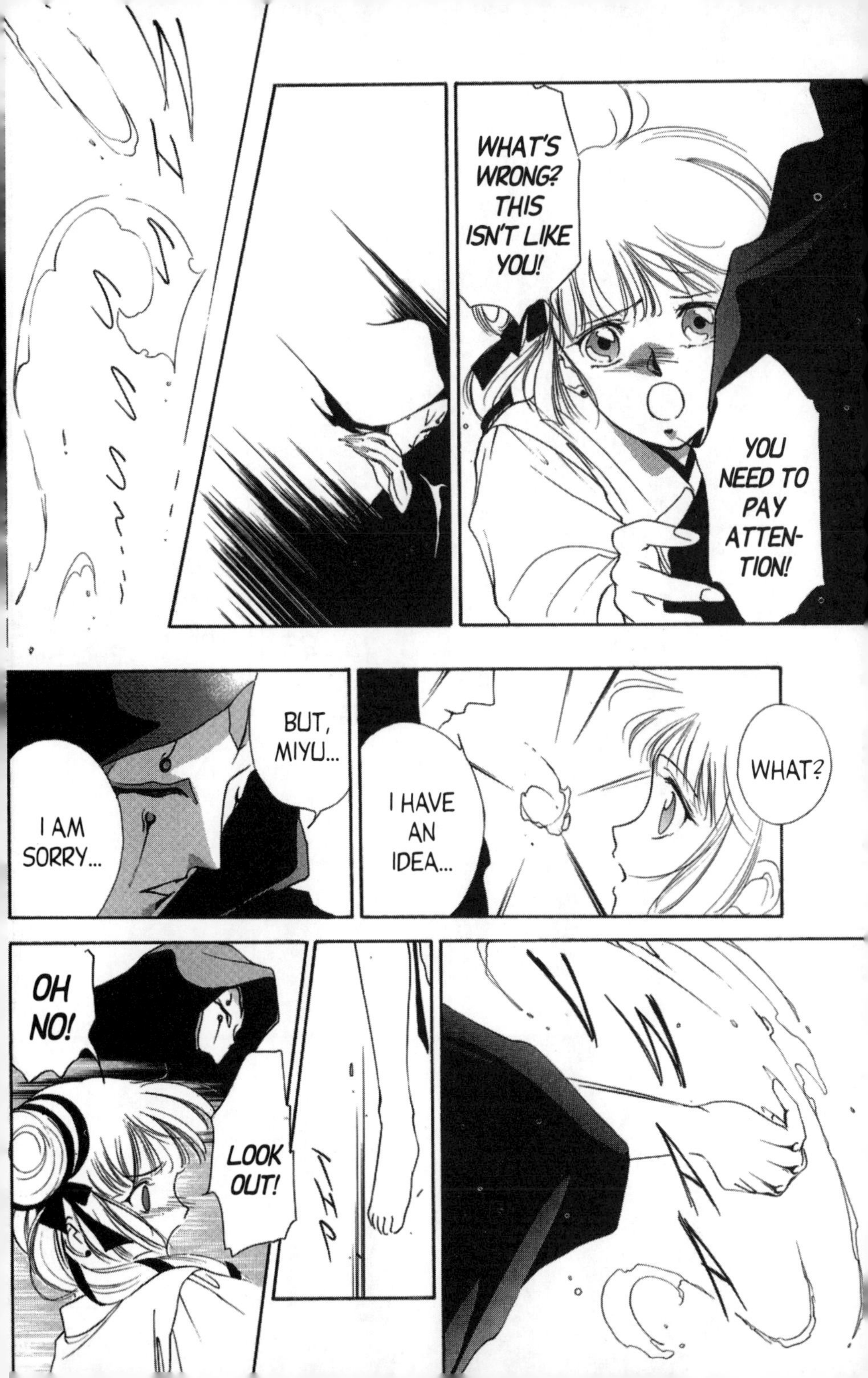

WHAT'S WRONG? THIS ISN'T LIKE YOU!
YOU NEED TO PAY ATTEN-TION!
WHAT?
I HAVE AN IDEA...
BUT, MIYU...
I AM SORRY...
OH NO!
LOOK OUT!

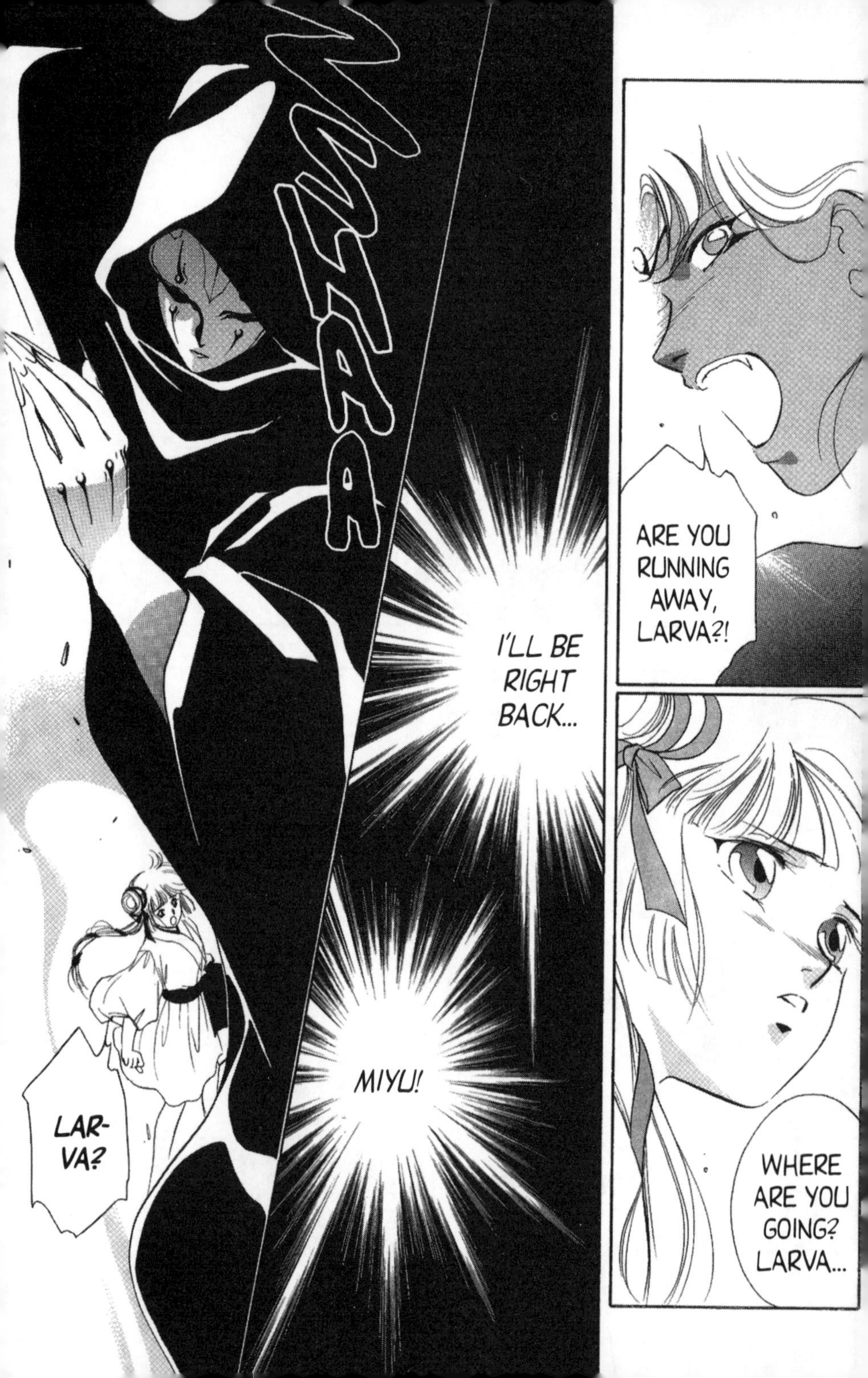
ARE YOU RUNNING AWAY, LARVA?!
WHERE ARE YOU GOING? LARVA...
I'LL BE RIGHT BACK...
MIYU!
LAR-VA?

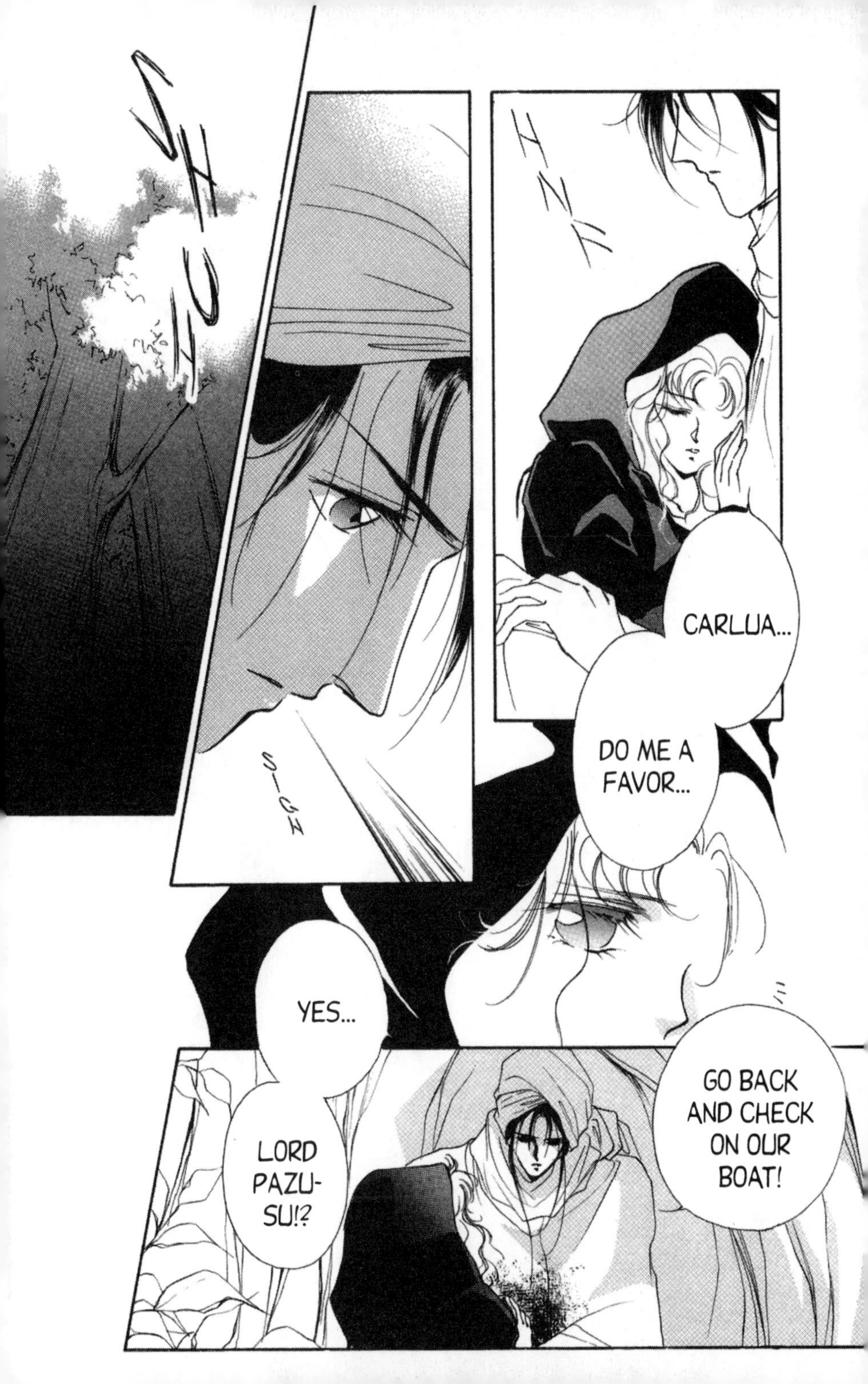
CARLUA...
DO ME A FAVOR...
SIGH
YES...
GO BACK AND CHECK ON OUR BOAT!
LORD PAZU-SU!?

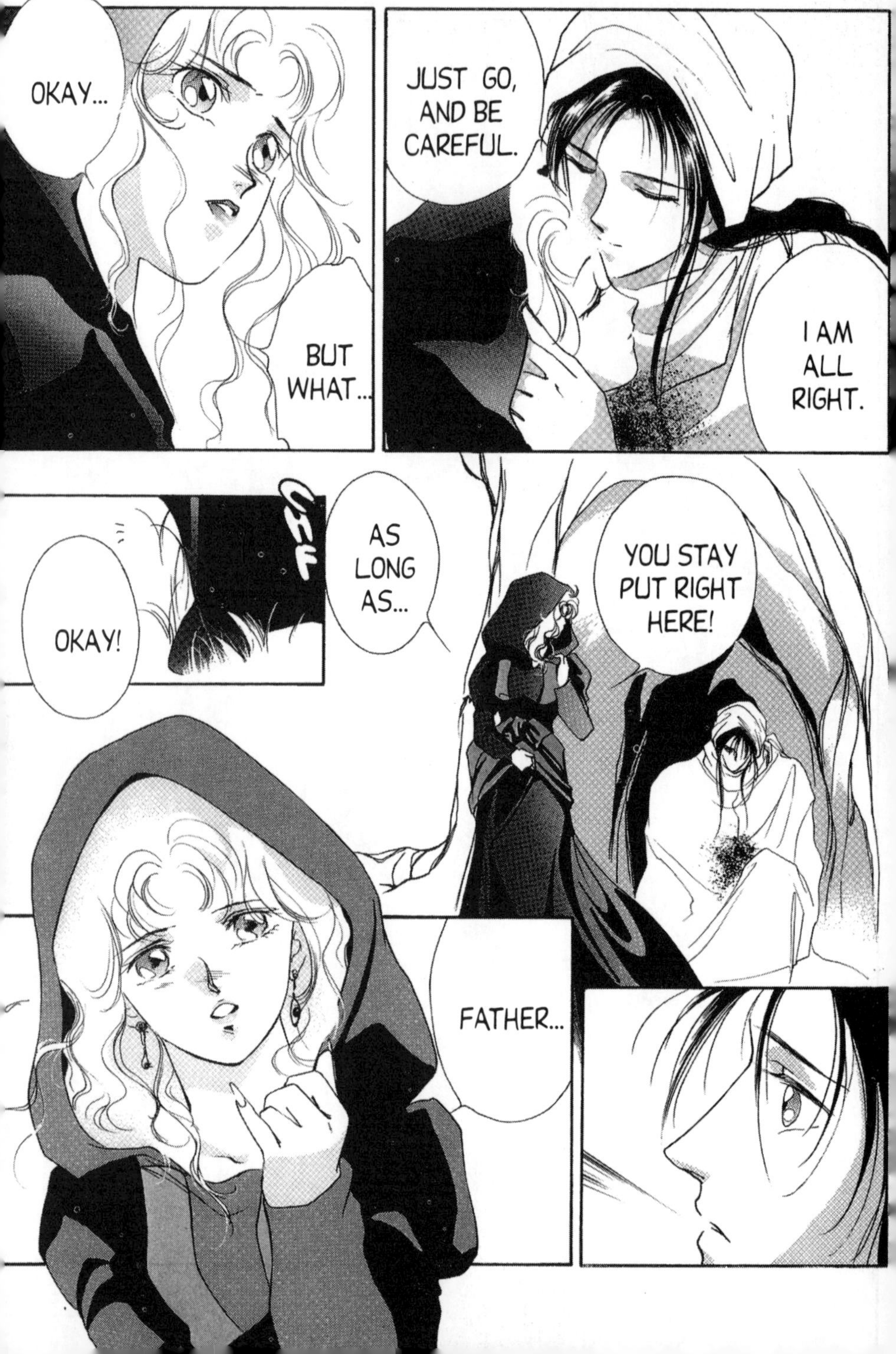
OKAY...
BUT WHAT...
JUST GO, AND BE CAREFUL.
I AM ALL RIGHT.
OKAY!
CHF
AS LONG AS...
YOU STAY PUT RIGHT HERE!
FATHER...

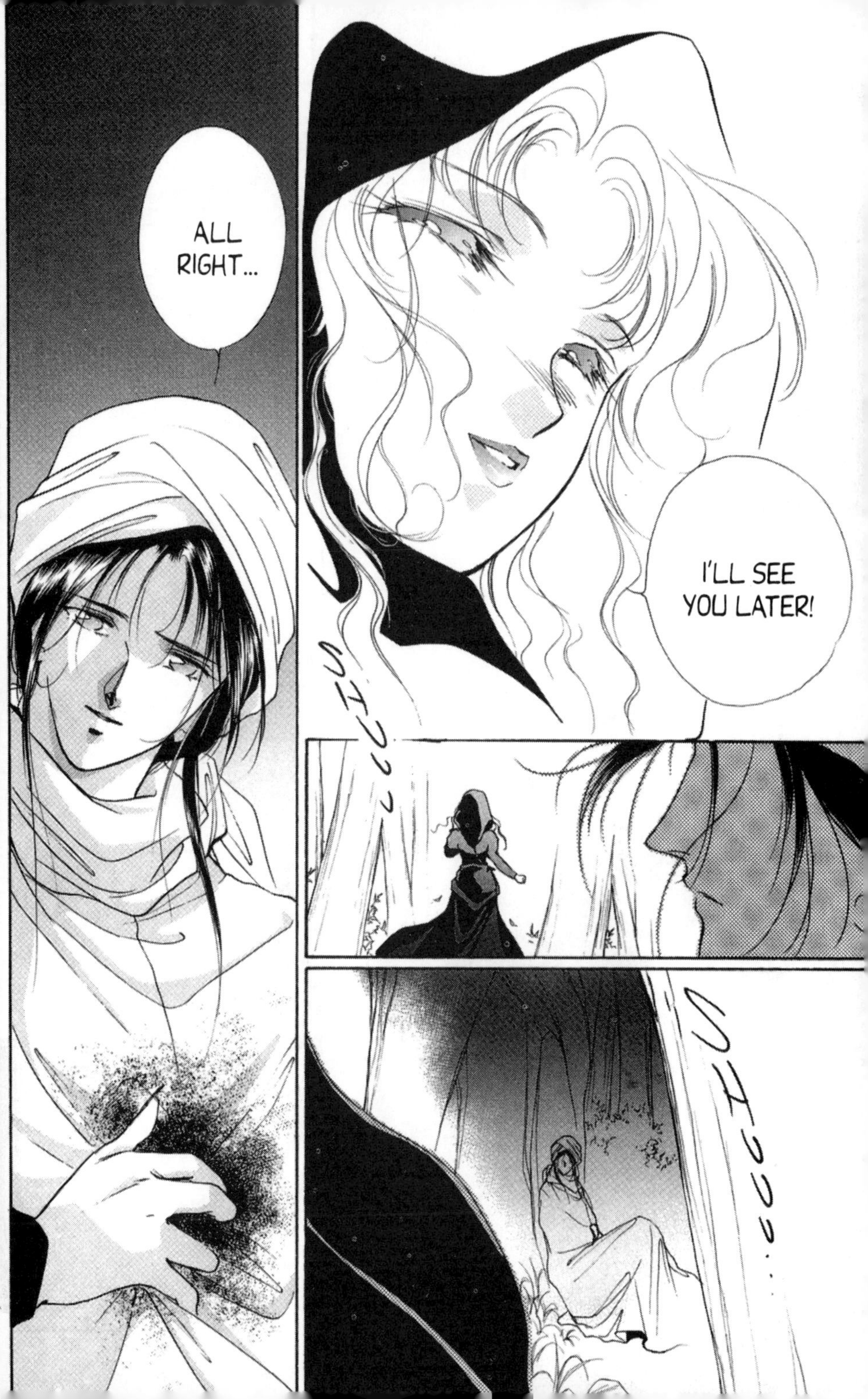
I'LL SEE YOU LATER!
ALL RIGHT...
SHUUUU
SHUUUU...

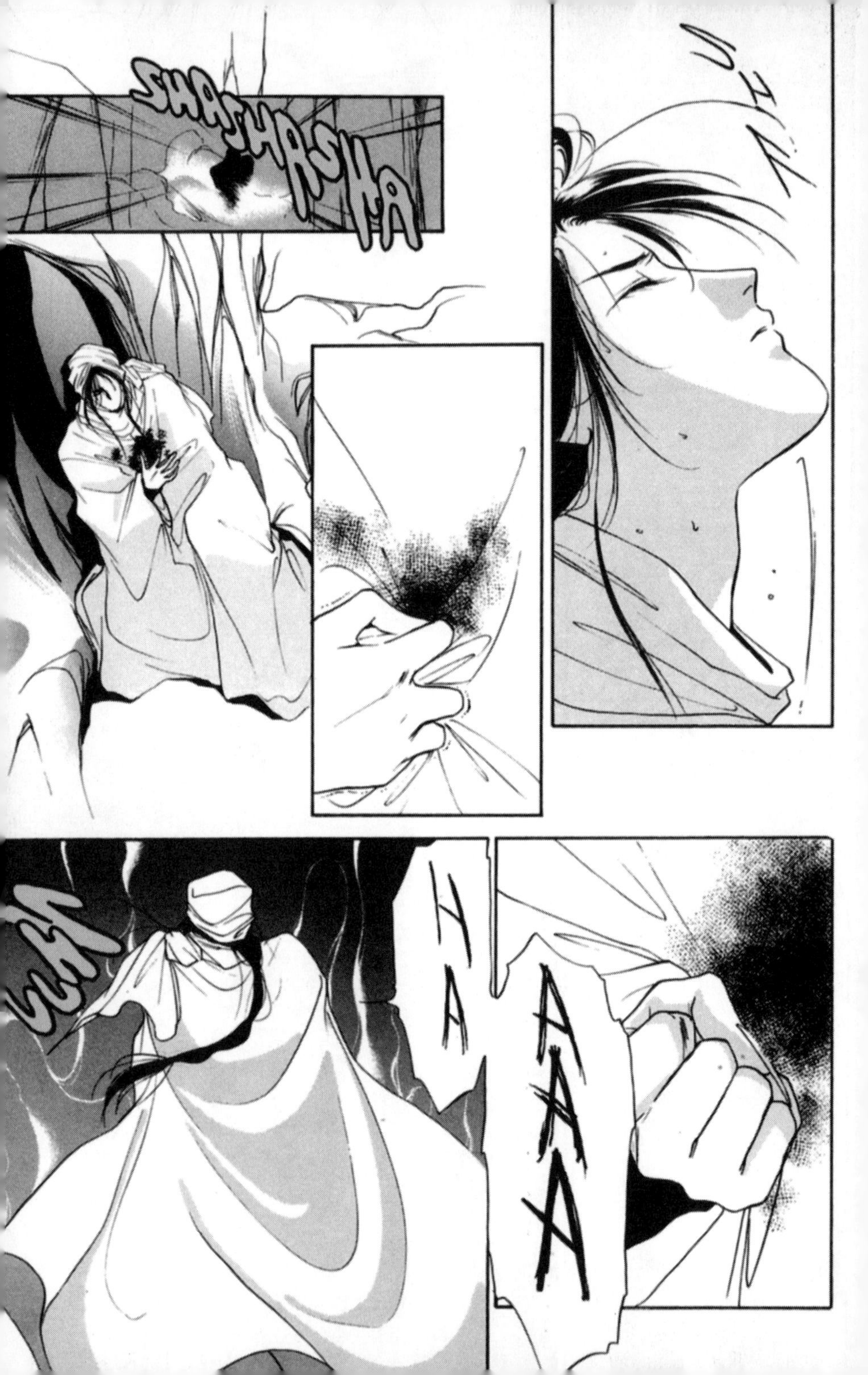
SHASHASHA
HAA
AAAAAA

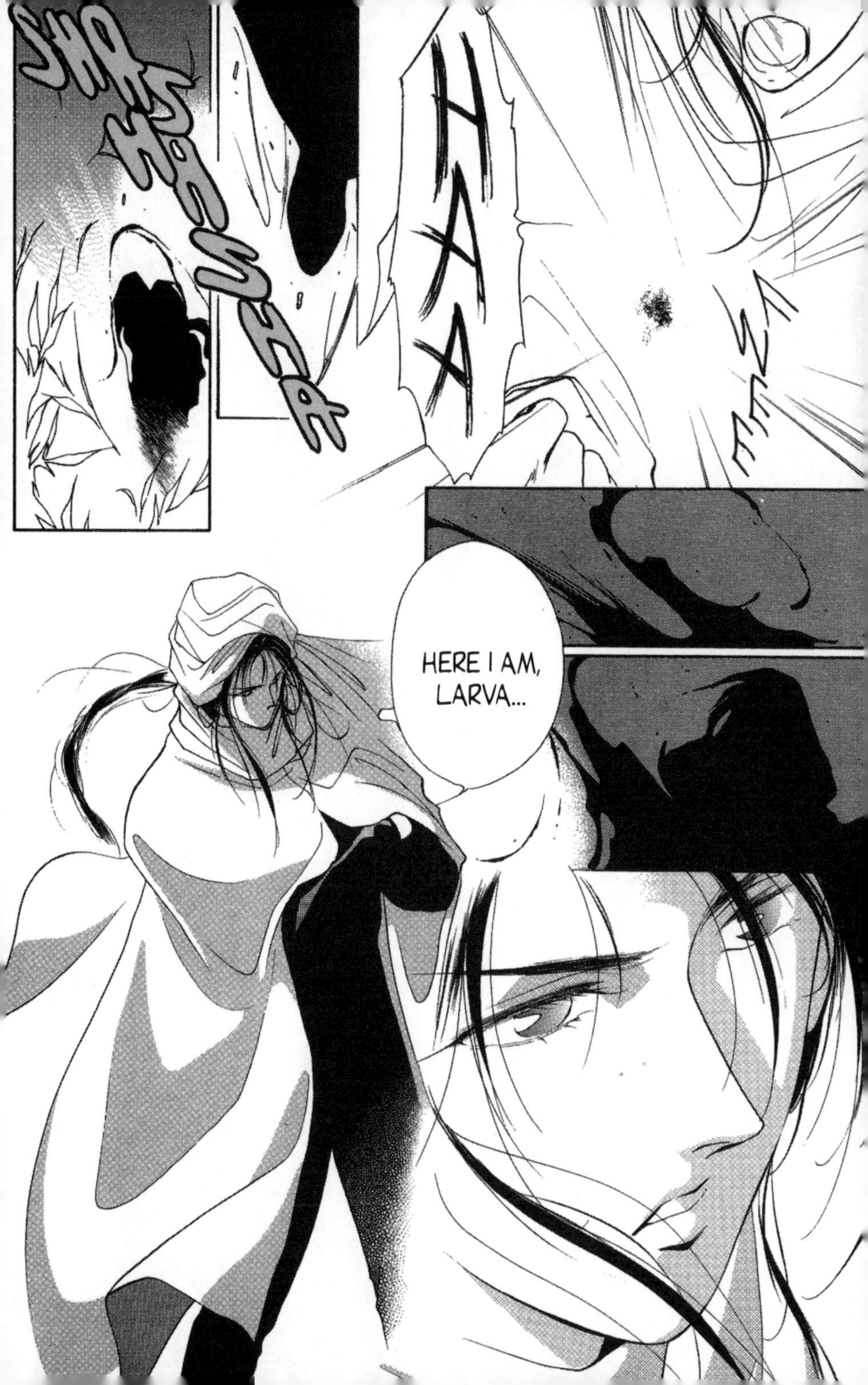
HAAA
VSEE
HERE I AM, LARVA...

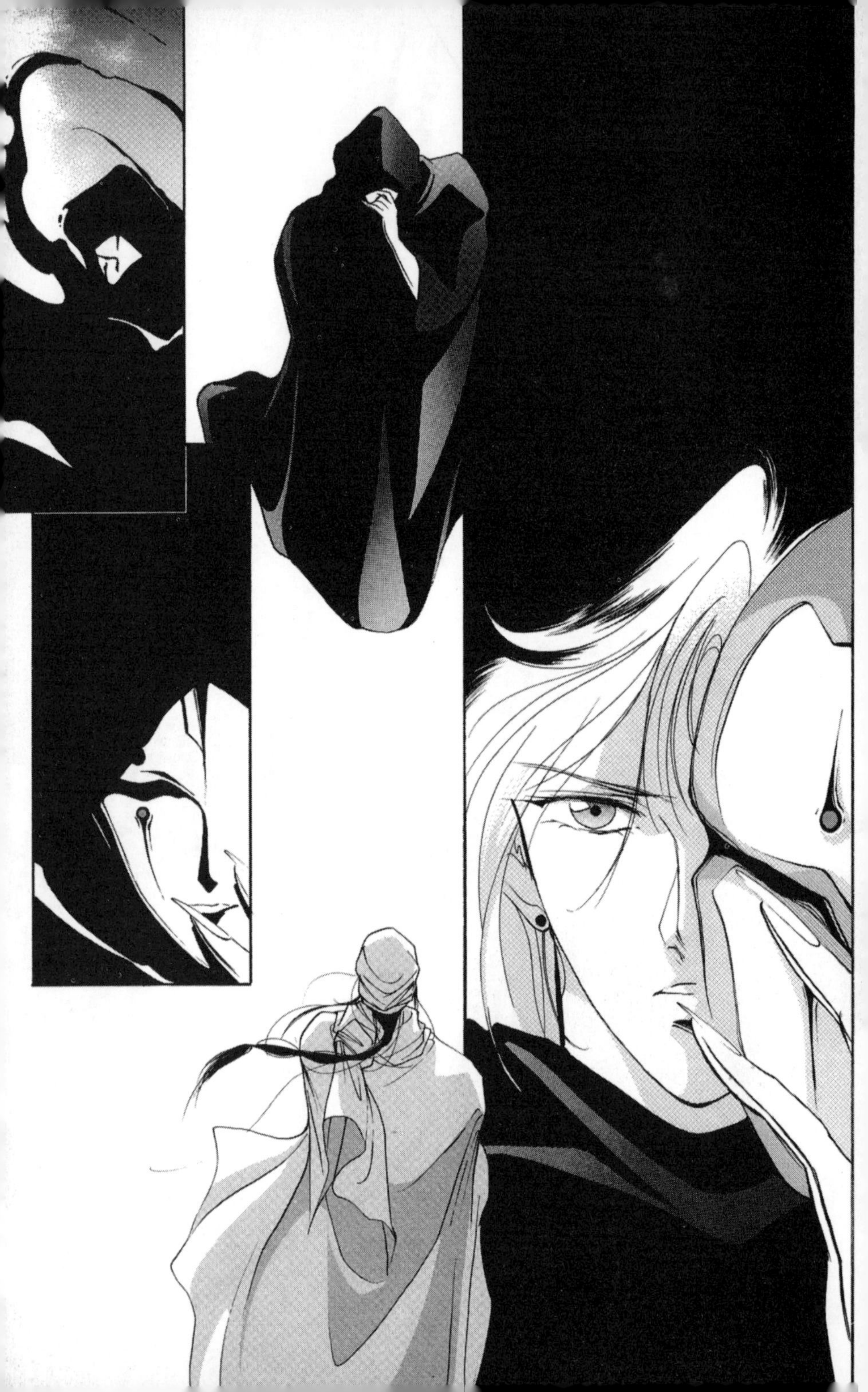

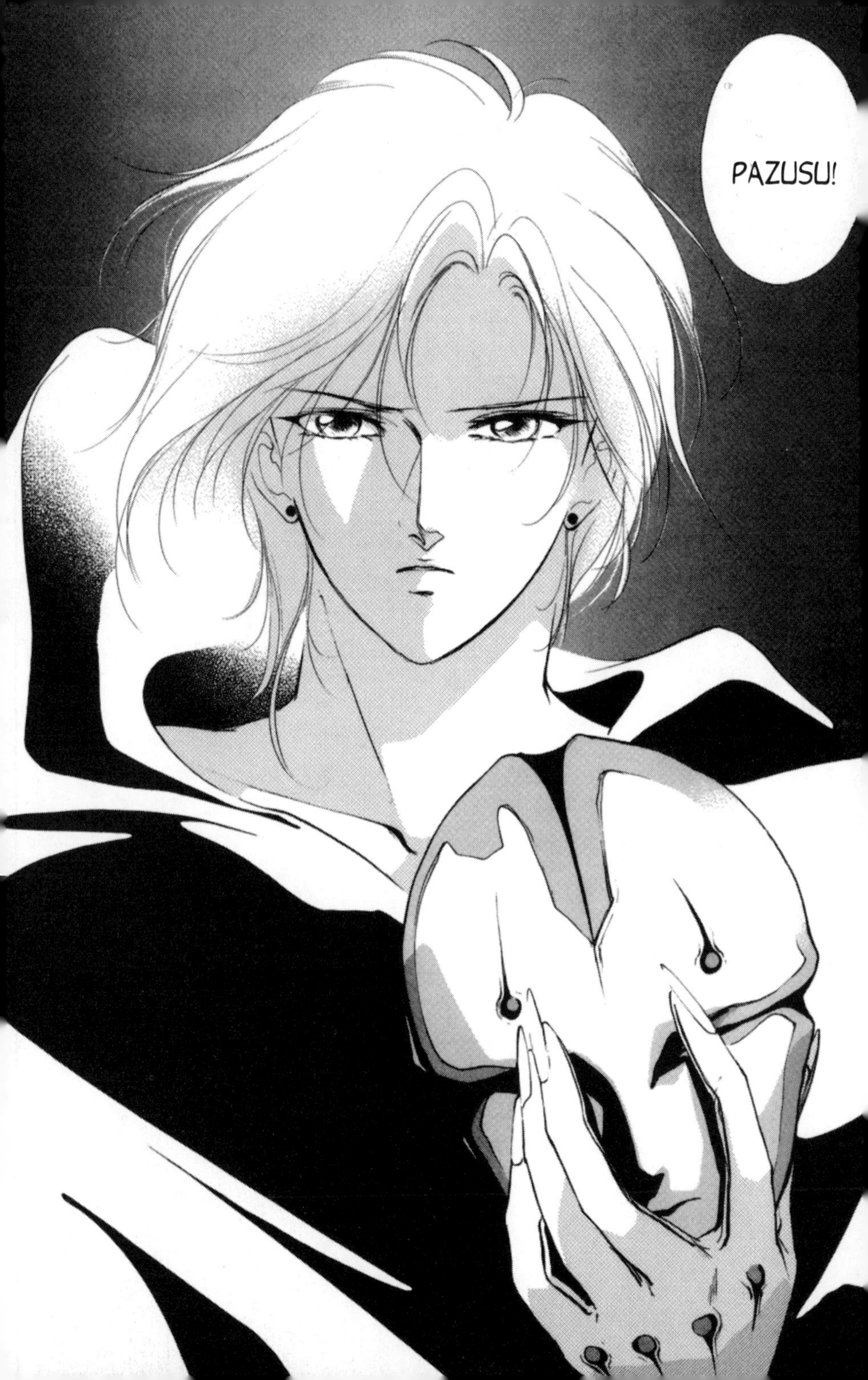
PAZUSU!

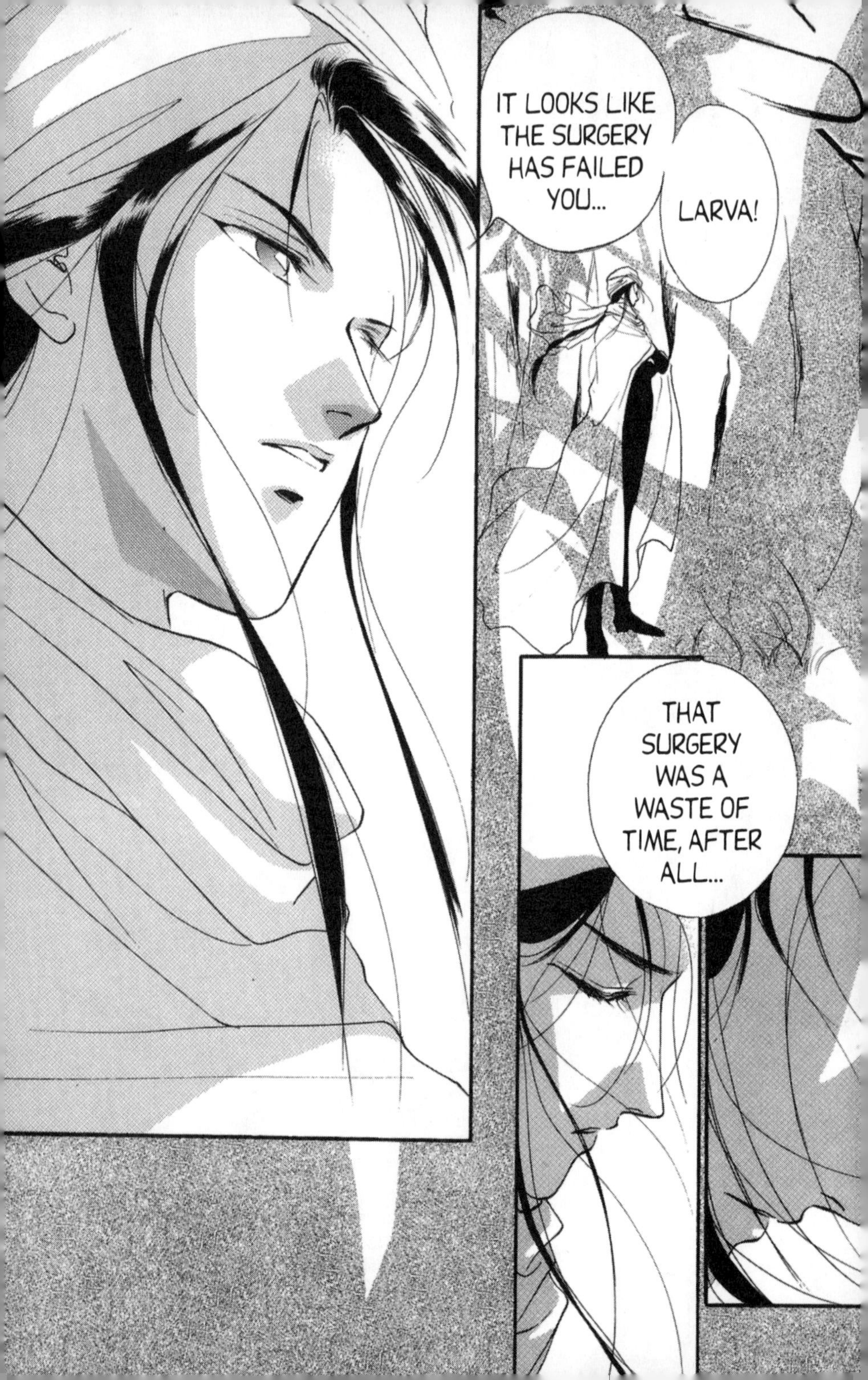
LARVA!
IT LOOKS LIKE THE SURGERY HAS FAILED YOU...
THAT SURGERY WAS A WASTE OF TIME, AFTER ALL...

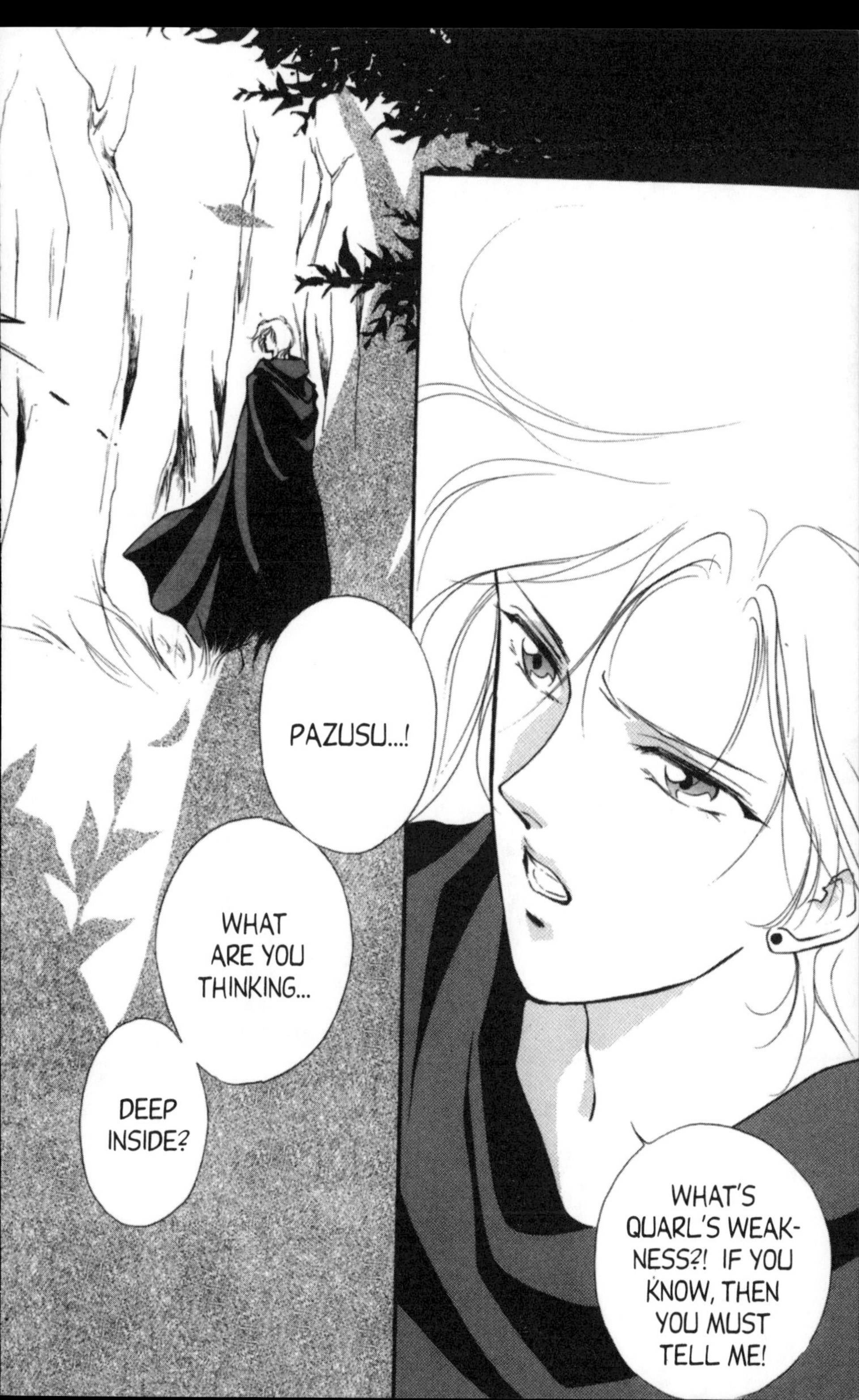
PAZUSU...!
WHAT ARE YOU THINKING...
DEEP INSIDE?
WHAT'S QUARL'S WEAKNESS?! IF YOU KNOW, THEN YOU MUST TELL ME!

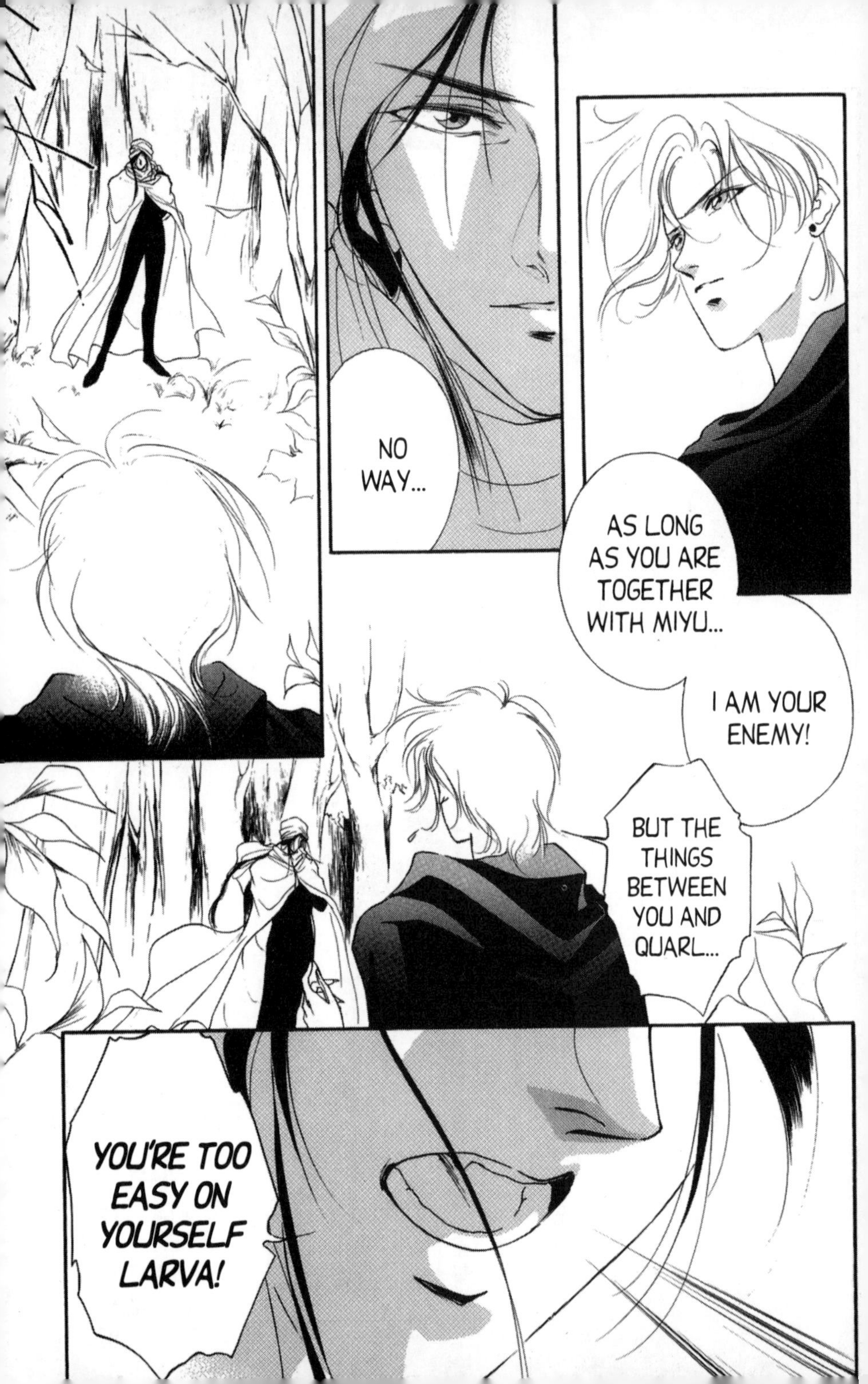
NO WAY...
AS LONG AS YOU ARE TOGETHER WITH MIYU...
I AM YOUR ENEMY!
BUT THE THINGS BETWEEN YOU AND QUARL...
YOU'RE TOO EASY ON YOURSELF LARVA!

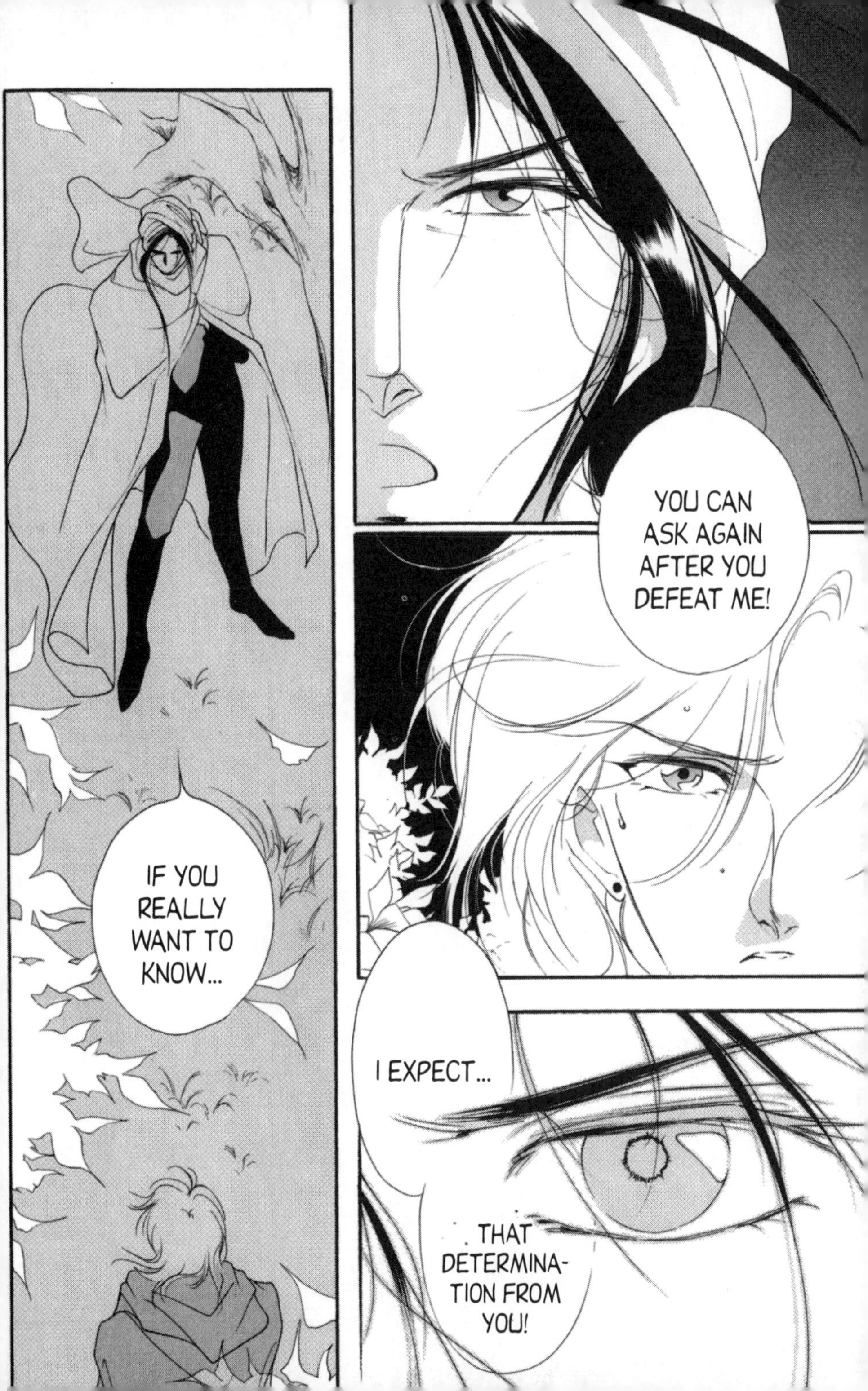
IF YOU REALLY WANT TO KNOW...
YOU CAN ASK AGAIN AFTER YOU DEFEAT ME!
I EXPECT...
THAT DETERMINATION FROM YOU!

THAT IS TRUE...

BUT EVEN IF I FIGHT PAZUSU...

WOULD I BE ABLE TO DEFEAT HIM?

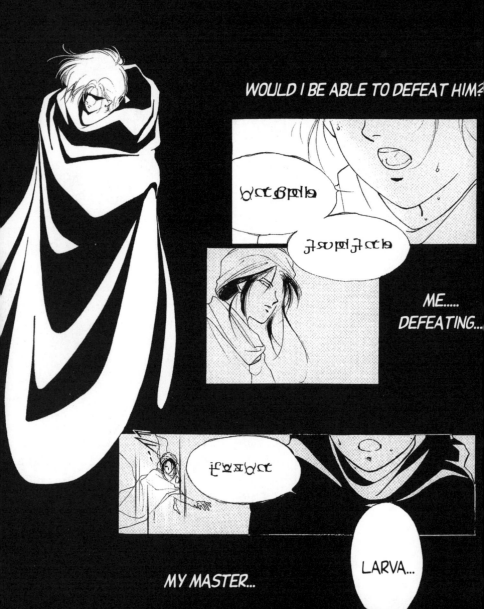

ME.....
DEFEATING...

MY MASTER...

LARVA...

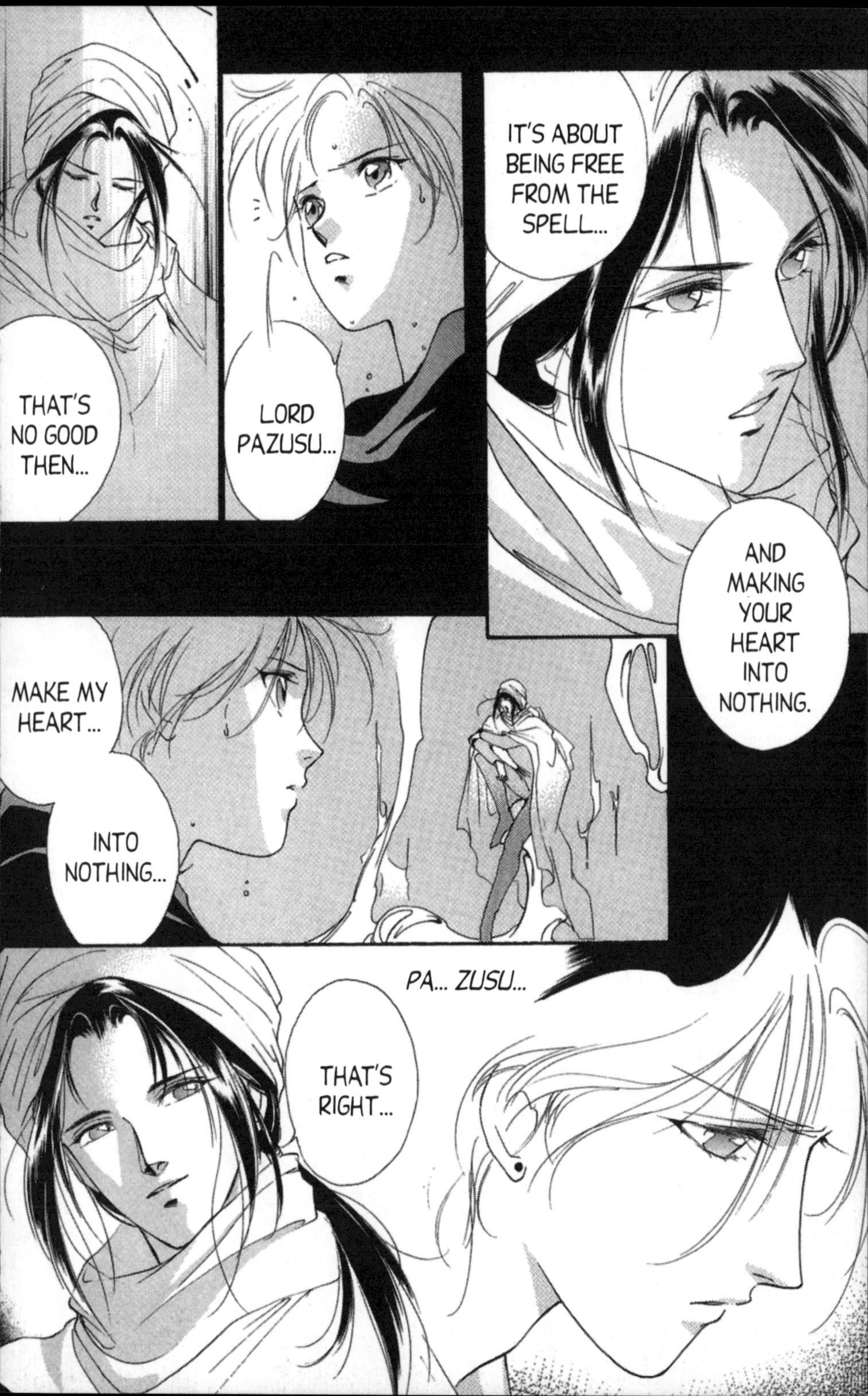

THAT'S NO GOOD THEN...
LORD PAZUSU...
IT'S ABOUT BEING FREE FROM THE SPELL...
AND MAKING YOUR HEART INTO NOTHING.
MAKE MY HEART...
INTO NOTHING...
PA... ZUSU...
THAT'S RIGHT...

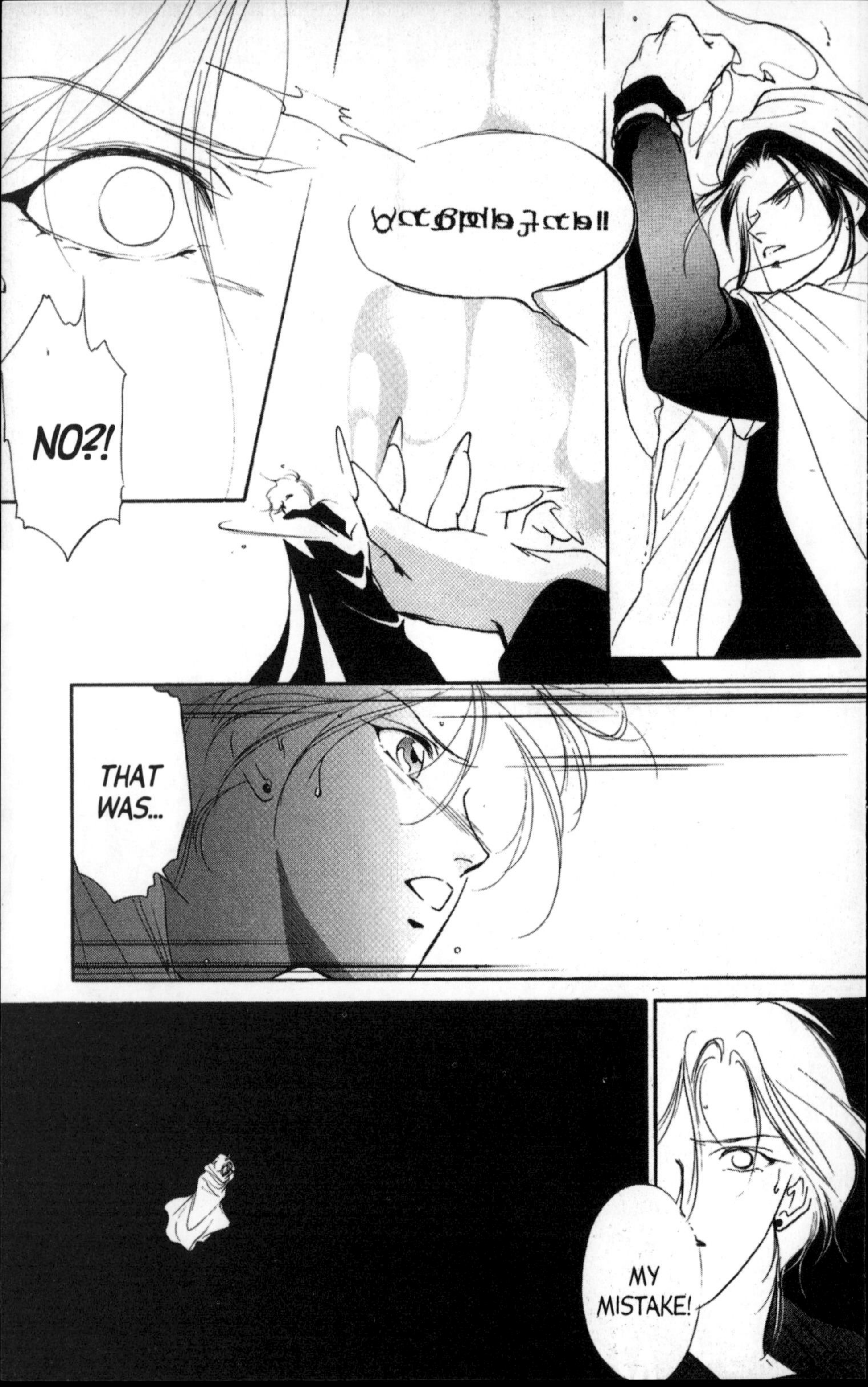
NO?!
THAT WAS...
MY MISTAKE!

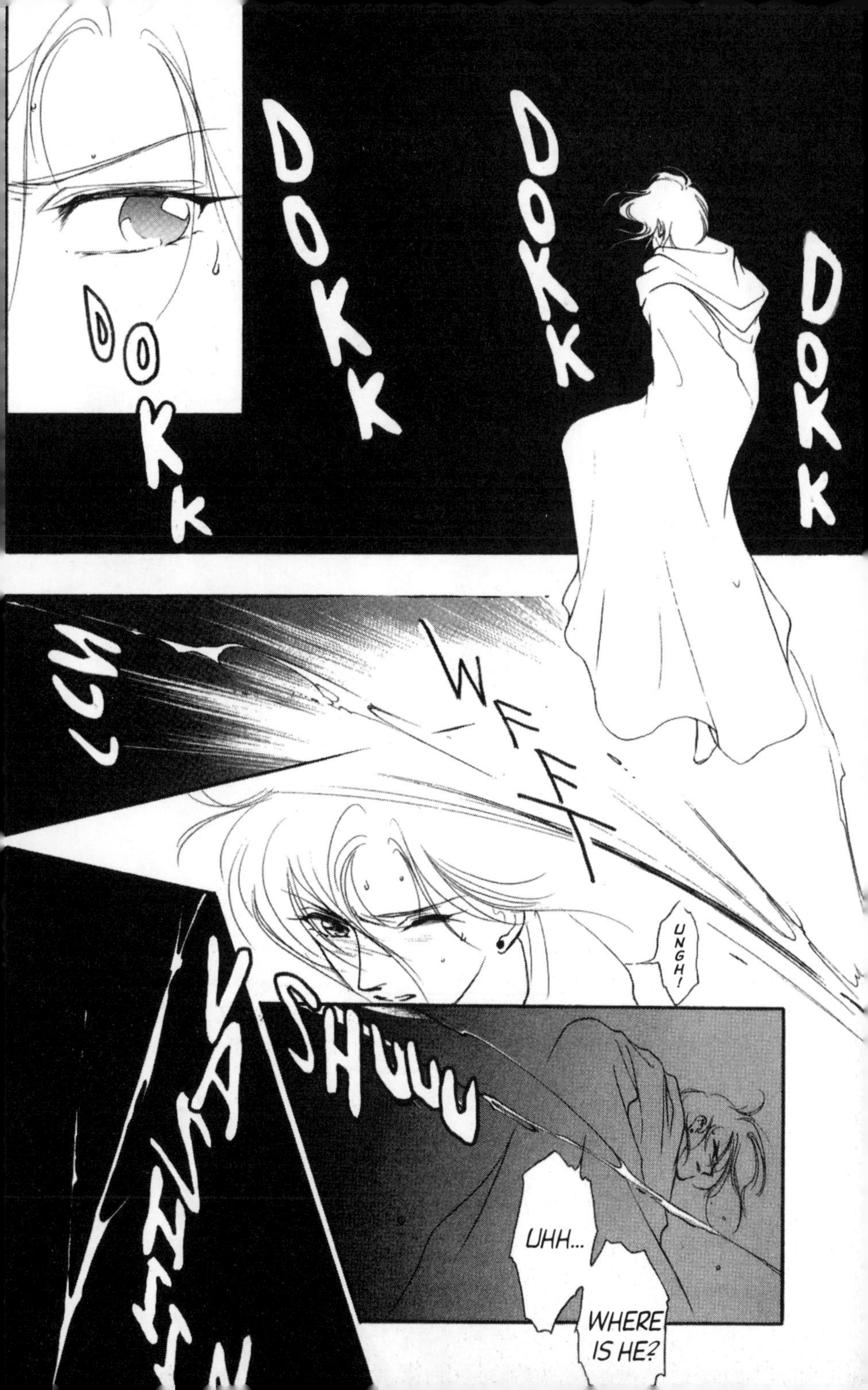
DOKK
DOKK
DOKK
DOKK
WFFT
UNGH!
SHUUU
UHH...
WHERE IS HE?

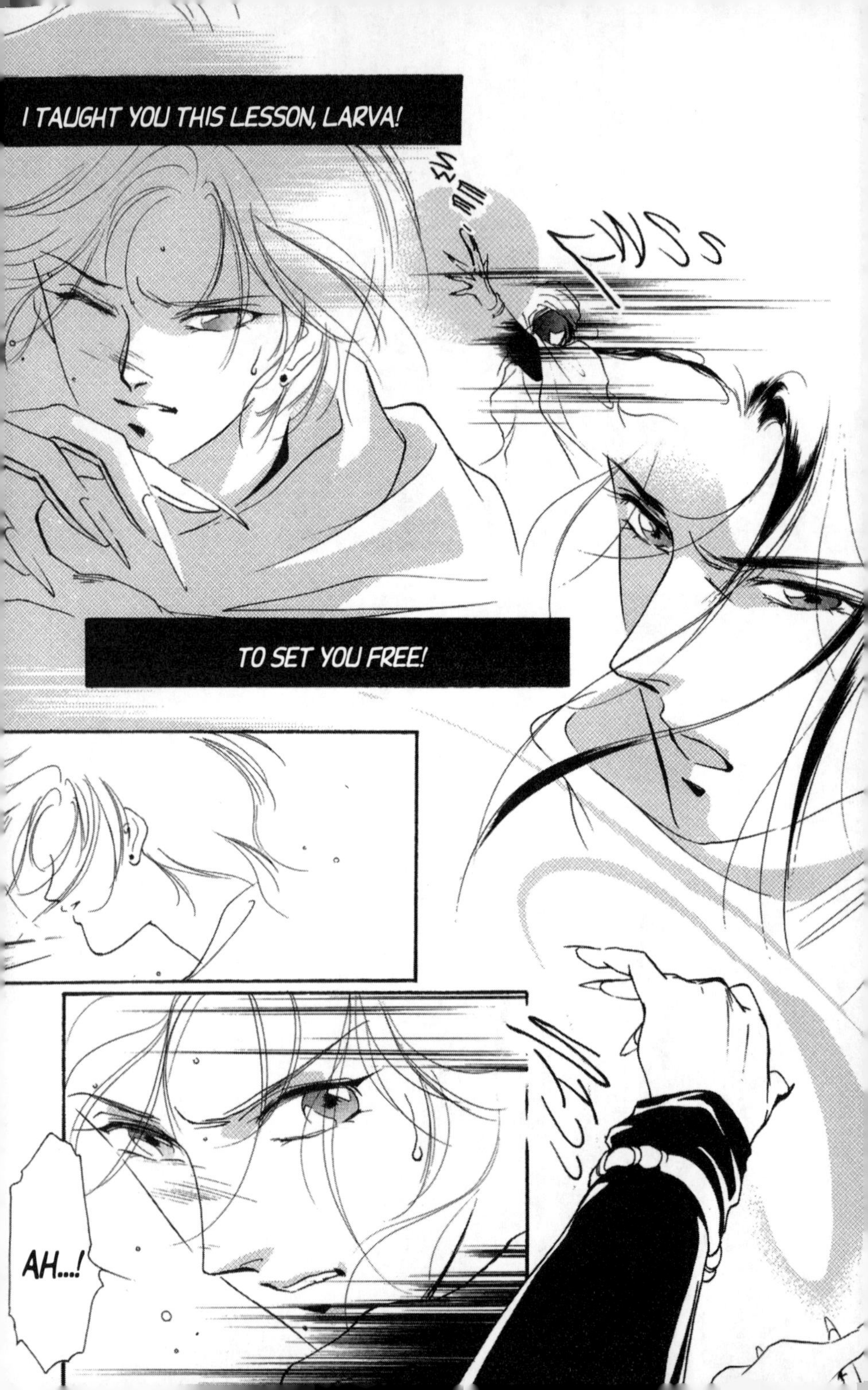
I TAUGHT YOU THIS LESSON, LARVA!
TO SET YOU FREE!
AH...!

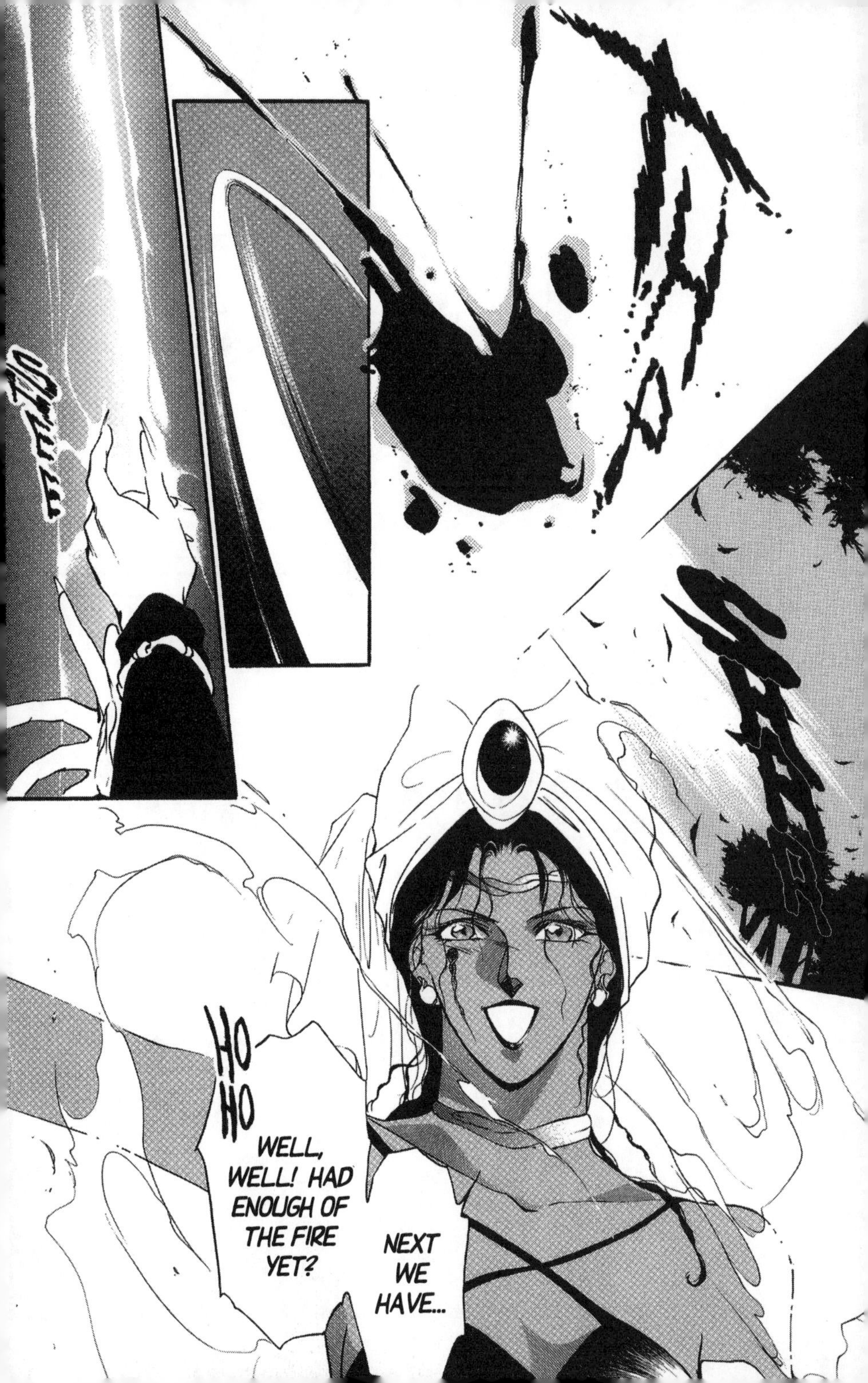
HO HO
WELL, WELL! HAD ENOUGH OF THE FIRE YET?
NEXT WE HAVE...

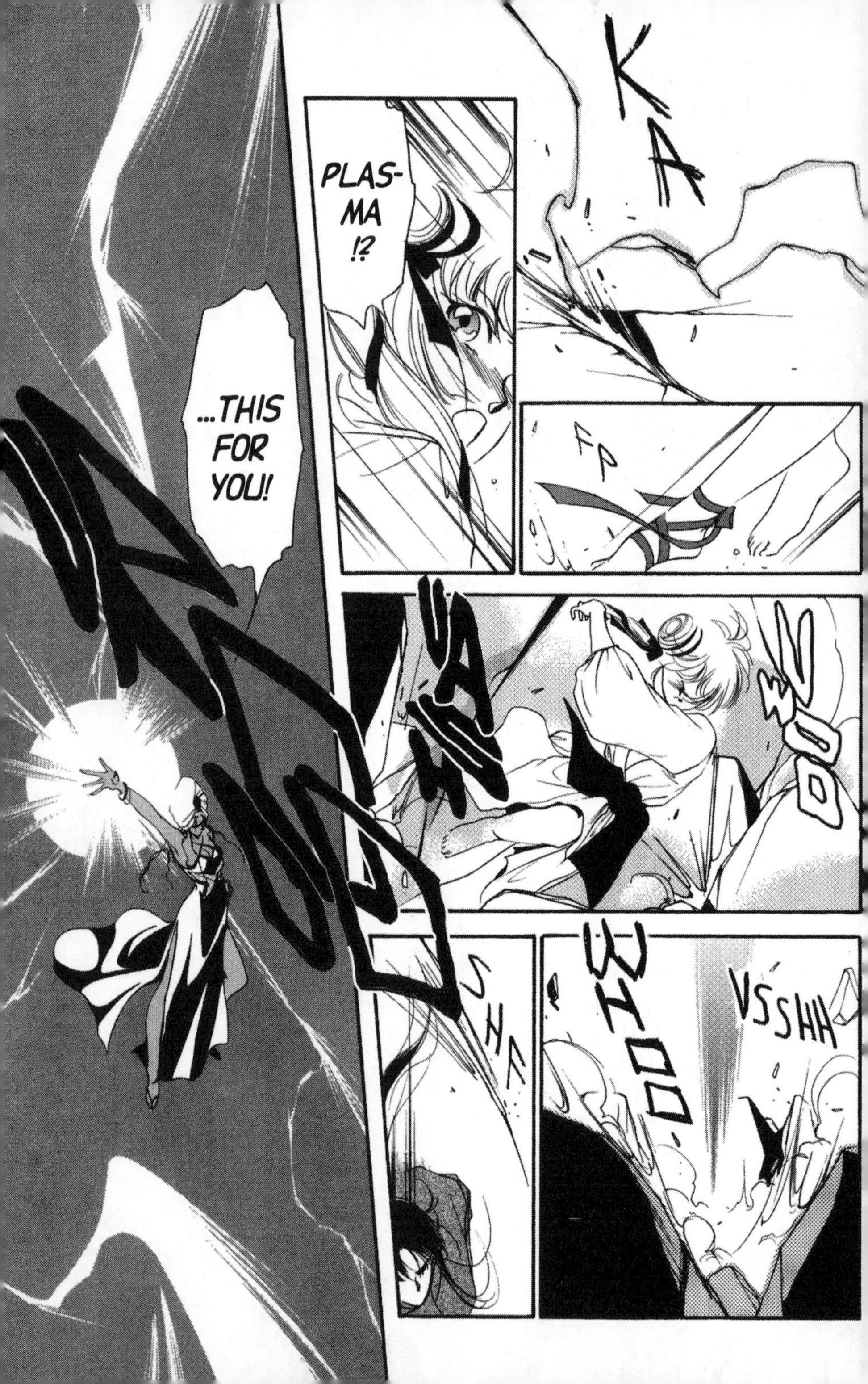
KA
PLAS-
MA
!?
FP
...THIS
FOR
YOU!
VSSHH
SHF

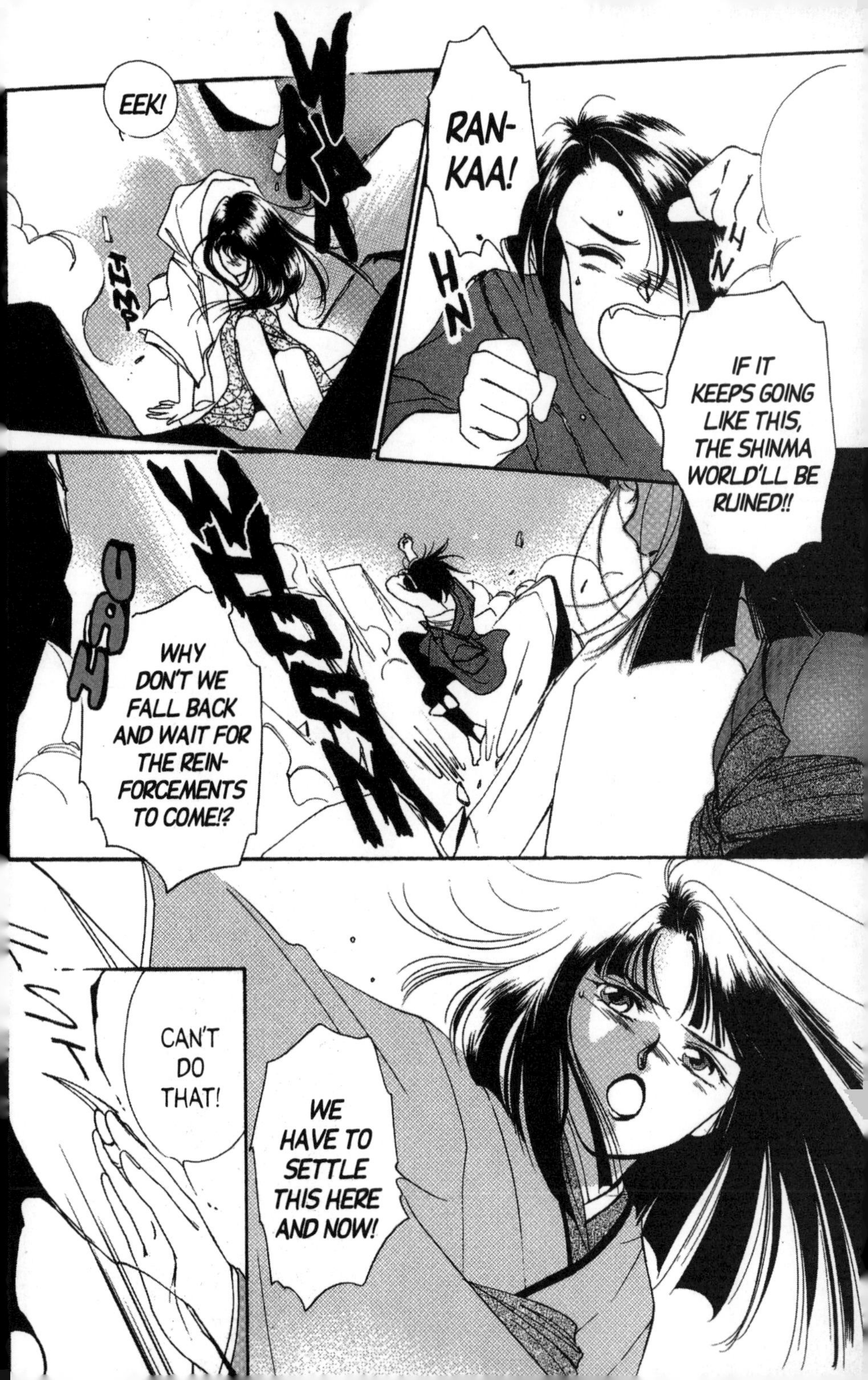
RAN-
KAA!
HN
HN
EEK!
IF IT KEEPS GOING LIKE THIS, THE SHINMA WORLD'LL BE RUINED!!
WHY DON'T WE FALL BACK AND WAIT FOR THE REIN-FORCEMENTS TO COME!?
CAN'T DO THAT!
WE HAVE TO SETTLE THIS HERE AND NOW!

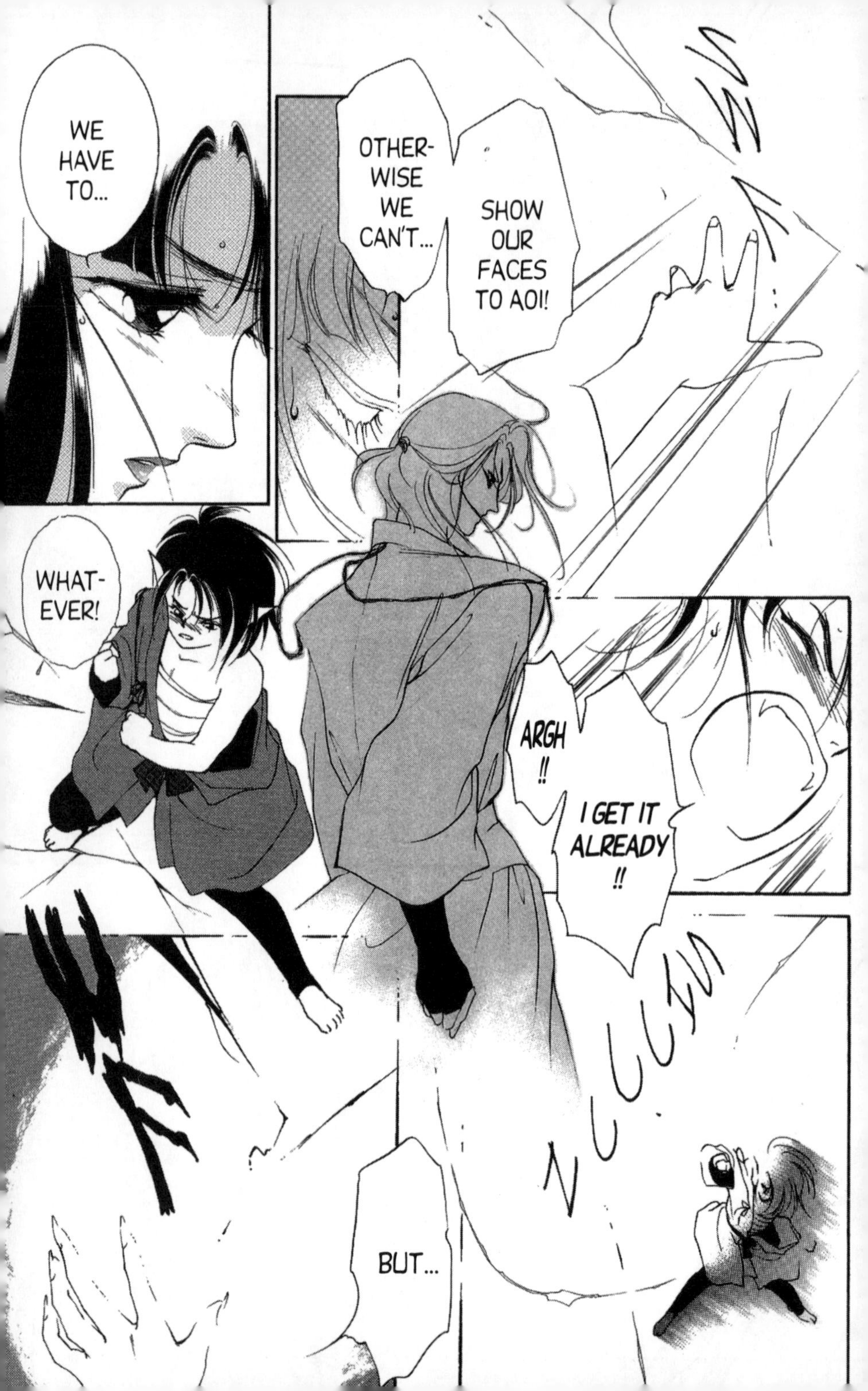
SHOW OUR FACES TO AOI!
OTHER-WISE WE CAN'T...
WE HAVE TO...
ARGH !!
I GET IT ALREADY !!
WHAT-EVER!
BUT...

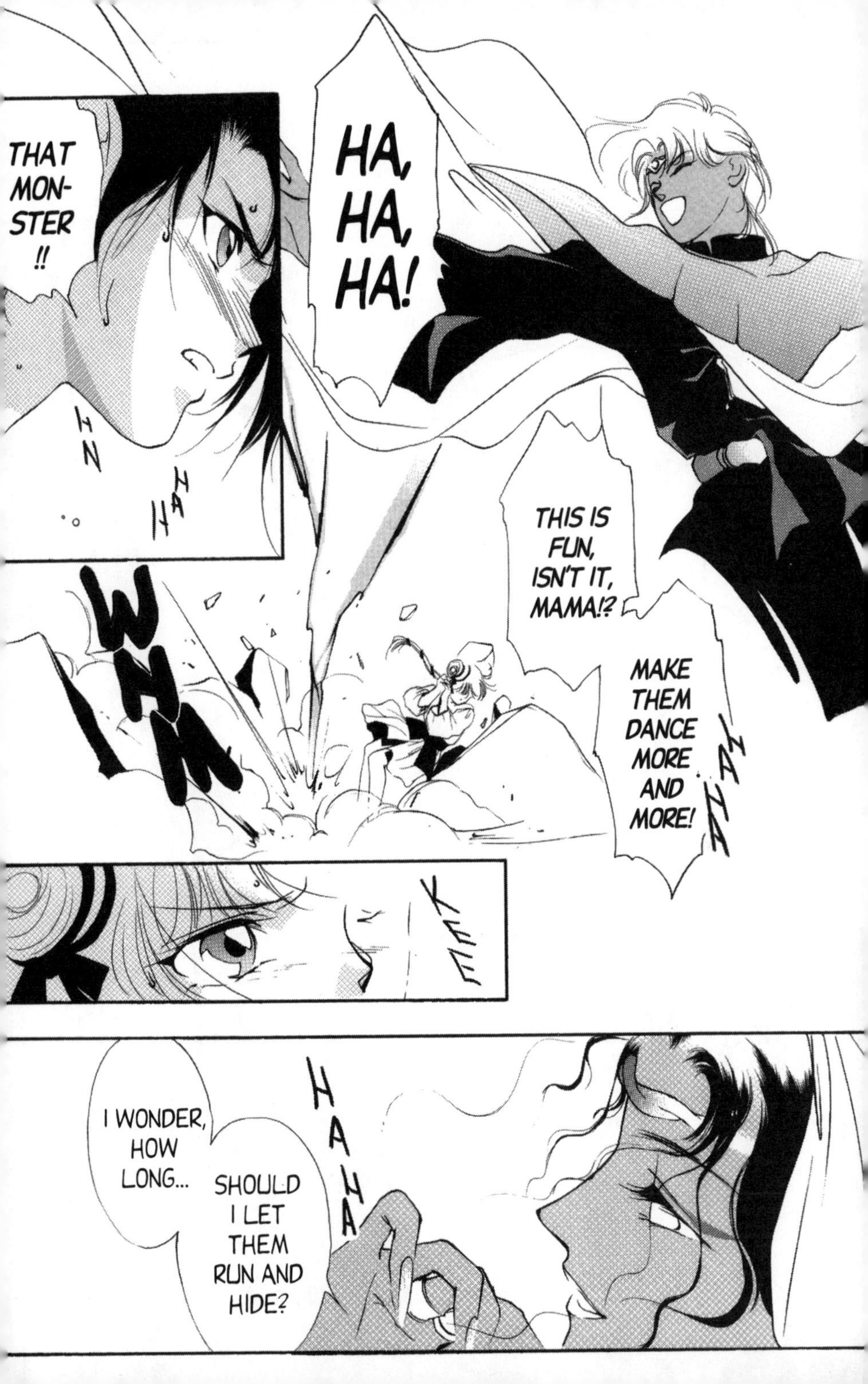
HA, HA, HA!
THAT MON-STER!!
HN
HA HA
THIS IS FUN, ISN'T IT, MAMA!?
MAKE THEM DANCE MORE AND MORE!
HA HA HA
I WONDER, HOW LONG...
SHOULD I LET THEM RUN AND HIDE?
HAHAHA

YES, BUT...

I DON'T HAVE A CHANCE TO ATTACK THEM!

ARE YOU OKAY YUI!?

YEAH!

THAT OLD BAT COULD KEEP THIS UP FOR- EVER!

EHH!

GHRRRRH!

DAMN!

LARVA...

WHERE ARE YOU WHEN WE NEED YOU?

DRRRRP

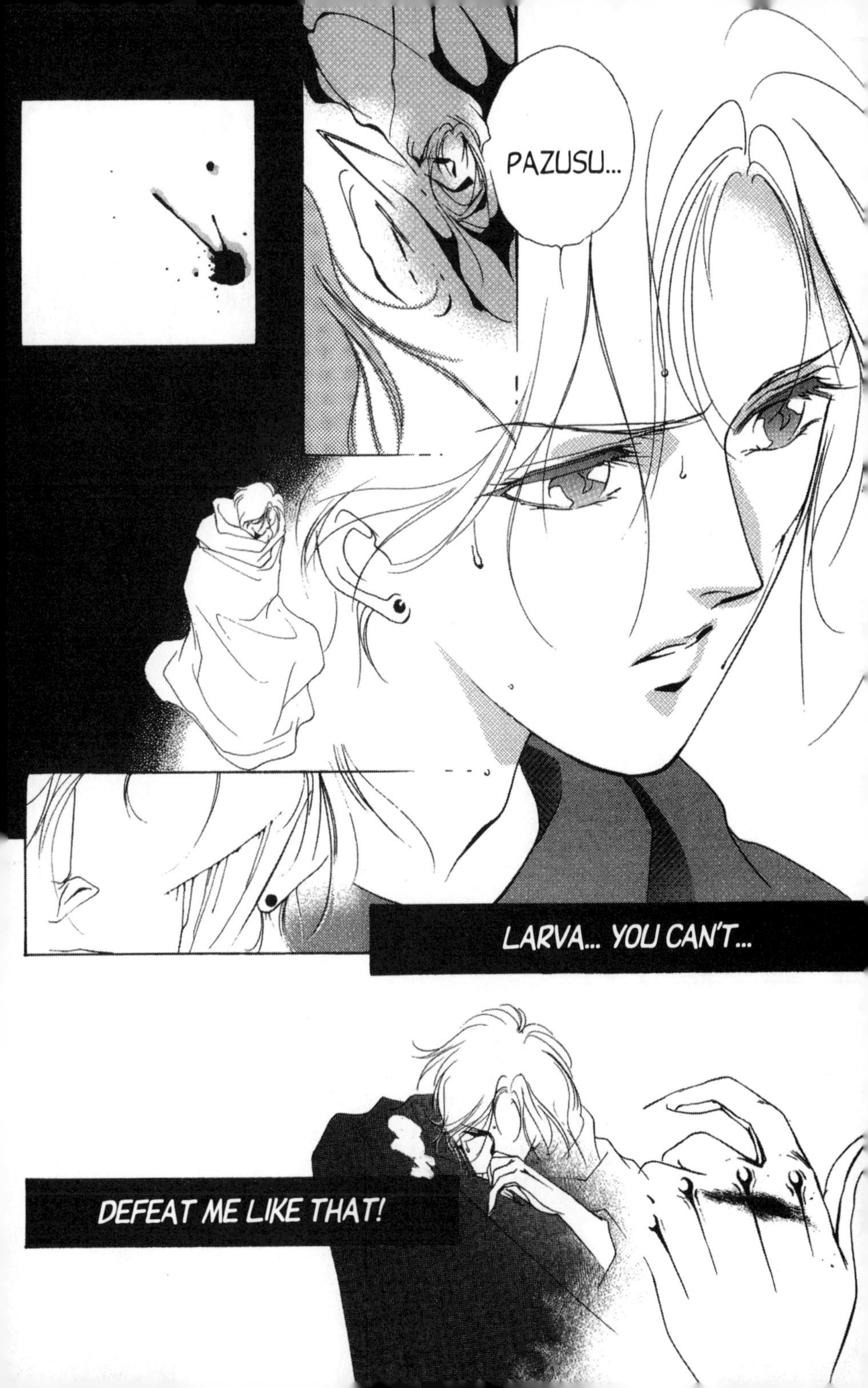
PAZUSU...
LARVA... YOU CAN'T...
DEFEAT ME LIKE THAT!

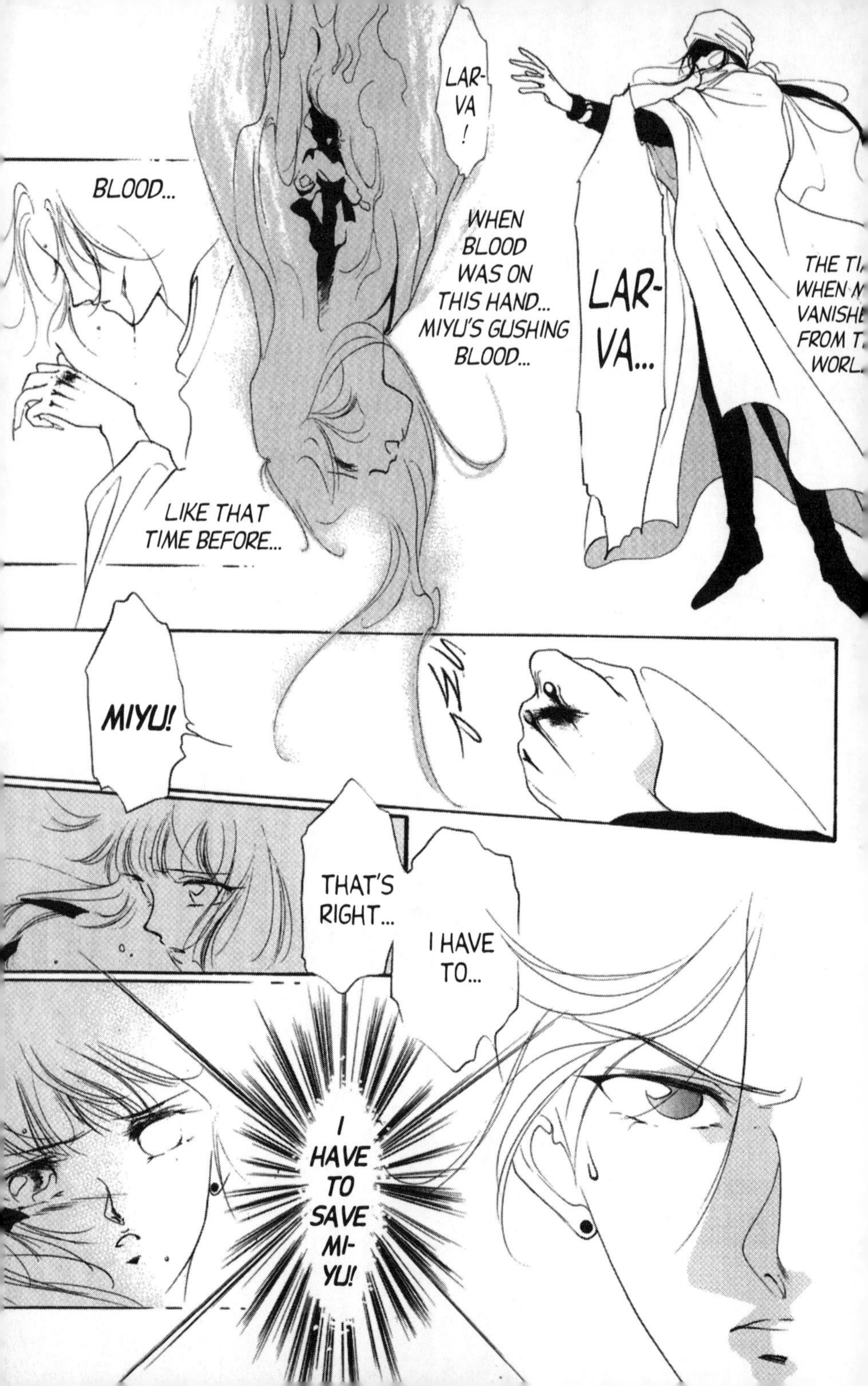
THE TI WHEN M VANISHE FROM T WORL
LAR-VA...
WHEN BLOOD WAS ON THIS HAND... MIYU'S GUSHING BLOOD...
LAR-VA!
BLOOD...
LIKE THAT TIME BEFORE...
MIYU!
THAT'S RIGHT...
I HAVE TO...
I HAVE TO SAVE MI-YU!

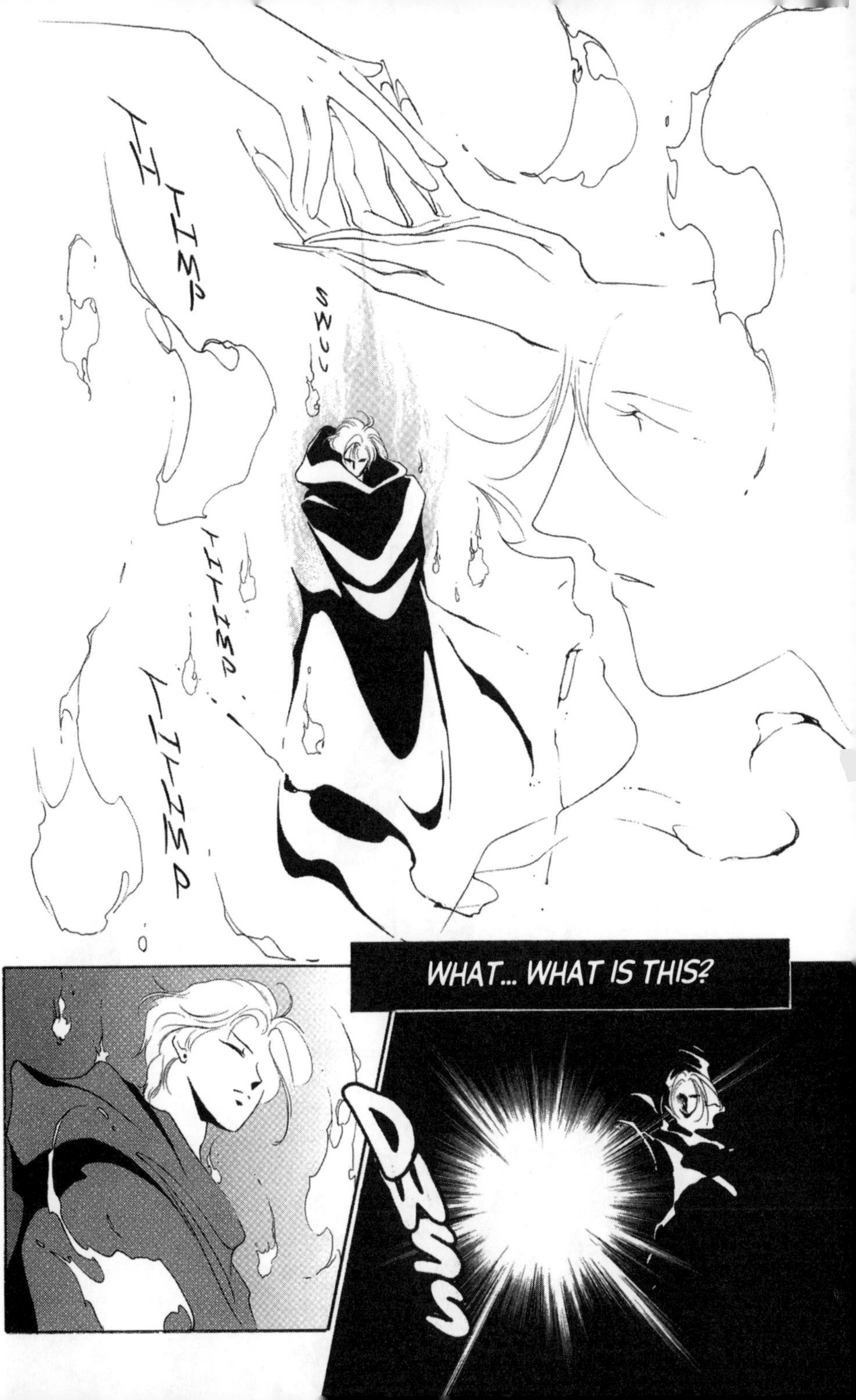
WHAT... WHAT IS THIS?

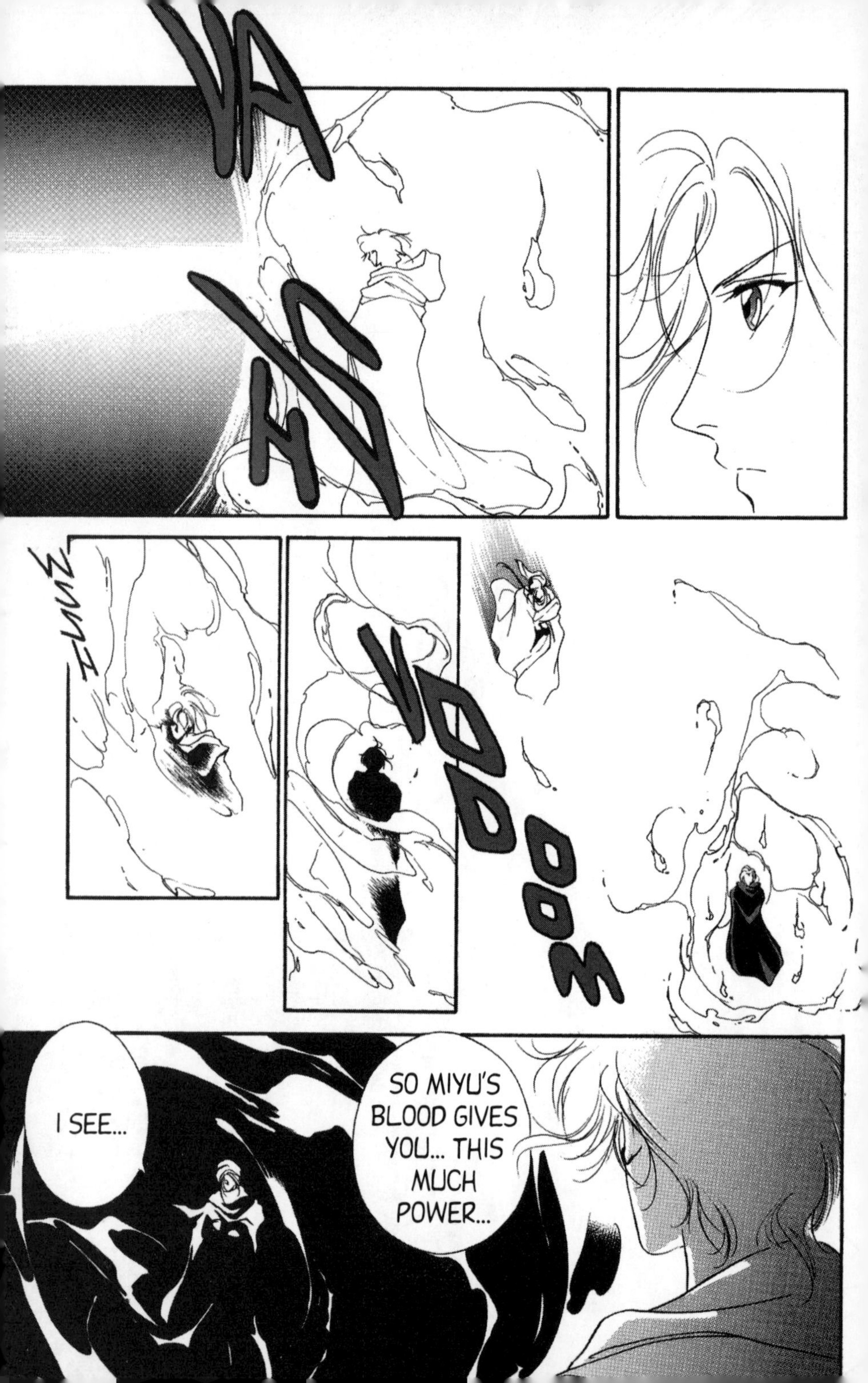
SO MIYU'S BLOOD GIVES YOU... THIS MUCH POWER...
I SEE...

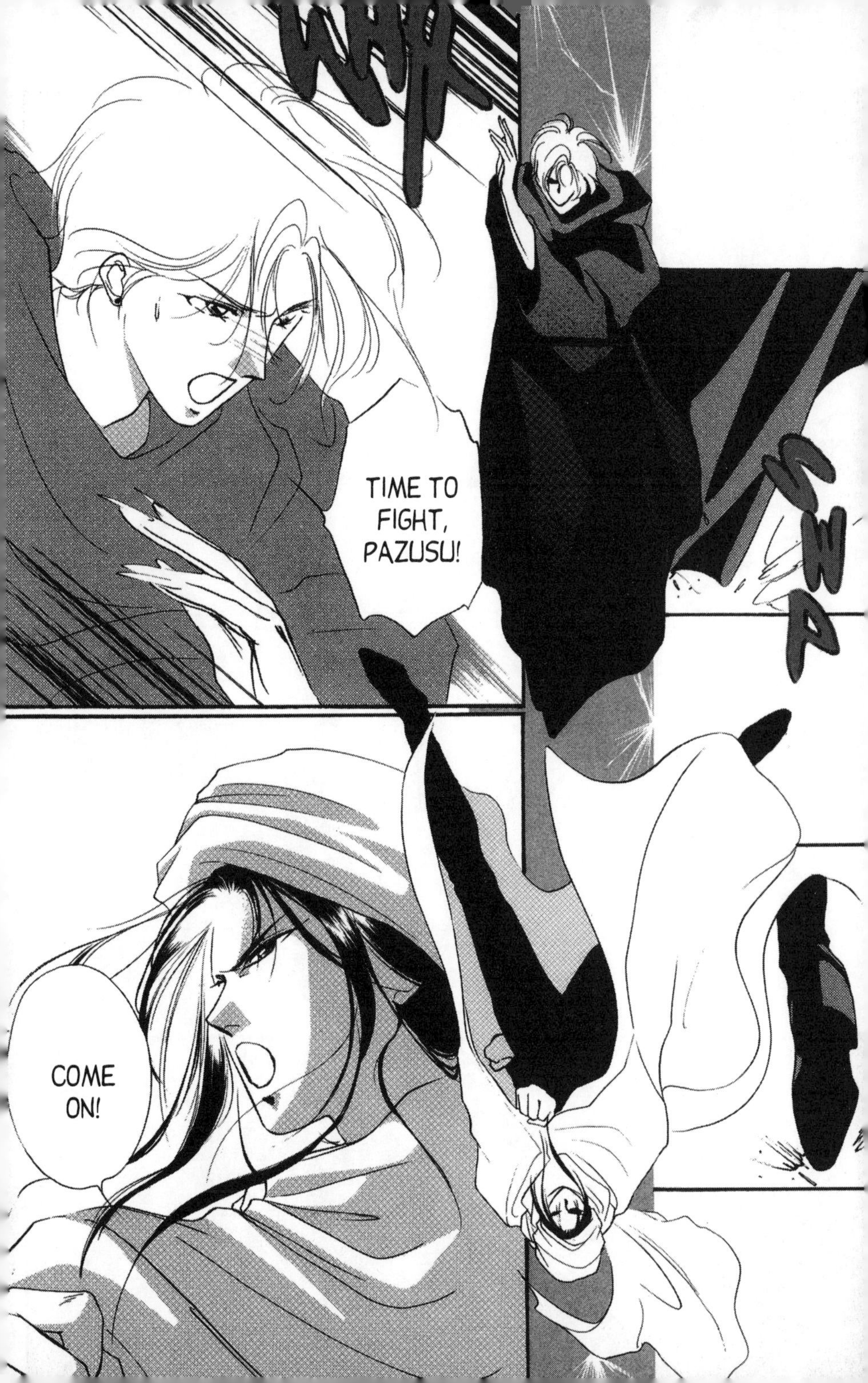
TIME TO FIGHT, PAZUSU!
COME ON!

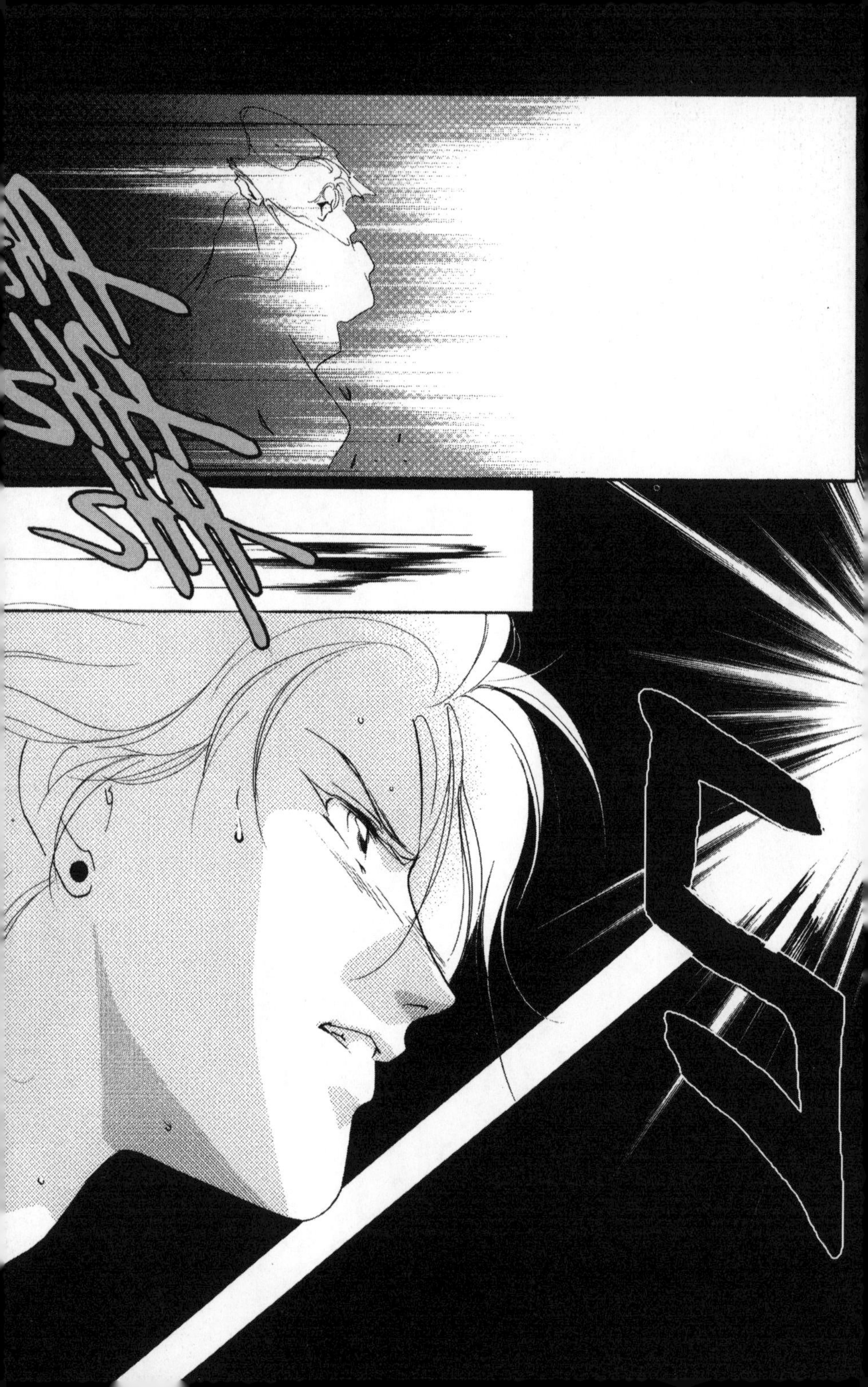

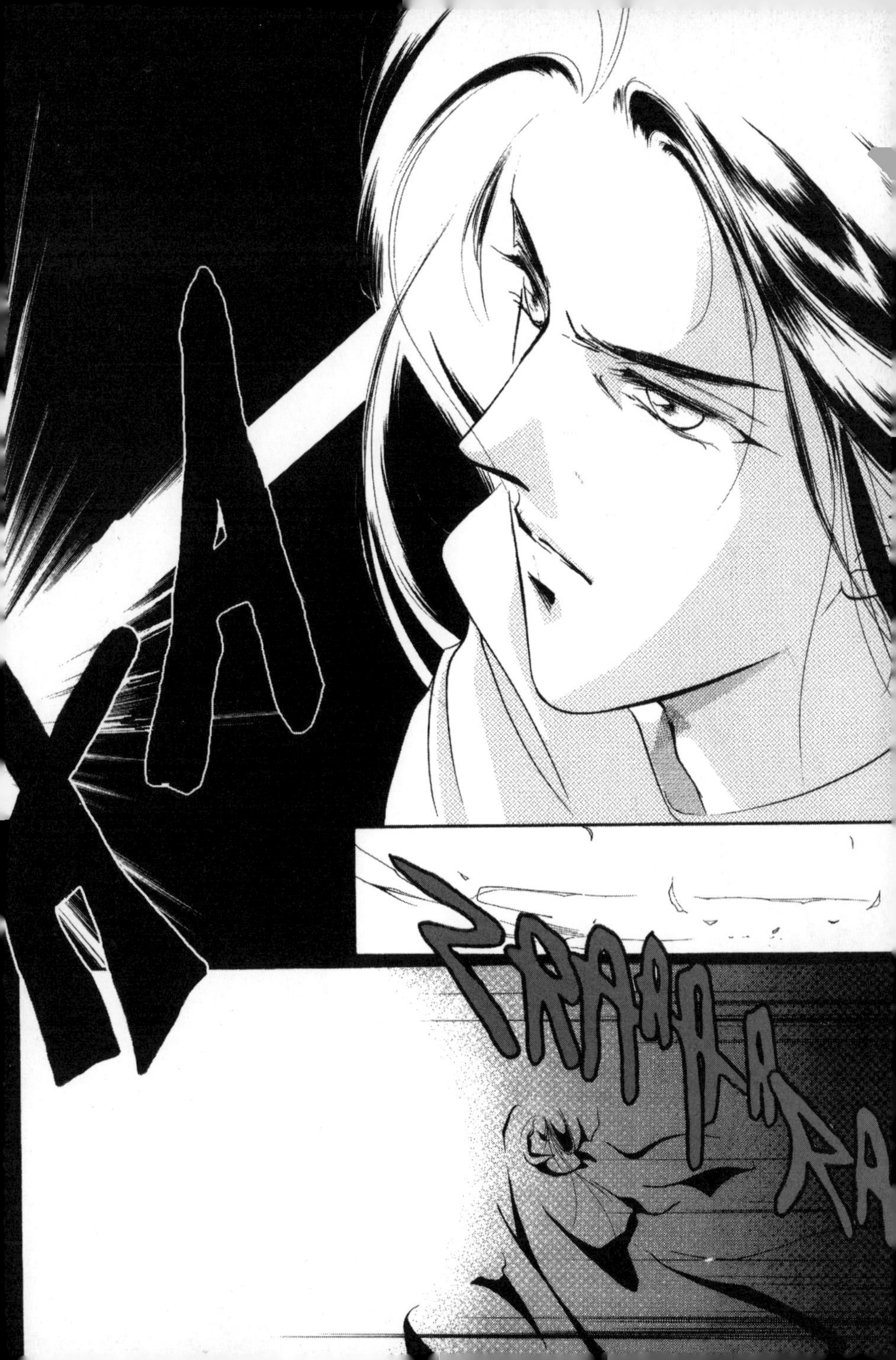
KA

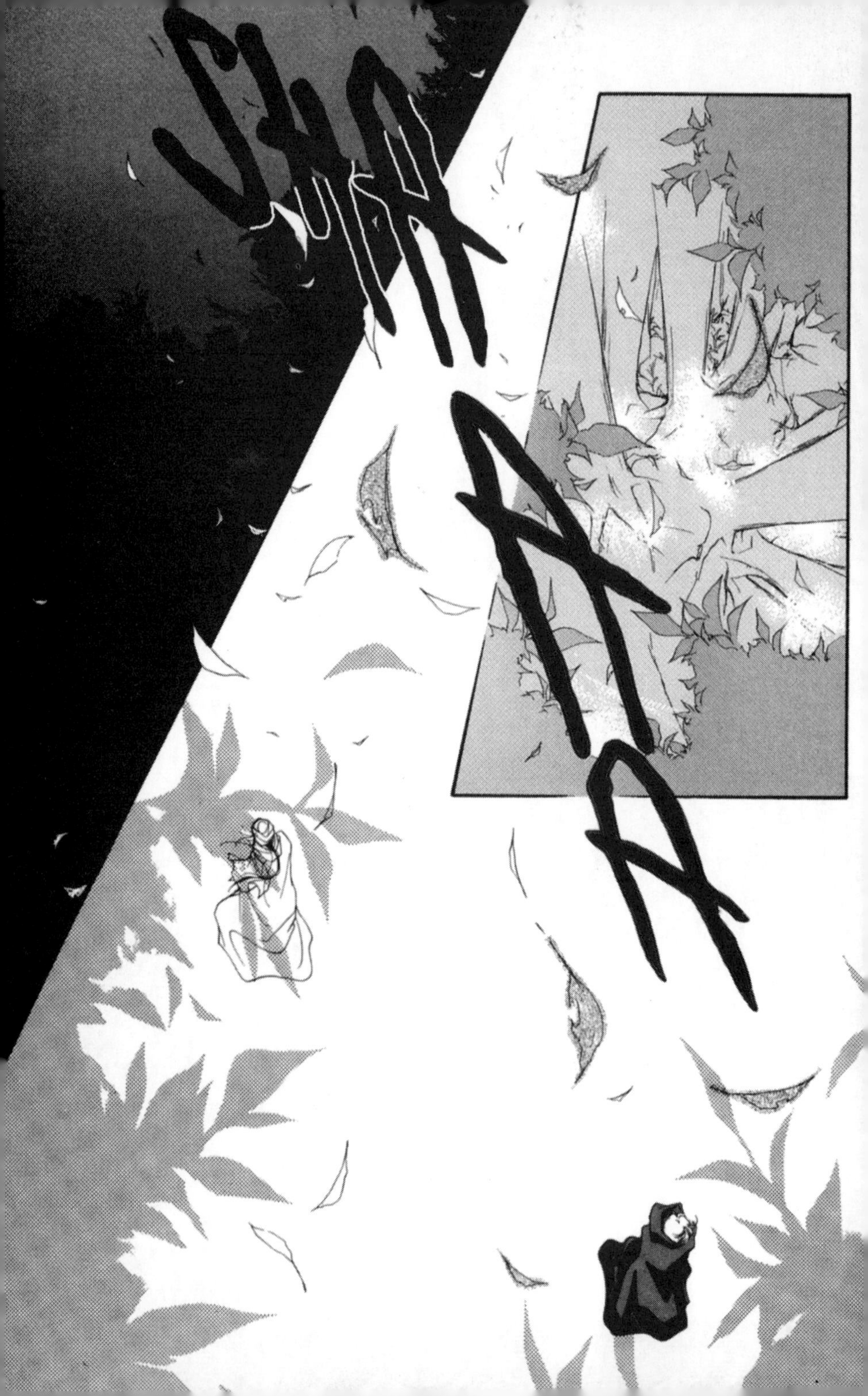
SHAAA

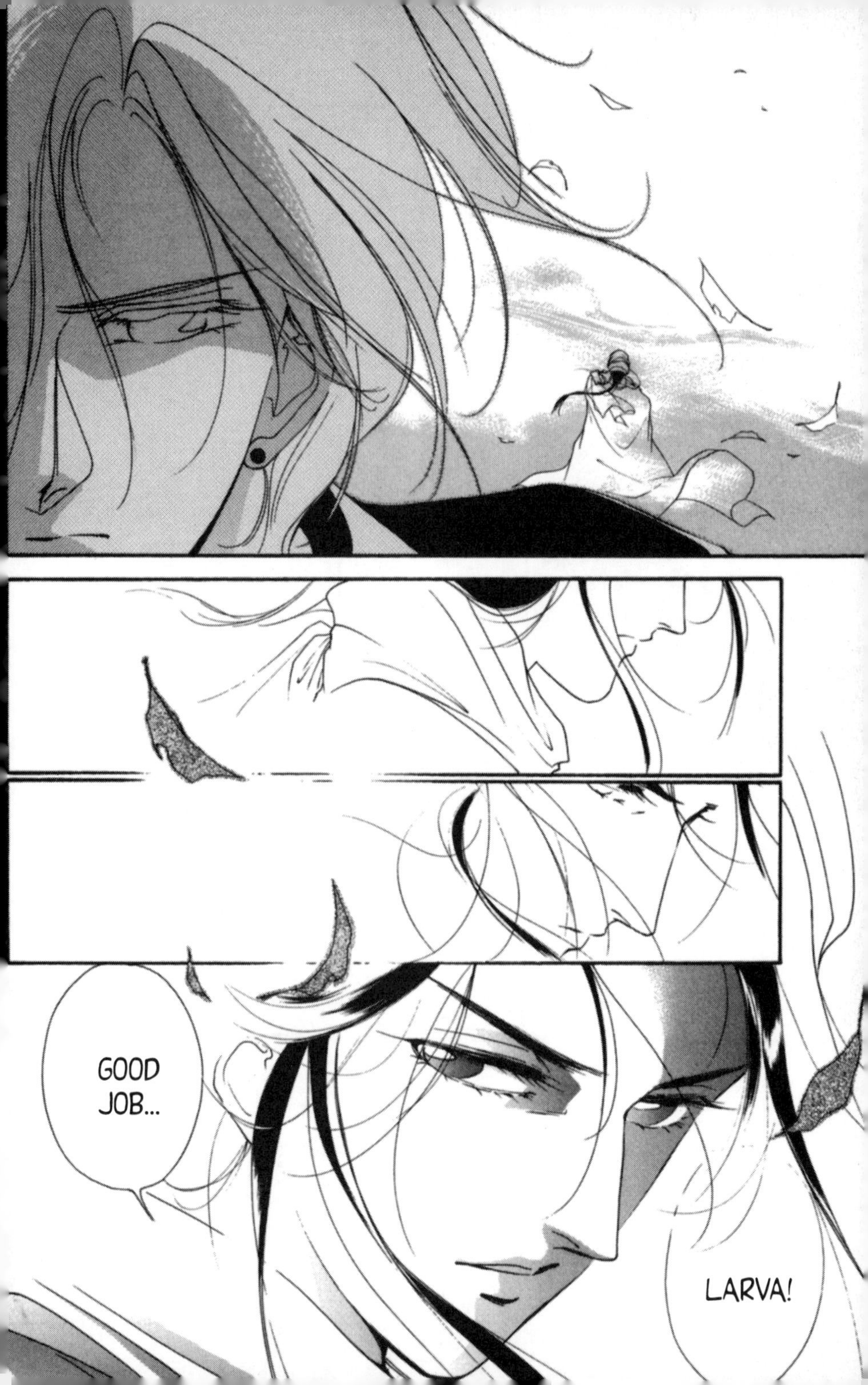
GOOD JOB...
LARVA!

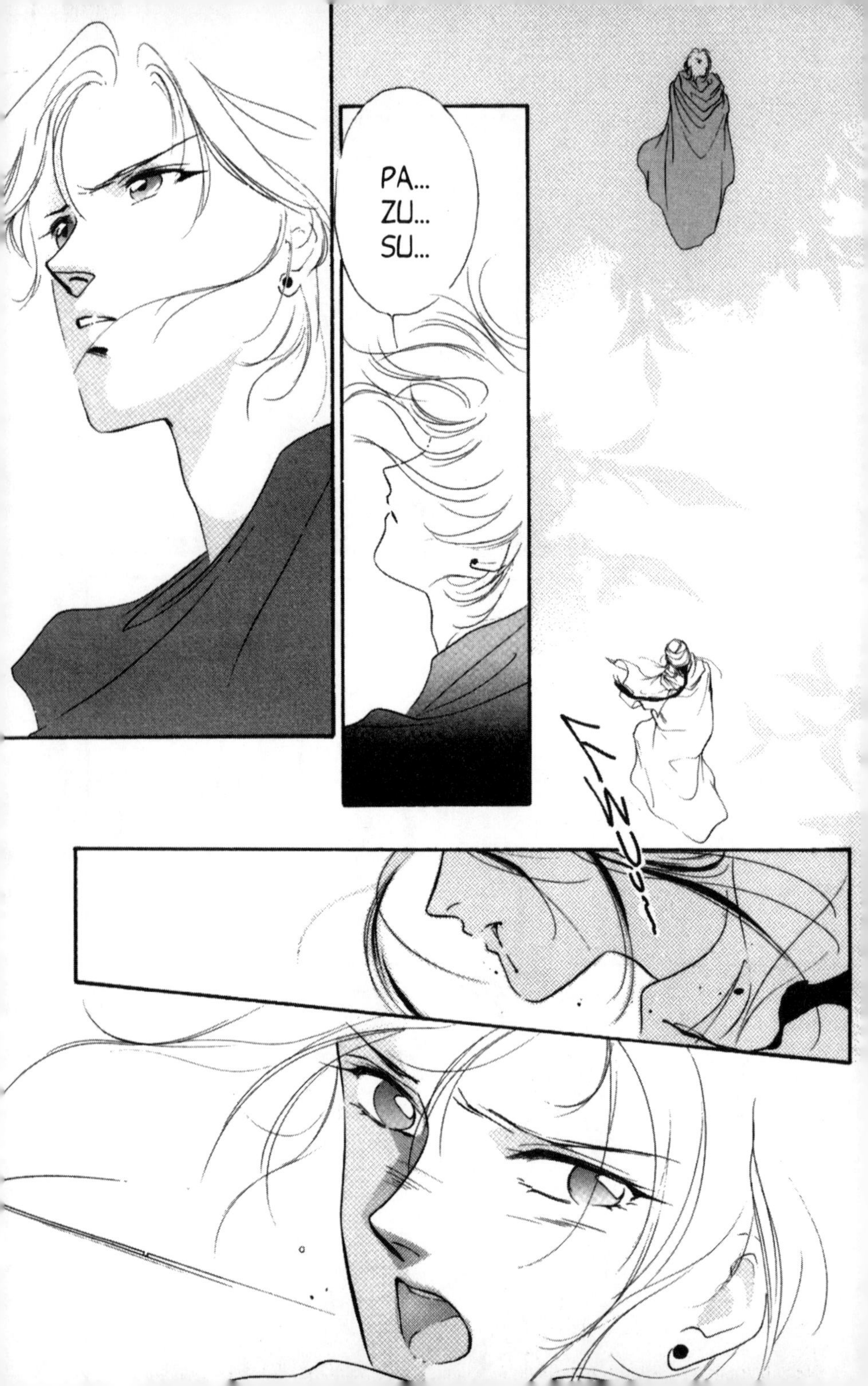
PA... ZU... SU...

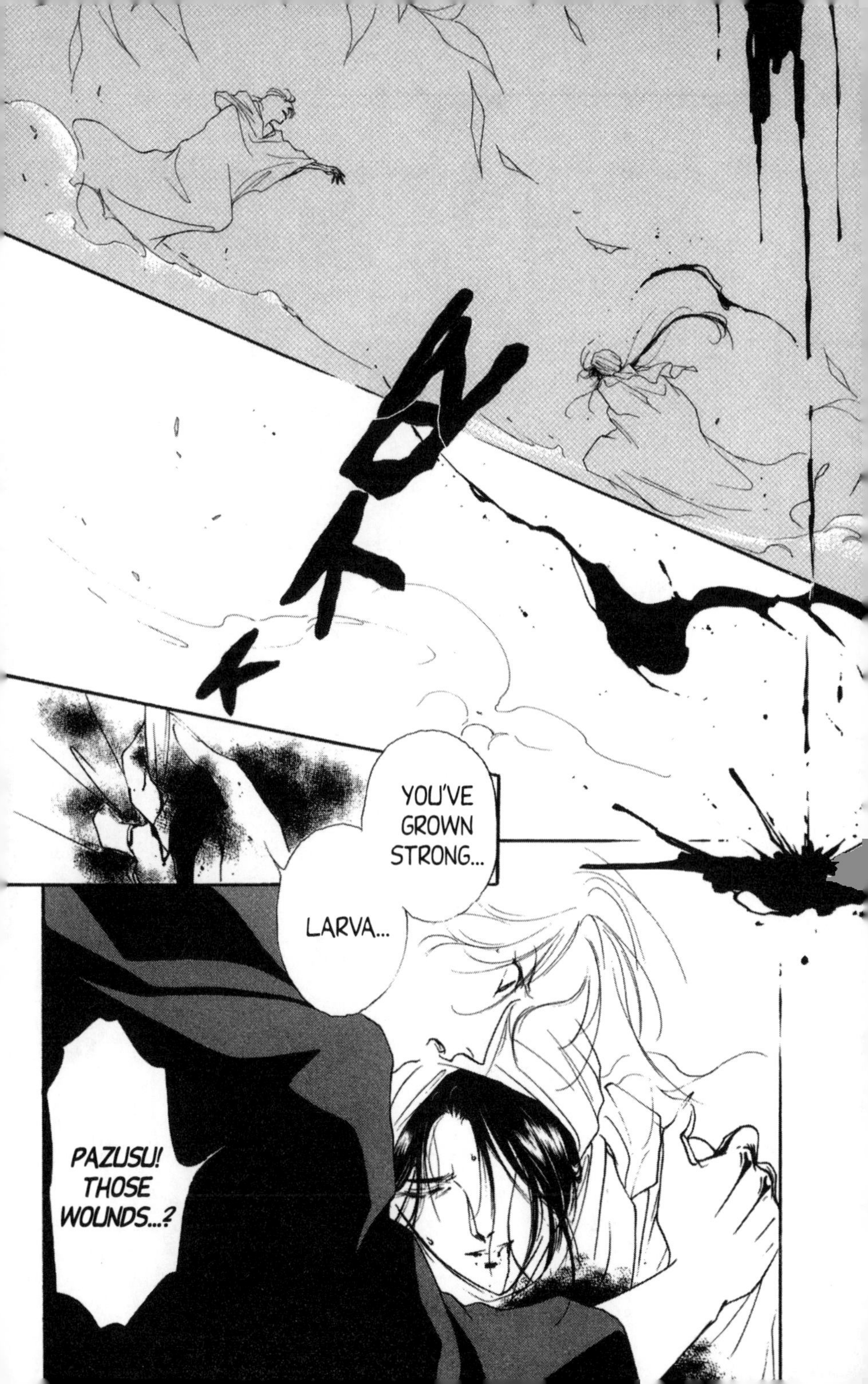
YOU'VE GROWN STRONG...
LARVA...
PAZUSU! THOSE WOUNDS...?

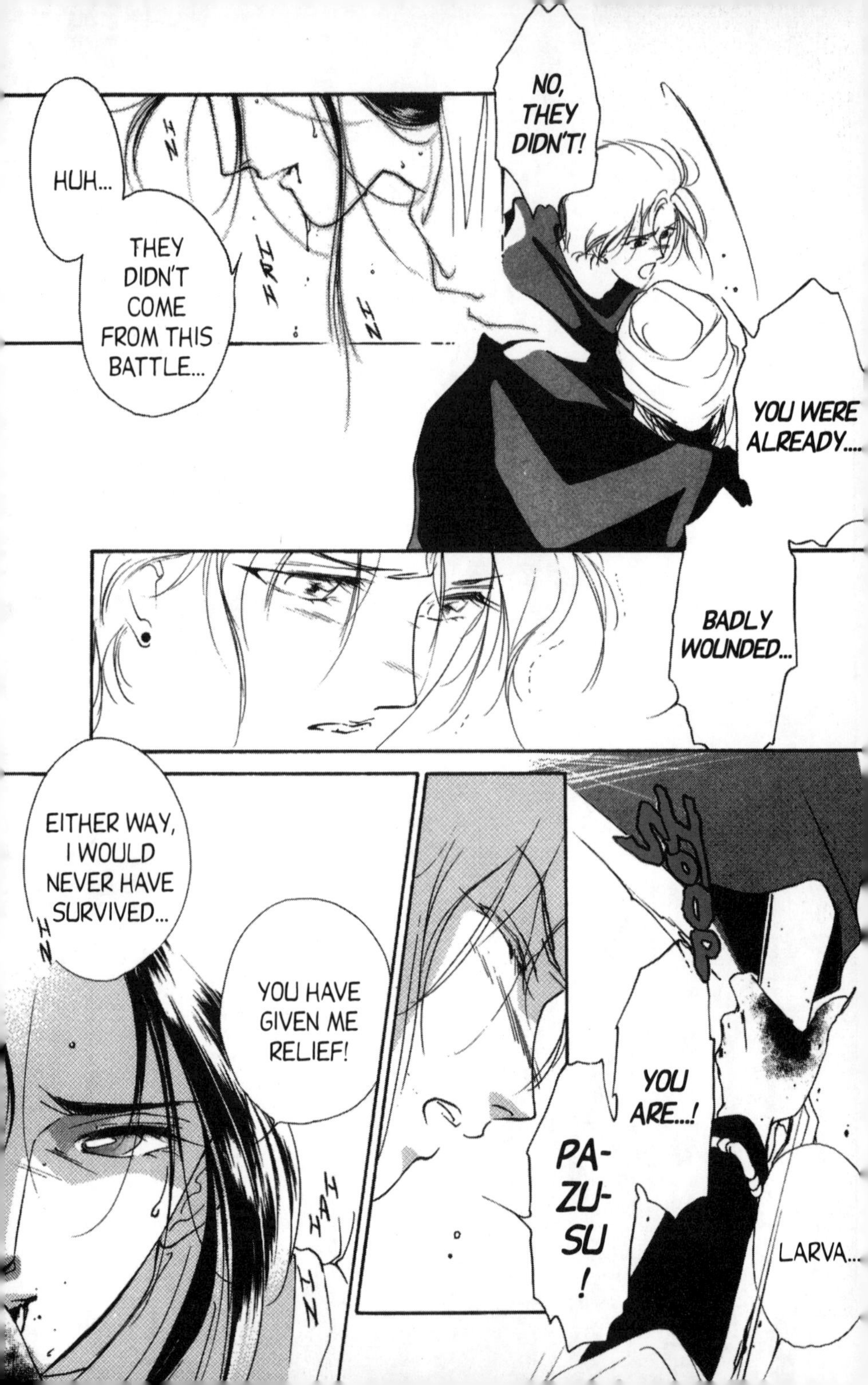
HUH...
THEY DIDN'T COME FROM THIS BATTLE...
HN HRH HN
NO, THEY DIDN'T!
YOU WERE ALREADY....
BADLY WOUNDED...
EITHER WAY, I WOULD NEVER HAVE SURVIVED...
HN
YOU HAVE GIVEN ME RELIEF!
HAH HN
SHOOP
YOU ARE...!
PA-ZU-SU!
LARVA...

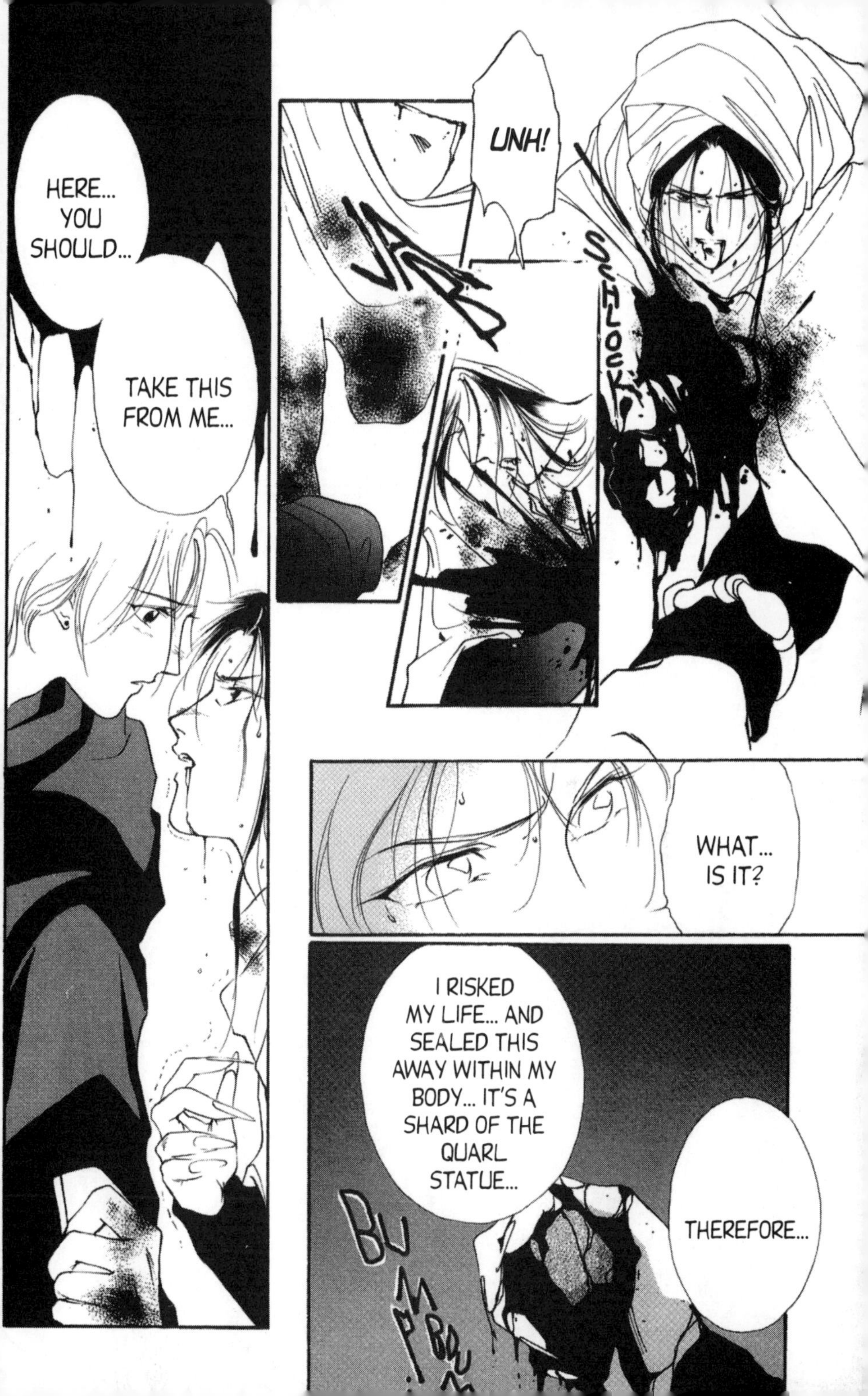
HERE... YOU SHOULD...
TAKE THIS FROM ME...
UNH!
SCHLOCK
WHAT... IS IT?
I RISKED MY LIFE... AND SEALED THIS AWAY WITHIN MY BODY... IT'S A SHARD OF THE QUARL STATUE...
THEREFORE...

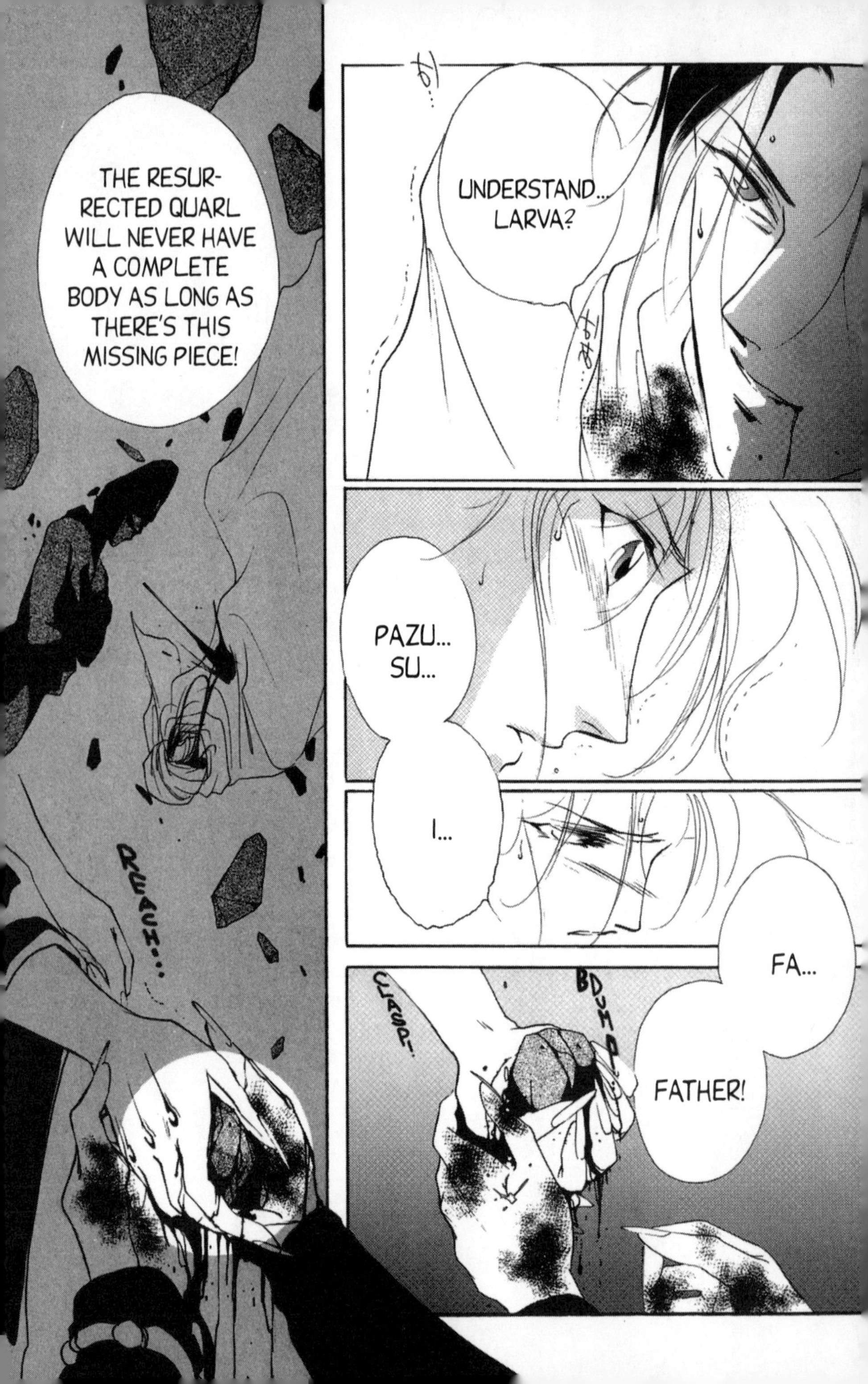
UNDERSTAND... LARVA?
PAZU... SU...
I...
FA...
FATHER!
BDUMP
CLASP!
THE RESUR-RECTED QUARL WILL NEVER HAVE A COMPLETE BODY AS LONG AS THERE'S THIS MISSING PIECE!
REACH...

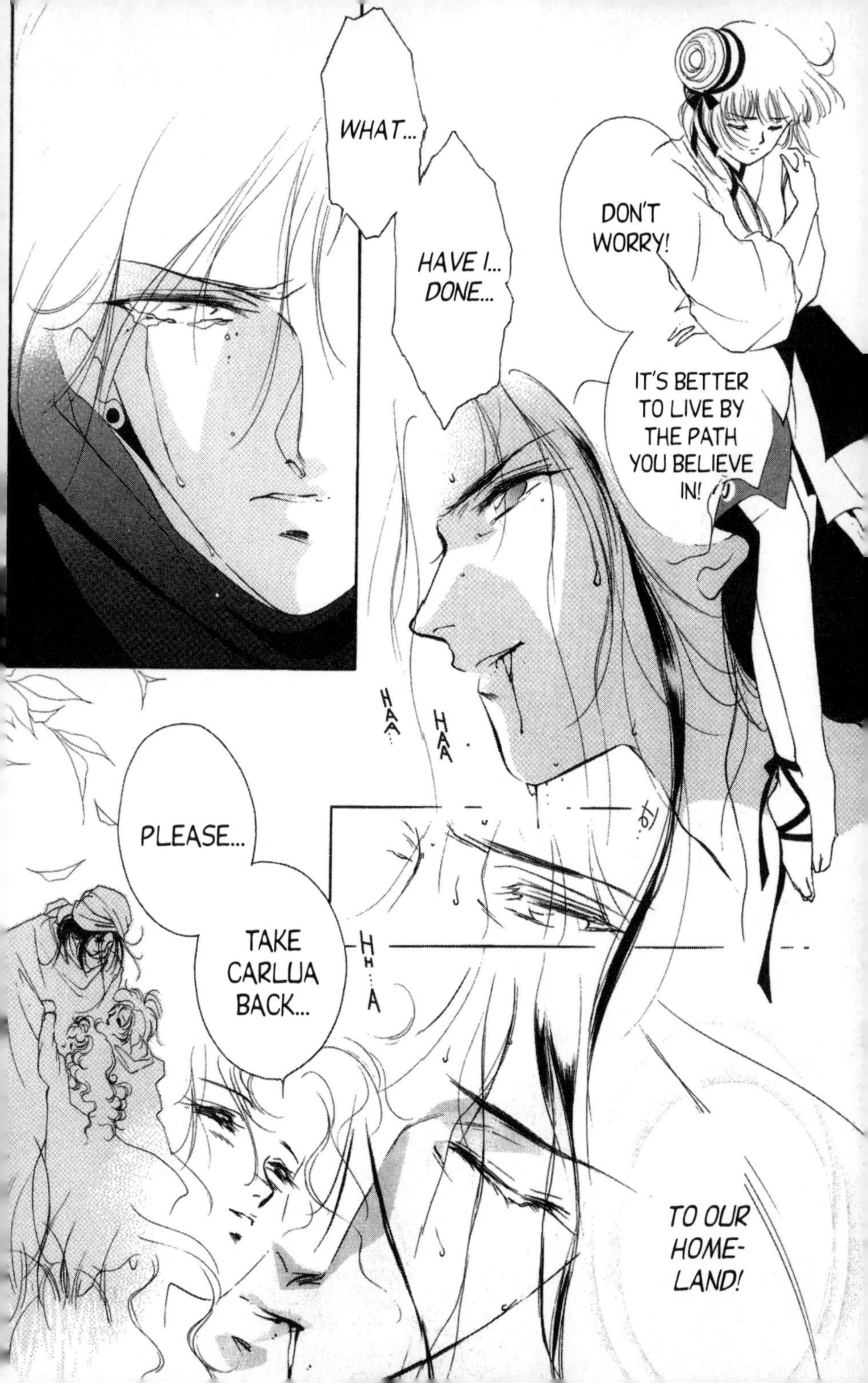
DON'T WORRY!
IT'S BETTER TO LIVE BY THE PATH YOU BELIEVE IN!
WHAT...
HAVE I... DONE...
HAA
HAA
TO OUR HOME-LAND!
H...A
PLEASE...
TAKE CARLUA BACK...

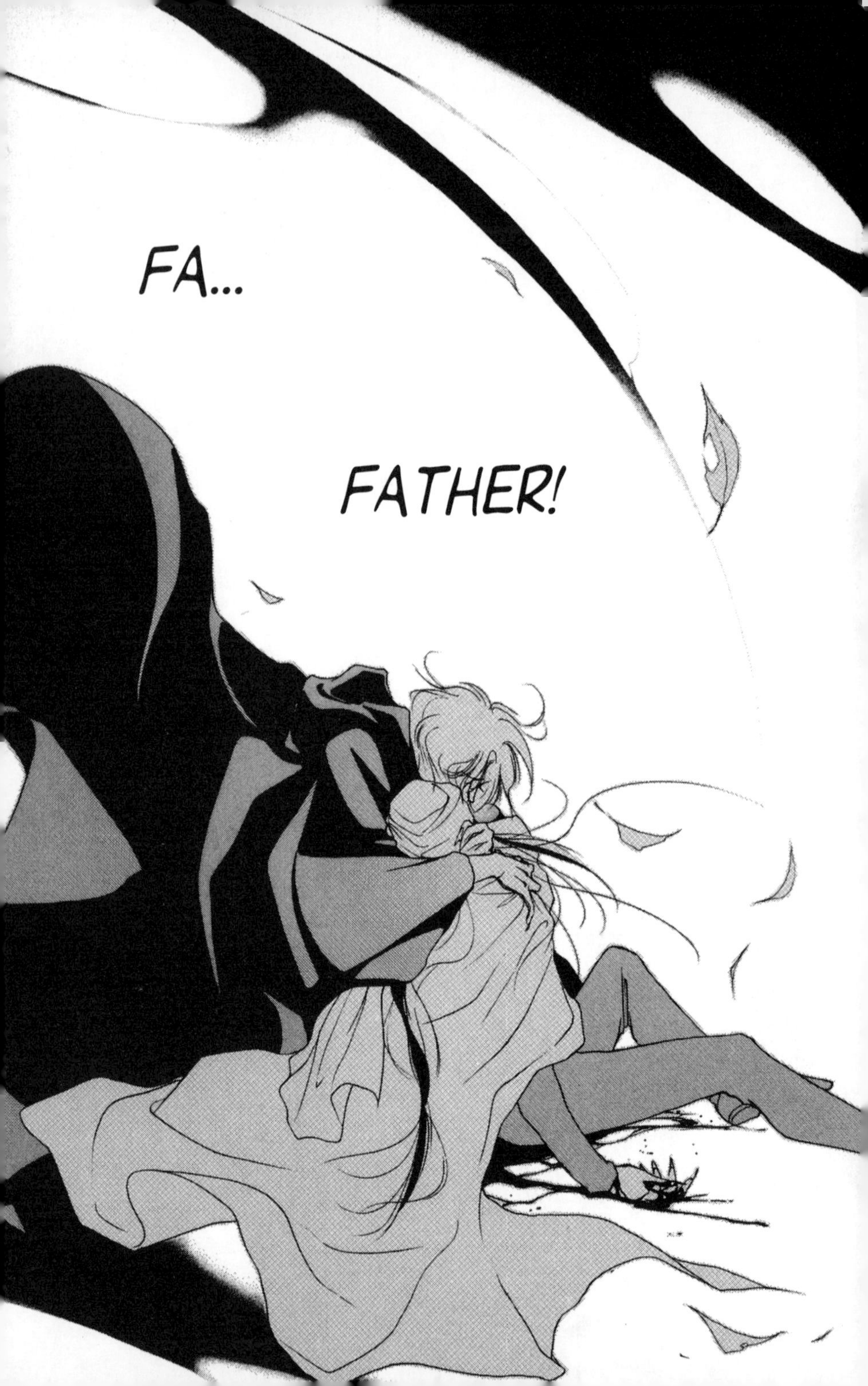
FA...
FATHER!

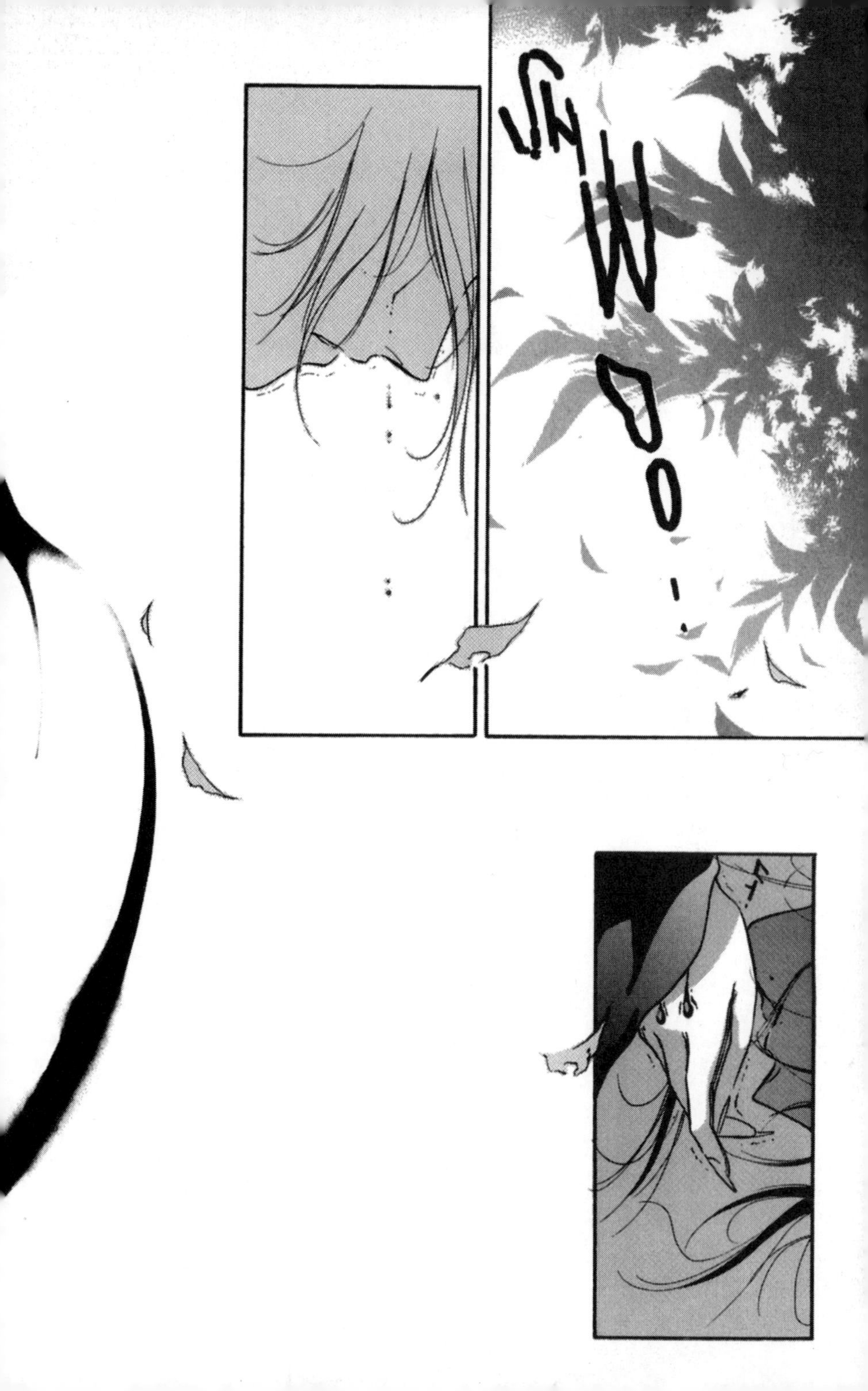
SHWOO...

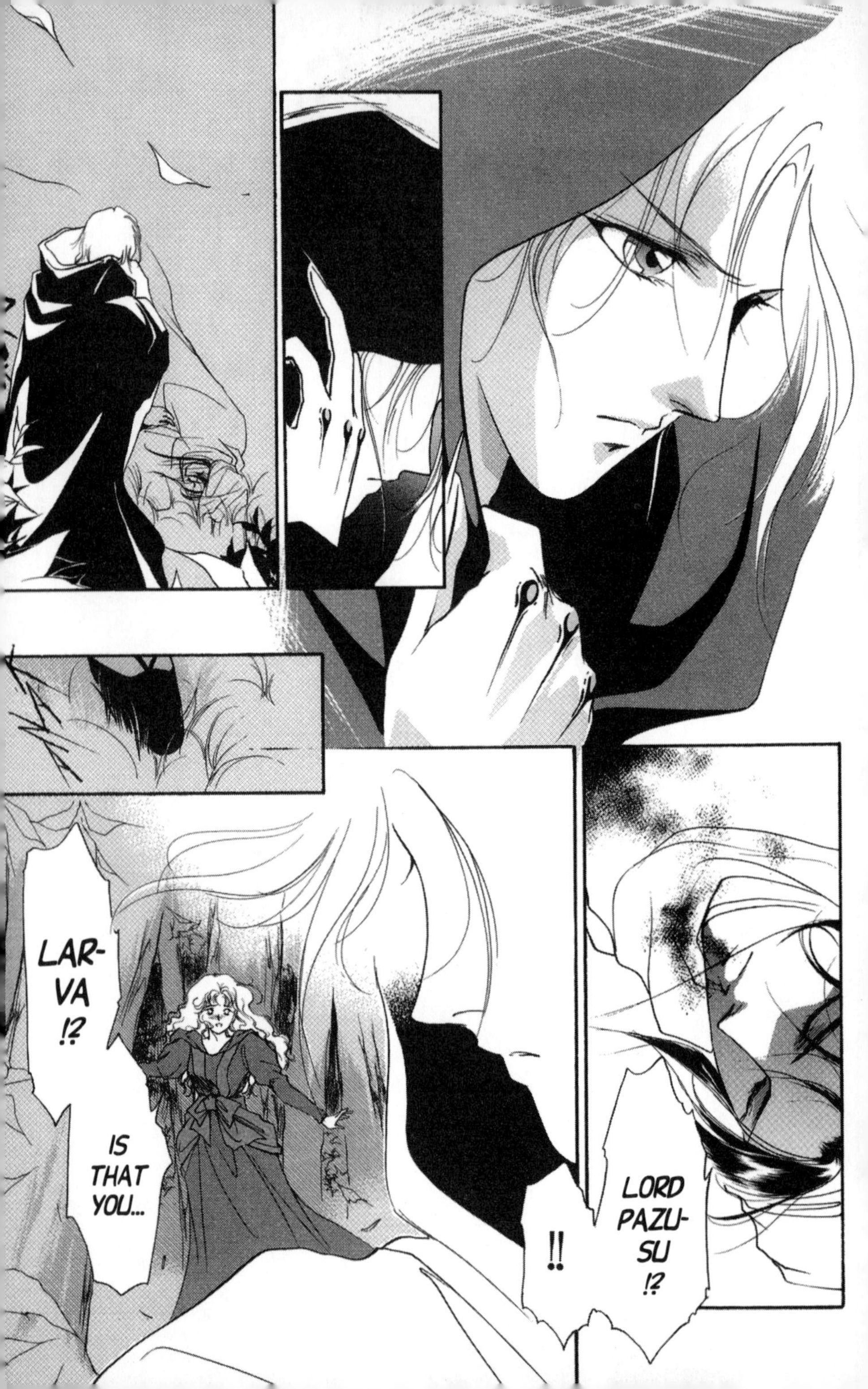
LORD PAZU-SU !?
!!
LAR-VA !?
IS THAT YOU...

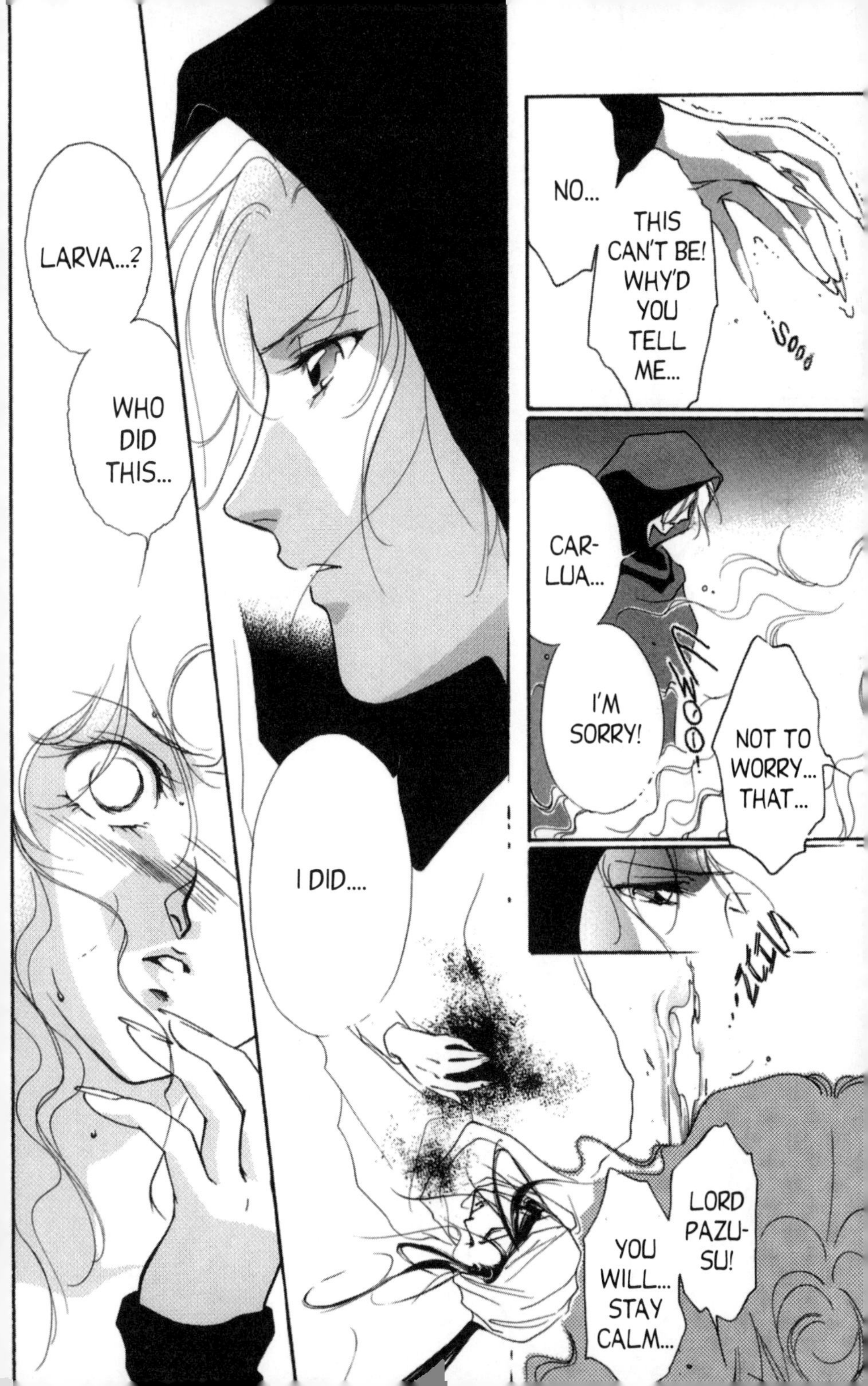
LARVA...?
WHO DID THIS...
I DID....
NO...
THIS CAN'T BE! WHY'D YOU TELL ME...
...SOOO
CAR-LUA...
I'M SORRY!
NOT TO WORRY... THAT...
LORD PAZU-SU!
YOU WILL... STAY CALM...

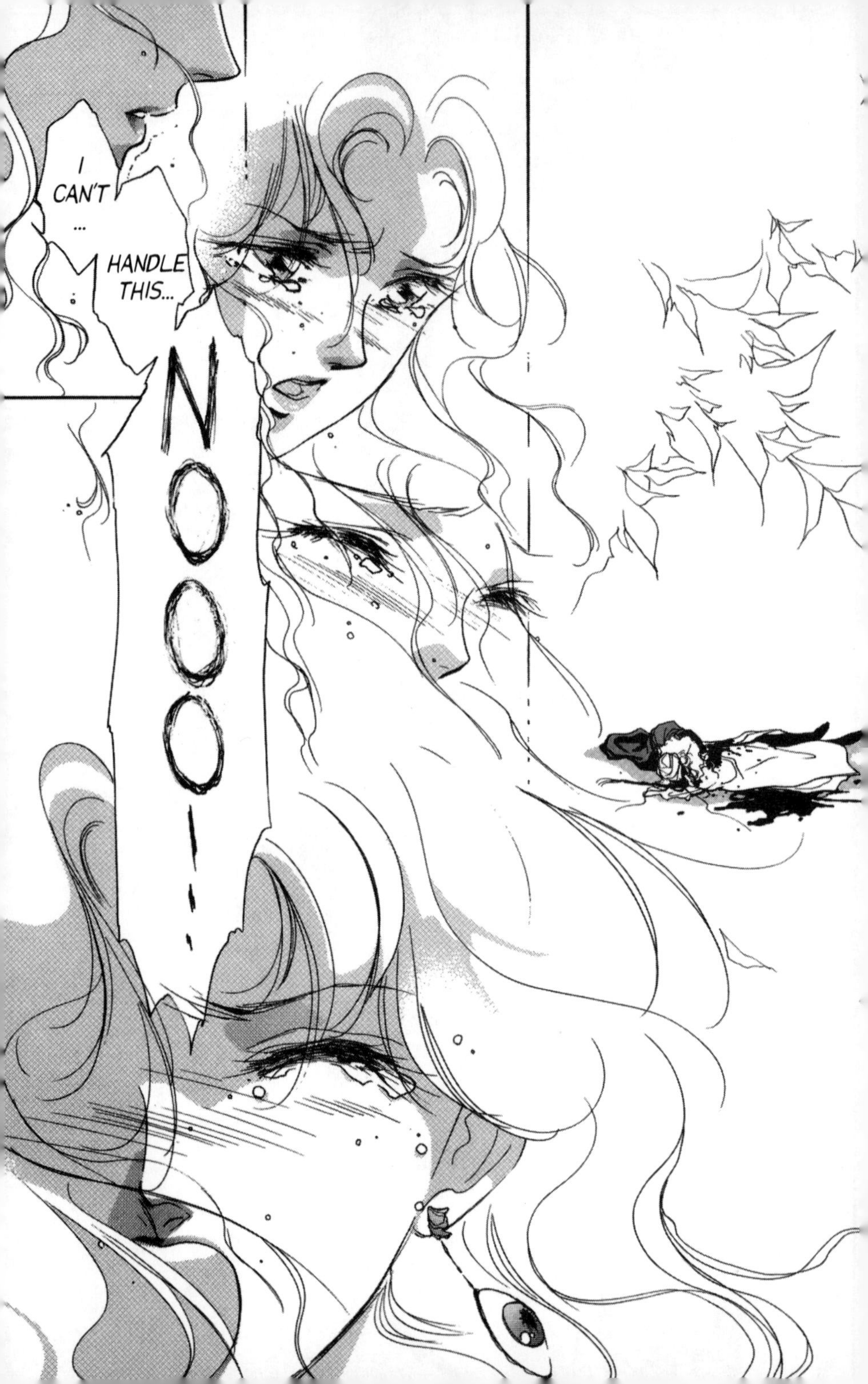
I CAN'T ... HANDLE THIS...
NOOO!!

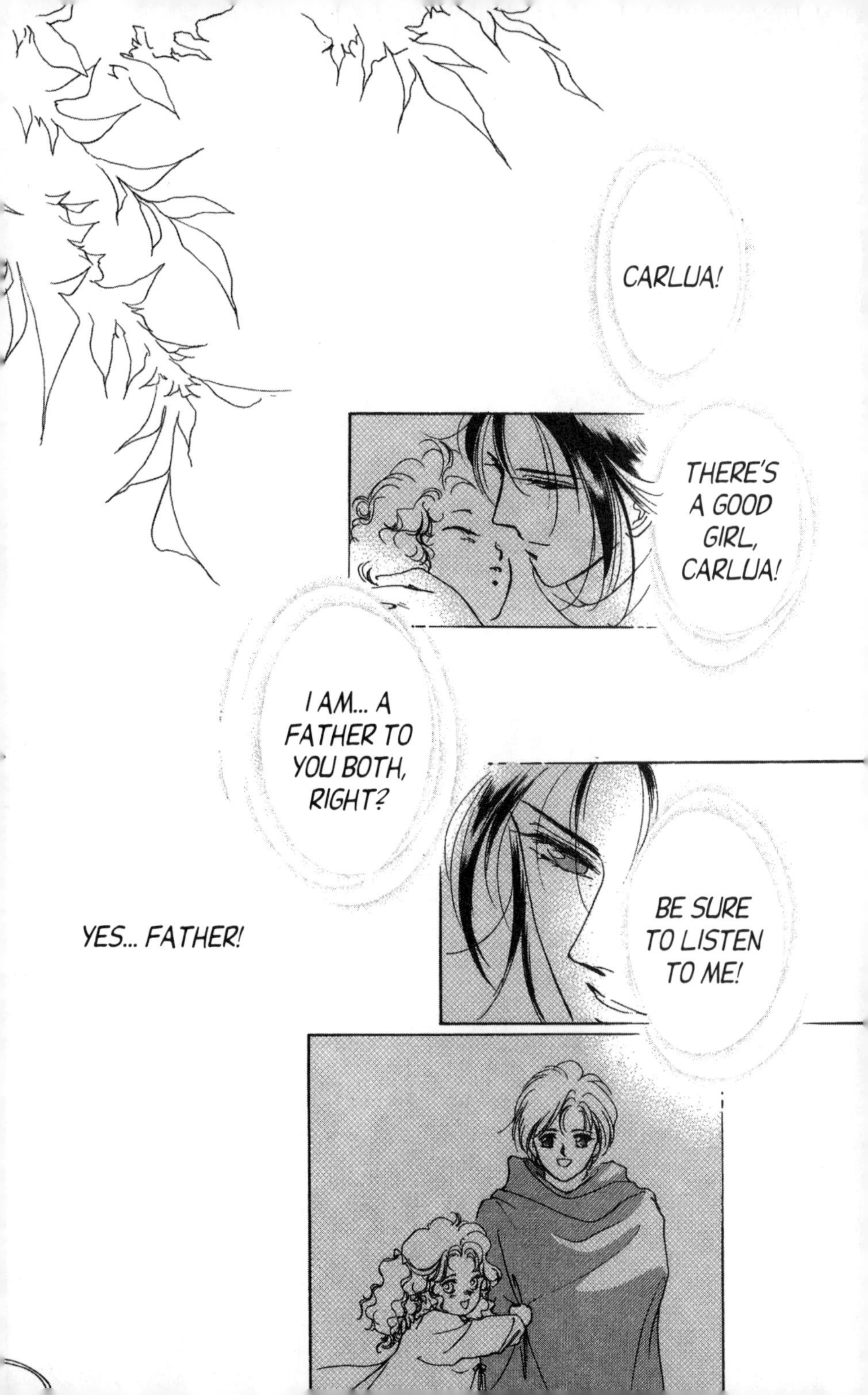
CARLUA!
THERE'S A GOOD GIRL, CARLUA!
I AM... A FATHER TO YOU BOTH, RIGHT?
BE SURE TO LISTEN TO ME!
YES... FATHER!

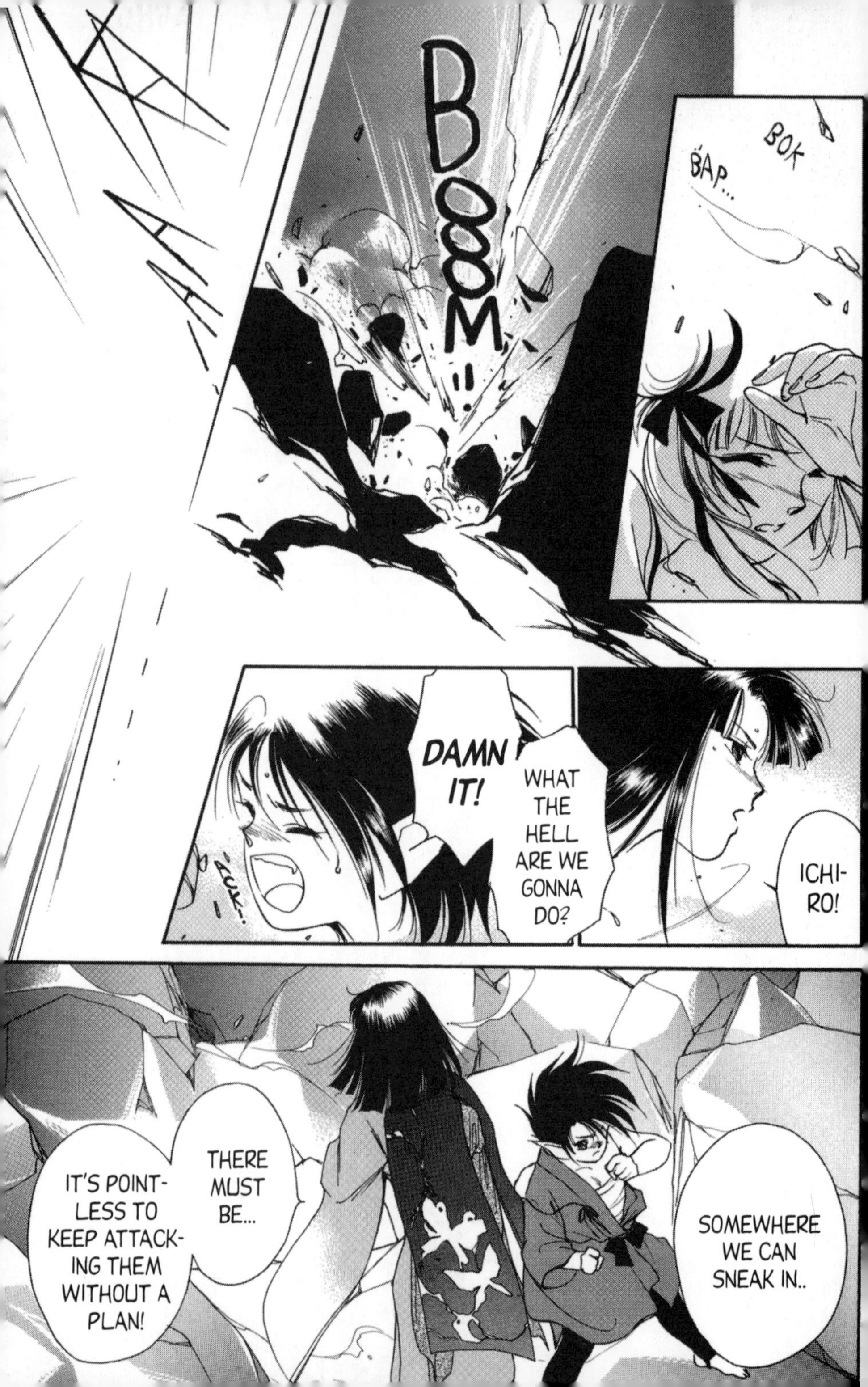

BOK
BAP...
BOOM!!
ICHI-RO!
DAMN IT!
WHAT THE HELL ARE WE GONNA DO?
SOMEWHERE WE CAN SNEAK IN..
THERE MUST BE...
IT'S POINT-LESS TO KEEP ATTACK-ING THEM WITHOUT A PLAN!

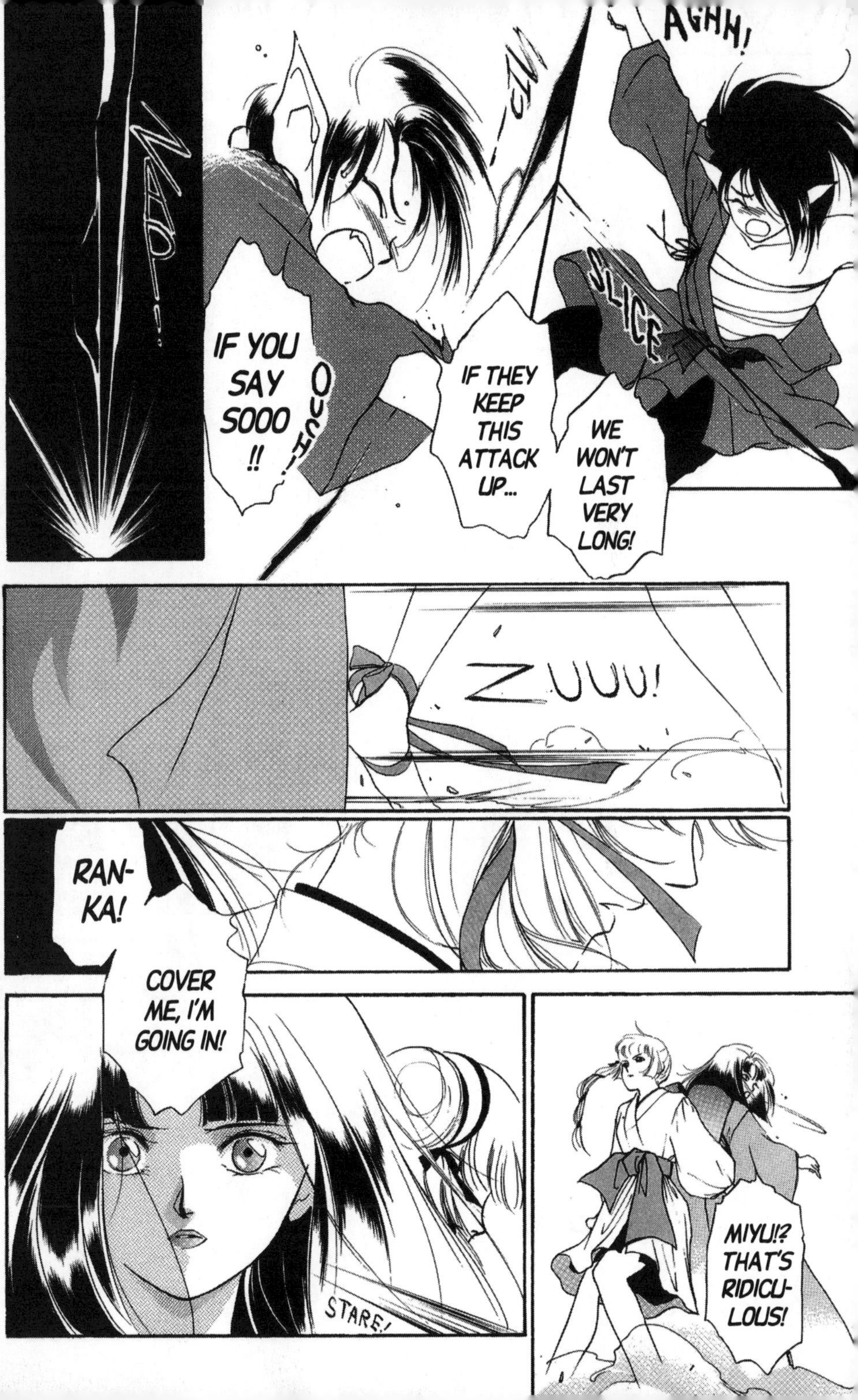
ZAAP
OUCH...
IF YOU SAY SOOO!!
AGHH!
SLICE
IF THEY KEEP THIS ATTACK UP...
WE WON'T LAST VERY LONG!
ZUUU!
RAN-KA!
COVER ME, I'M GOING IN!
STARE!
MIYU!? THAT'S RIDICULOUS!

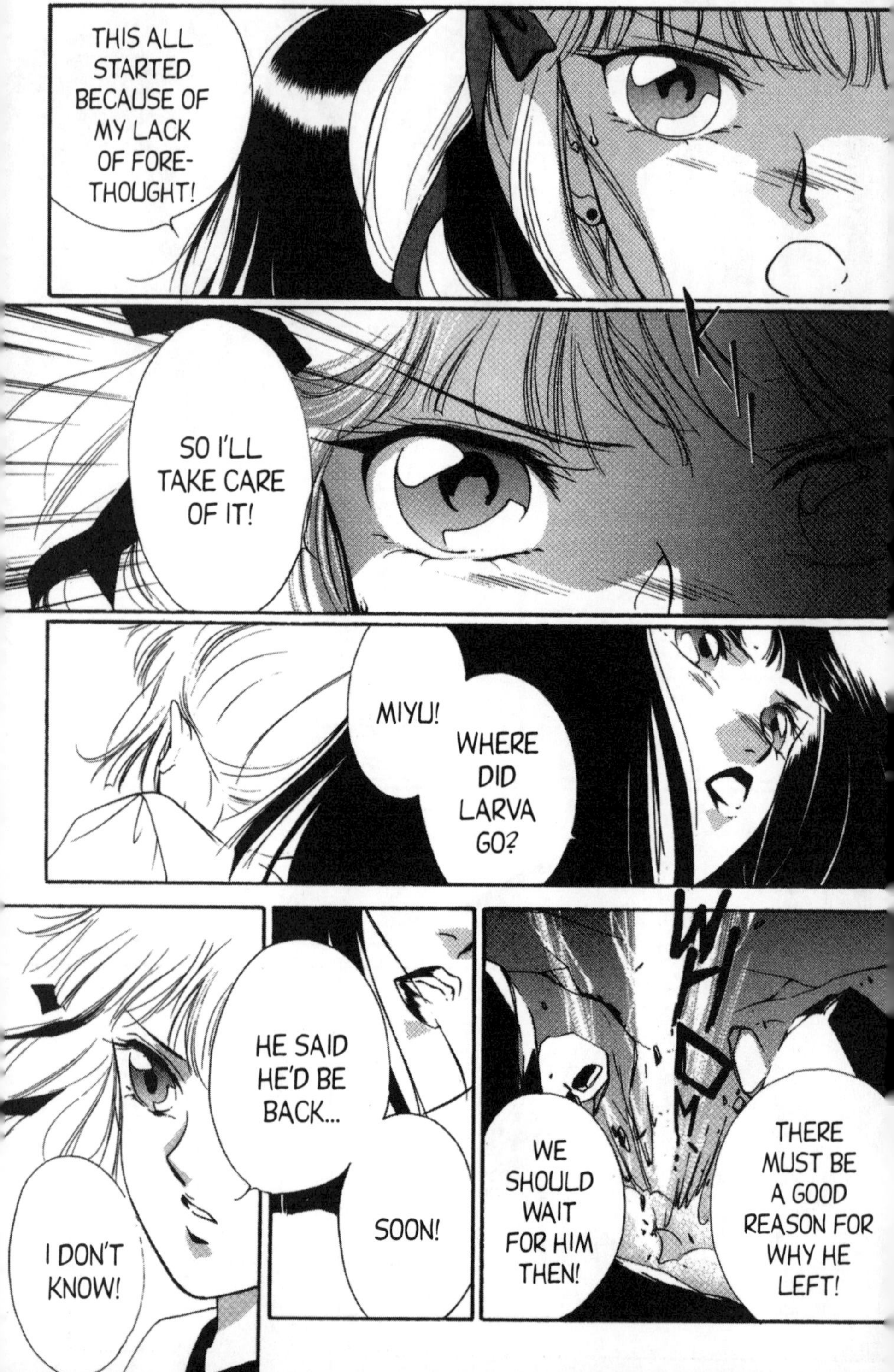
THIS ALL STARTED BECAUSE OF MY LACK OF FORE-THOUGHT!
SO I'LL TAKE CARE OF IT!
MIYU!
WHERE DID LARVA GO?
I DON'T KNOW!
HE SAID HE'D BE BACK...
SOON!
THERE MUST BE A GOOD REASON FOR WHY HE LEFT!
WE SHOULD WAIT FOR HIM THEN!

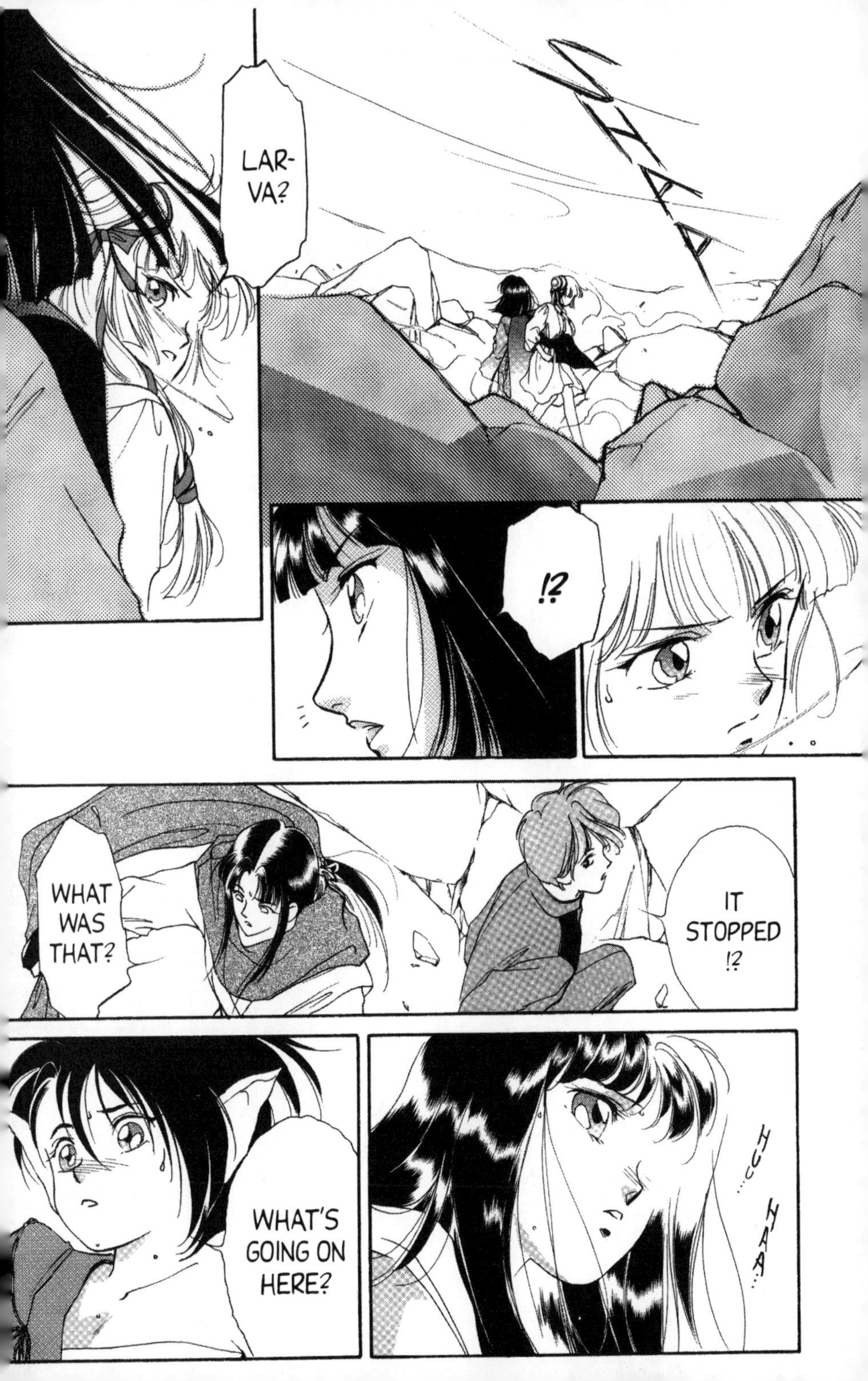
CHAAA
LAR-VA?
!?
IT STOPPED !?
WHAT WAS THAT?
WHAT'S GOING ON HERE?

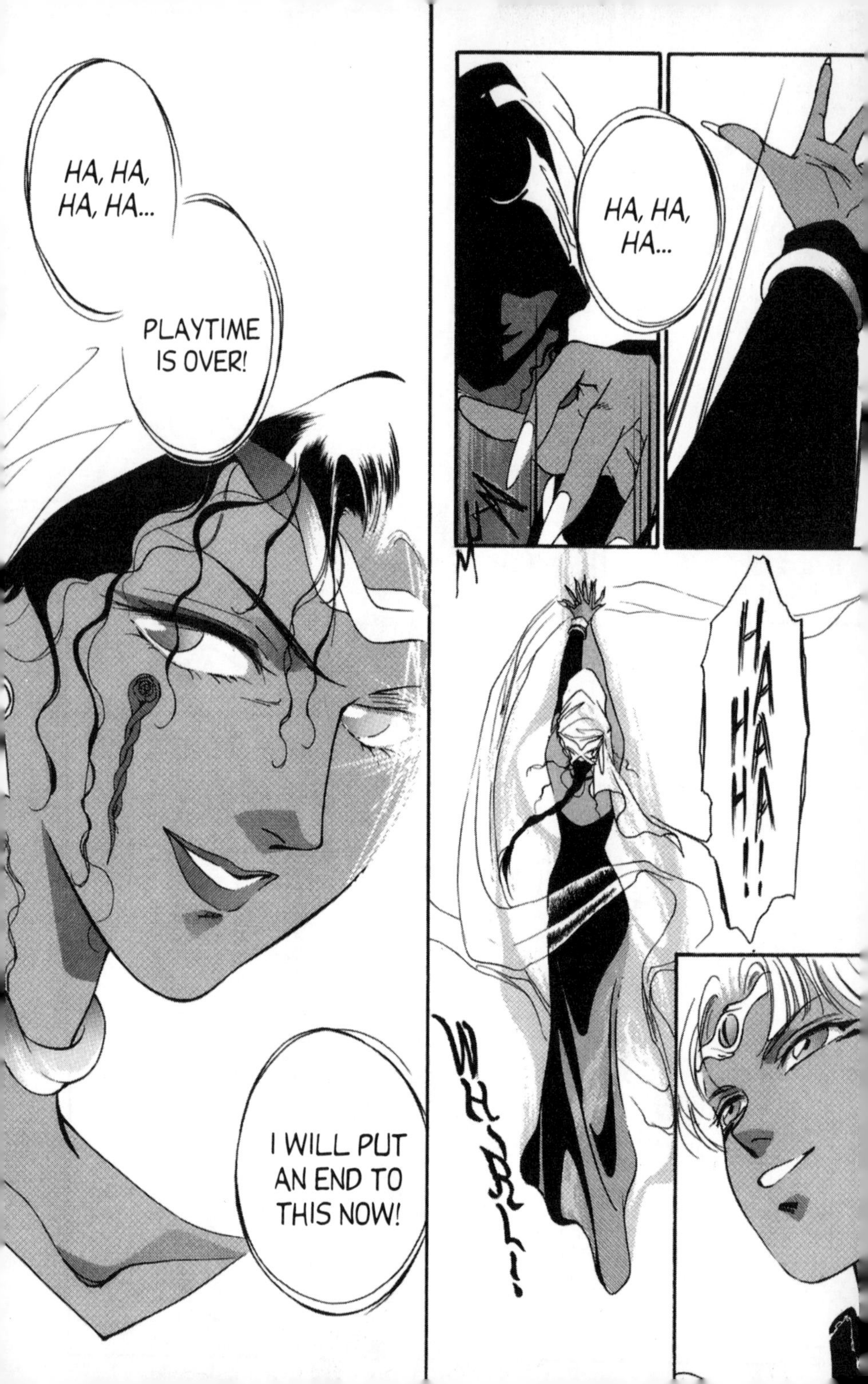
HA, HA, HA, HA...
PLAYTIME IS OVER!
I WILL PUT AN END TO THIS NOW!
HA, HA, HA...
HAHAHAHA!!
SHIRL-!

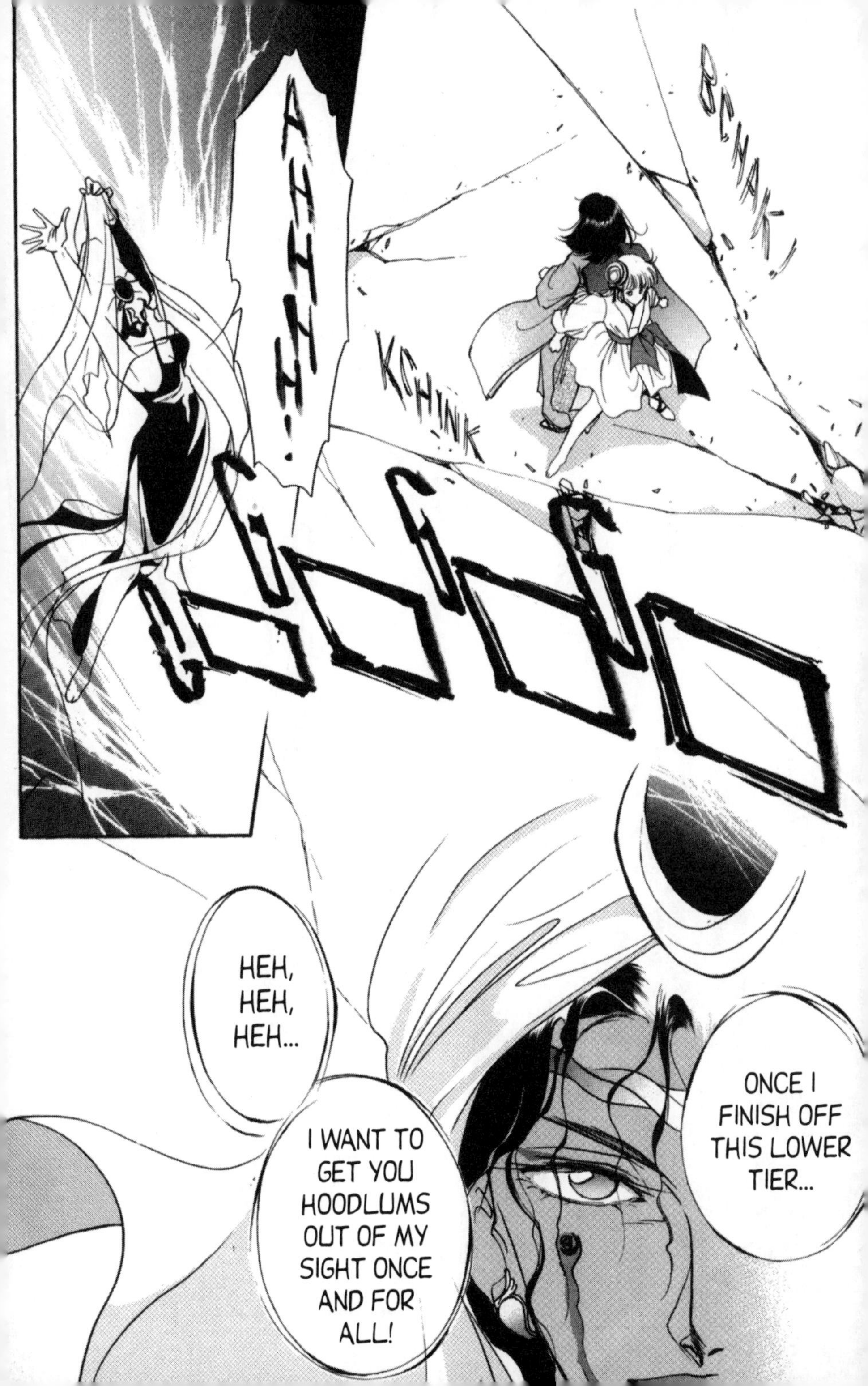
BCHAK!
KCHINK
AHHHH!
GOGOGO
HEH, HEH, HEH...
ONCE I FINISH OFF THIS LOWER TIER...
I WANT TO GET YOU HOODLUMS OUT OF MY SIGHT ONCE AND FOR ALL!

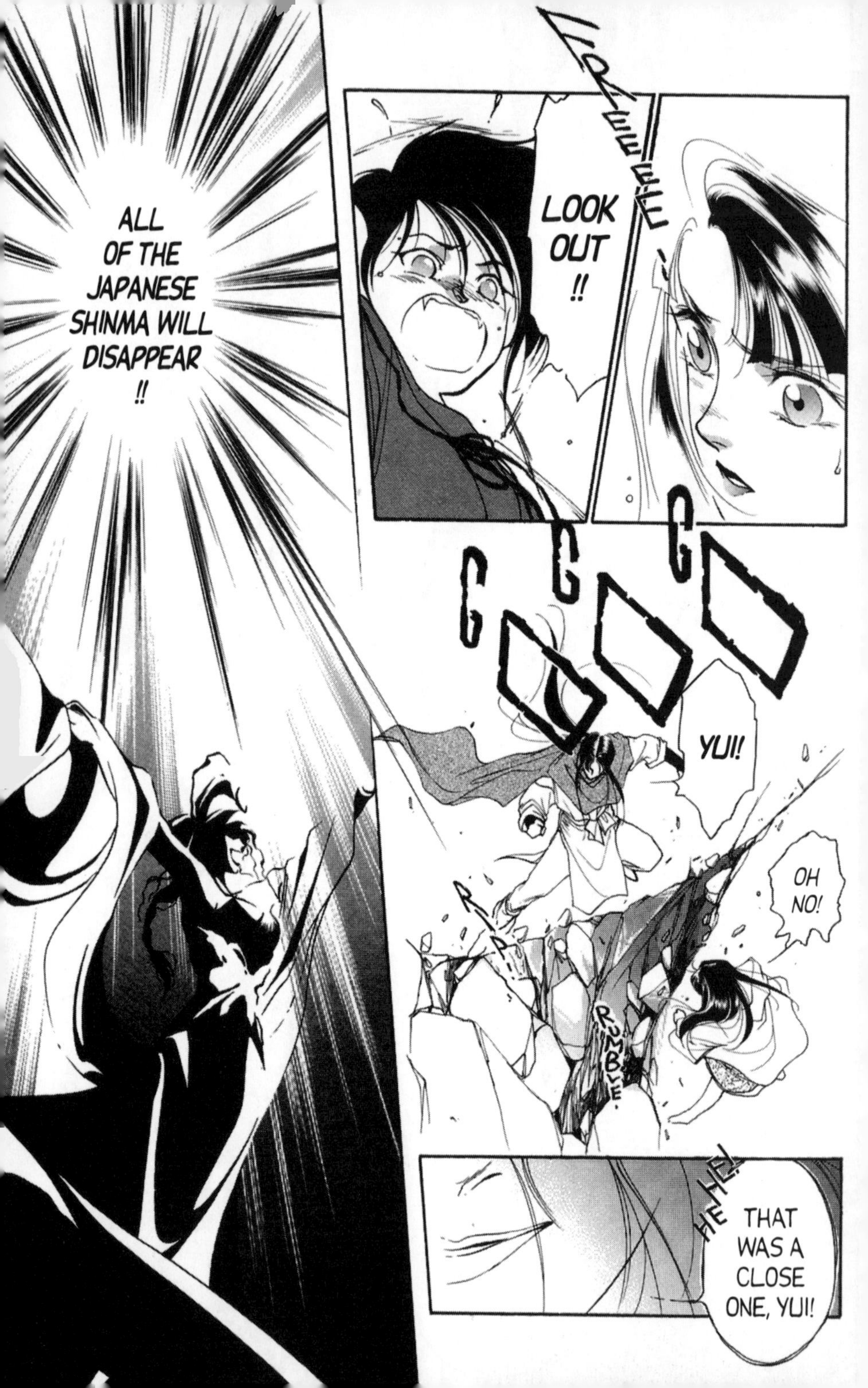
FREEEE
LOOK OUT !!
ALL OF THE JAPANESE SHINMA WILL DISAPPEAR !!
G G G
YUI!
OH NO!
RUMBLE
HEHE!
THAT WAS A CLOSE ONE, YUI!

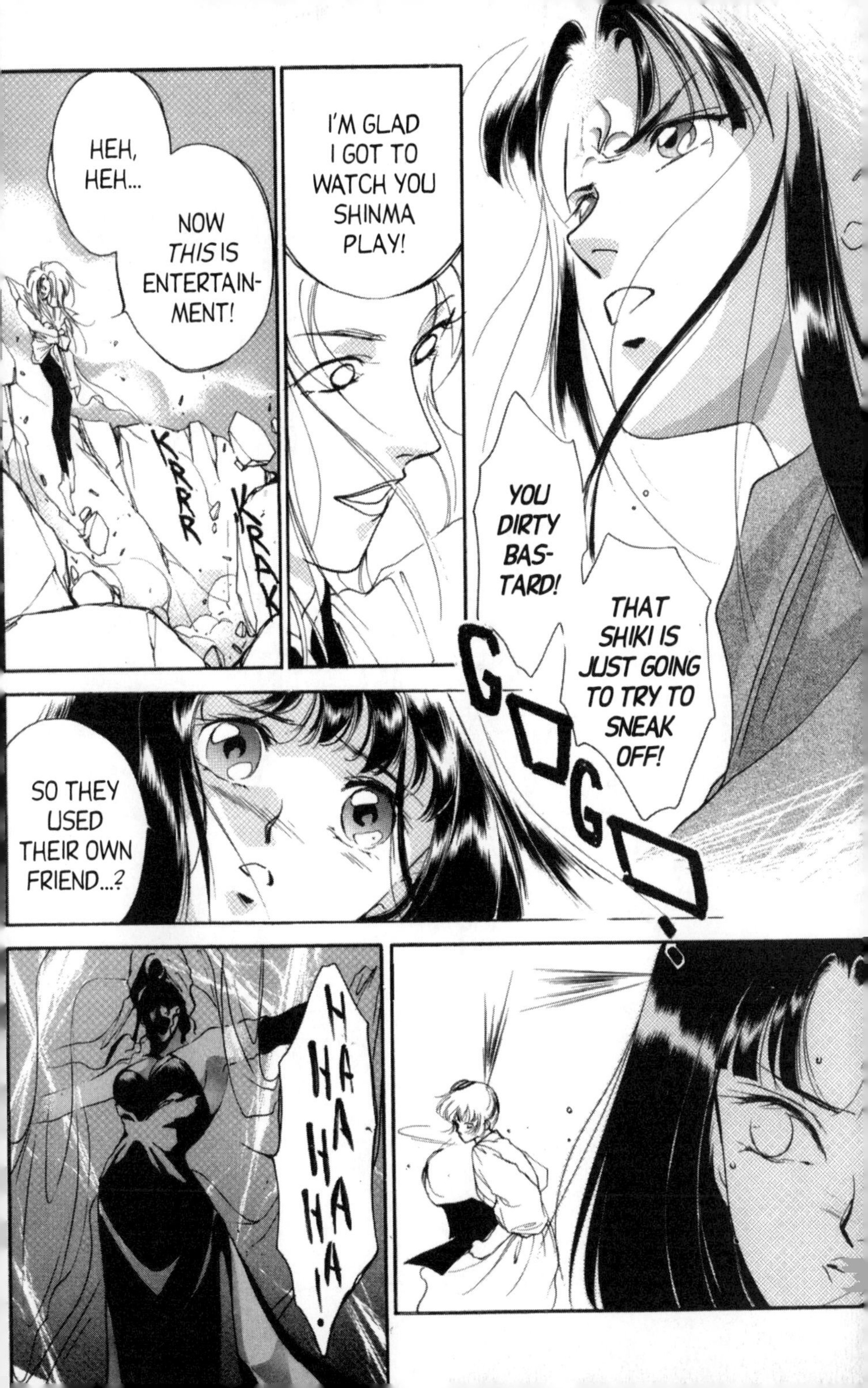
HEH, HEH...
NOW *THIS* IS ENTERTAIN-MENT!
KRRRR
KRAK
I'M GLAD I GOT TO WATCH YOU SHINMA PLAY!
YOU DIRTY BAS-TARD!
THAT SHIKI IS JUST GOING TO TRY TO SNEAK OFF!
GOGO
SO THEY USED THEIR OWN FRIEND...?
HAHAHA HAHAHA!

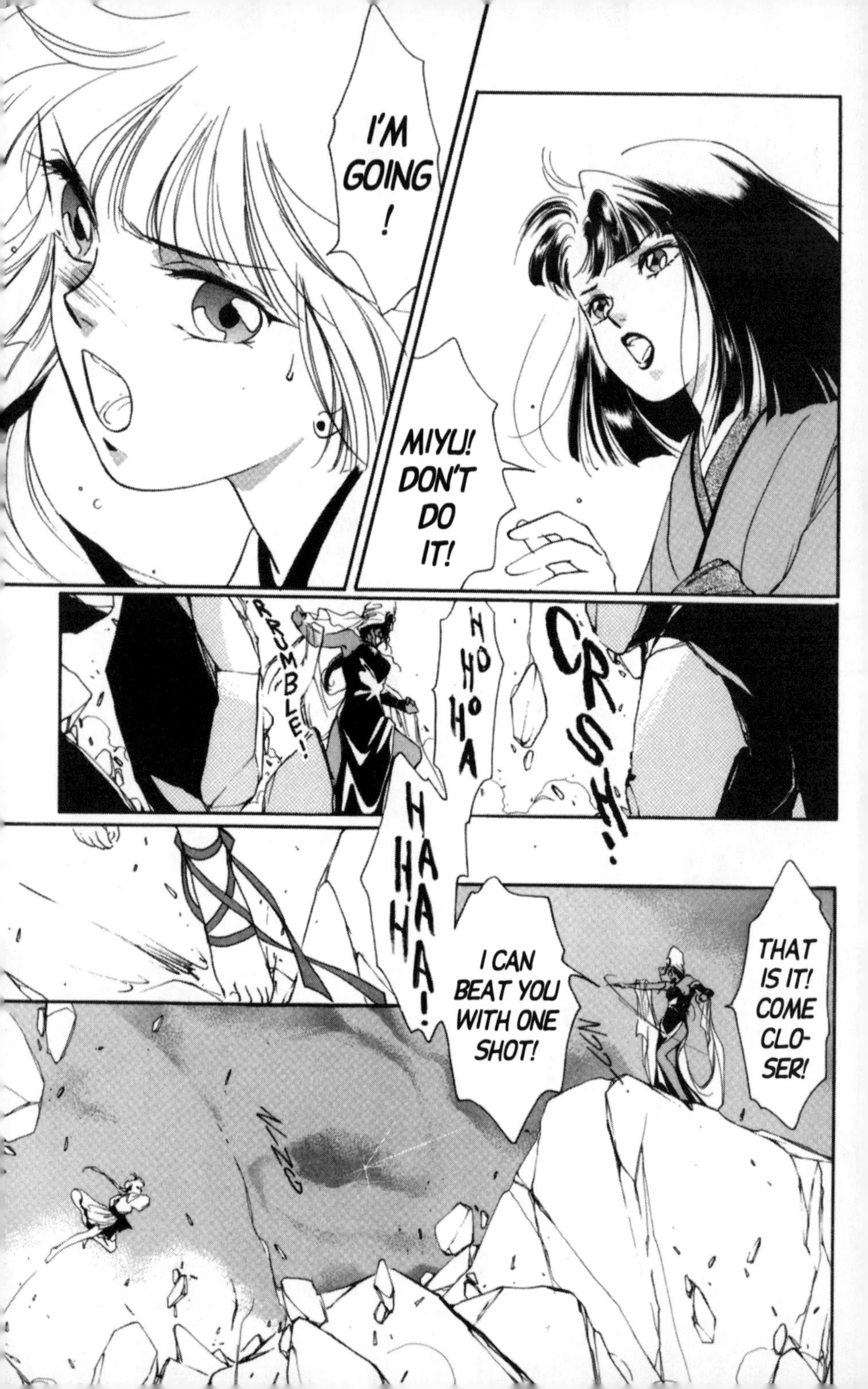
I'M GOING!
MIYU! DON'T DO IT!
RRUMBLE!
HOHOHOHA
CRSH!!
HAHAHAHA!
I CAN BEAT YOU WITH ONE SHOT!
THAT IS IT! COME CLO- SER!

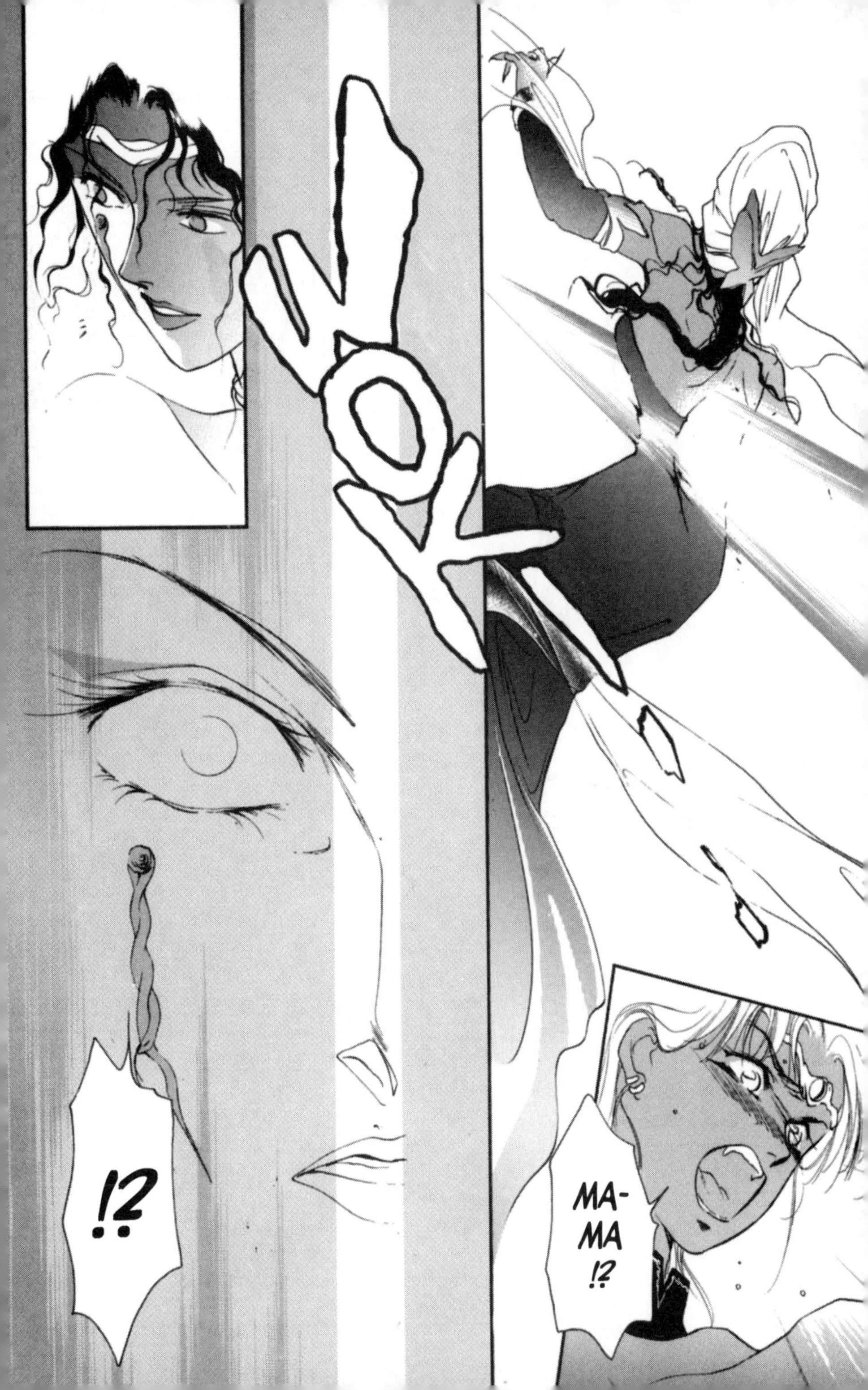
MA-
MA
!?
KOK
!?

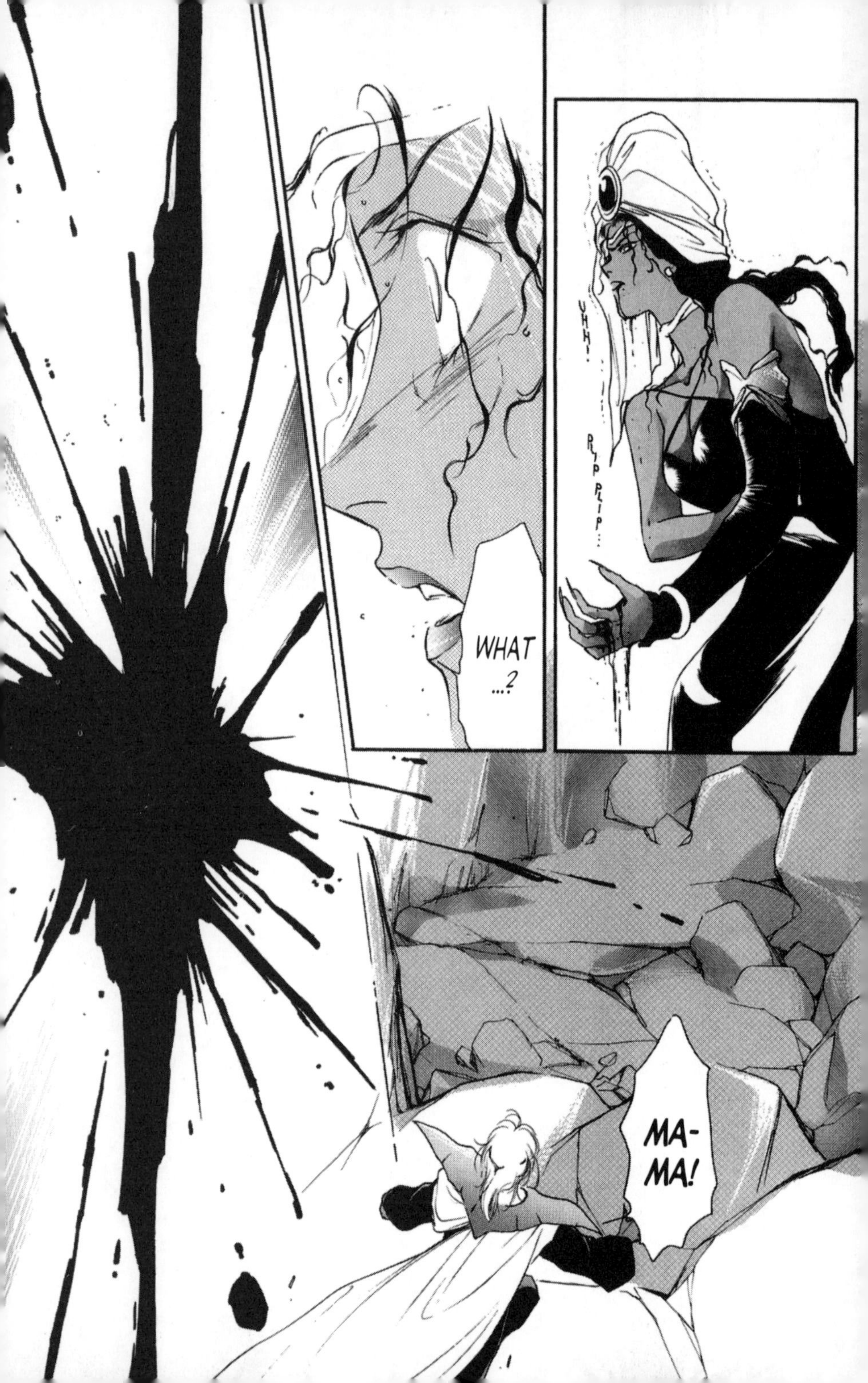
UHH!
PLIP PLIP...
WHAT ...?
MA-MA!

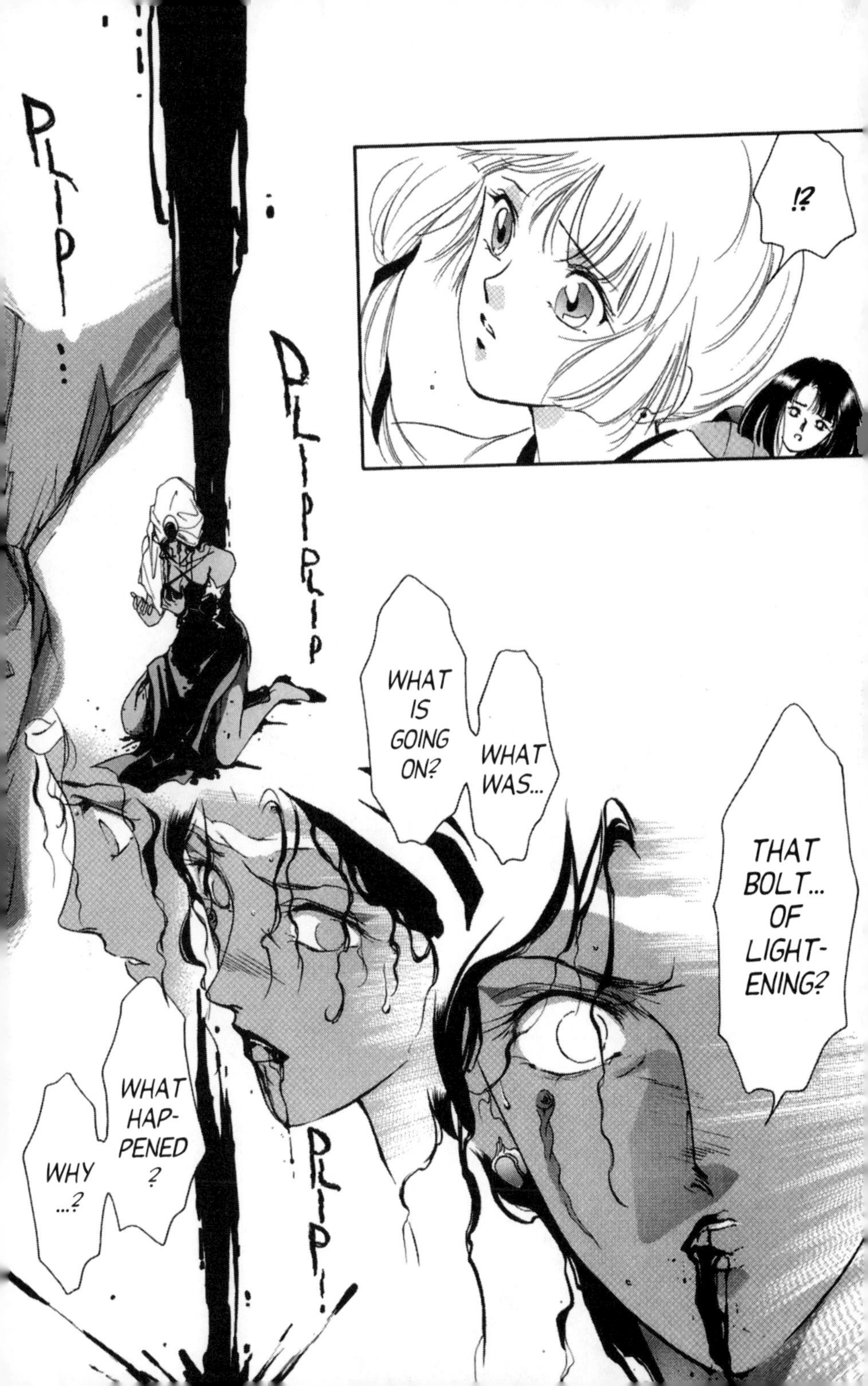
!?
PLIP...
PLIPPLIP
WHAT IS GOING ON?
WHAT WAS...
THAT BOLT... OF LIGHT-ENING?
PLIP!!
WHAT HAP-PENED?
WHY ...?

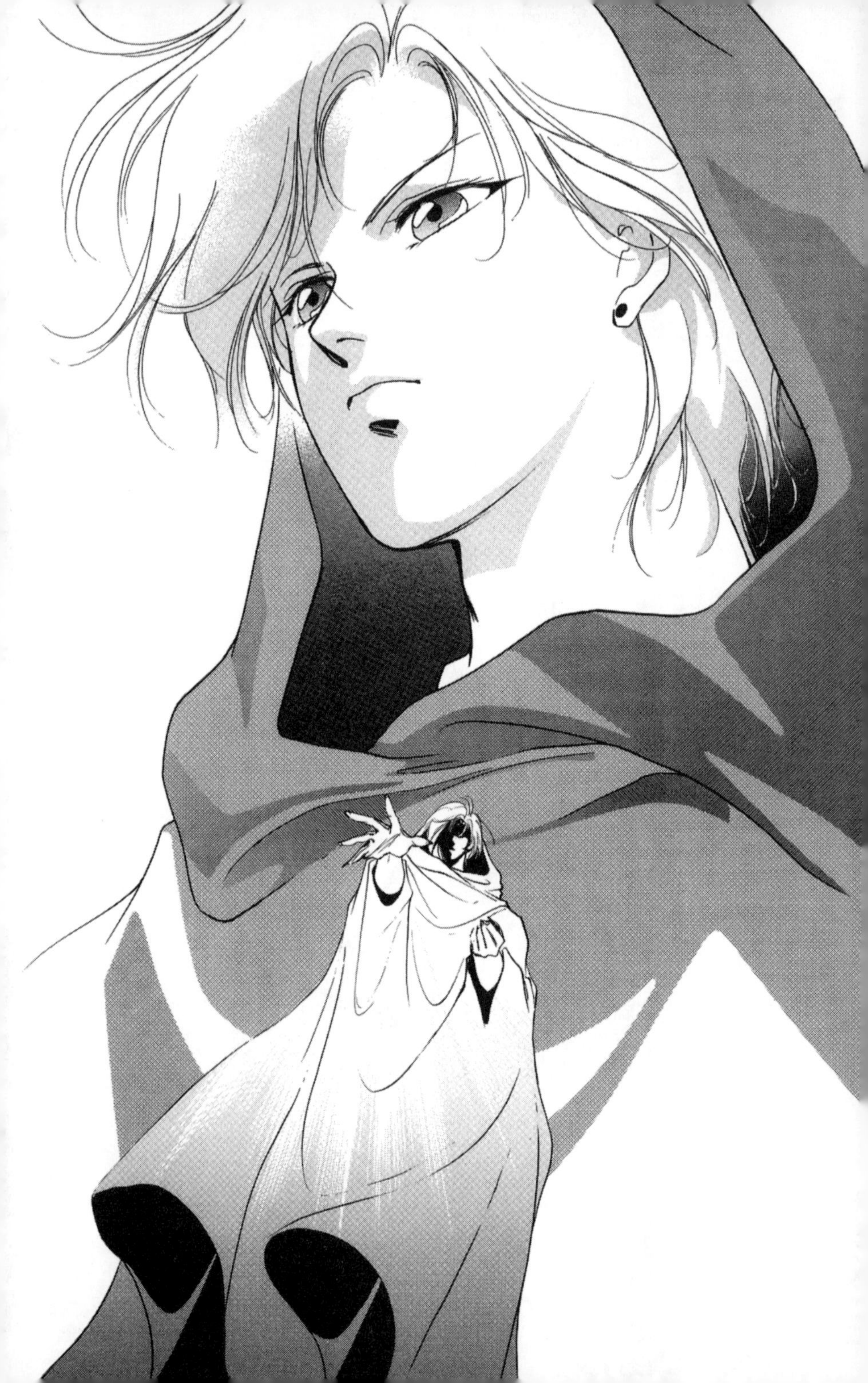

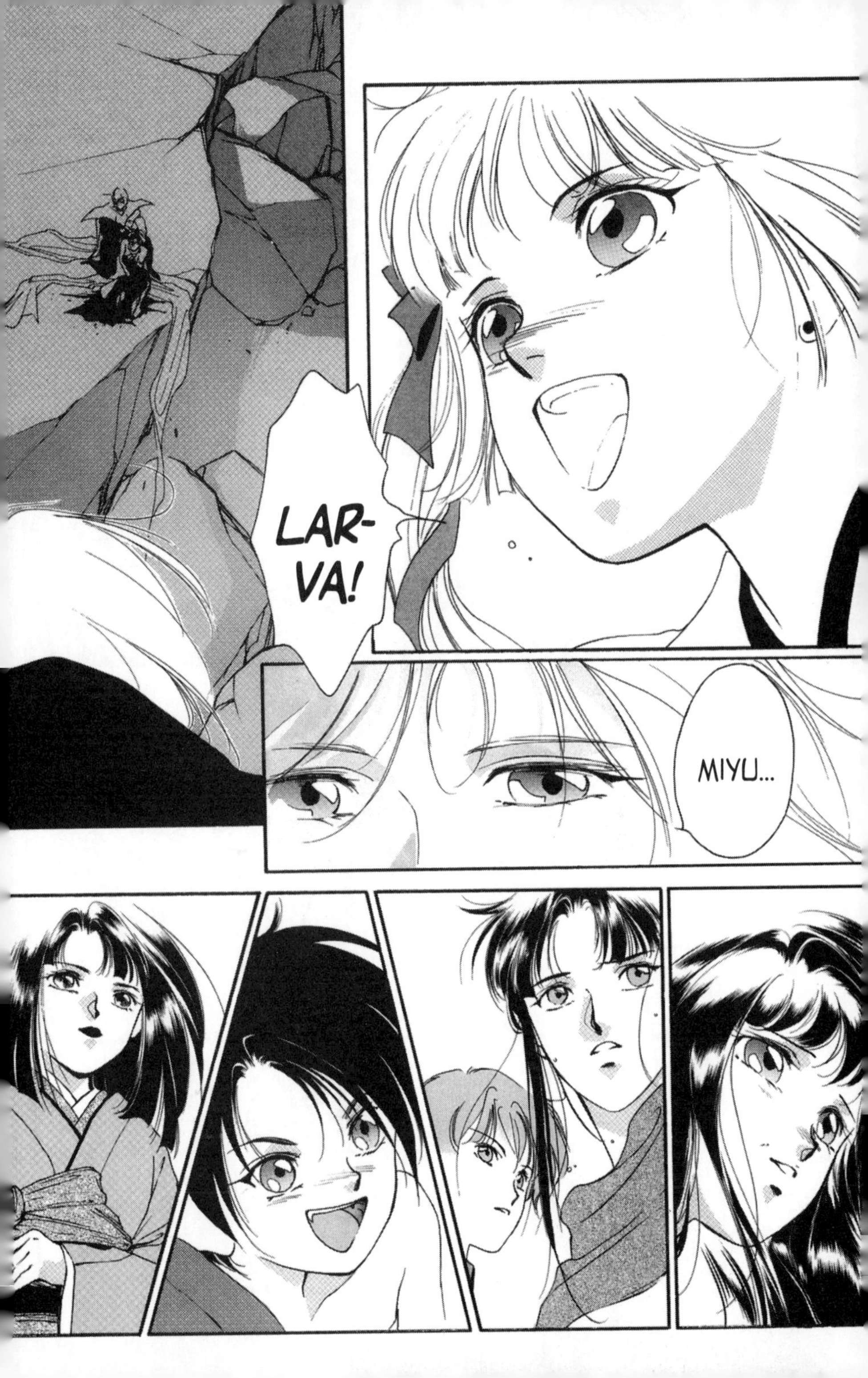
MIYU...
LAR-VA!

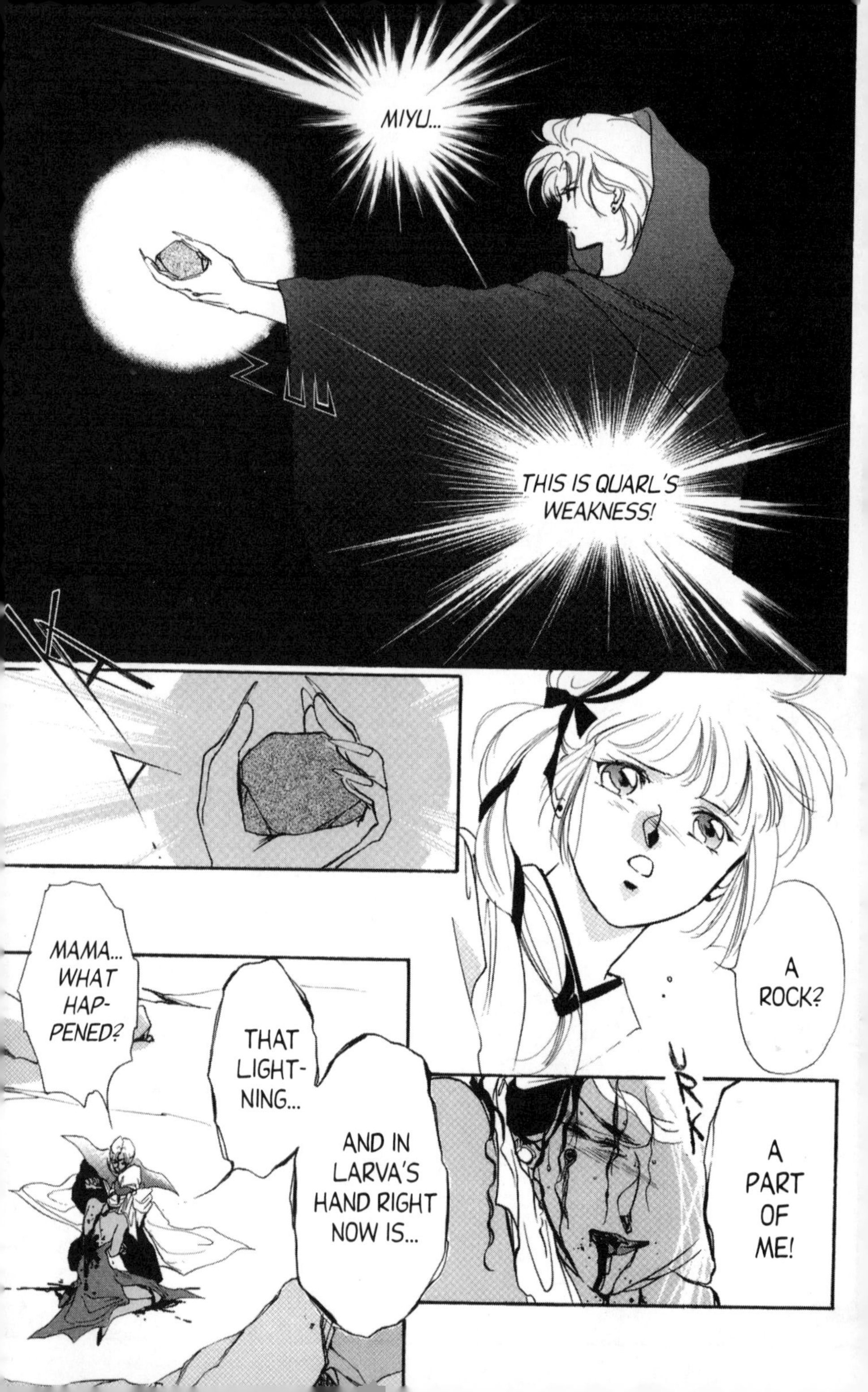
MIYU...
THIS IS QUARL'S WEAKNESS!
ZUU
A ROCK?
MAMA... WHAT HAP-PENED?
THAT LIGHT-NING...
AND IN LARVA'S HAND RIGHT NOW IS...
URK
A PART OF ME!

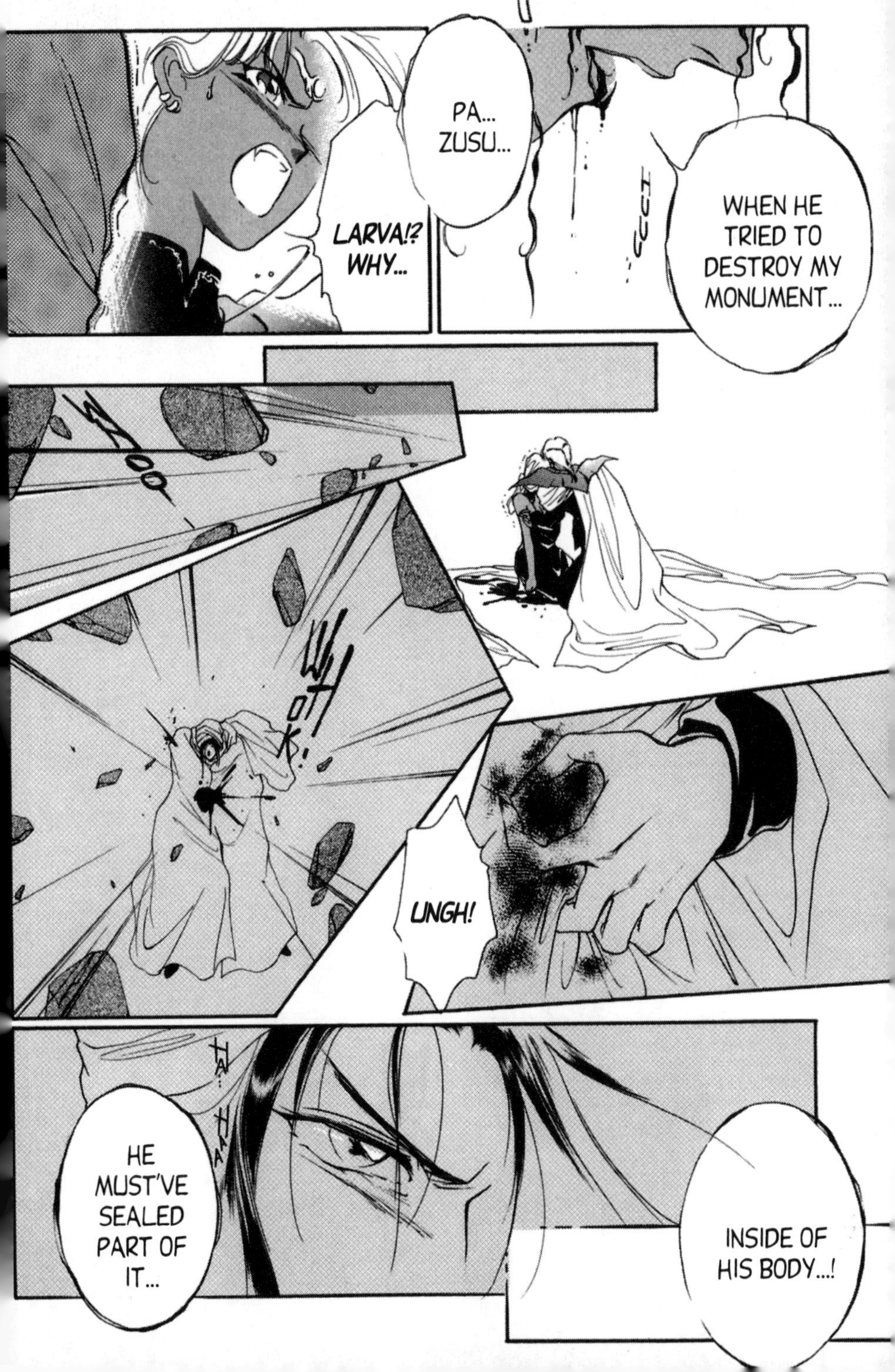
PA... ZUSU...
WHEN HE TRIED TO DESTROY MY MONUMENT...
LARVA!? WHY...
UNGH!
HE MUST'VE SEALED PART OF IT...
INSIDE OF HIS BODY...!

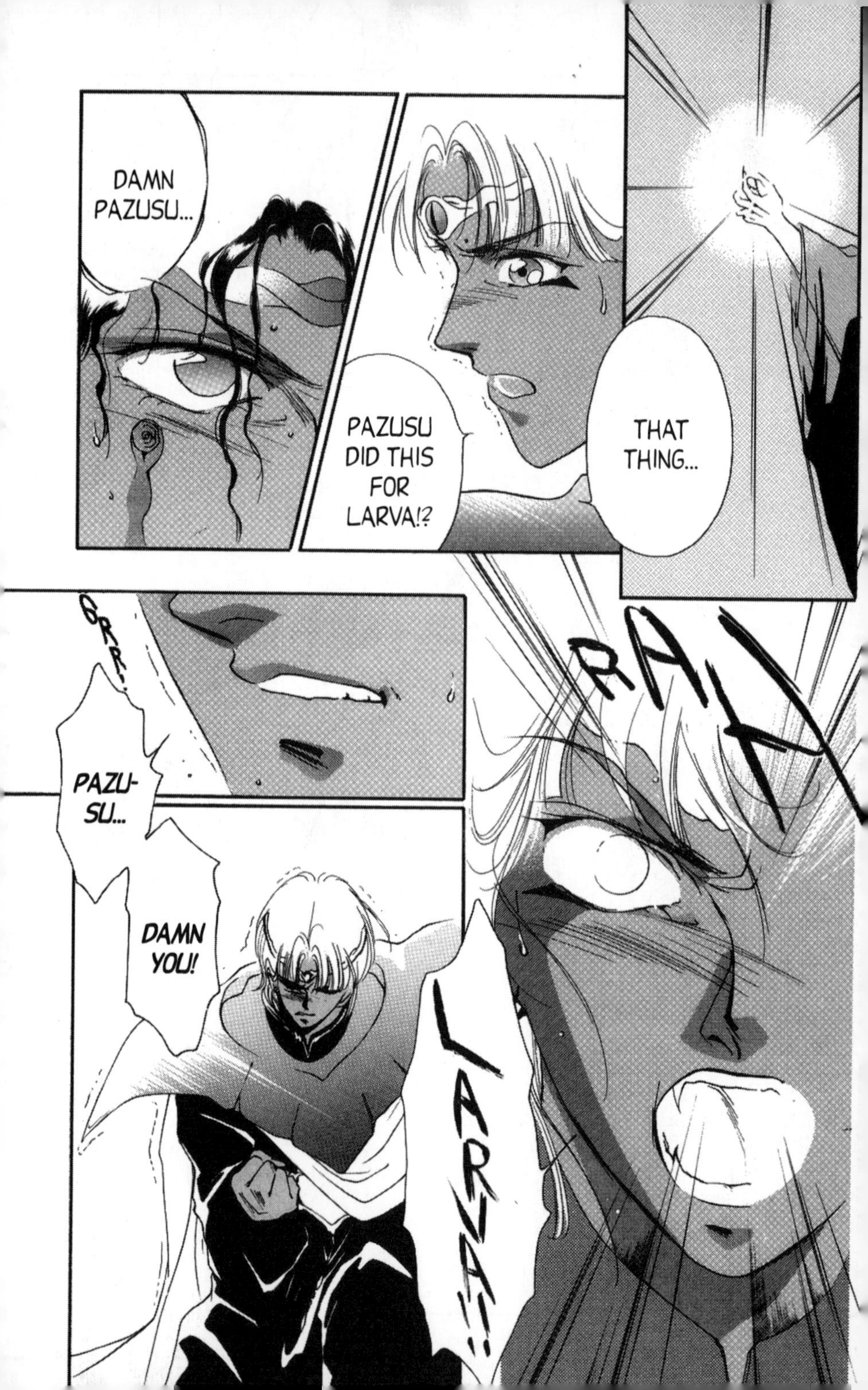
THAT THING...
PAZUSU DID THIS FOR LARVA!?
DAMN PAZUSU...
RAI
LARVA!!!
GRRR
PAZU-SU...
DAMN YOU!

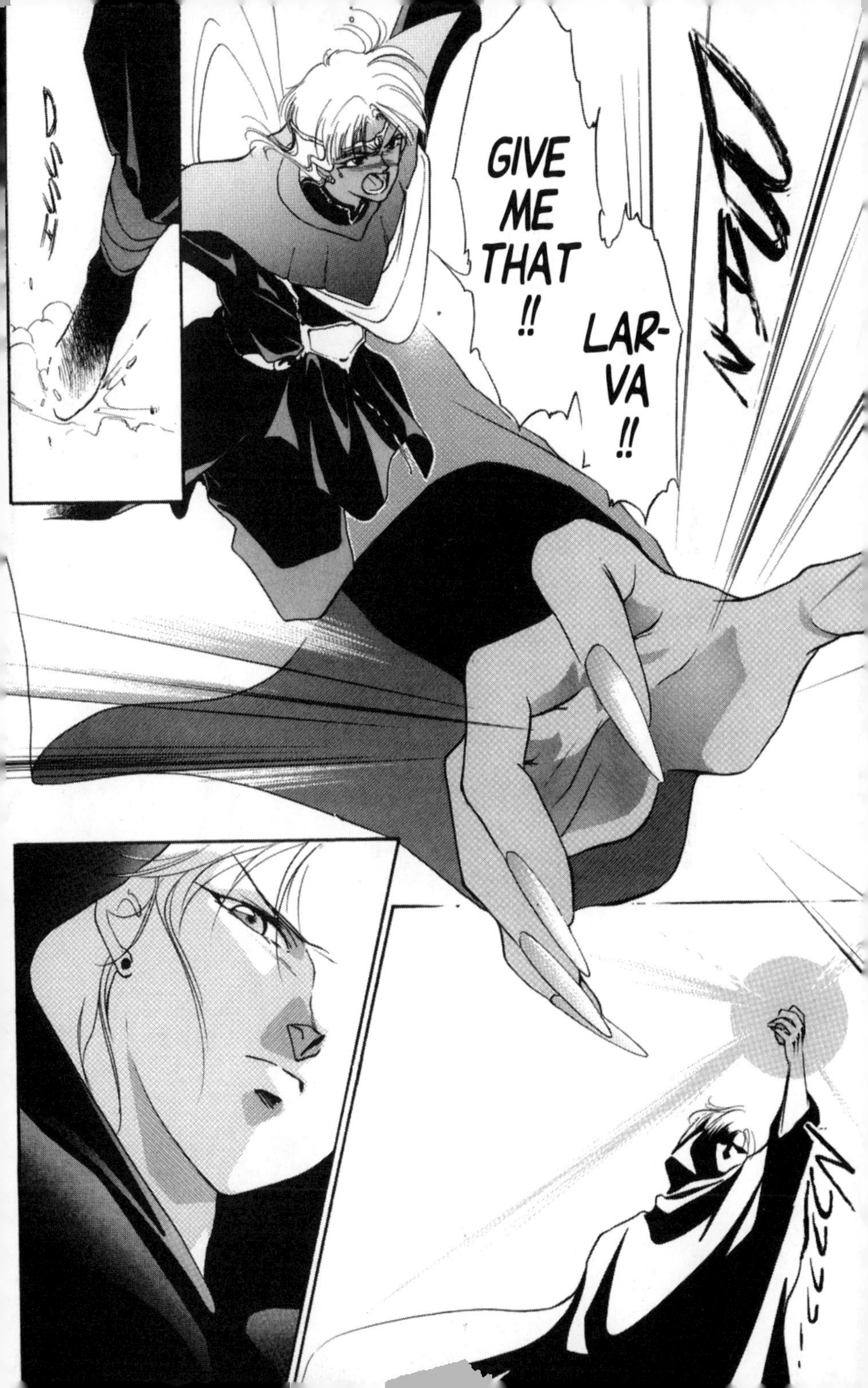
GIVE ME THAT !!
LAR-VA !!

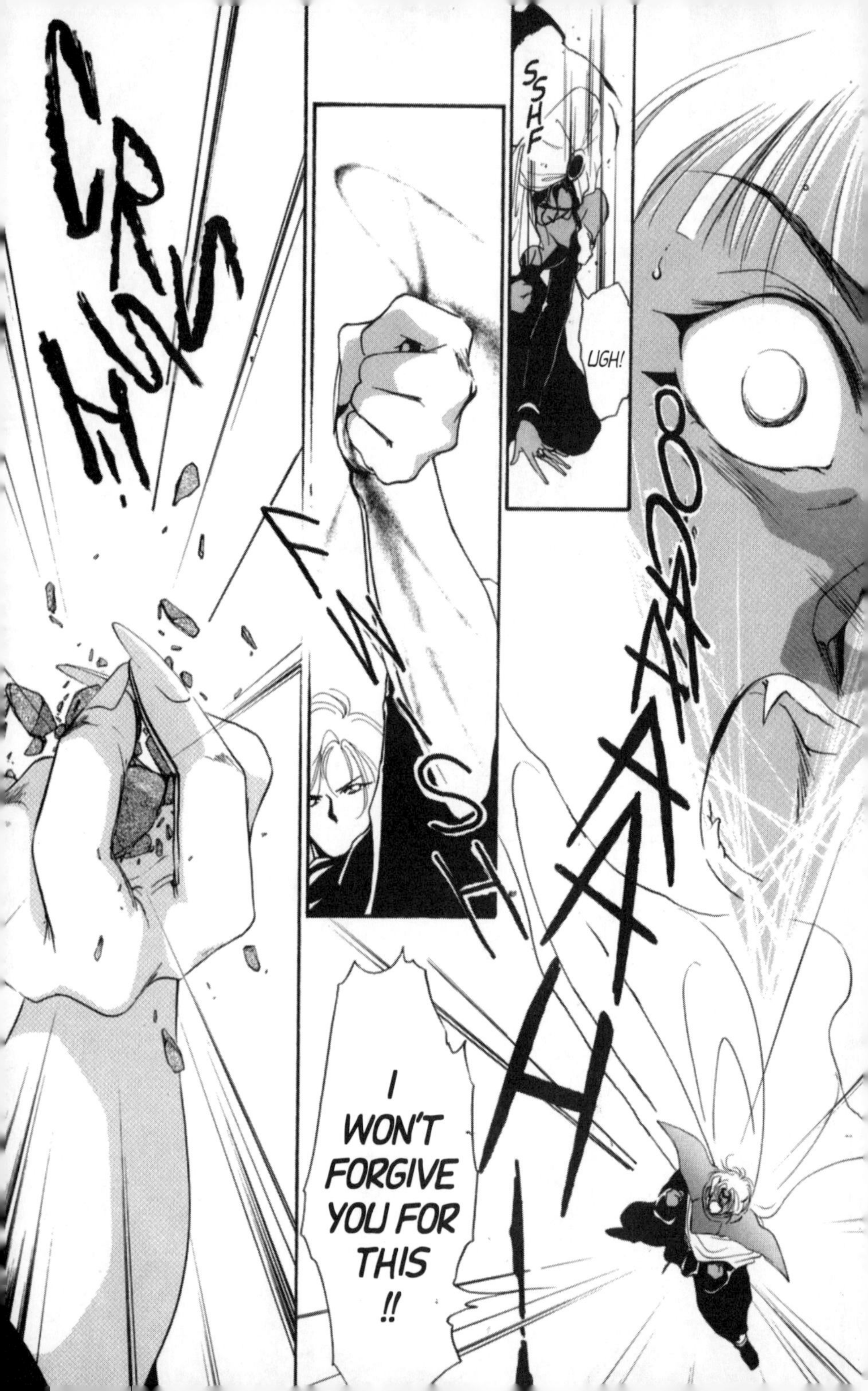
SSHF
UGH!
HAAAAGOO
I WON'T FORGIVE YOU FOR THIS !!
CRUSH!!

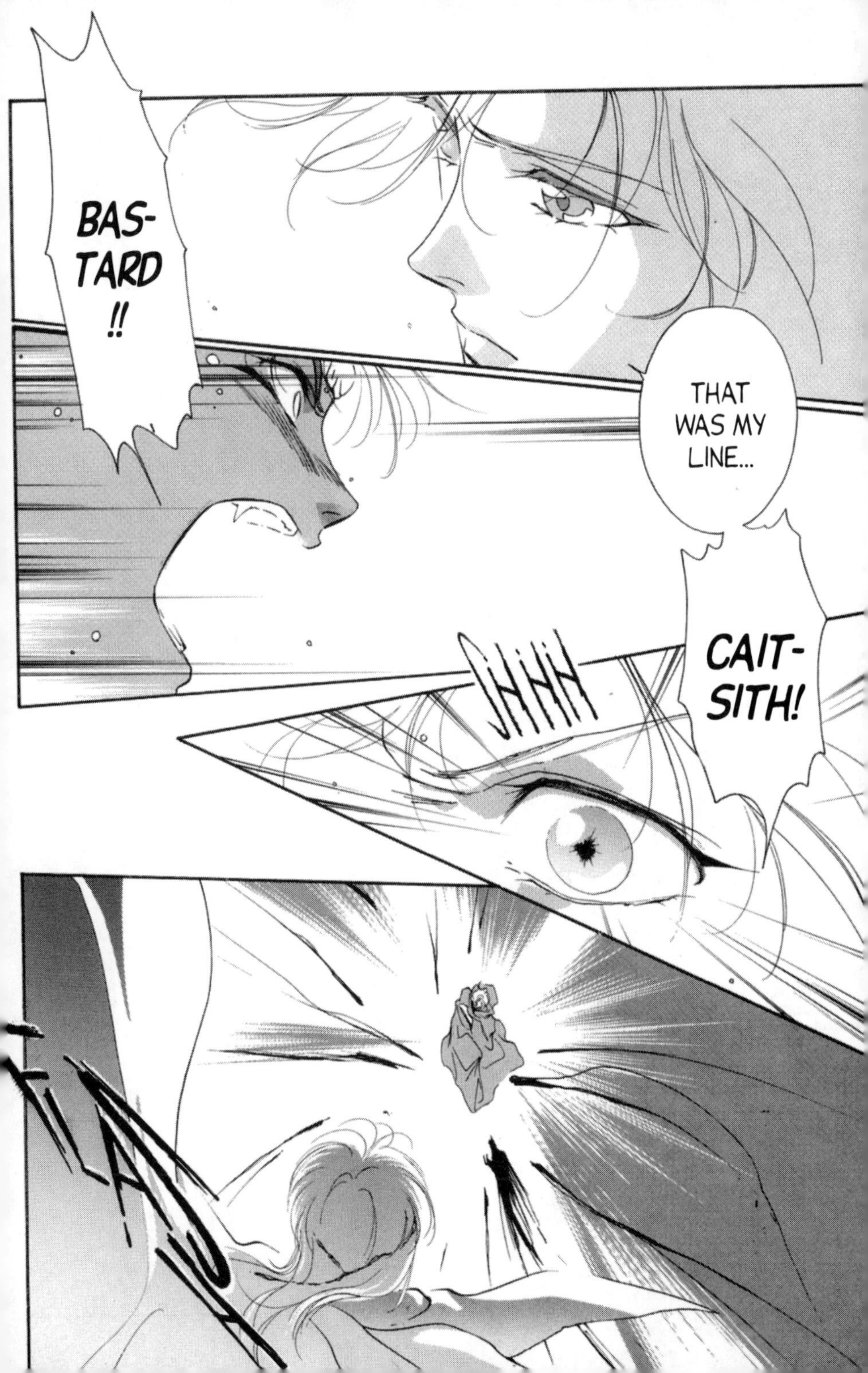
BAS-
TARD
!!
THAT WAS MY LINE...
CAIT-
SITH!

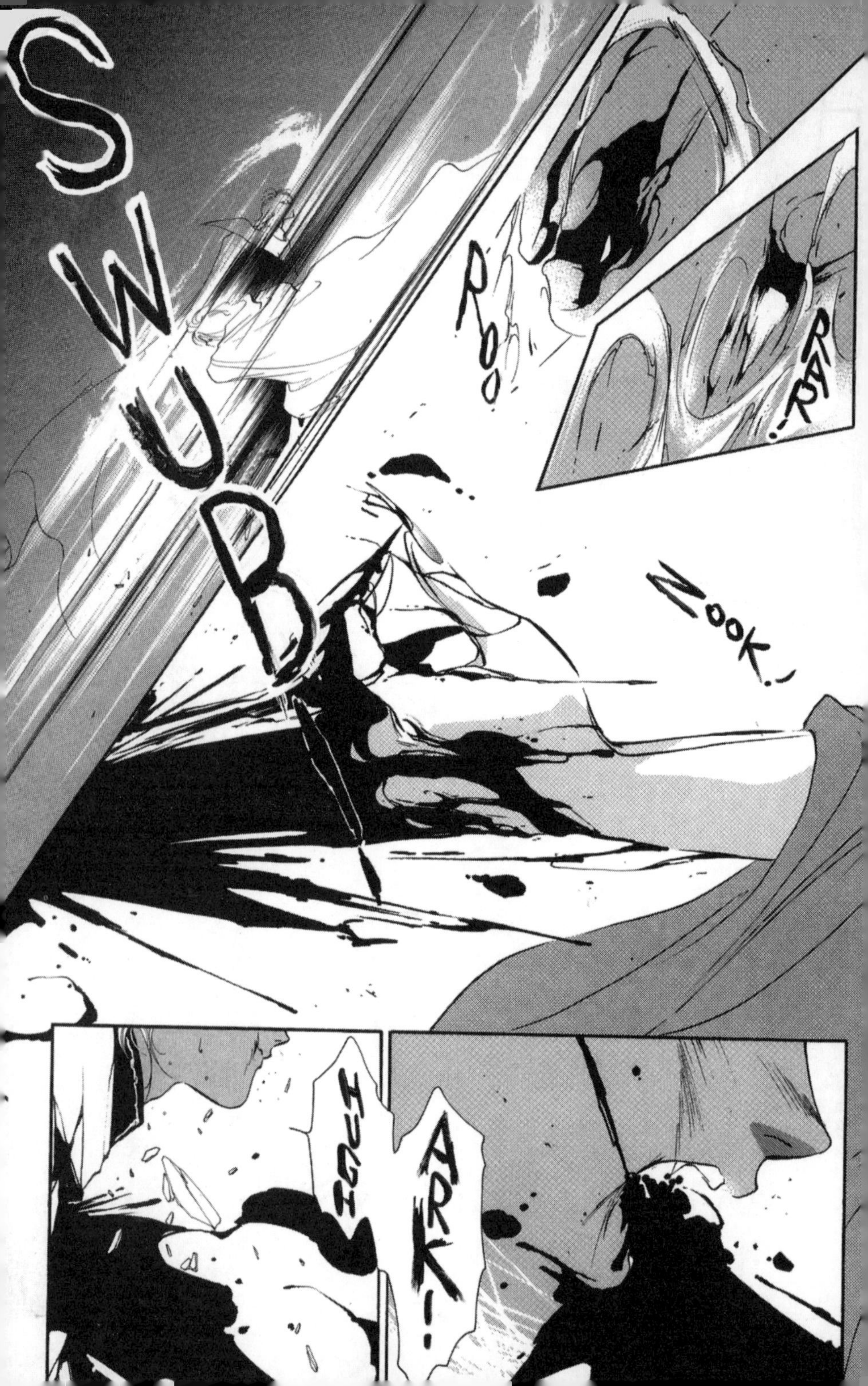
RAR..
ROO..
ZOOK..
SWUB
ARK!
HUGH

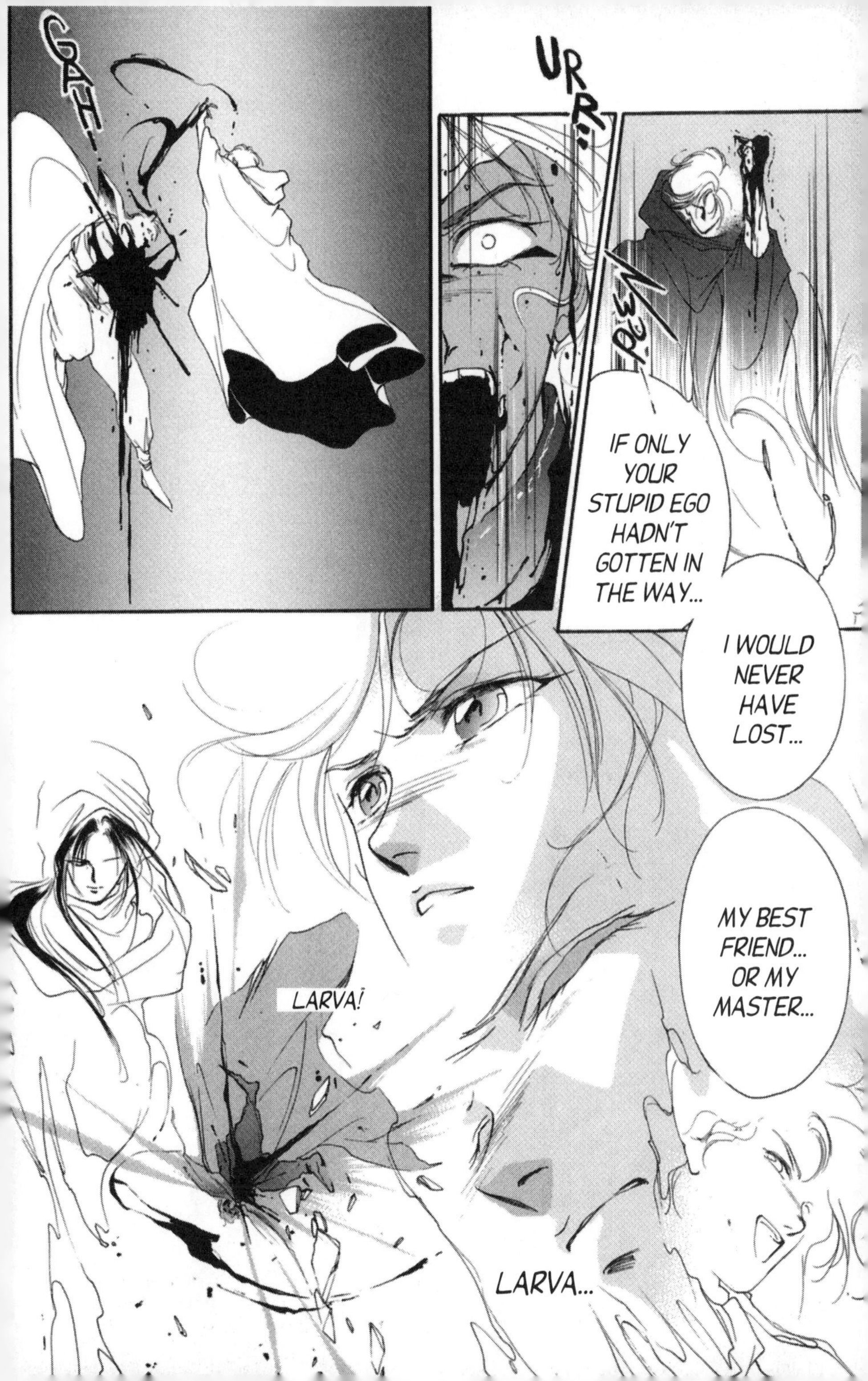
URR...
DEW
IF ONLY YOUR STUPID EGO HADN'T GOTTEN IN THE WAY...
GAH!
I WOULD NEVER HAVE LOST...
MY BEST FRIEND... OR MY MASTER...
LARVA!
LARVA...

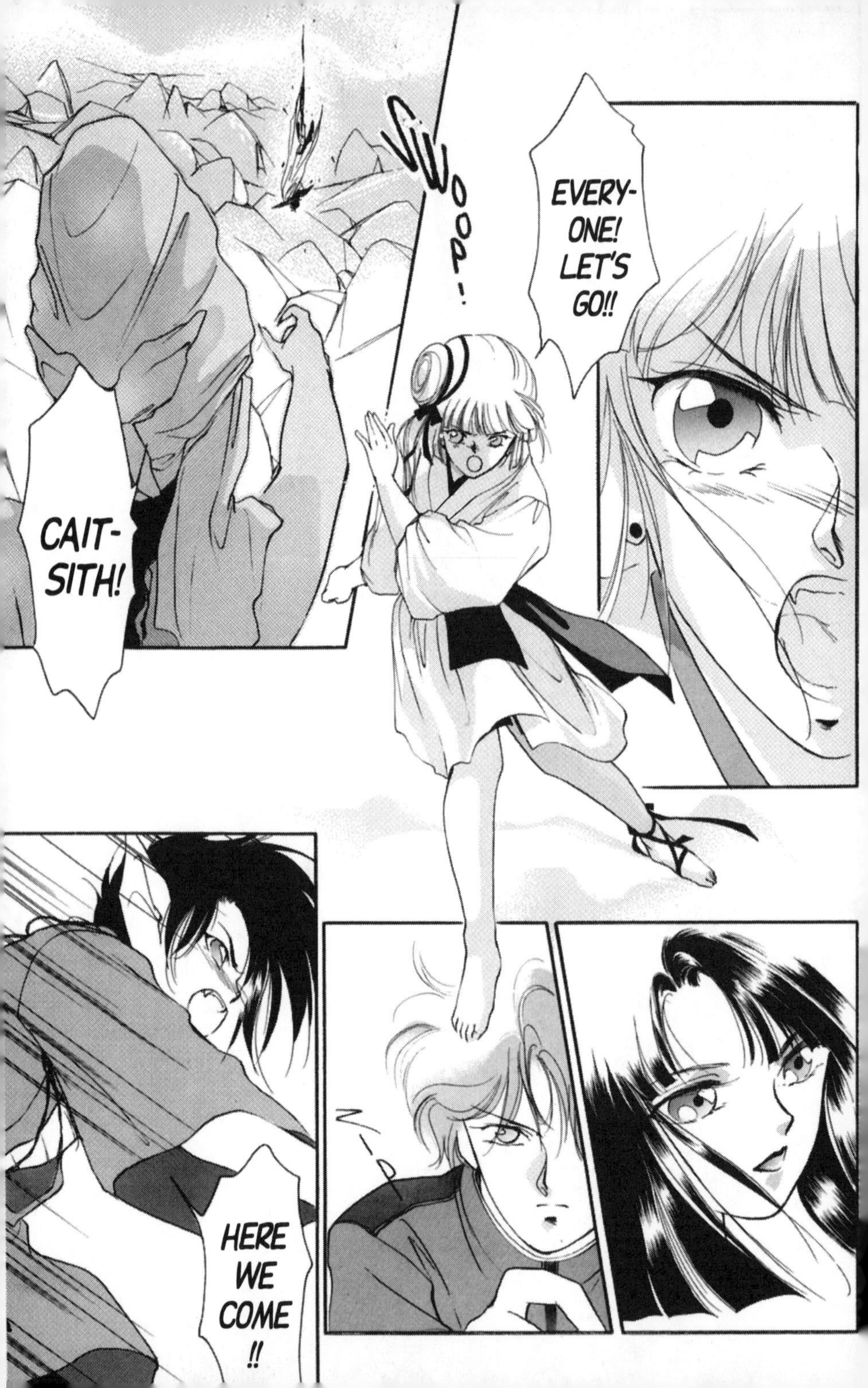
SWOOP!!
EVERY-ONE! LET'S GO!!
CAIT-SITH!
HERE WE COME !!

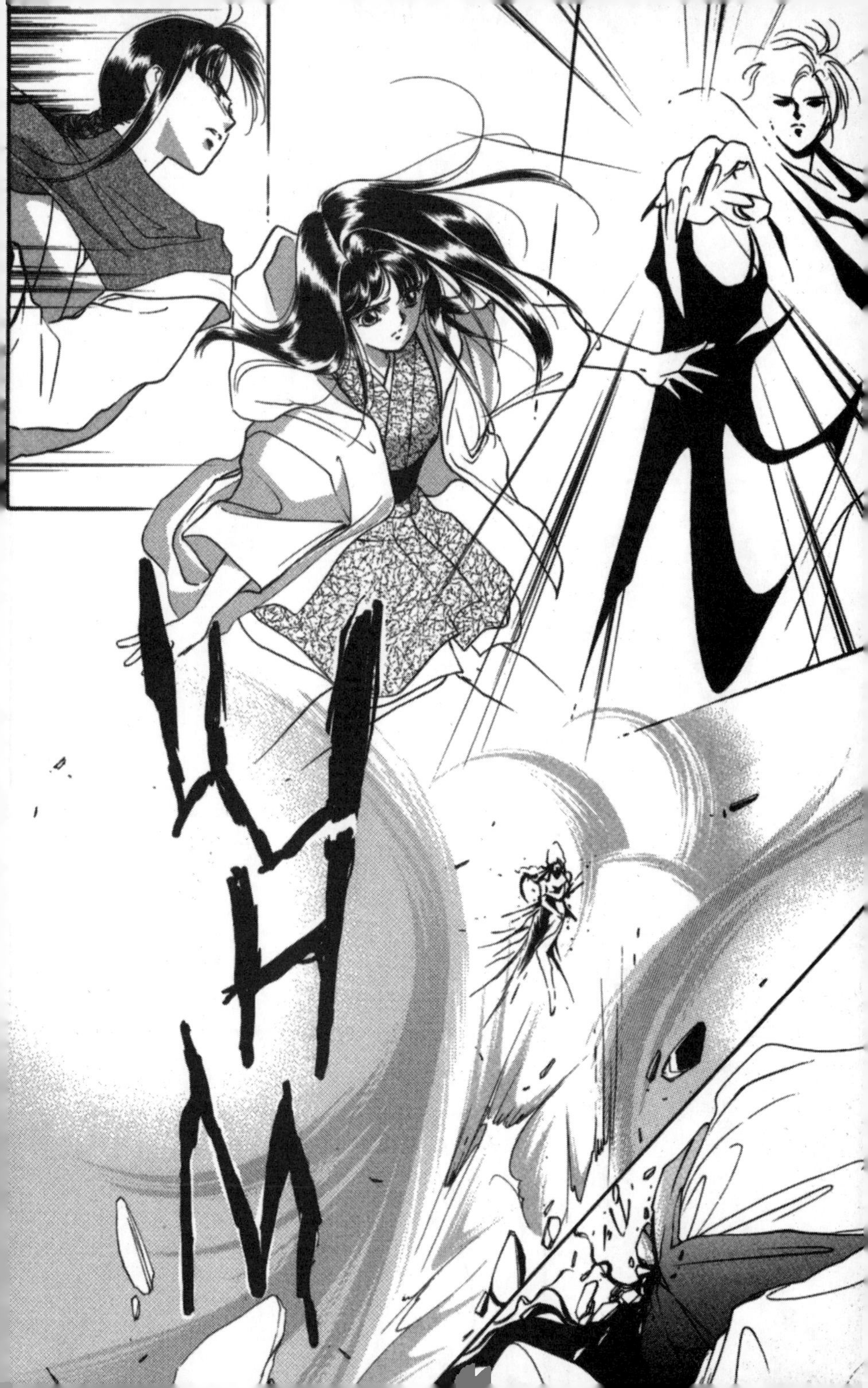
WHM

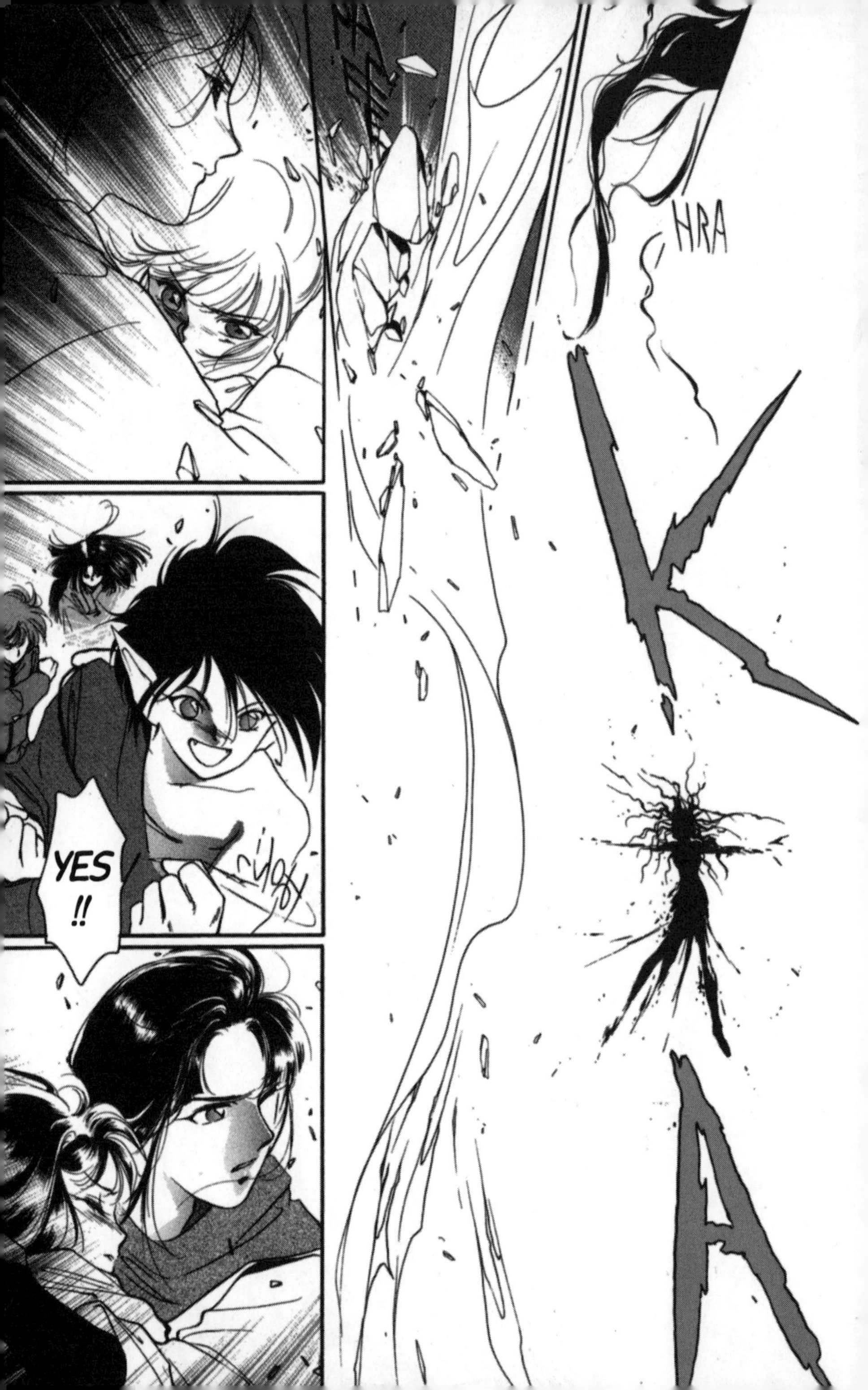
HRA
KA
YES !!

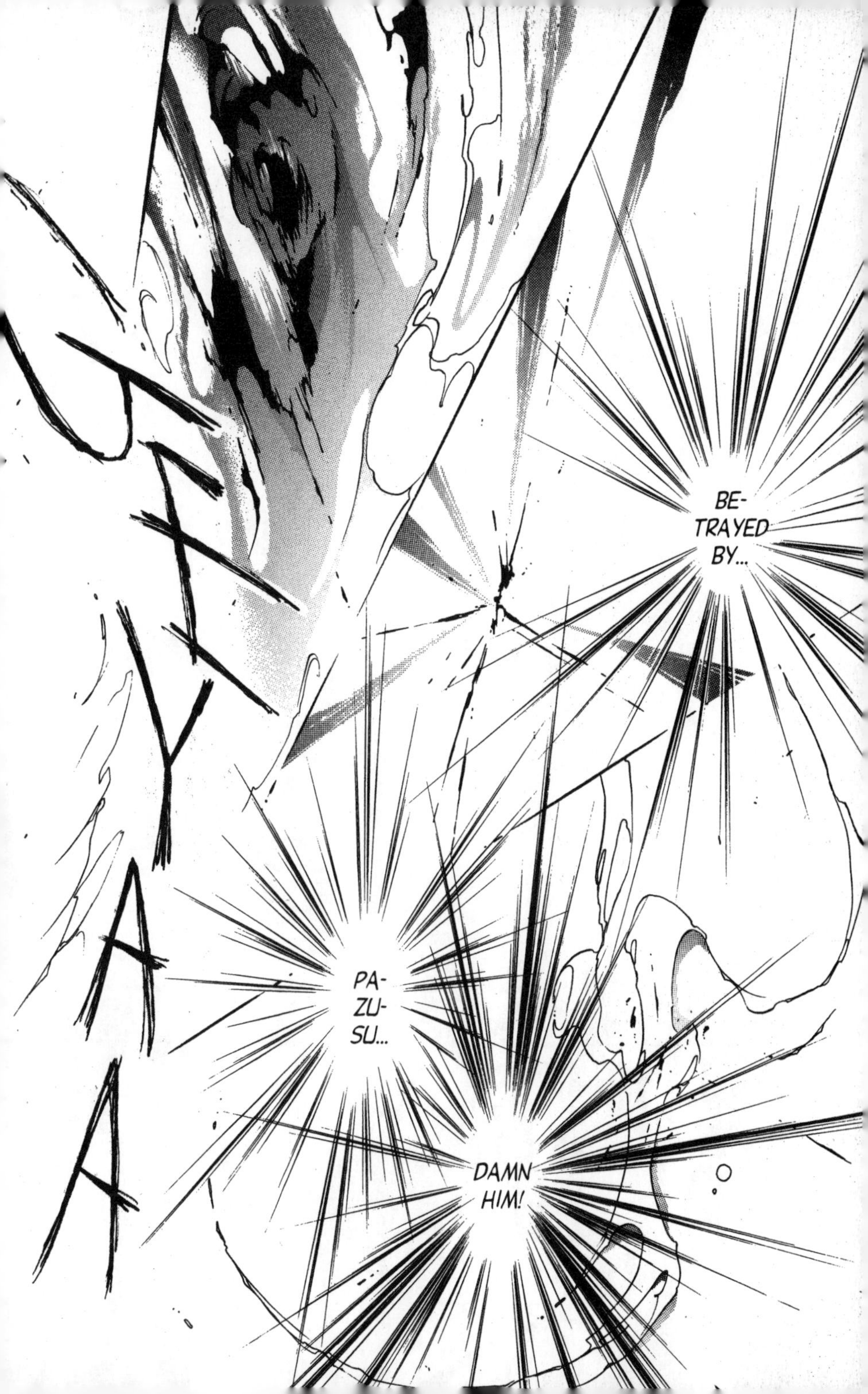
BE-TRAYED BY...
PA-ZU-SU...
DAMN HIM!

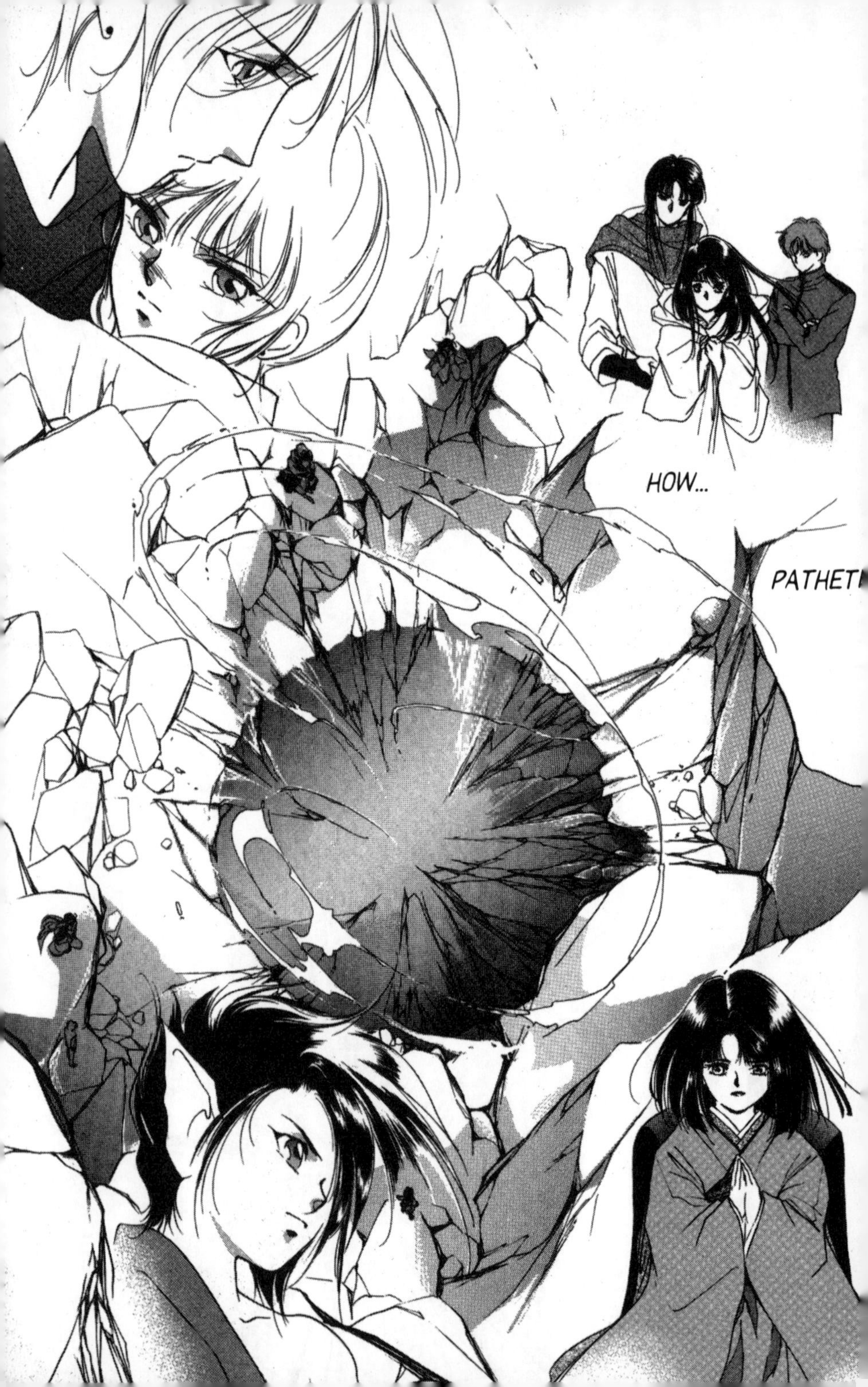
HOW...
PATHETI

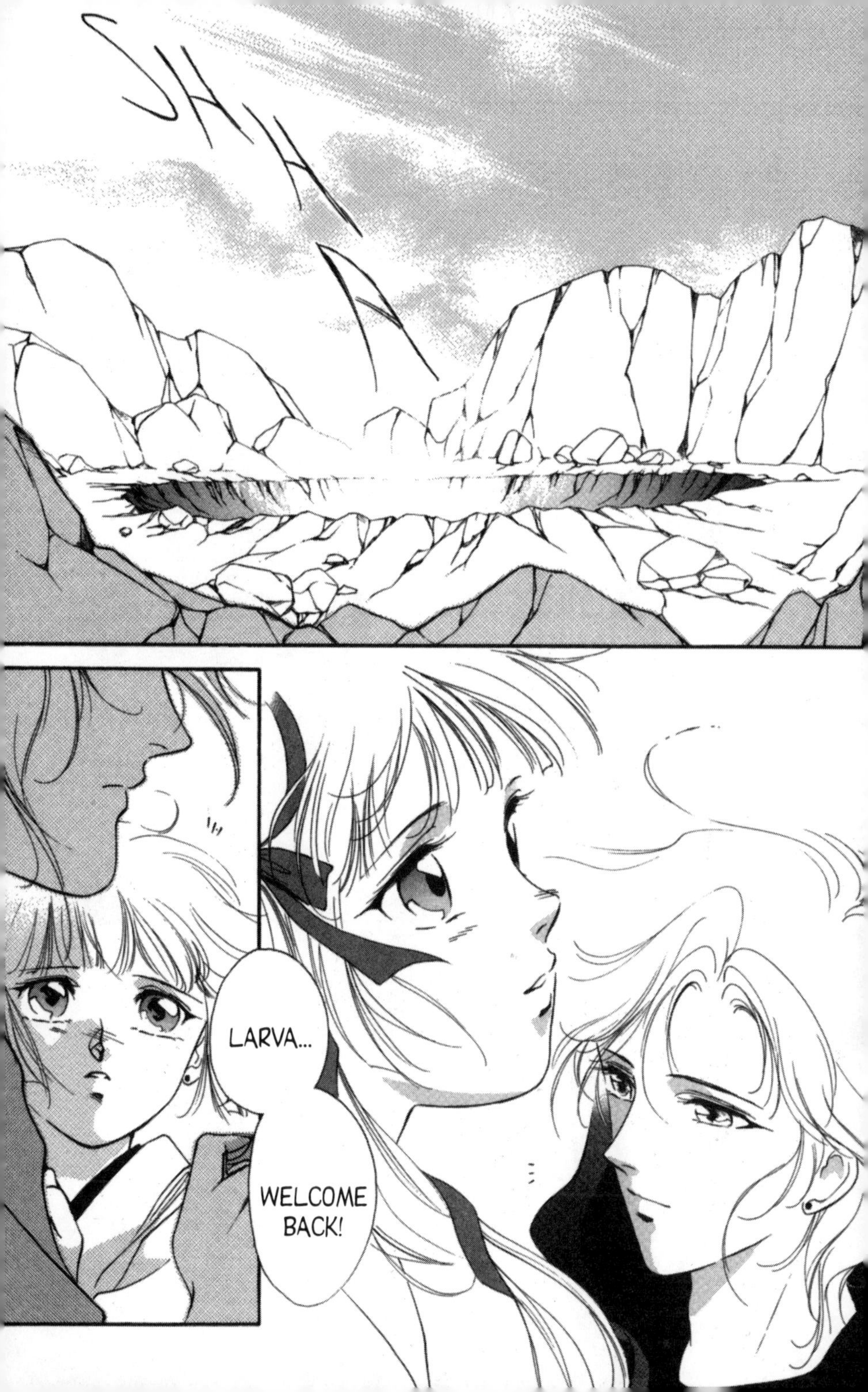
SHAAA
LARVA...
WELCOME BACK!

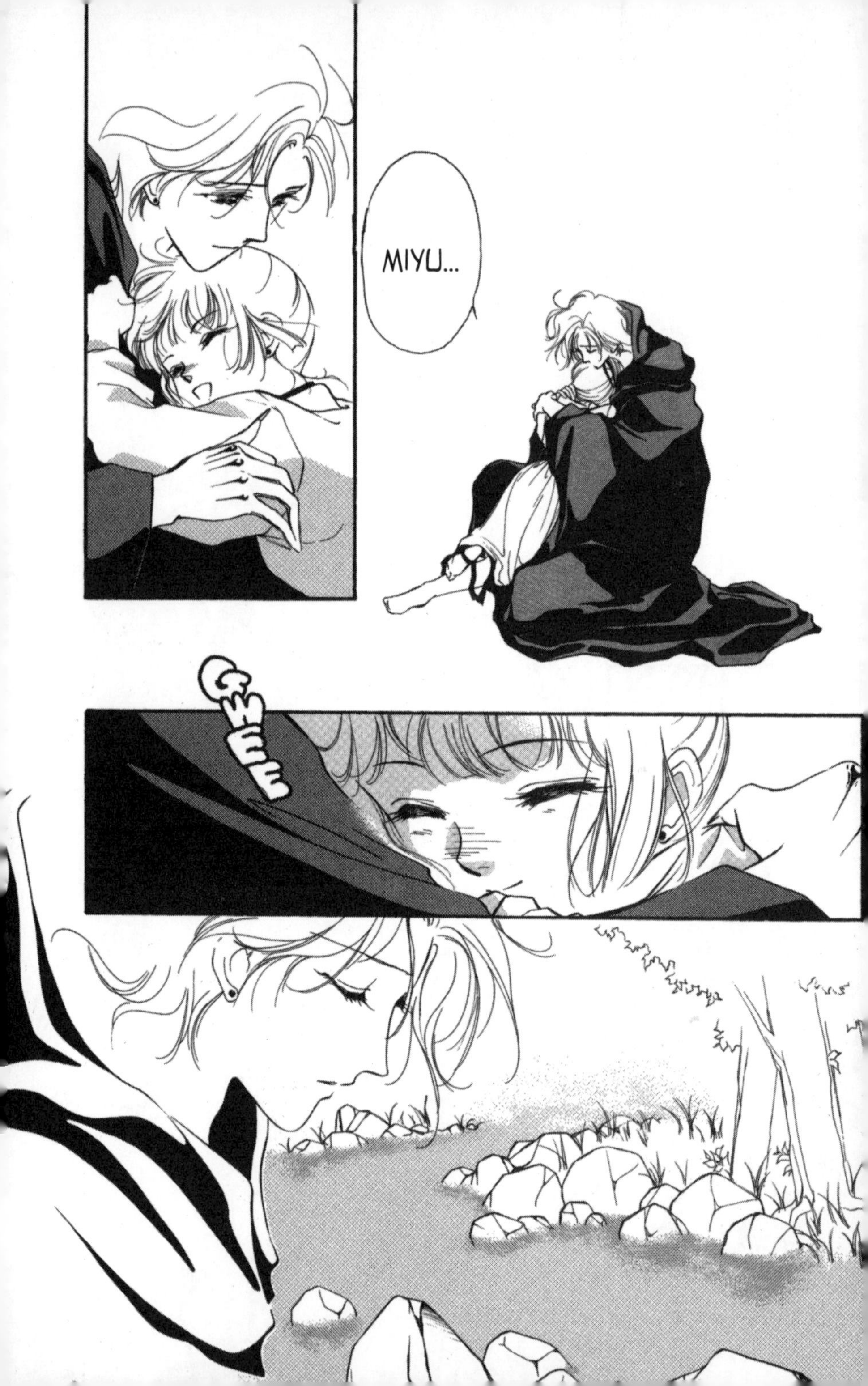
MIYU...
GYEE

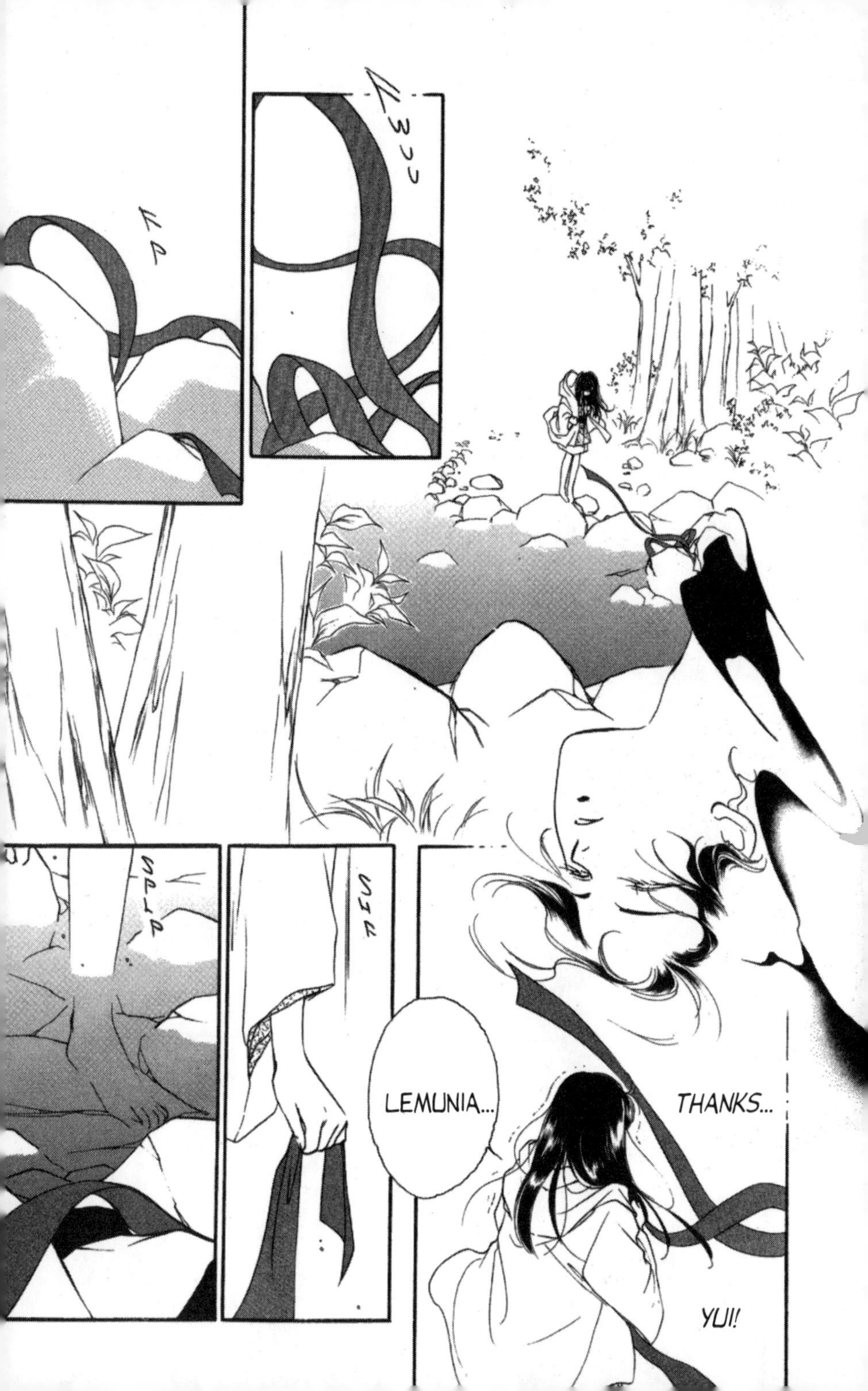
THANKS...
LEMUNIA...
YUI!

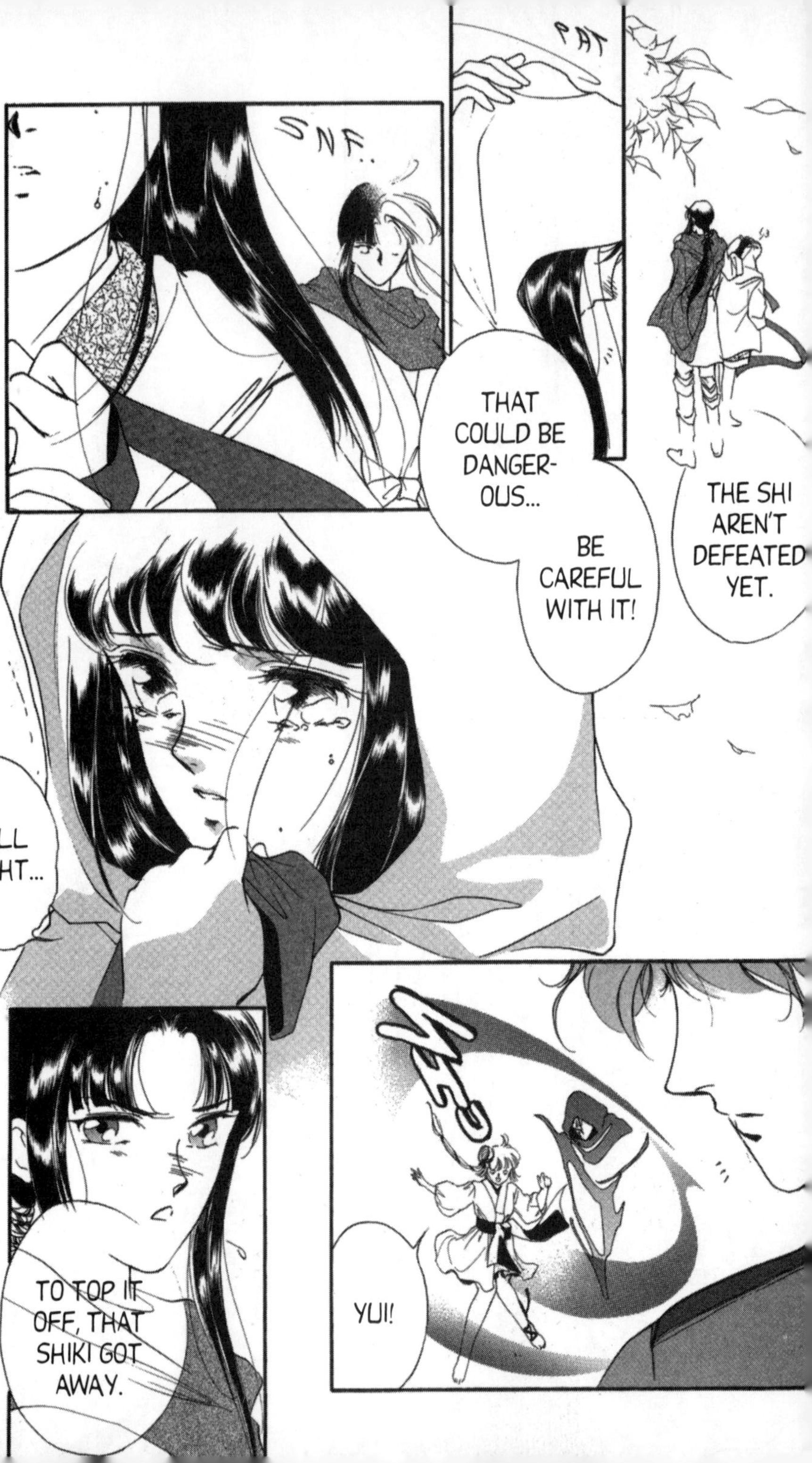
PAT
THE SHI AREN'T DEFEATED YET.
THAT COULD BE DANGER-OUS...
BE CAREFUL WITH IT!
SNF..
ALL RIGHT...
YUI!
TO TOP IT OFF, THAT SHIKI GOT AWAY.

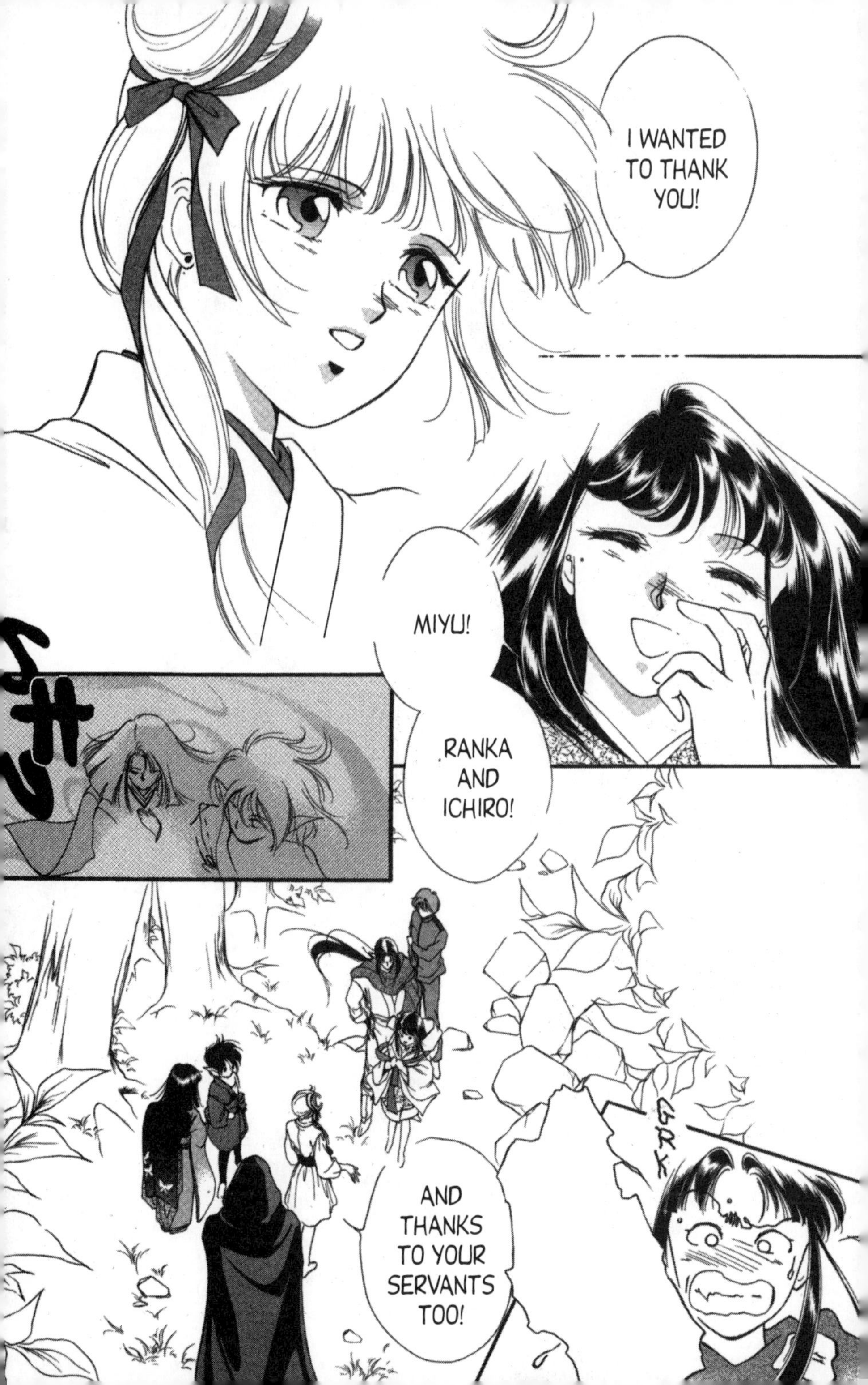
I WANTED TO THANK YOU!
MIYU!
RANKA AND ICHIRO!
AND THANKS TO YOUR SERVANTS TOO!
GRR

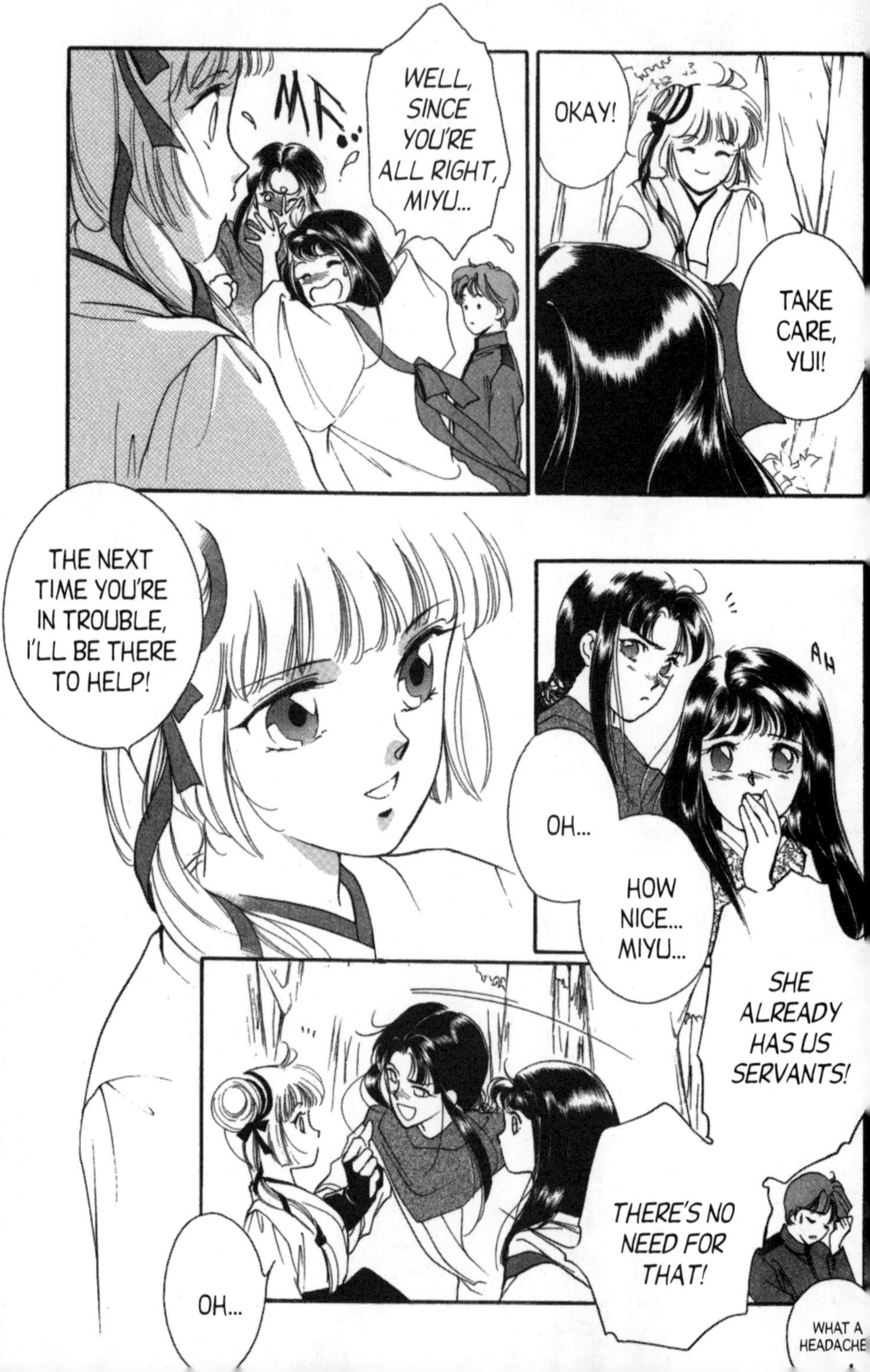
MF
WELL, SINCE YOU'RE ALL RIGHT, MIYU...
OKAY!
TAKE CARE, YUI!
THE NEXT TIME YOU'RE IN TROUBLE, I'LL BE THERE TO HELP!
AH
OH...
HOW NICE... MIYU...
SHE ALREADY HAS US SERVANTS!
THERE'S NO NEED FOR THAT!
OH...
WHAT A HEADACHE

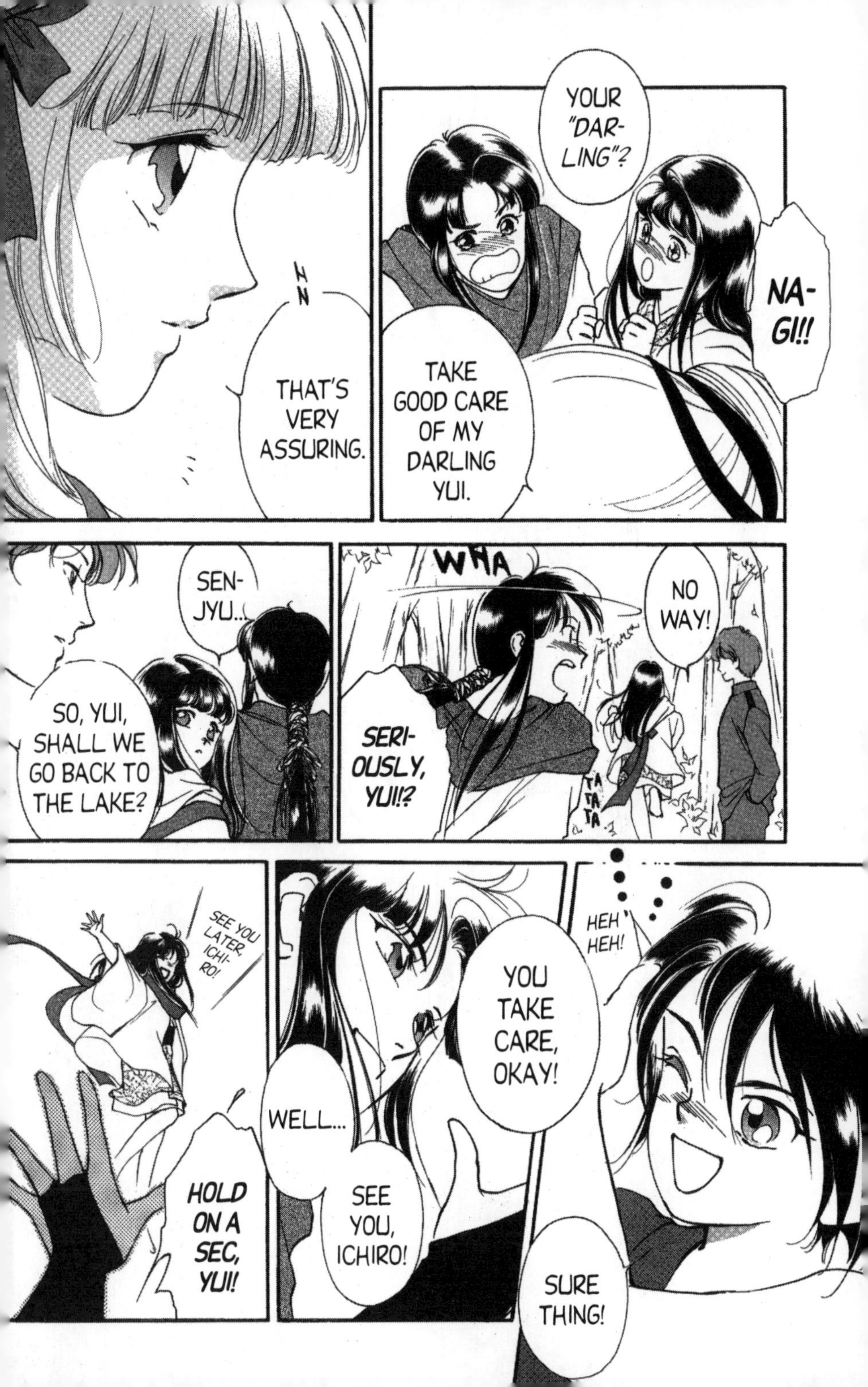
HN
THAT'S VERY ASSURING.
TAKE GOOD CARE OF MY DARLING YUI.
YOUR "DARLING"?
NA-GI!!
SO, YUI, SHALL WE GO BACK TO THE LAKE?
SEN-JYU...
WHA
NO WAY!
SERIOUSLY, YUI!?
TA TA TA
SEE YOU LATER, ICHIRO!
HOLD ON A SEC, YUI!
WELL...
SEE YOU, ICHIRO!
YOU TAKE CARE, OKAY!
HEH HEH!
SURE THING!

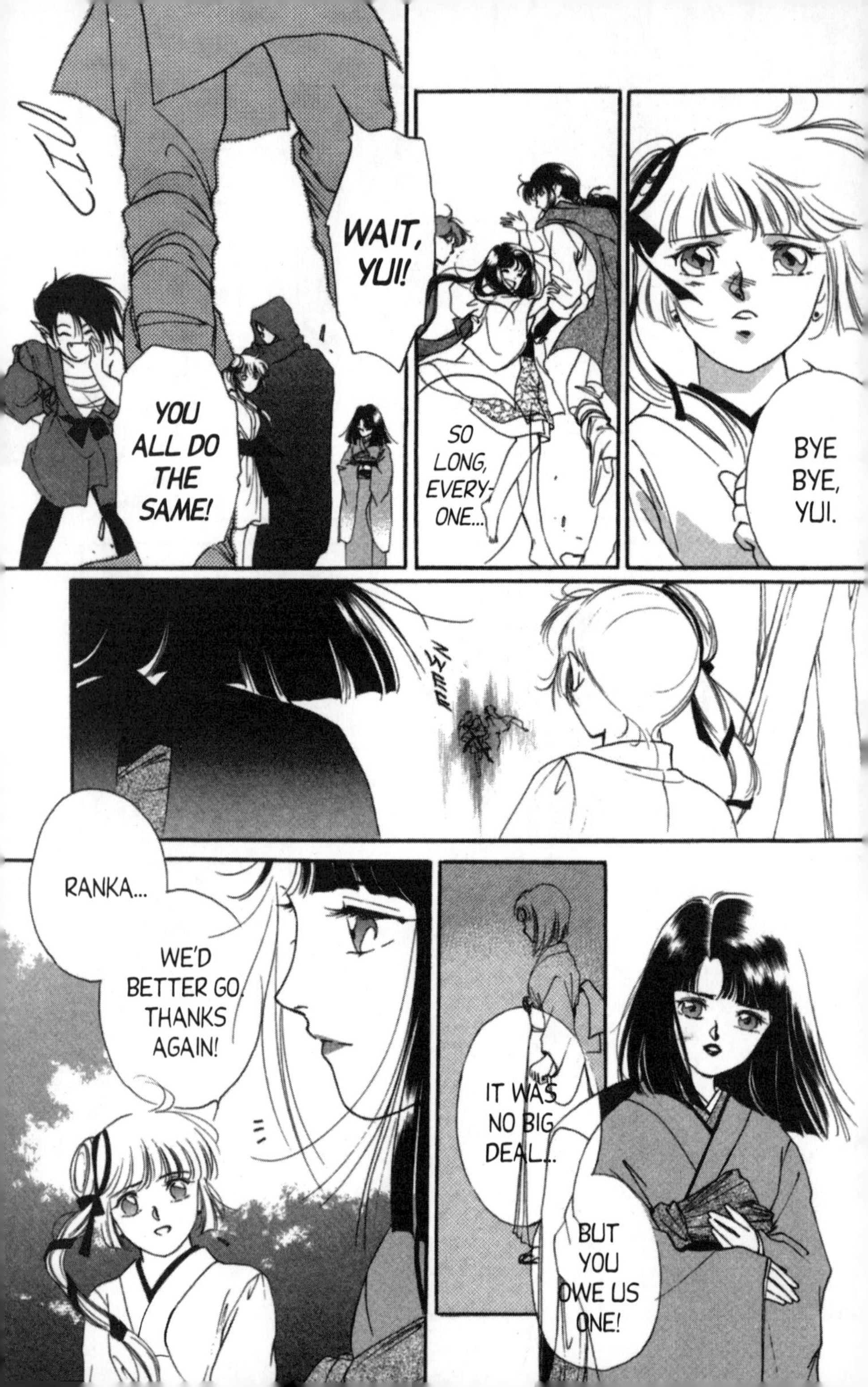
WAIT, YUI!
YOU ALL DO THE SAME!
SO LONG, EVERY-ONE...
BYE BYE, YUI.
RANKA...
WE'D BETTER GO. THANKS AGAIN!
IT WAS NO BIG DEAL...
BUT YOU OWE US ONE!

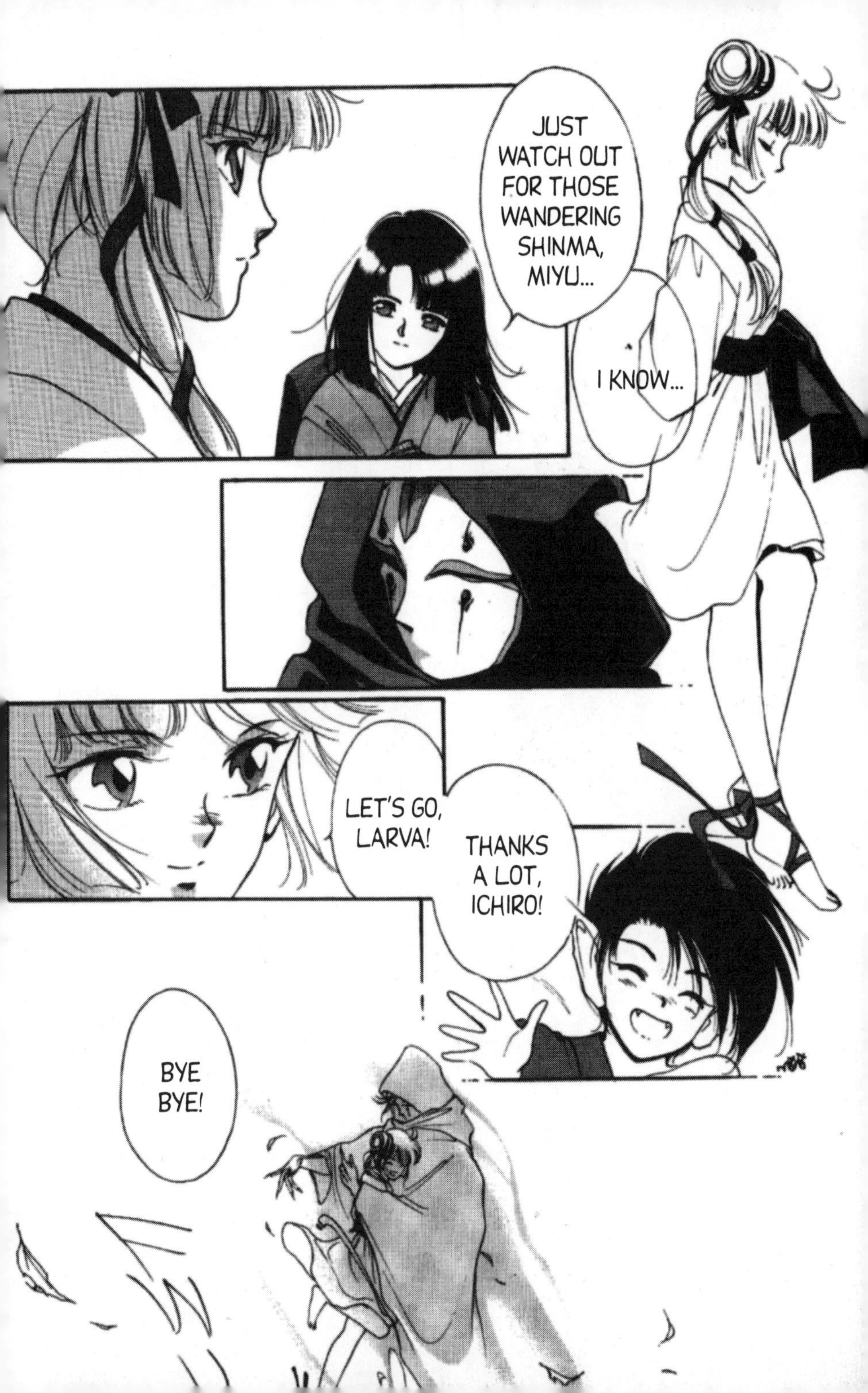
JUST WATCH OUT FOR THOSE WANDERING SHINMA, MIYU...
I KNOW...
THANKS A LOT, ICHIRO!
LET'S GO, LARVA!
BYE BYE!

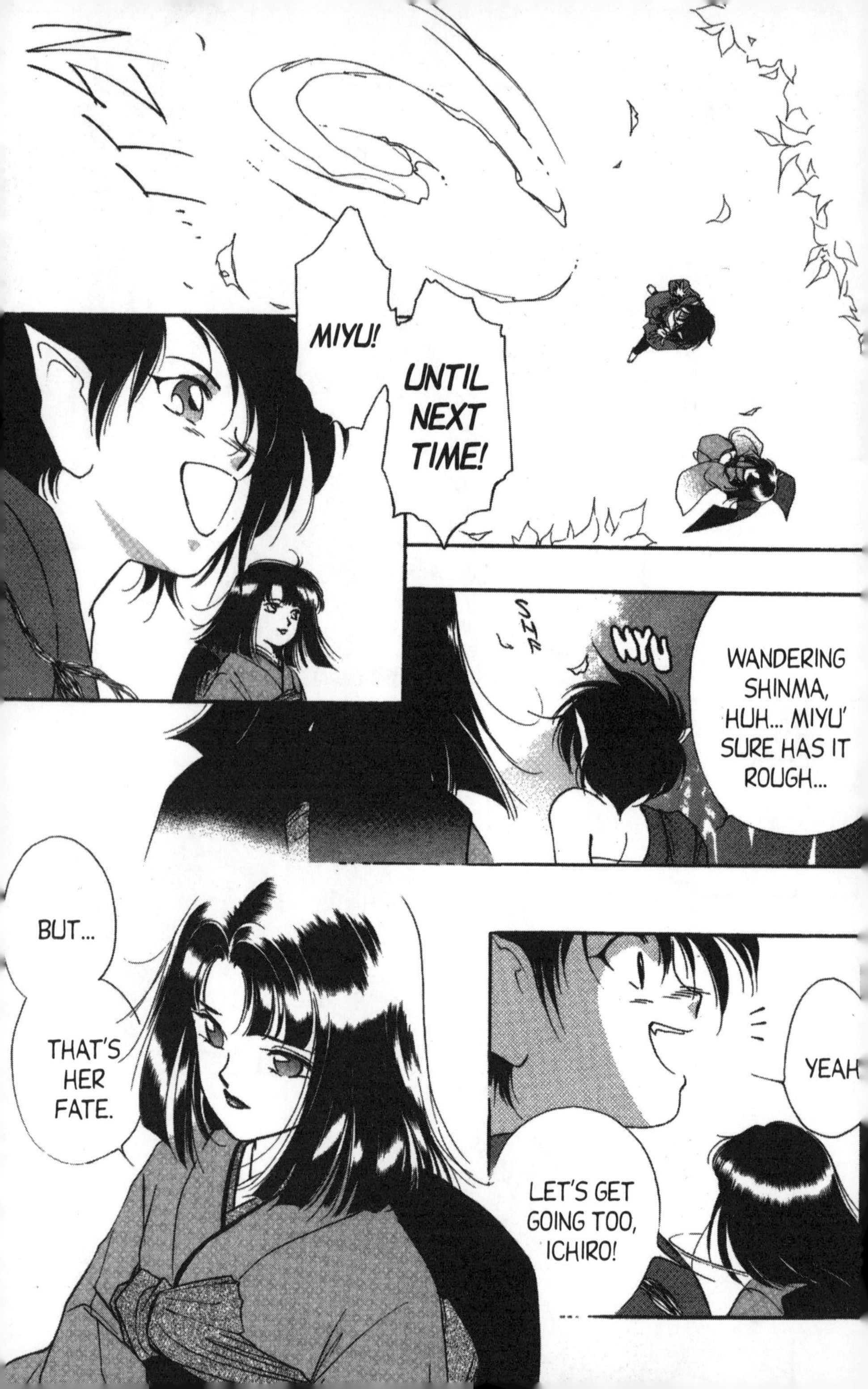
MIYU!
UNTIL NEXT TIME!
SHR
HYU
WANDERING SHINMA, HUH... MIYU' SURE HAS IT ROUGH...
BUT...
THAT'S HER FATE.
YEAH
LET'S GET GOING TOO, ICHIRO!

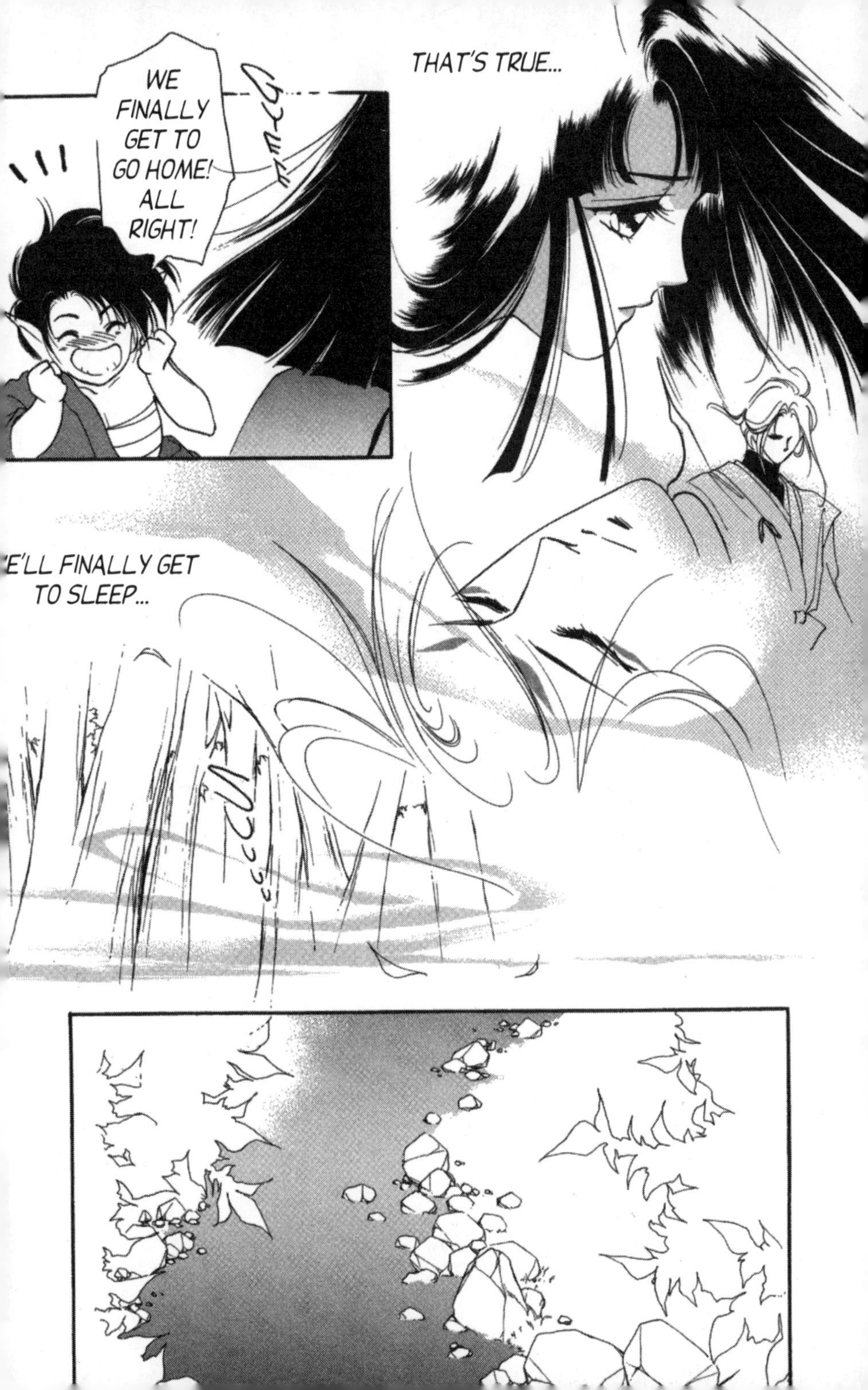
WE FINALLY GET TO GO HOME! ALL RIGHT!
THAT'S TRUE...
'E'LL FINALLY GET TO SLEEP...

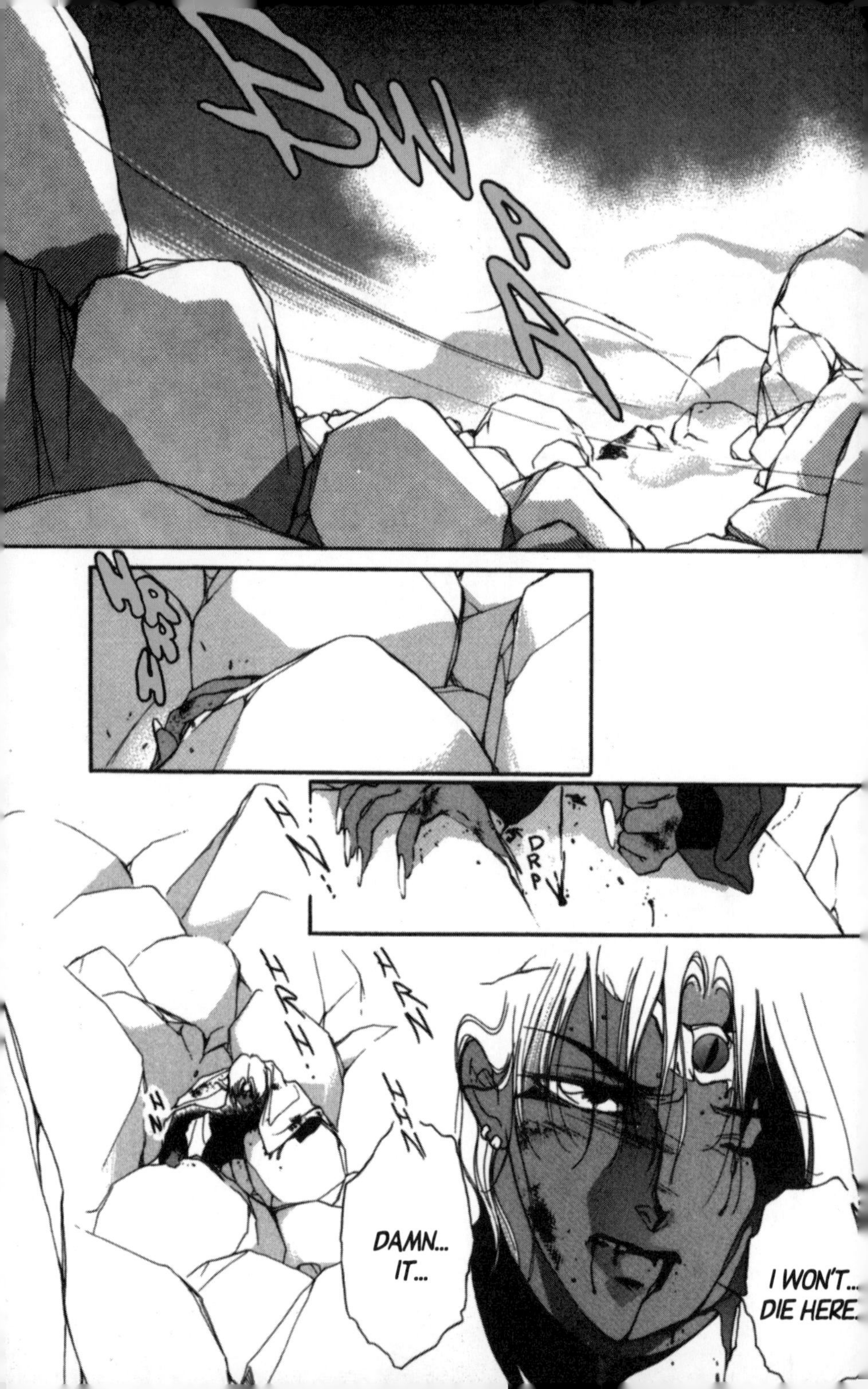
BWAA
HAAH
HN...
DRP
HRN
HRH..
HN
HN
DAMN... IT...
I WON'T... DIE HERE.

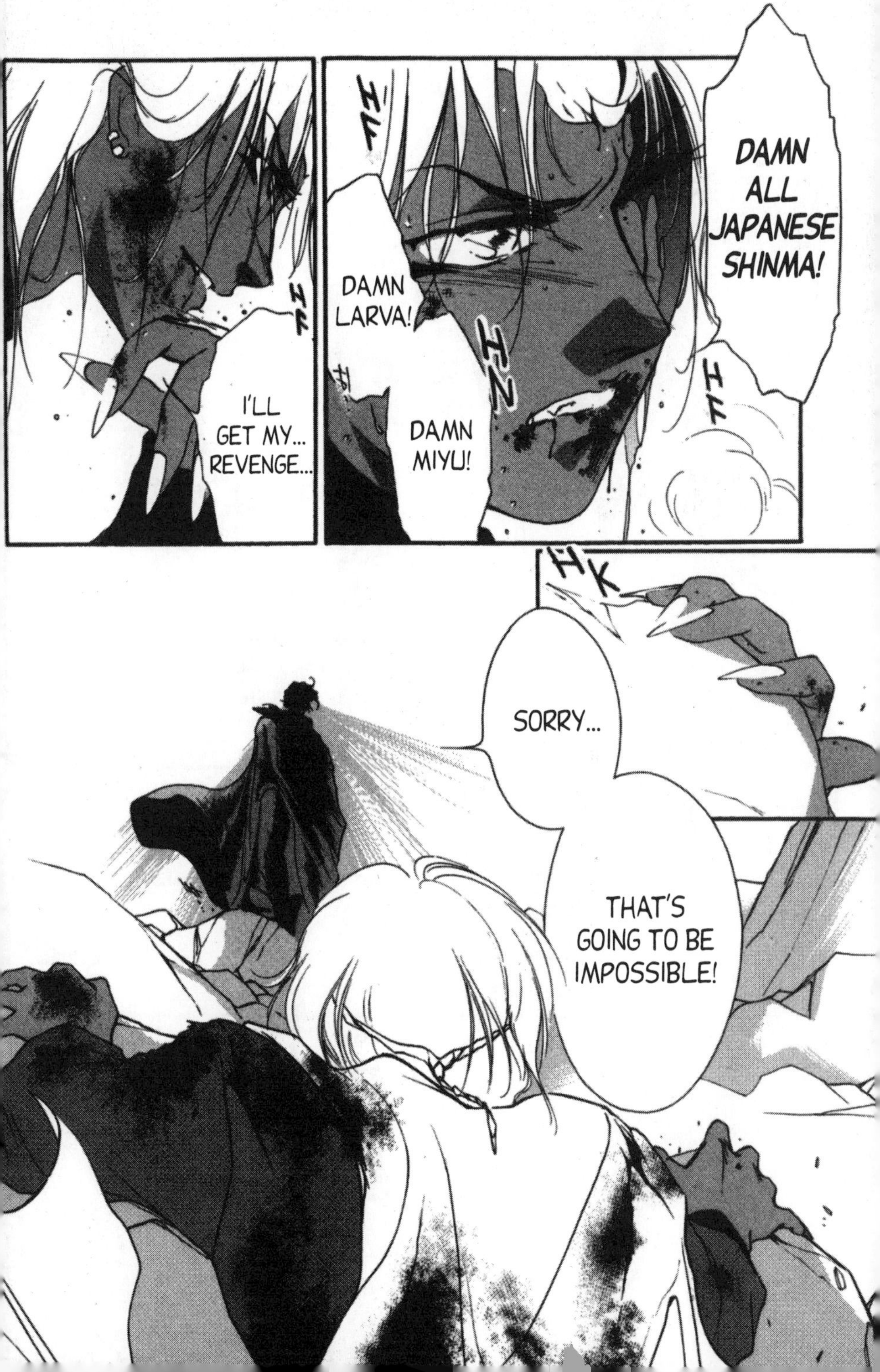
DAMN ALL JAPANESE SHINMA!
HF
HN
DAMN LARVA!
DAMN MIYU!
HF
HF
I'LL GET MY... REVENGE...
HK
SORRY...
THAT'S GOING TO BE IMPOSSIBLE!

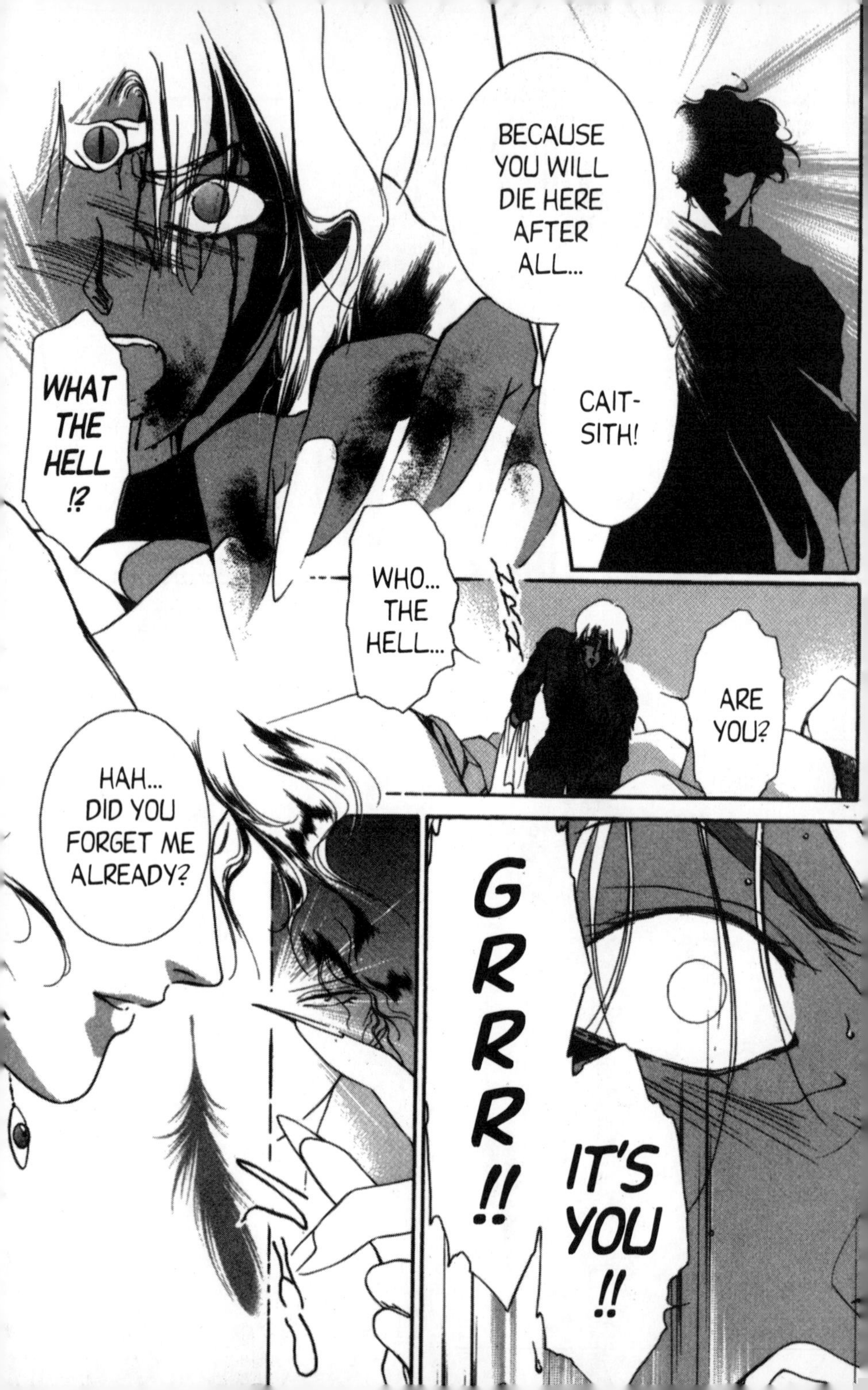
BECAUSE YOU WILL DIE HERE AFTER ALL...
CAIT-SITH!
WHAT THE HELL !?
WHO... THE HELL...
ARE YOU?
IT'S YOU !!
GRRR !!
HAH... DID YOU FORGET ME ALREADY?

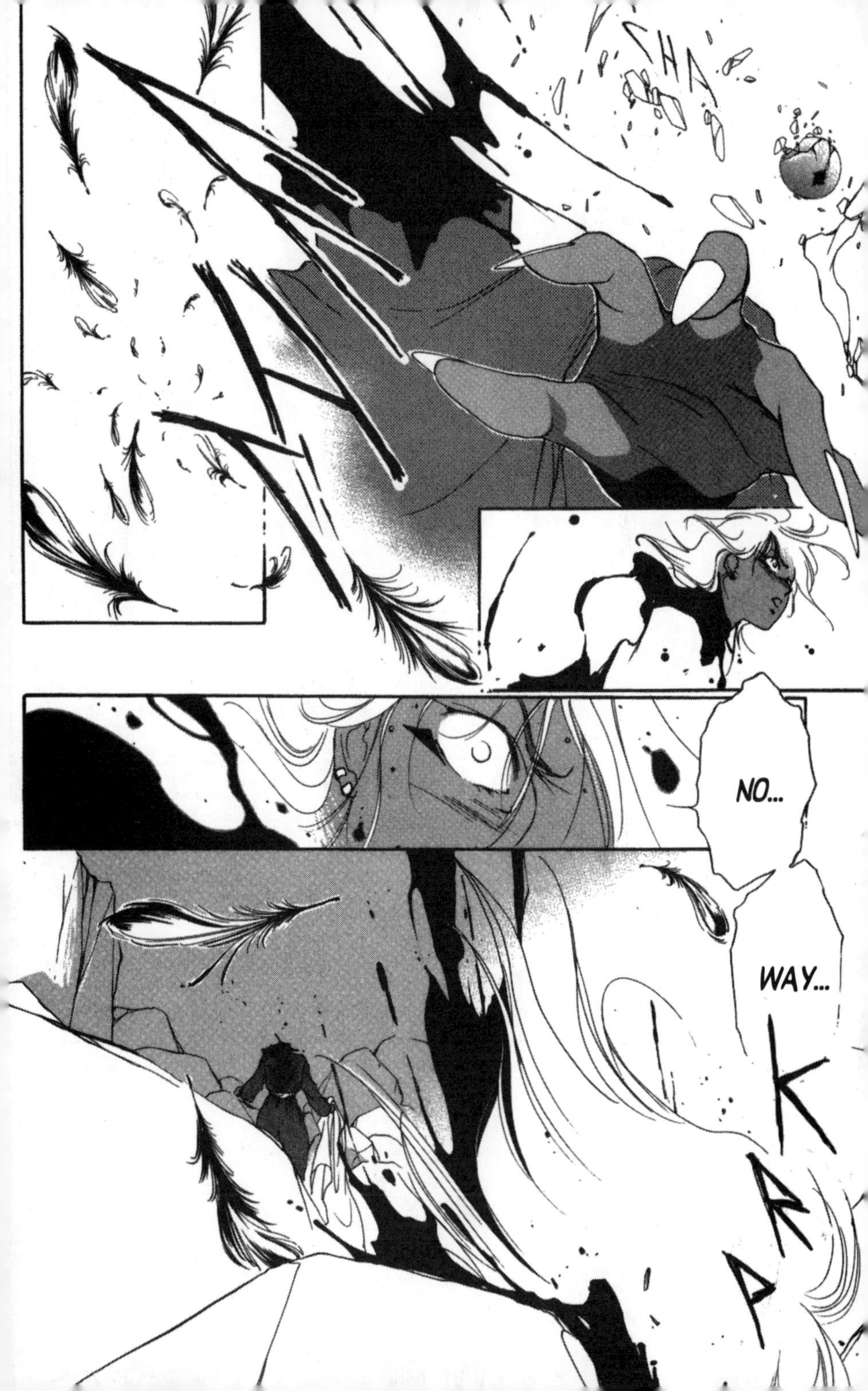
CHA
NO...
WAY...
KRAK

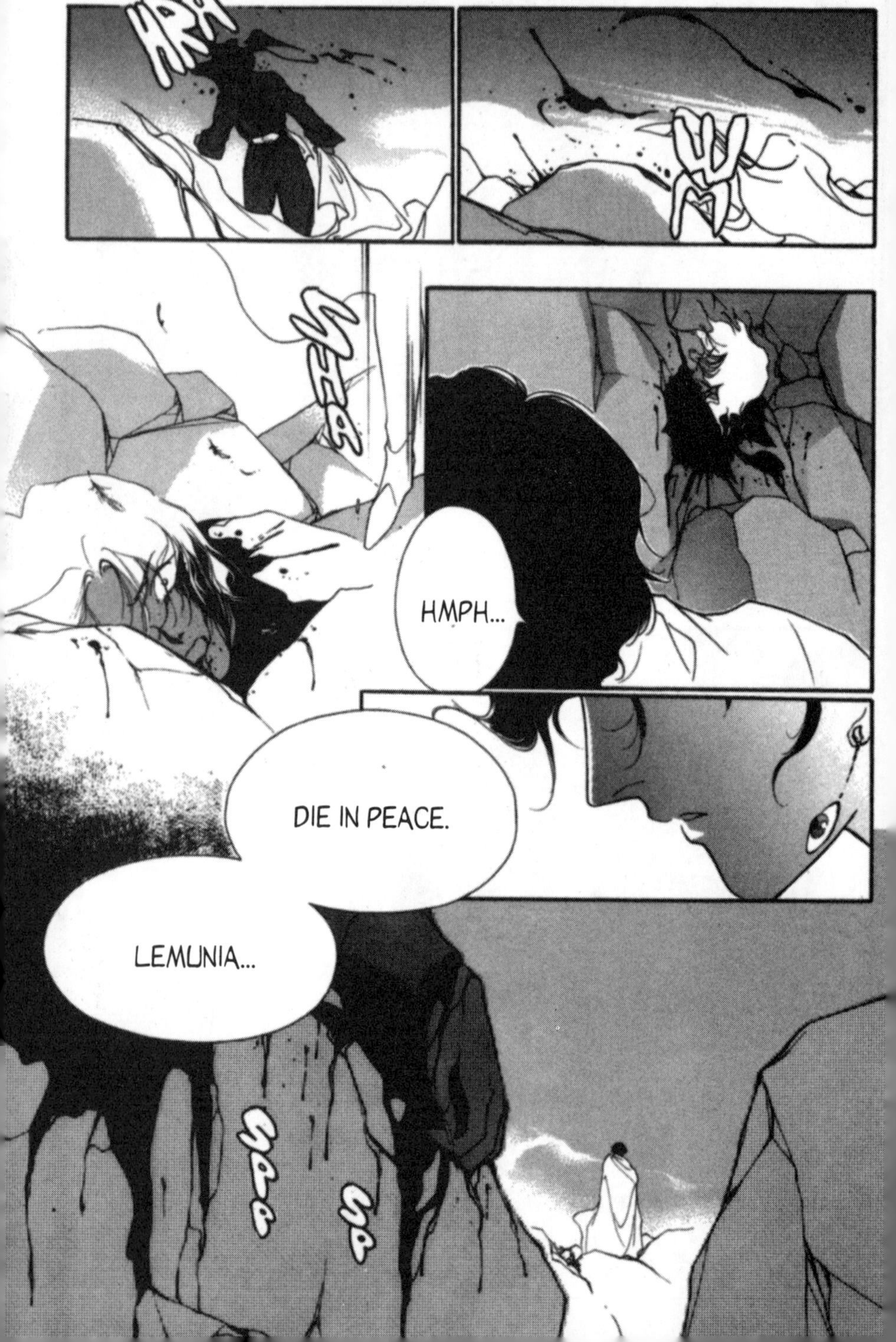
HMPH...
DIE IN PEACE.
LEMUNIA...

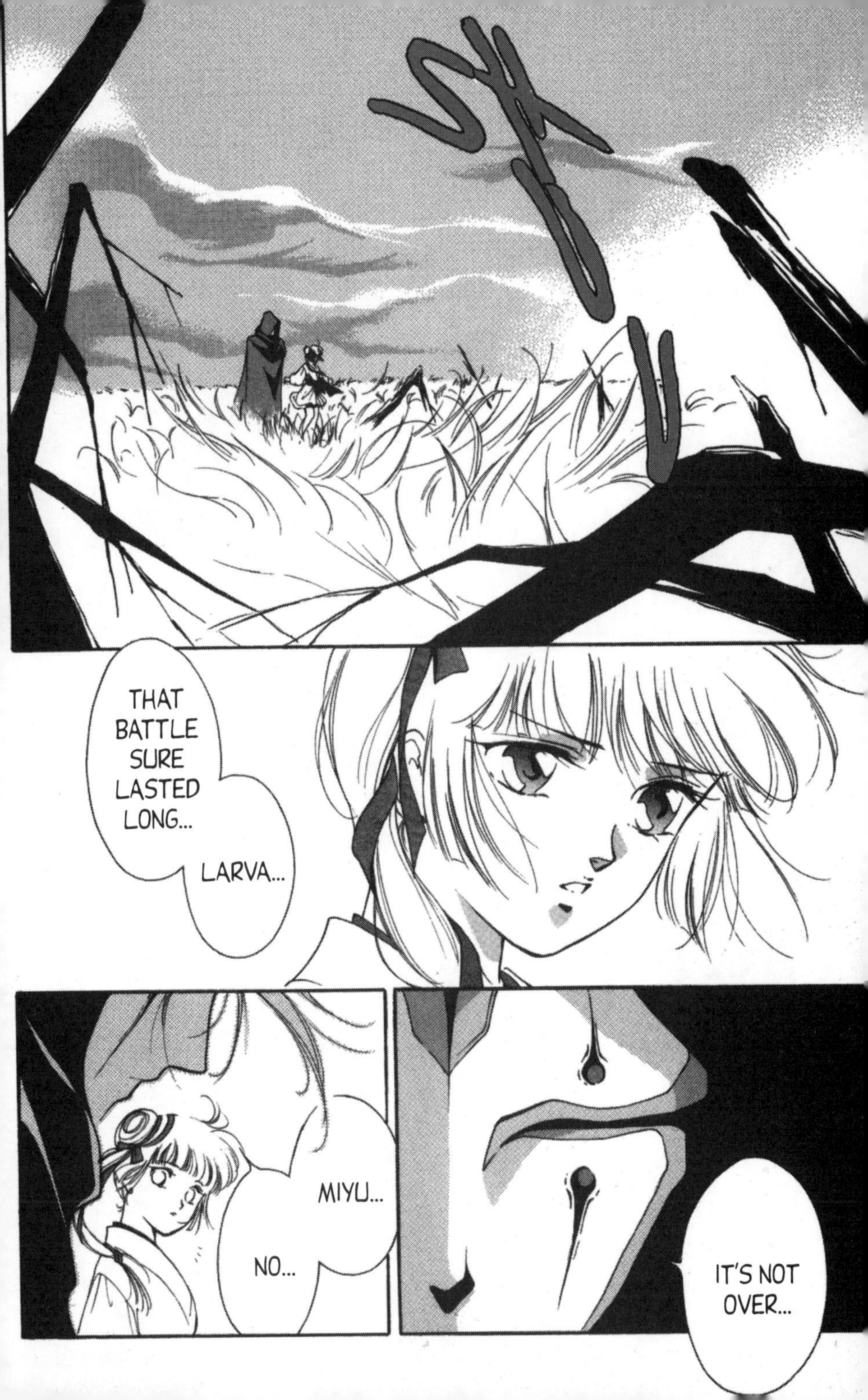
THAT BATTLE SURE LASTED LONG...
LARVA...
MIYU...
NO...
IT'S NOT OVER...

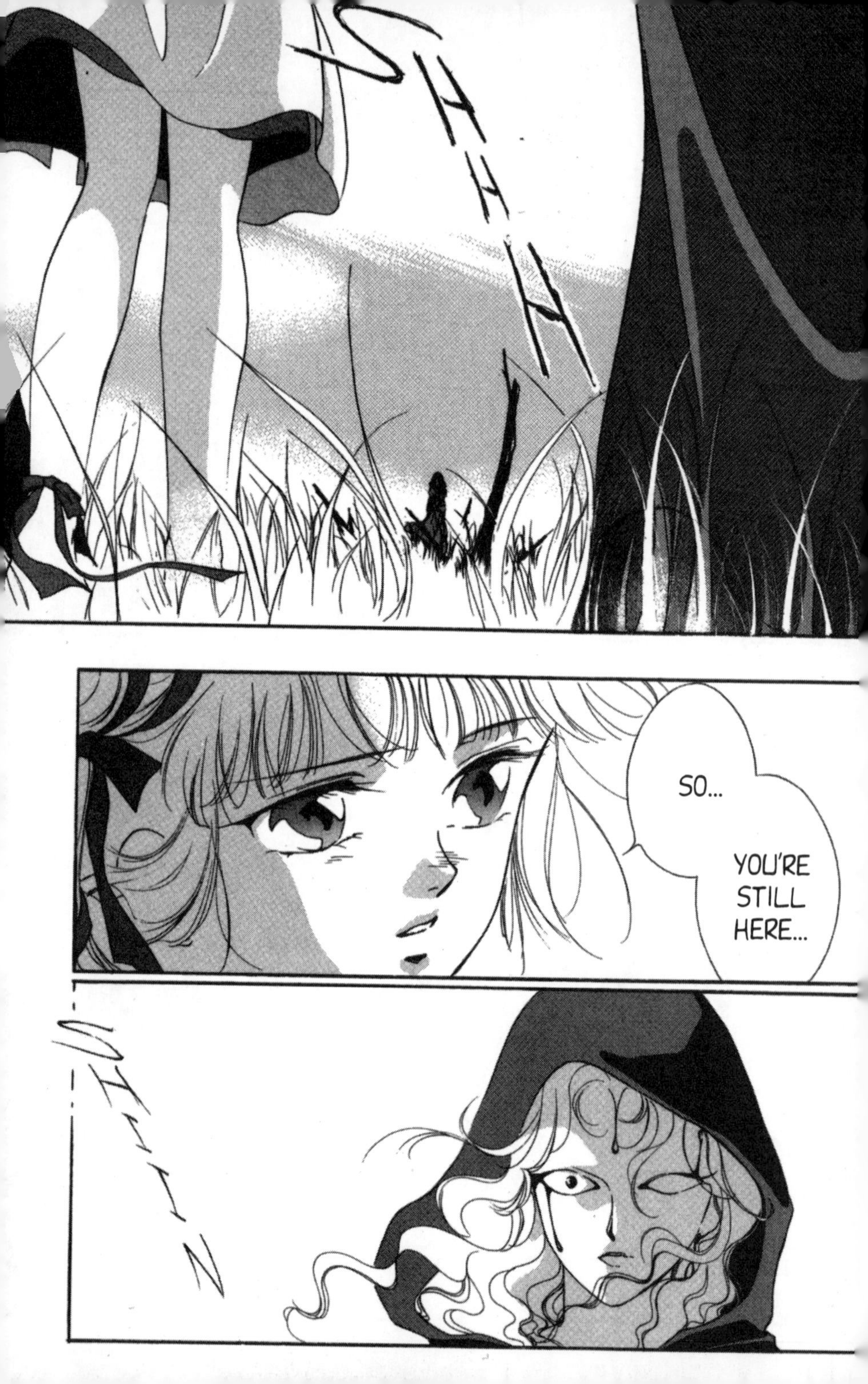
SO...
YOU'RE STILL HERE...

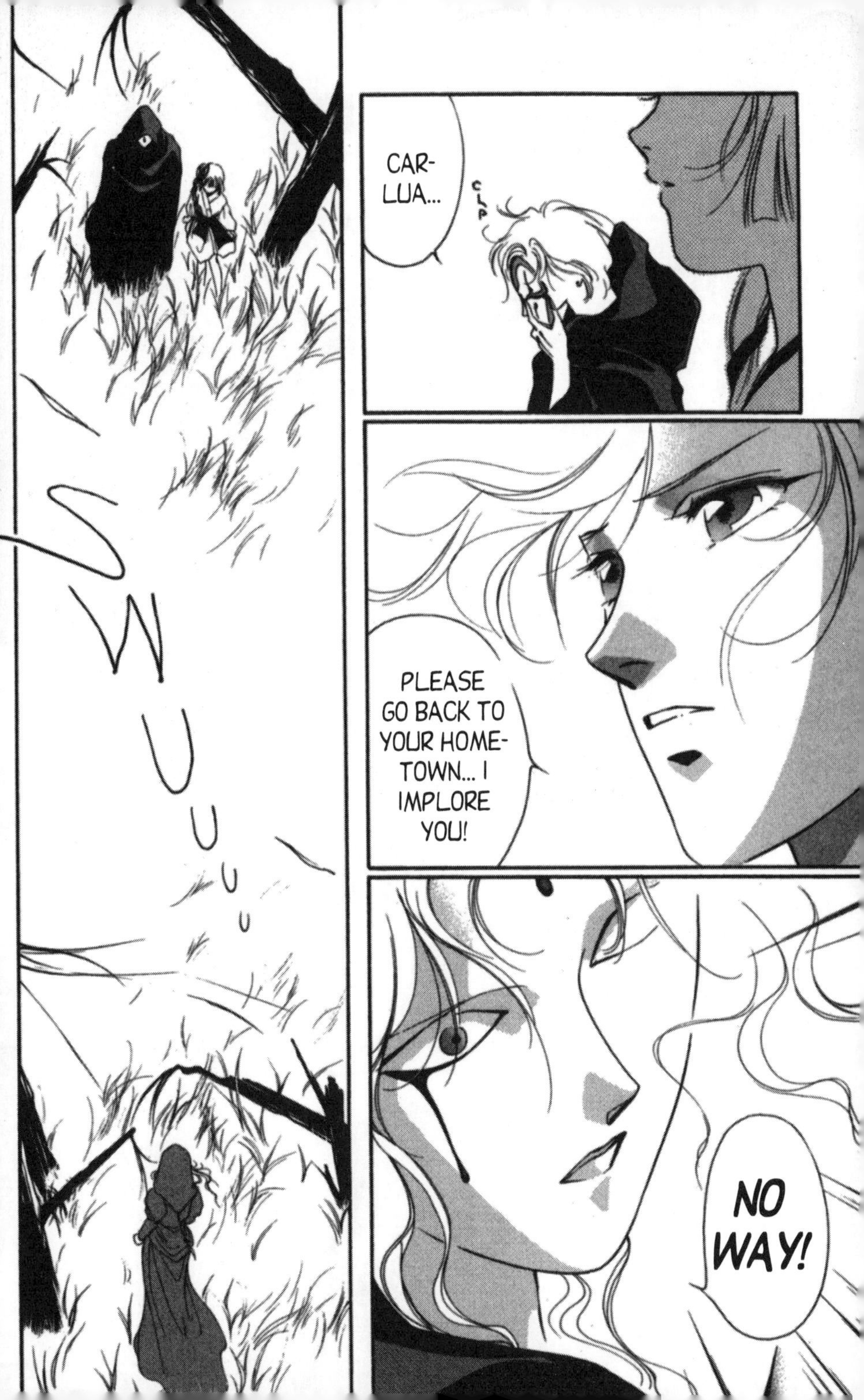
CAR-
LUA...
PLEASE GO BACK TO YOUR HOME-TOWN... I IMPLORE YOU!
NO WAY!
SWUUUU

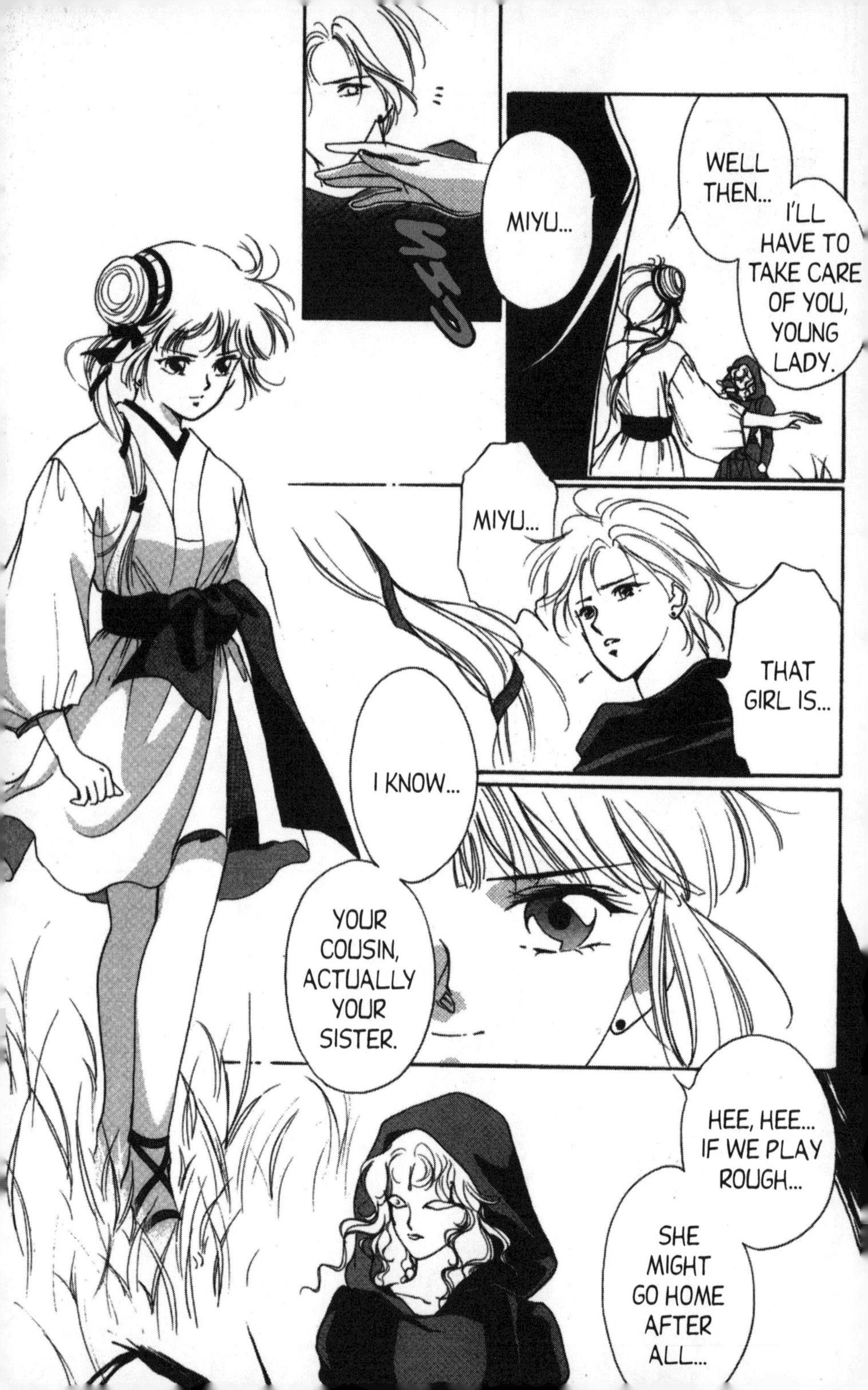
WELL THEN...
I'LL HAVE TO TAKE CARE OF YOU, YOUNG LADY.
MIYU...
MIYU...
THAT GIRL IS...
I KNOW...
YOUR COUSIN, ACTUALLY YOUR SISTER.
HEE, HEE... IF WE PLAY ROUGH...
SHE MIGHT GO HOME AFTER ALL...

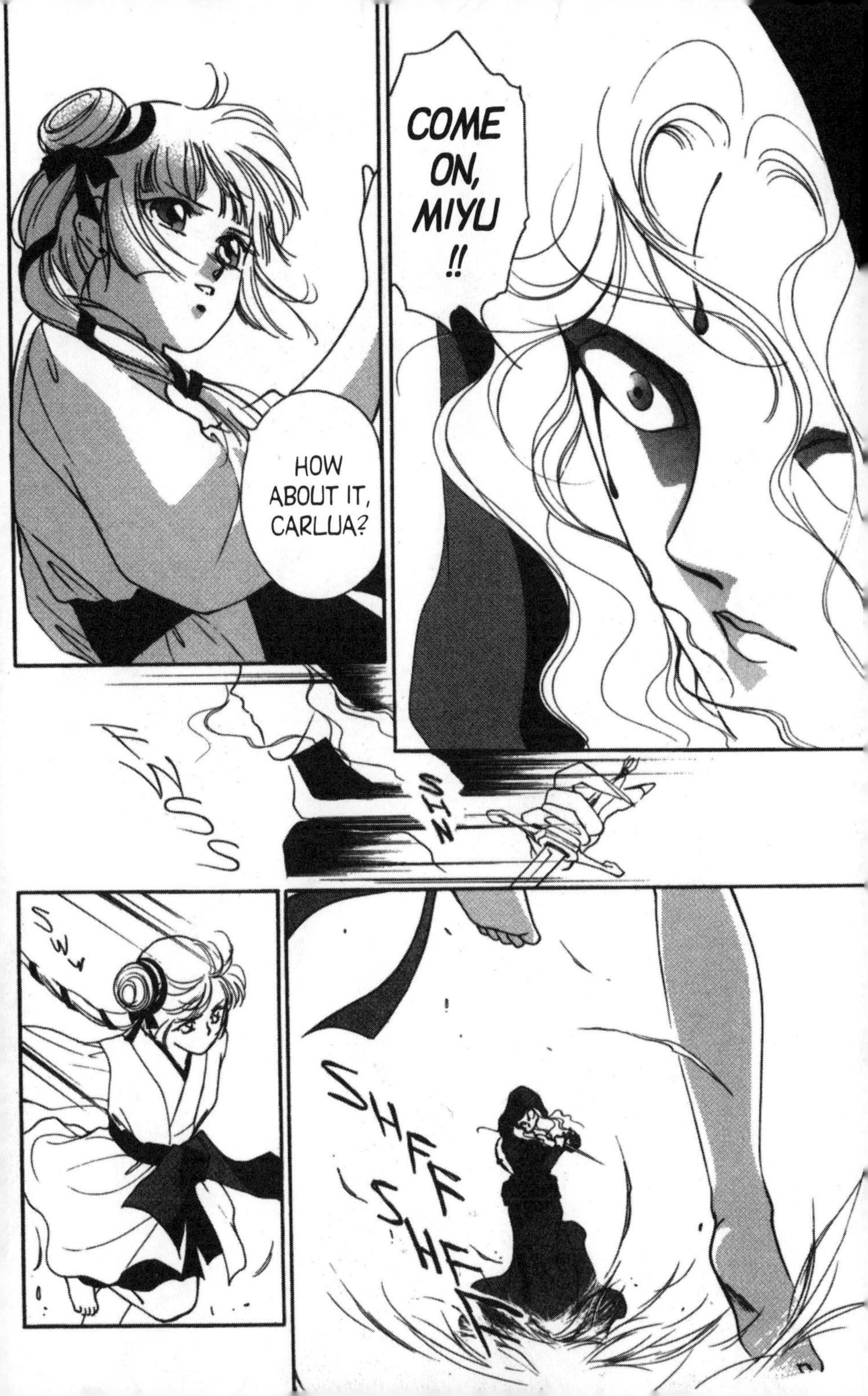
COME ON, MIYU!!
HOW ABOUT IT, CARLUA?
SHFF SHFF

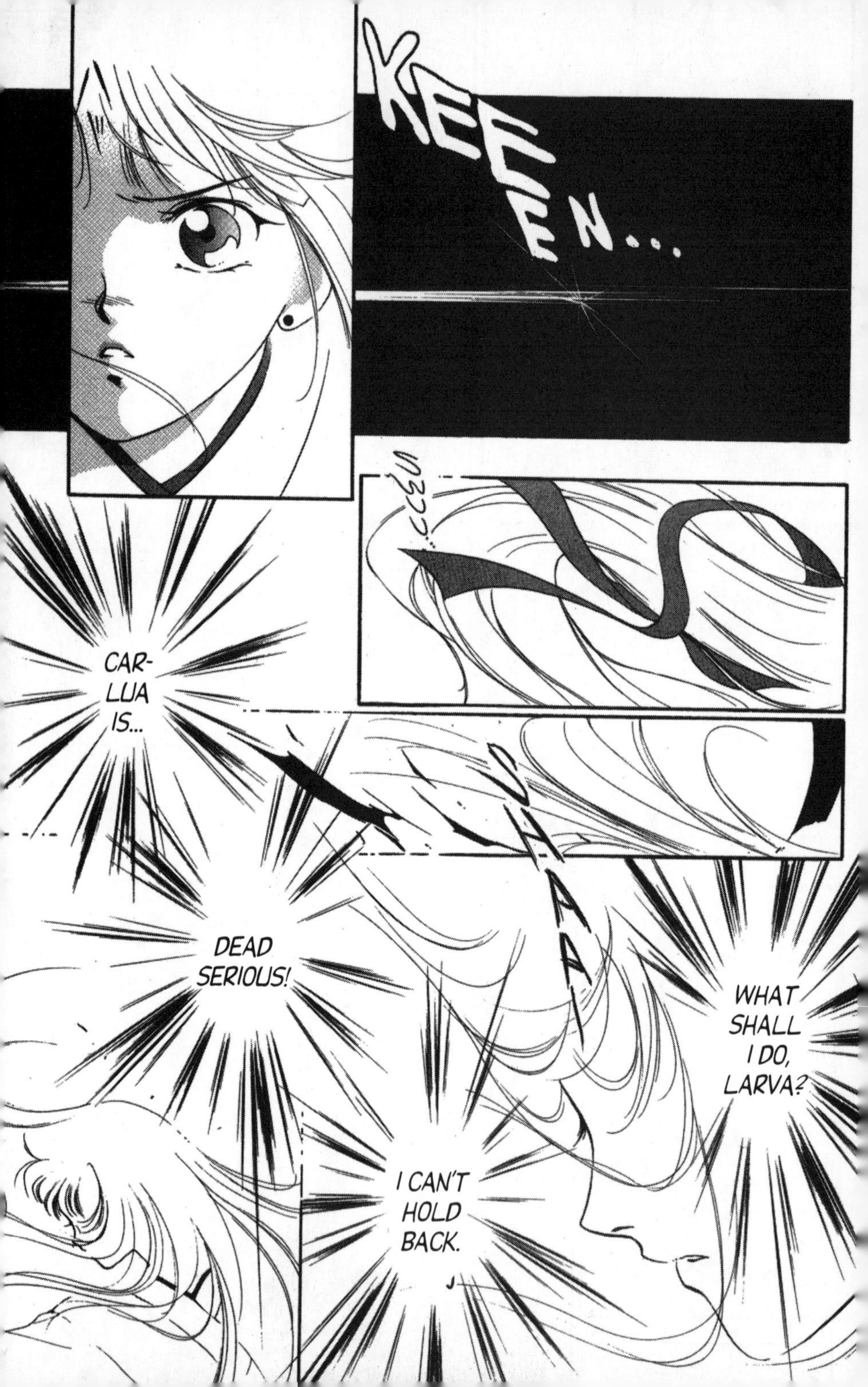
KEEEEN...
CAR-
LUA
IS...
DEAD
SERIOUS!
WHAT
SHALL
I DO,
LARVA?
I CAN'T
HOLD
BACK.

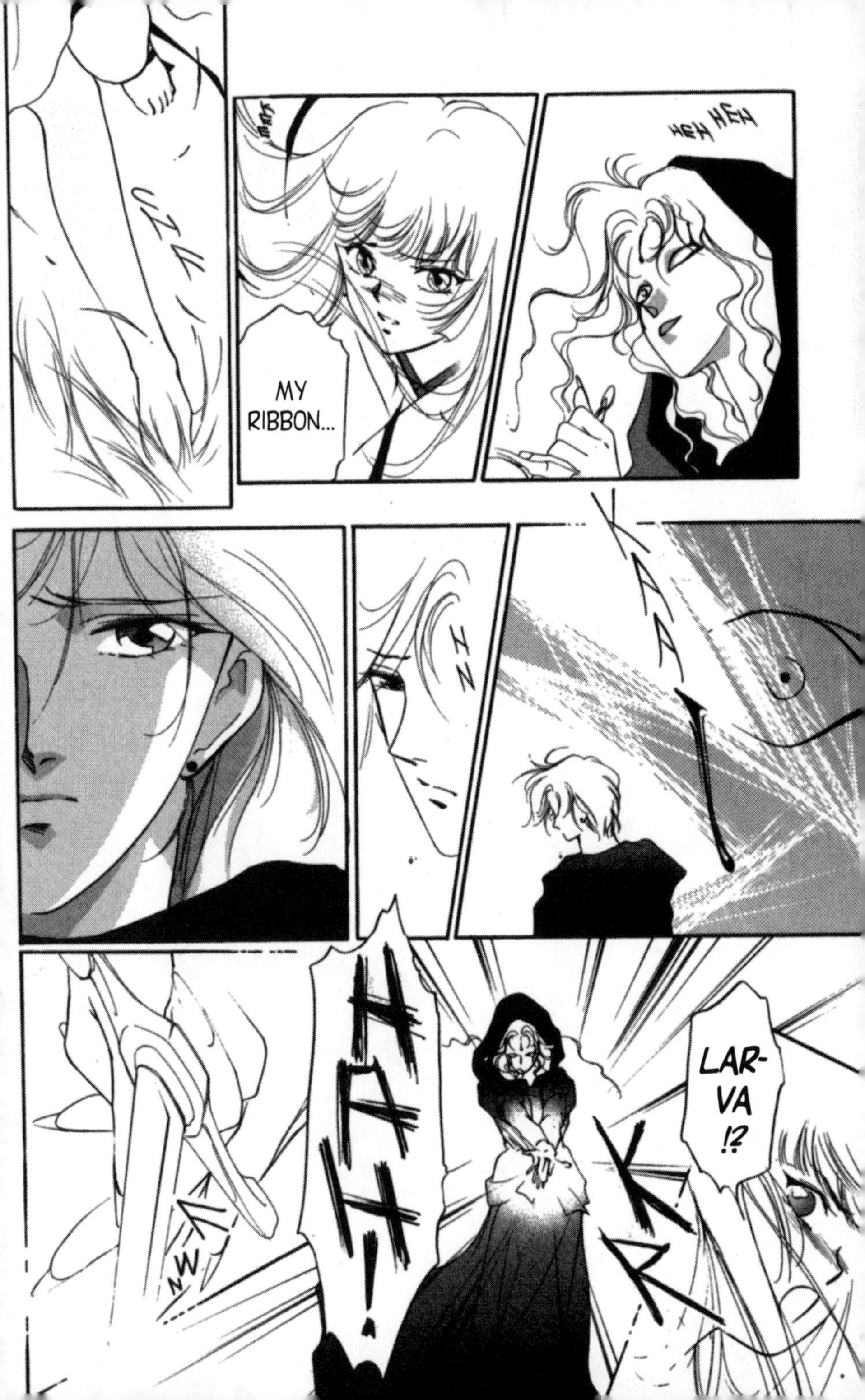
HEH HEH
MY RIBBON...
LAR-VA !?
HAH!

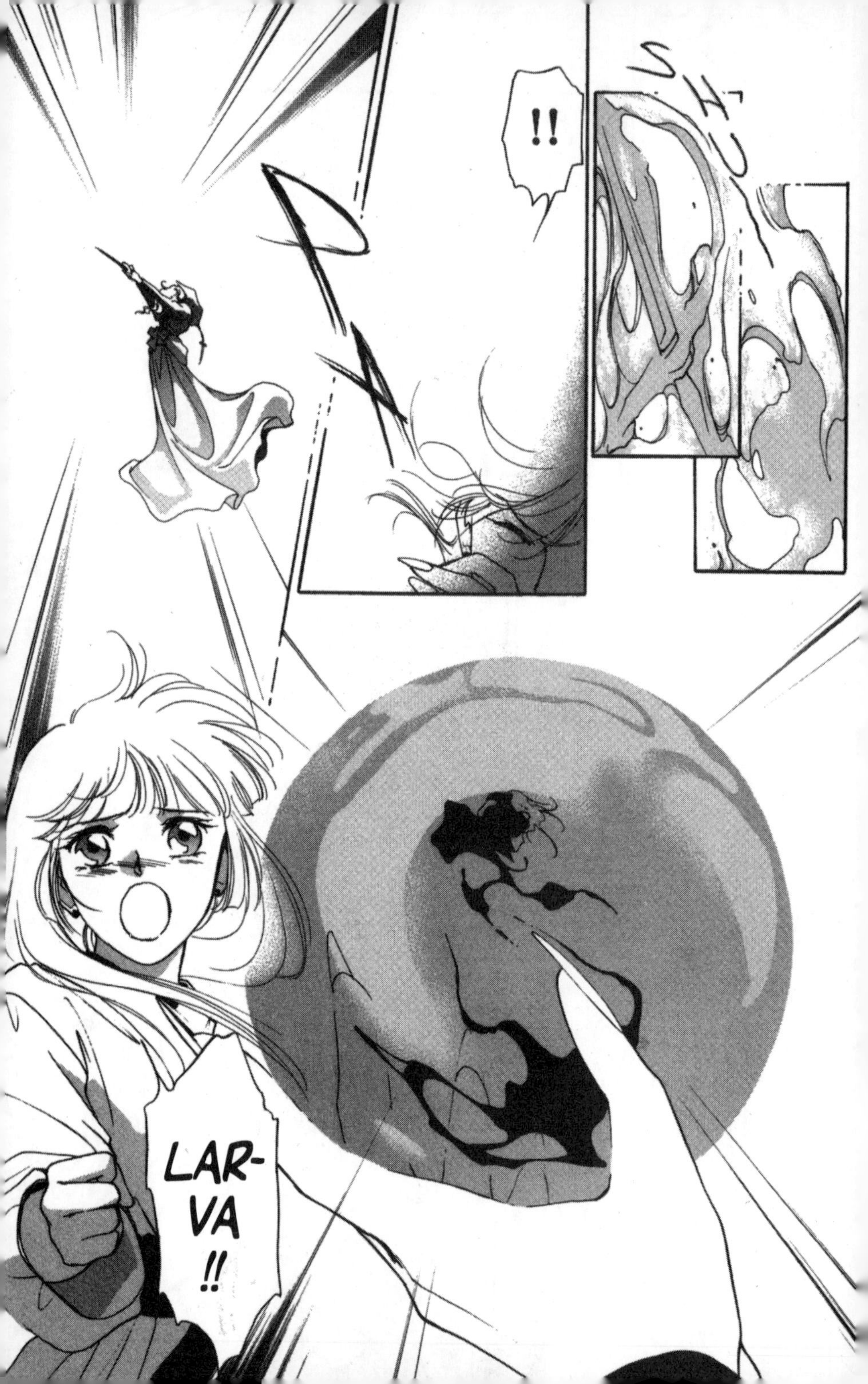
!!
LAR-
VA
!!

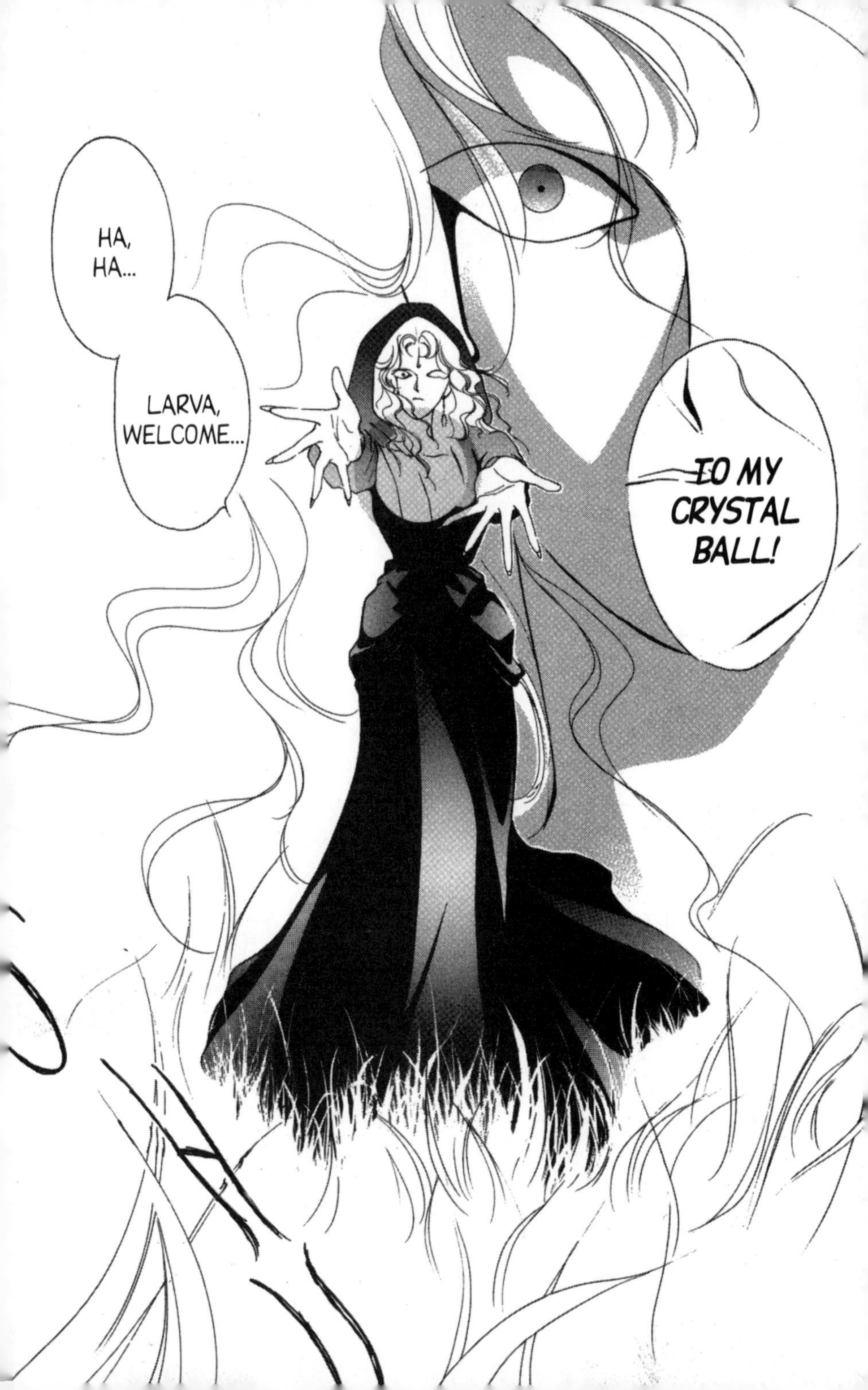
HA, HA...
LARVA, WELCOME...
TO MY CRYSTAL BALL!

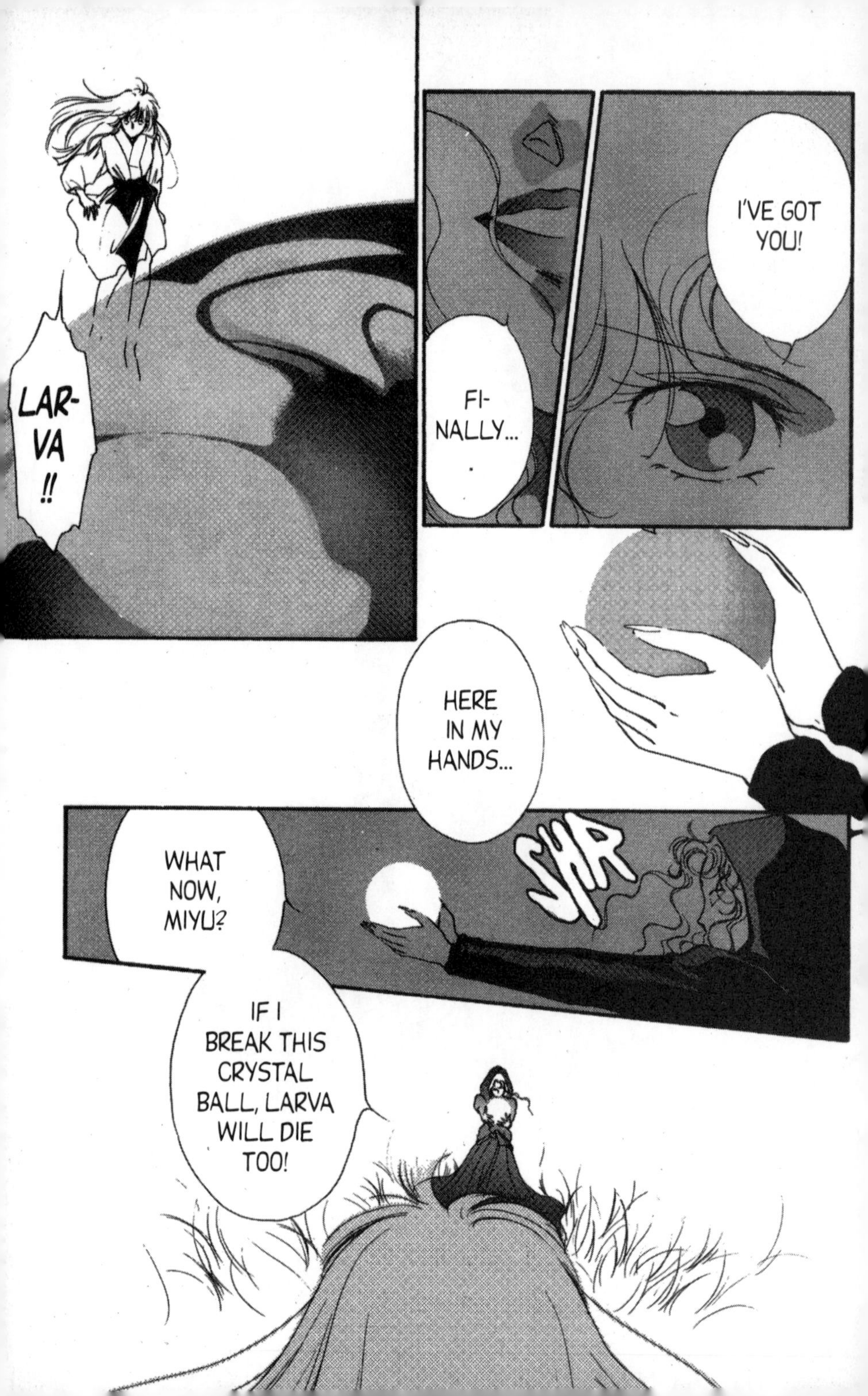
I'VE GOT YOU!
FI-NALLY....
LAR-VA!!
HERE IN MY HANDS...
SHR
WHAT NOW, MIYU?
IF I BREAK THIS CRYSTAL BALL, LARVA WILL DIE TOO!

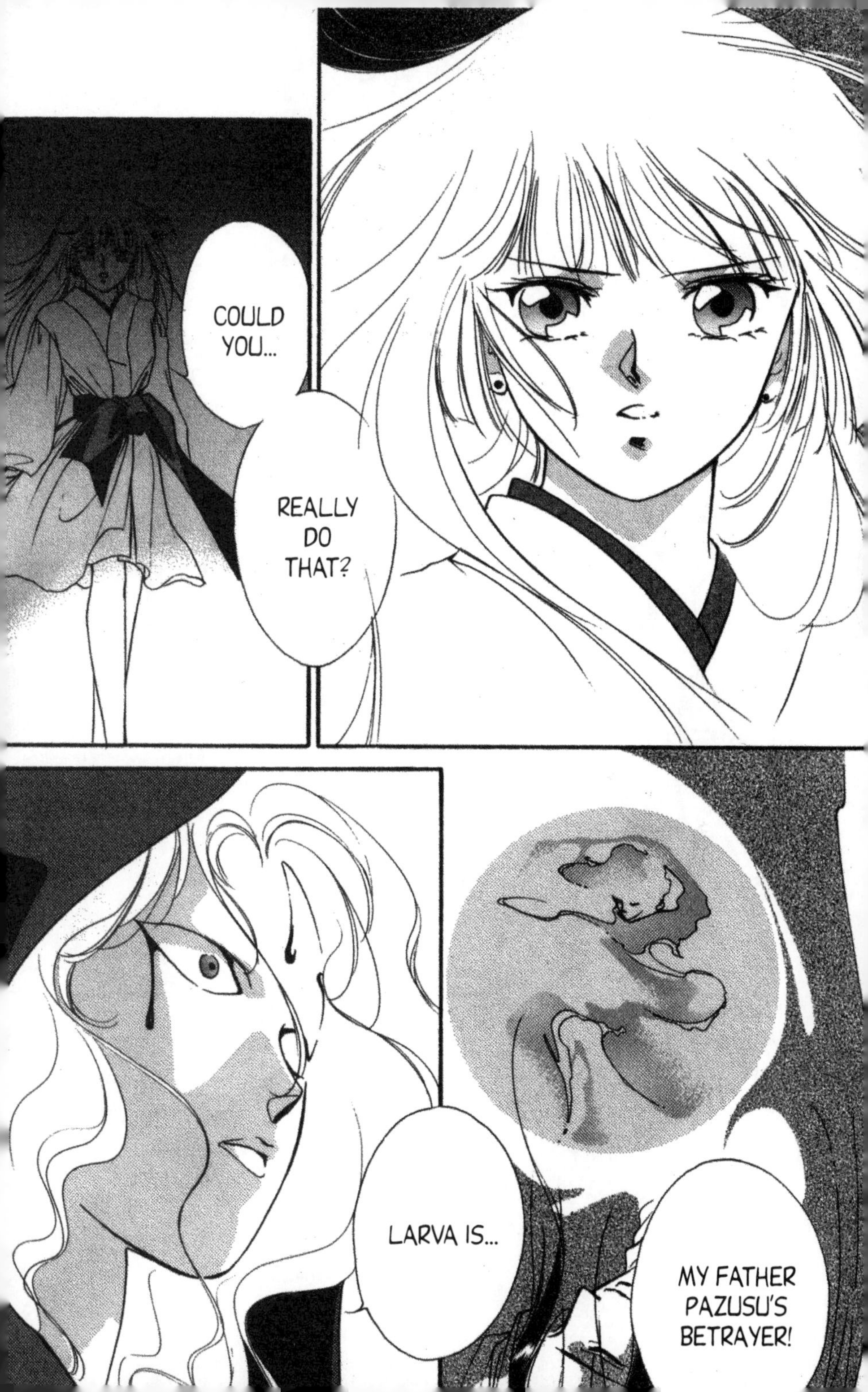
COULD YOU...
REALLY DO THAT?
MY FATHER PAZUSU'S BETRAYER!
LARVA IS...

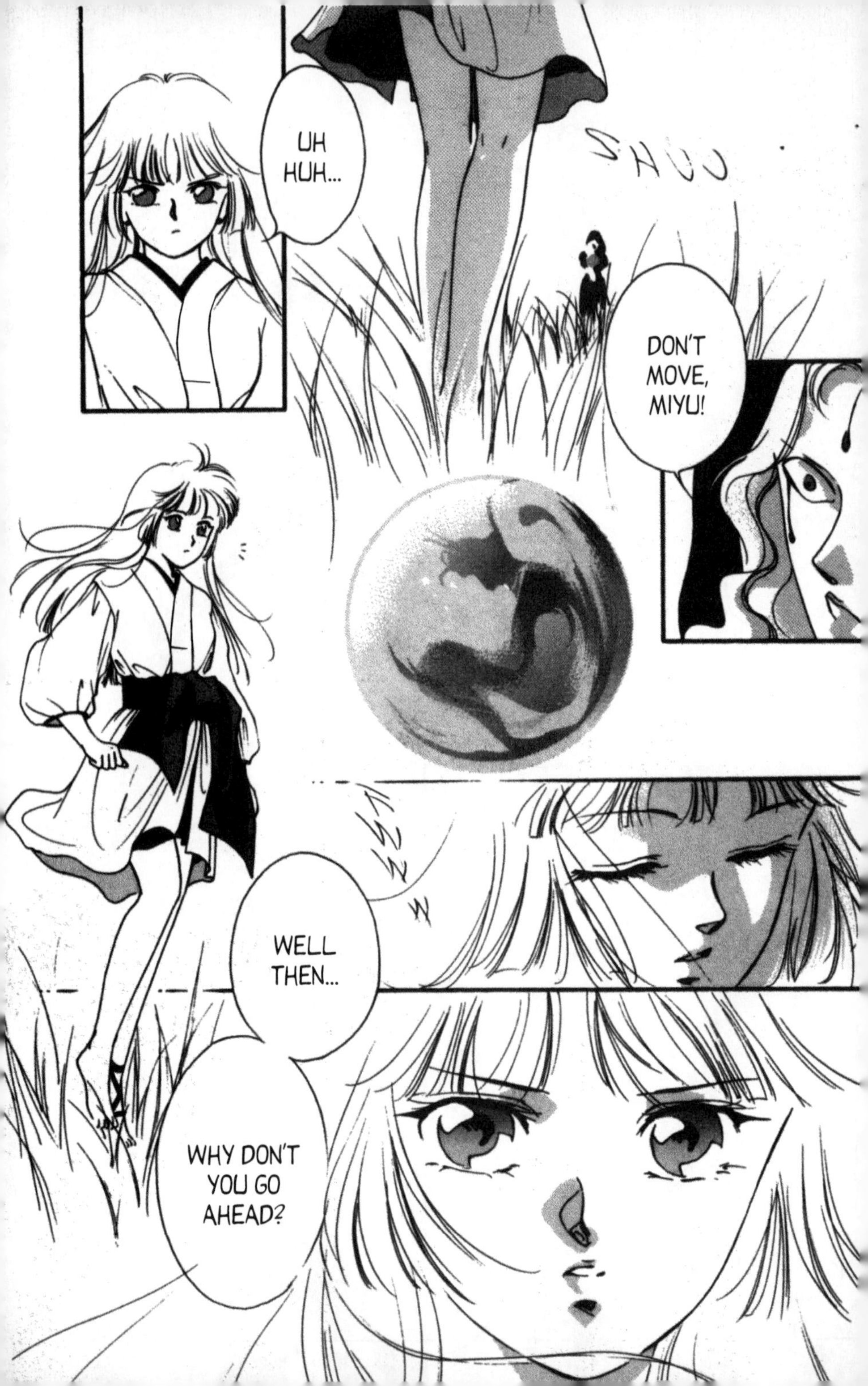
UH HUH...
DON'T MOVE, MIYU!
WELL THEN...
WHY DON'T YOU GO AHEAD?

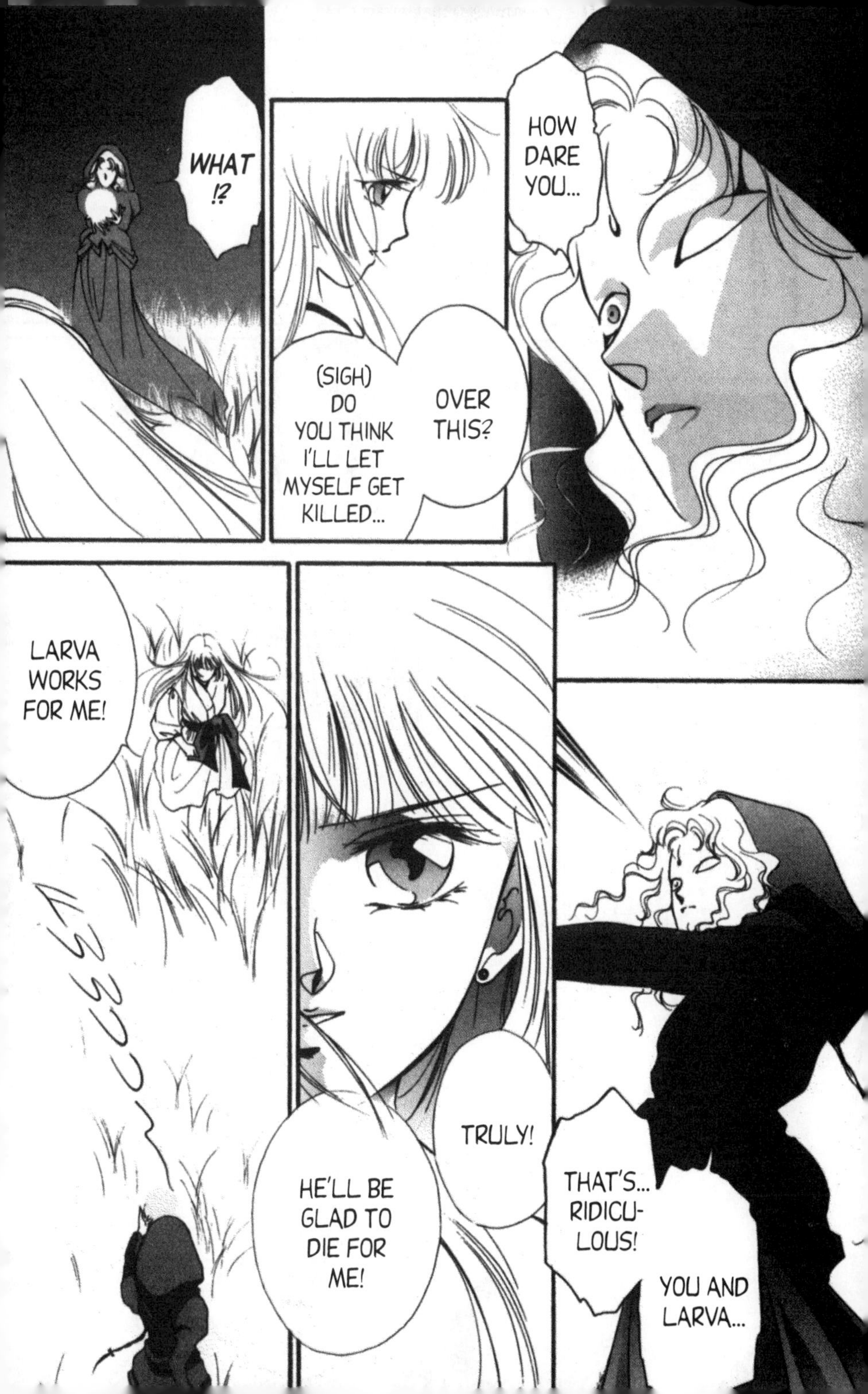
HOW DARE YOU...
(SIGH) DO YOU THINK I'LL LET MYSELF GET KILLED...
OVER THIS?
WHAT !?
THAT'S... RIDICU-LOUS!
YOU AND LARVA...
TRULY!
HE'LL BE GLAD TO DIE FOR ME!
LARVA WORKS FOR ME!

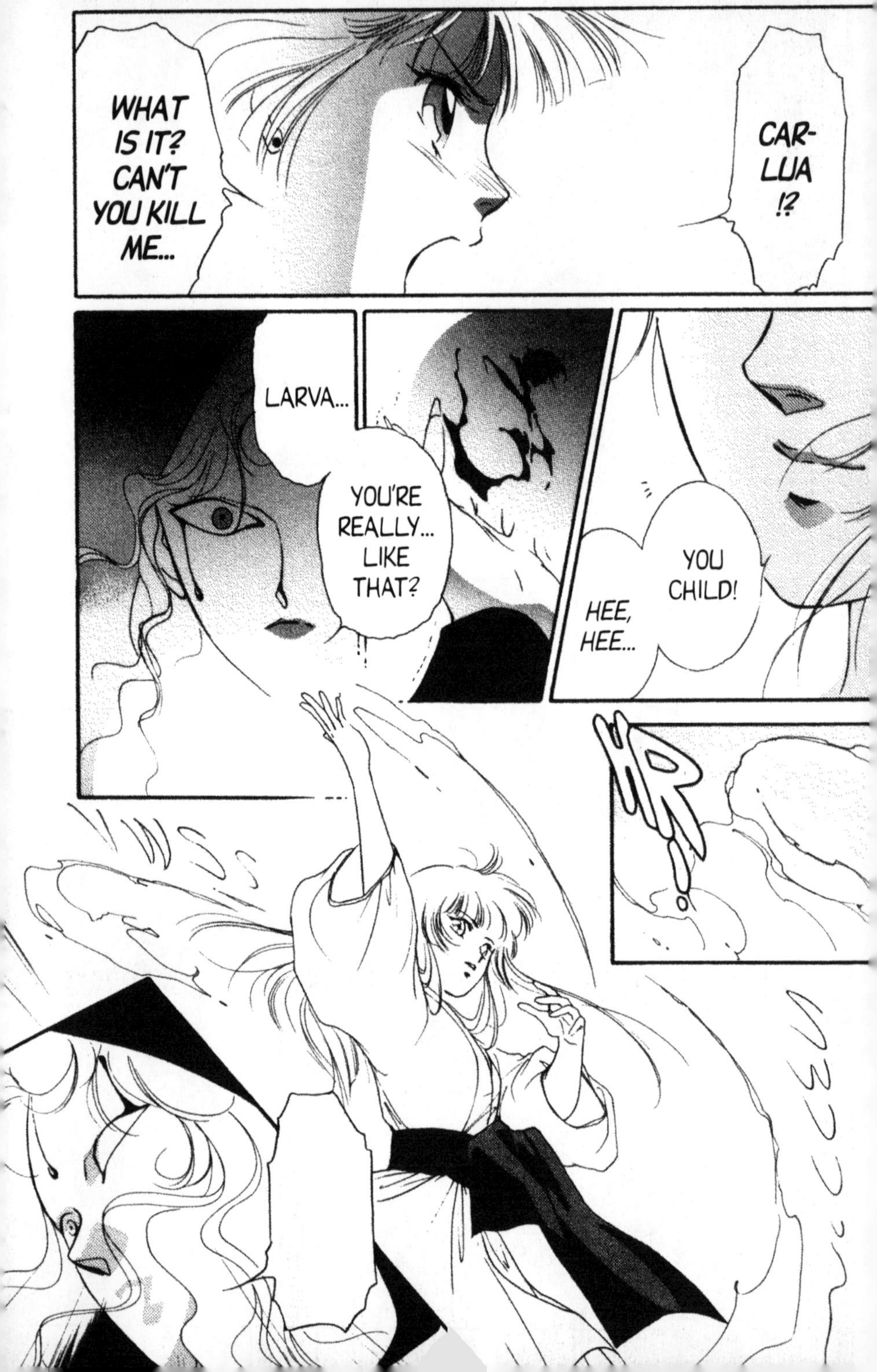
WHAT IS IT? CAN'T YOU KILL ME...
CAR-LUA!?
LARVA...
YOU'RE REALLY... LIKE THAT?
HEE, HEE...
YOU CHILD!
HR!

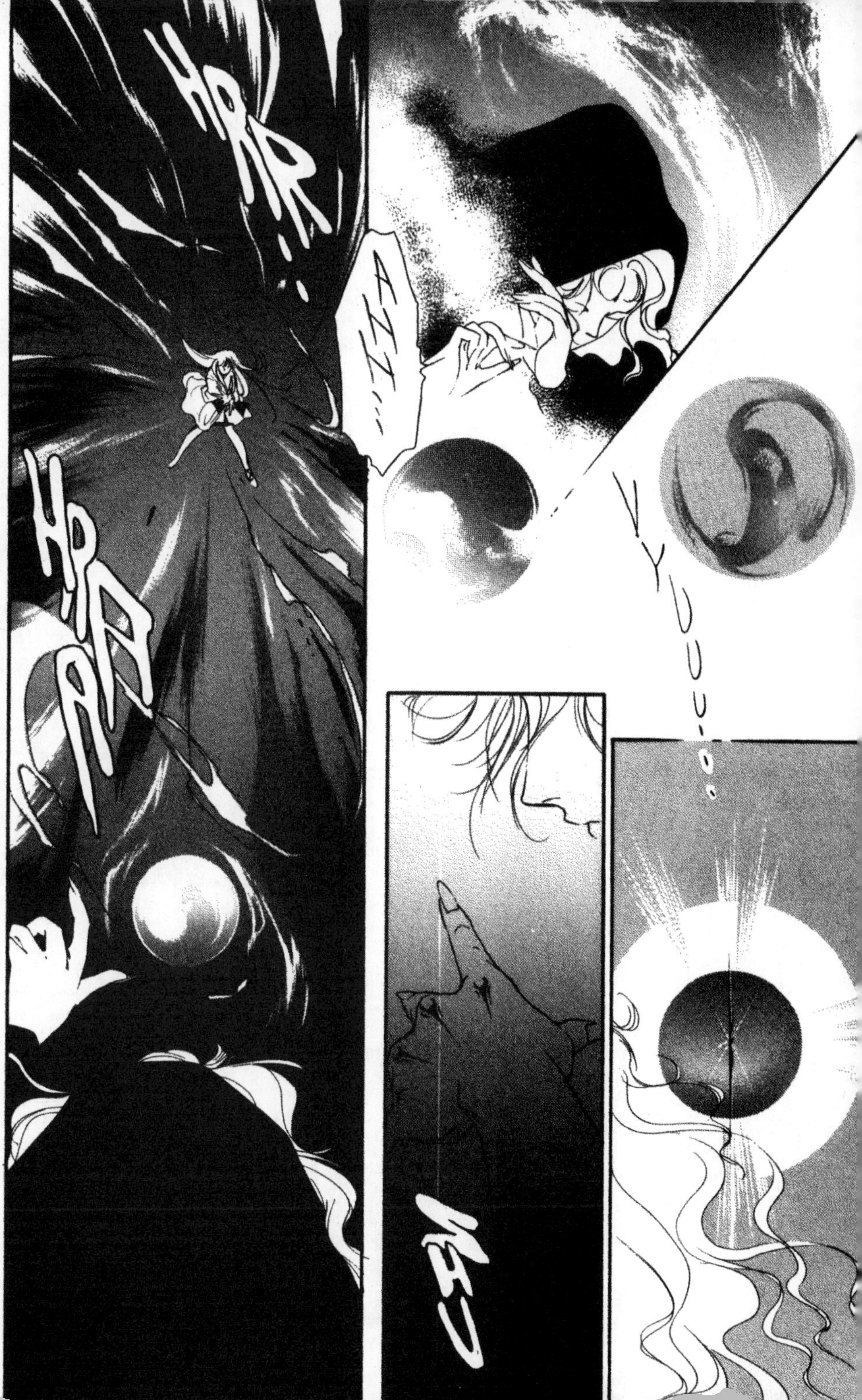
AHH...
VYUUUU...
HRRR...
HRRR

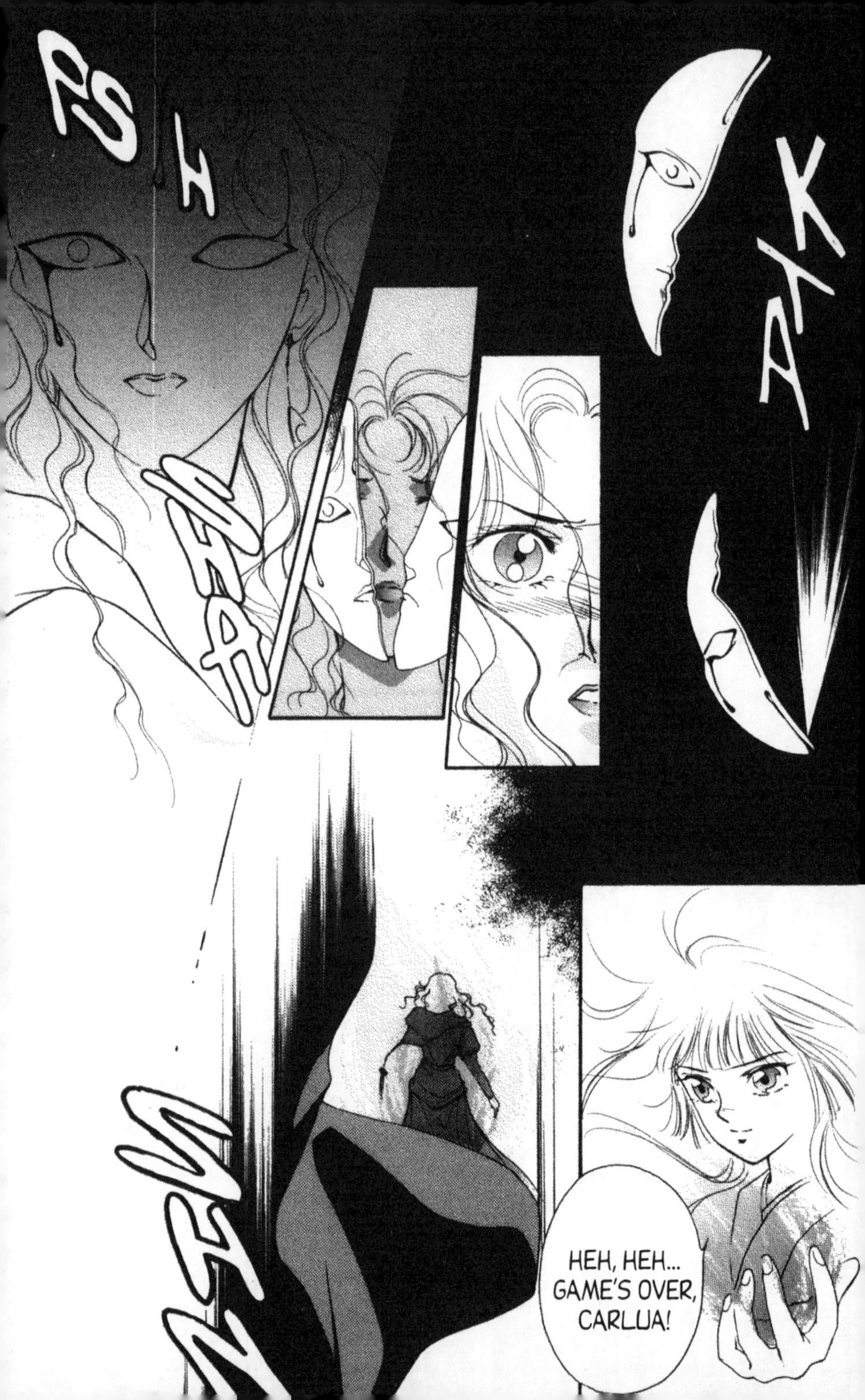

TAKK
PSSH
SHAA
SHIN
HEH, HEH... GAME'S OVER, CARLUA!

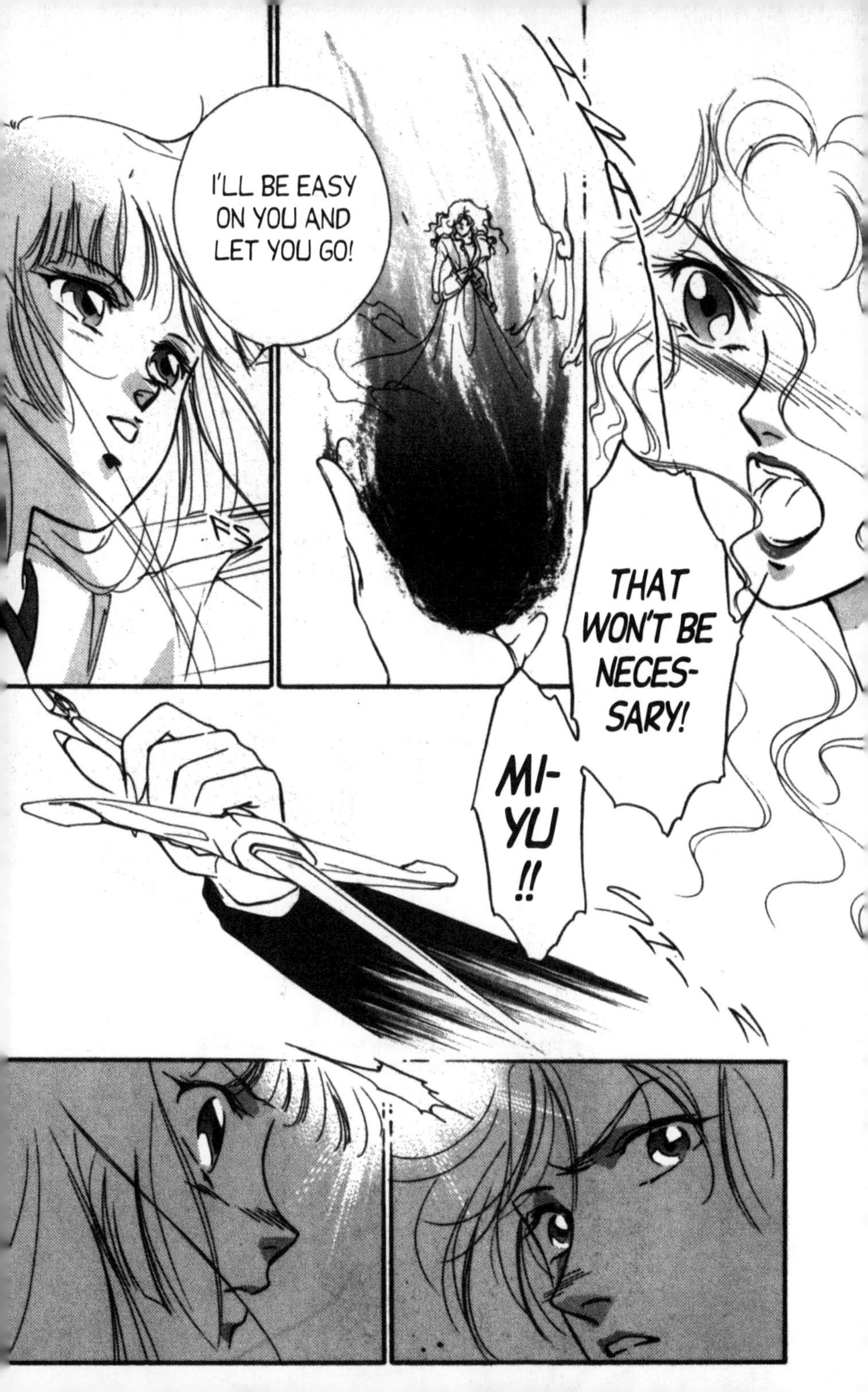
I'LL BE EASY ON YOU AND LET YOU GO!
FS
THAT WON'T BE NECES-SARY!
MI-YU!!

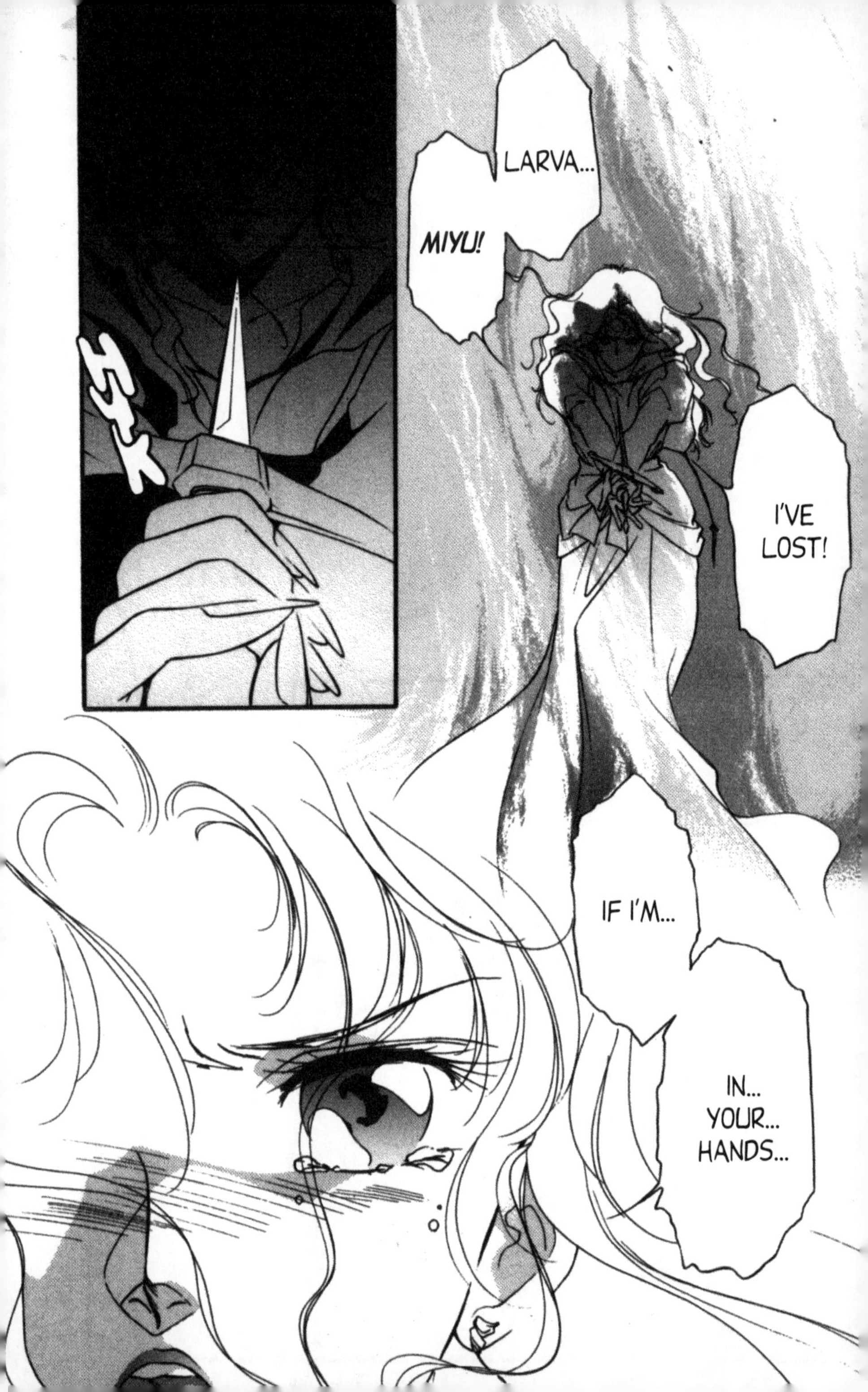
LARVA...
MIYU!
I'VE LOST!
IF I'M...
IN... YOUR... HANDS...

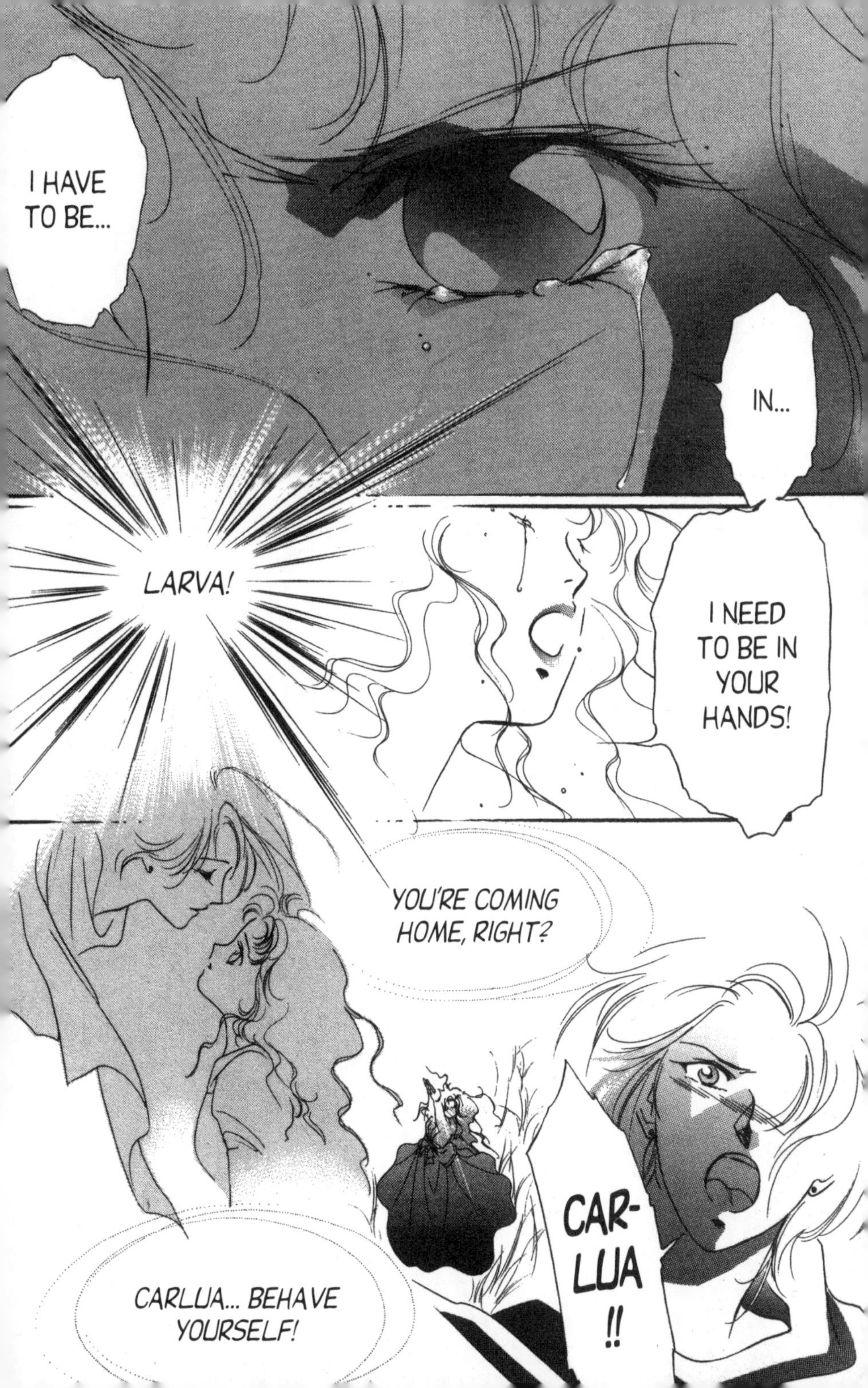
I HAVE TO BE...
IN...
LARVA!
I NEED TO BE IN YOUR HANDS!
YOU'RE COMING HOME, RIGHT?
CARLUA... BEHAVE YOURSELF!
CAR-LUA !!

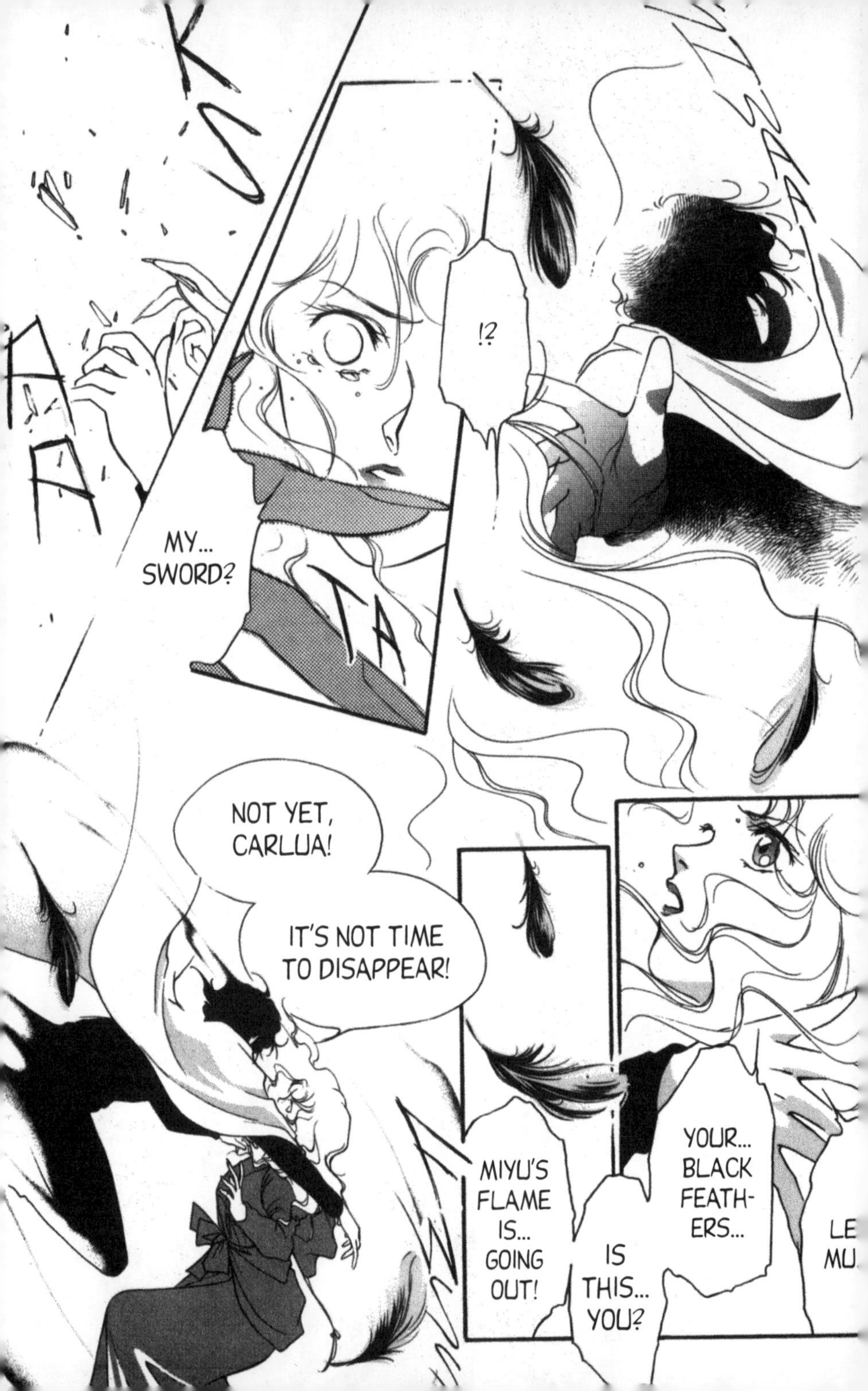
MY... SWORD?
TA
!?
NOT YET, CARLUA!
IT'S NOT TIME TO DISAPPEAR!
MIYU'S FLAME IS... GOING OUT!
YOUR... BLACK FEATH-ERS...
IS THIS... YOU?

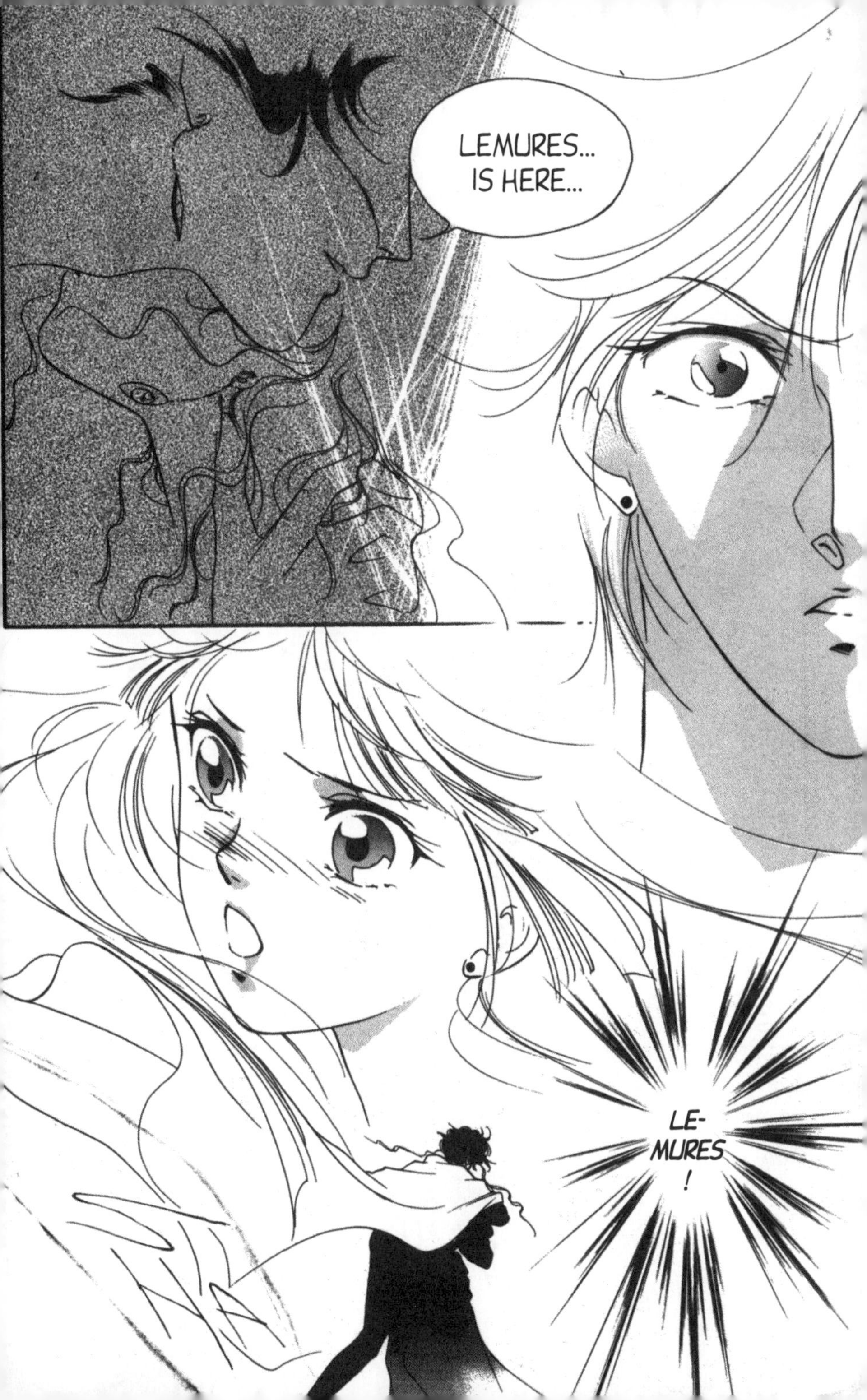
LEMURES... IS HERE...
LE-MURES!

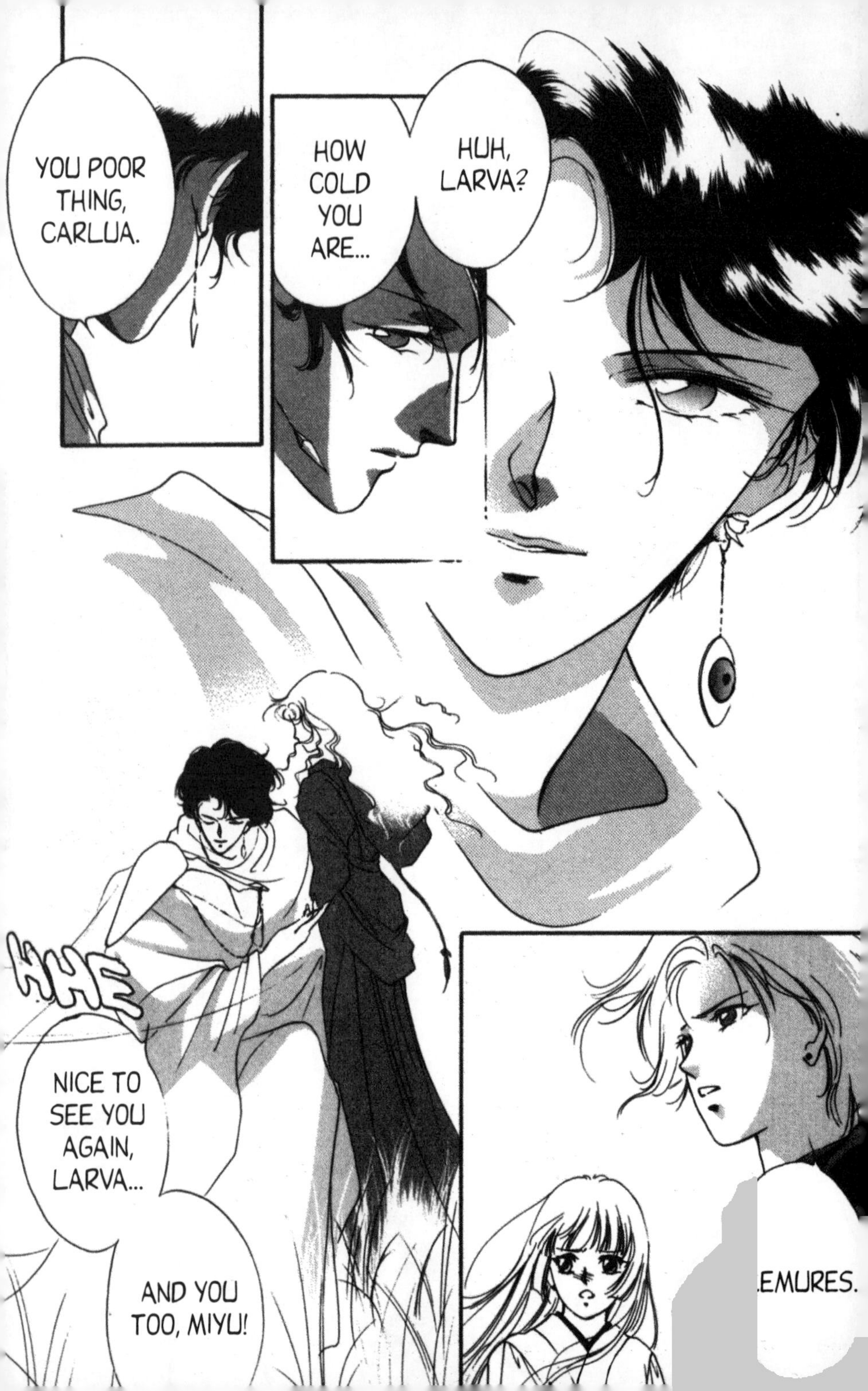
YOU POOR THING, CARLUA.
HOW COLD YOU ARE...
HUH, LARVA?
NICE TO SEE YOU AGAIN, LARVA...
AND YOU TOO, MIYU!
.EMURES.

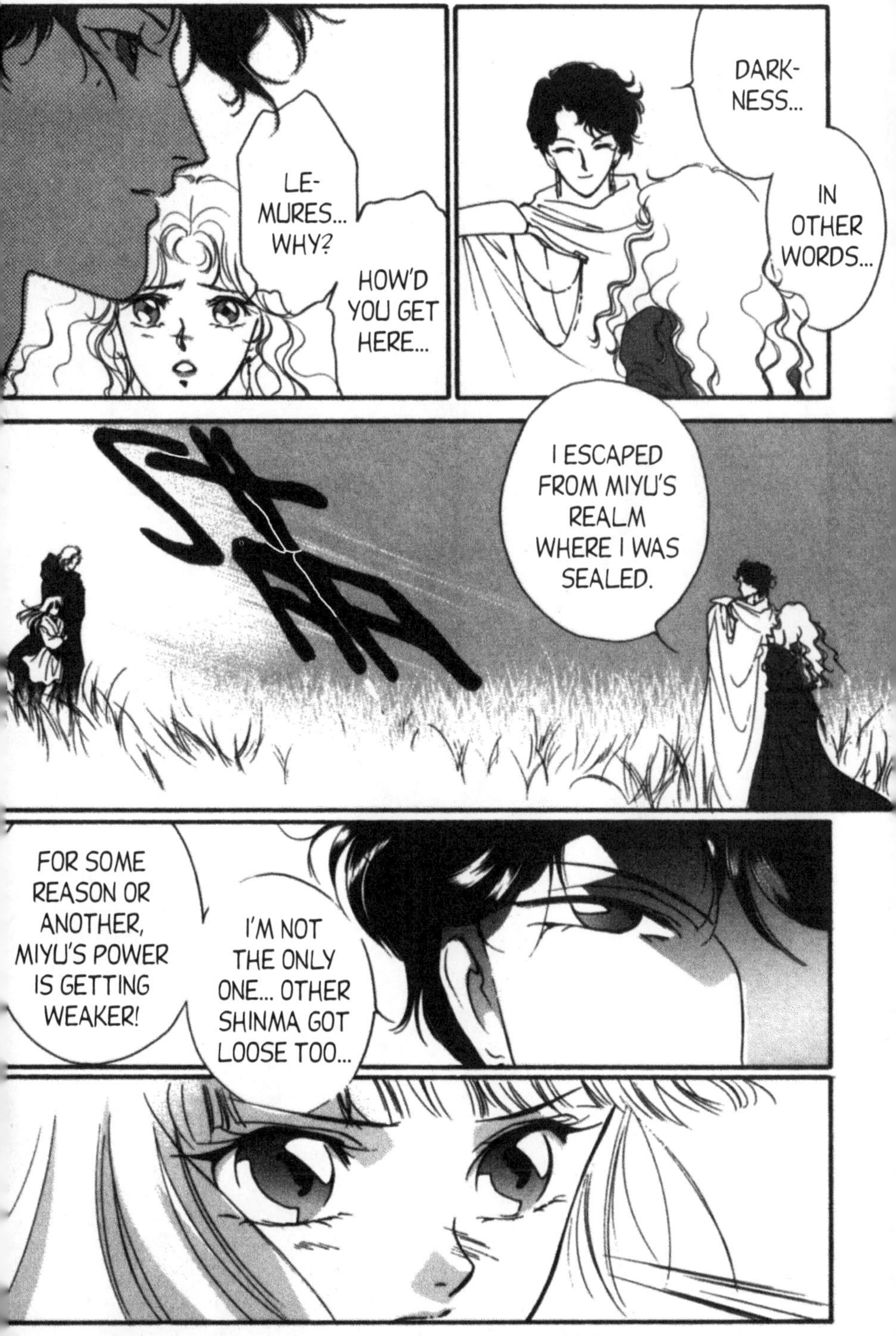
LE-MURES... WHY?
HOW'D YOU GET HERE...
DARK-NESS...
IN OTHER WORDS...
I ESCAPED FROM MIYU'S REALM WHERE I WAS SEALED.
FOR SOME REASON OR ANOTHER, MIYU'S POWER IS GETTING WEAKER!
I'M NOT THE ONLY ONE... OTHER SHINMA GOT LOOSE TOO...

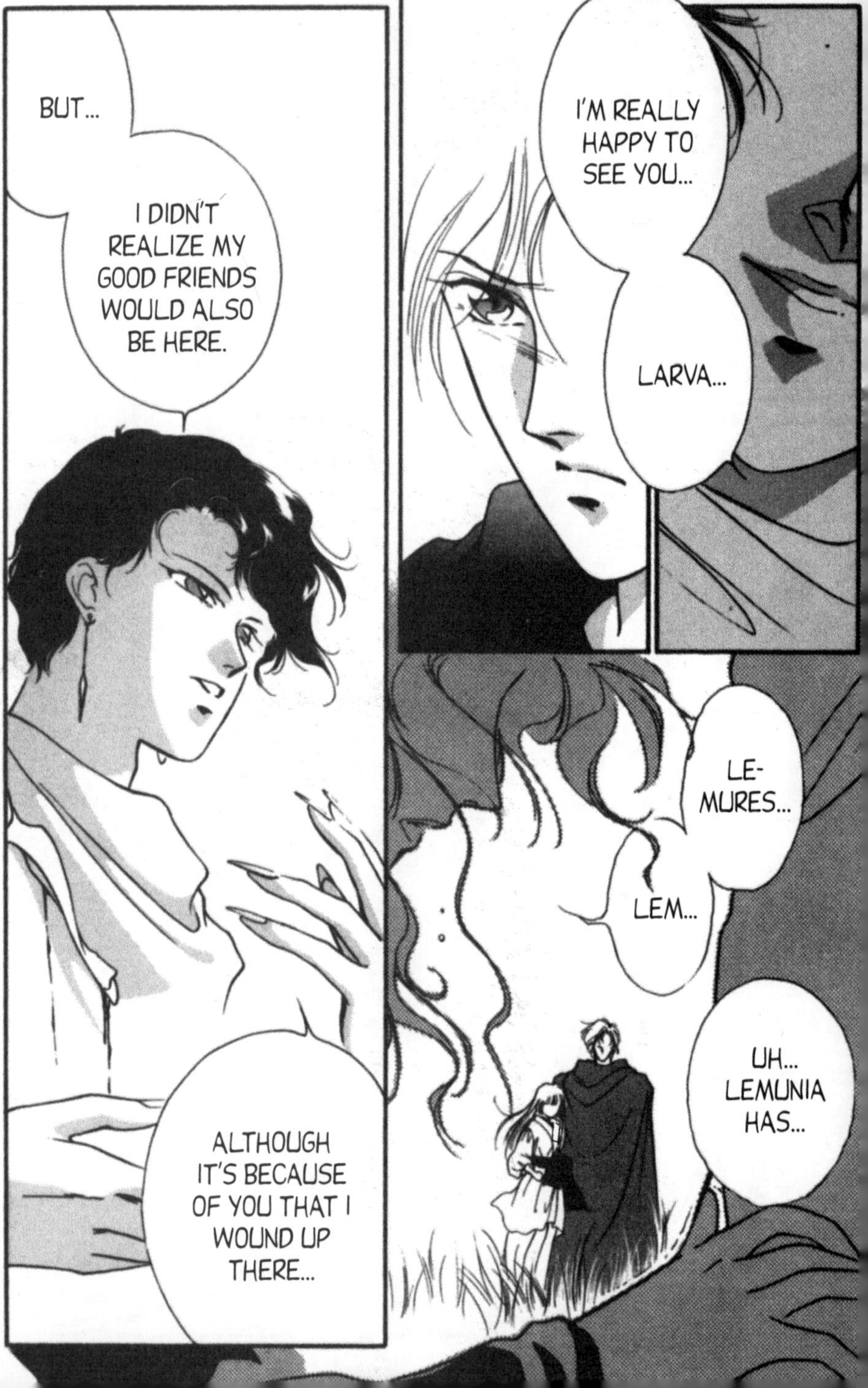
I'M REALLY HAPPY TO SEE YOU...
LARVA...
BUT...
I DIDN'T REALIZE MY GOOD FRIENDS WOULD ALSO BE HERE.
LE-MURES...
LEM...
UH... LEMUNIA HAS...
ALTHOUGH IT'S BECAUSE OF YOU THAT I WOUND UP THERE...

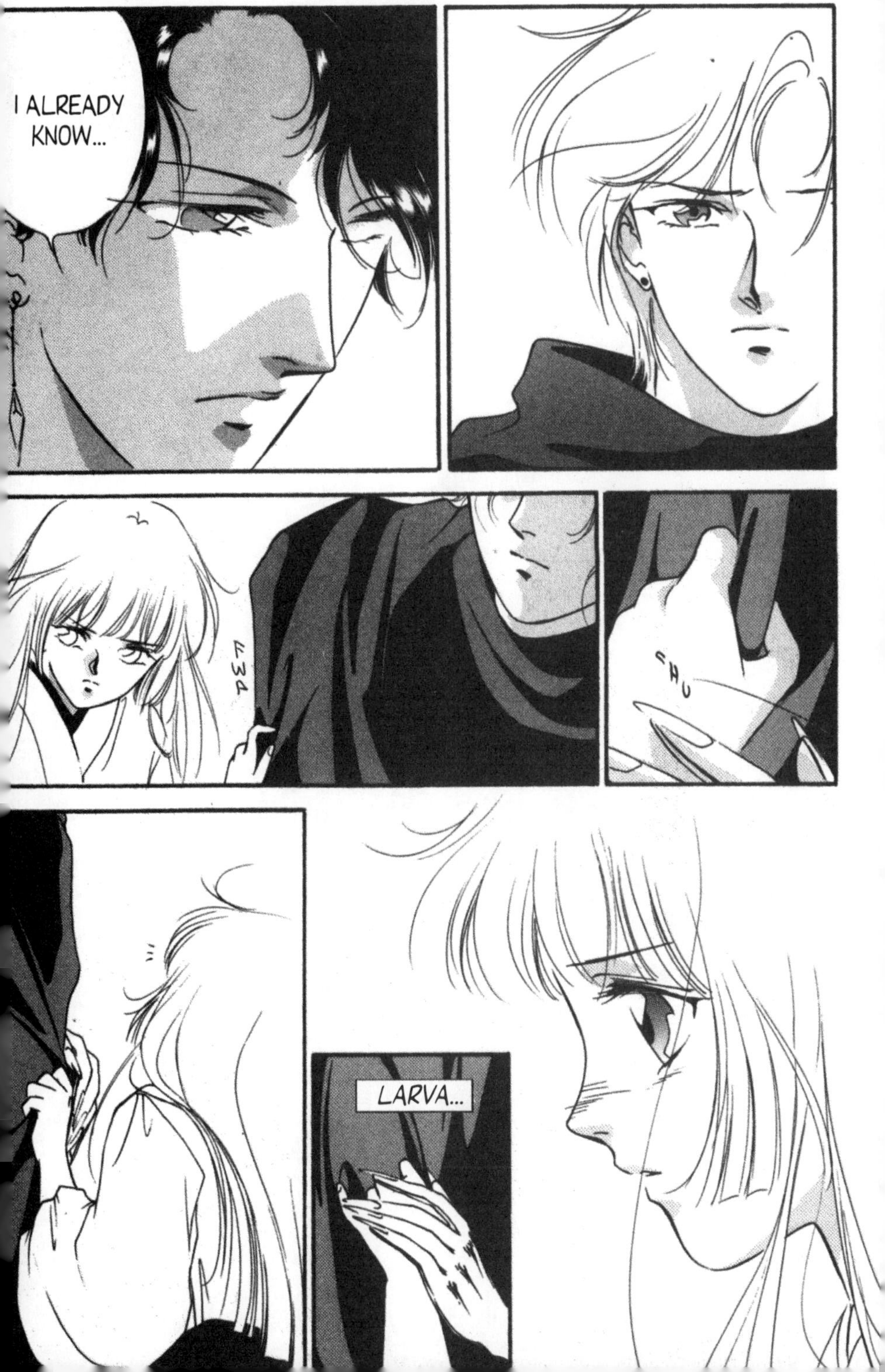
I ALREADY KNOW...
CHU
FWA
LARVA...

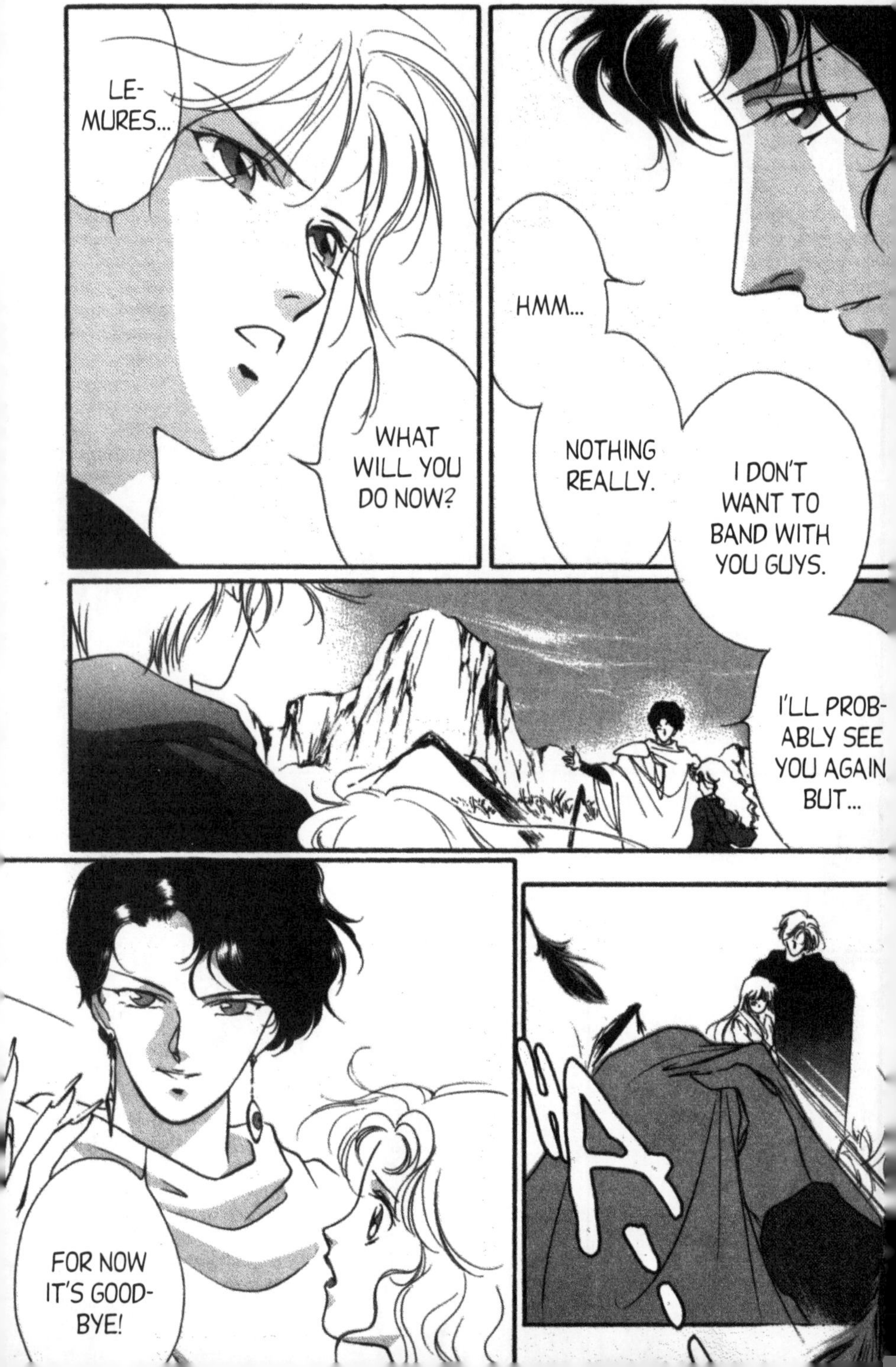
LE-
MURES...
WHAT WILL YOU DO NOW?
HMM...
NOTHING REALLY.
I DON'T WANT TO BAND WITH YOU GUYS.
I'LL PROBABLY SEE YOU AGAIN BUT...
FOR NOW IT'S GOOD-BYE!
HA...

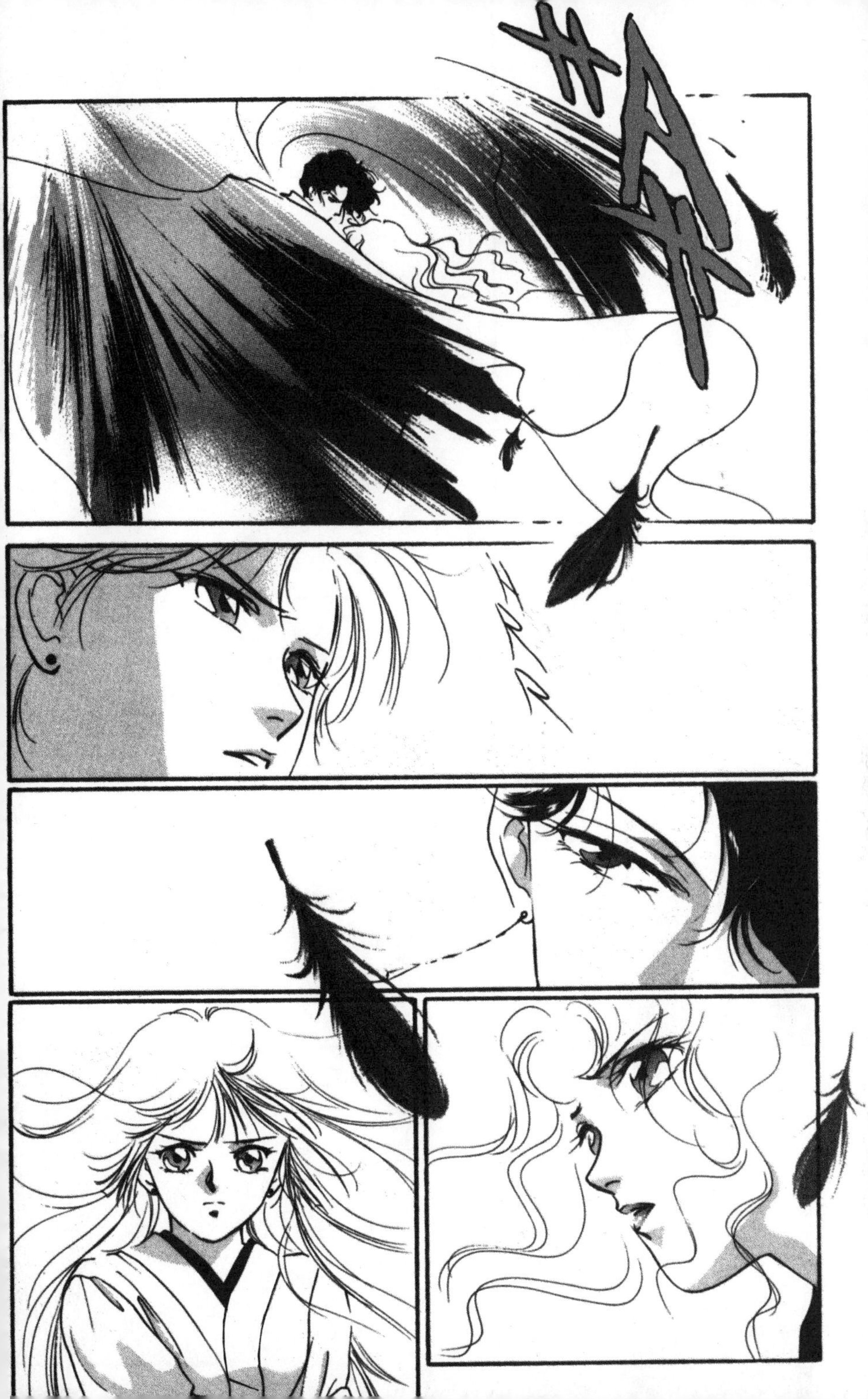

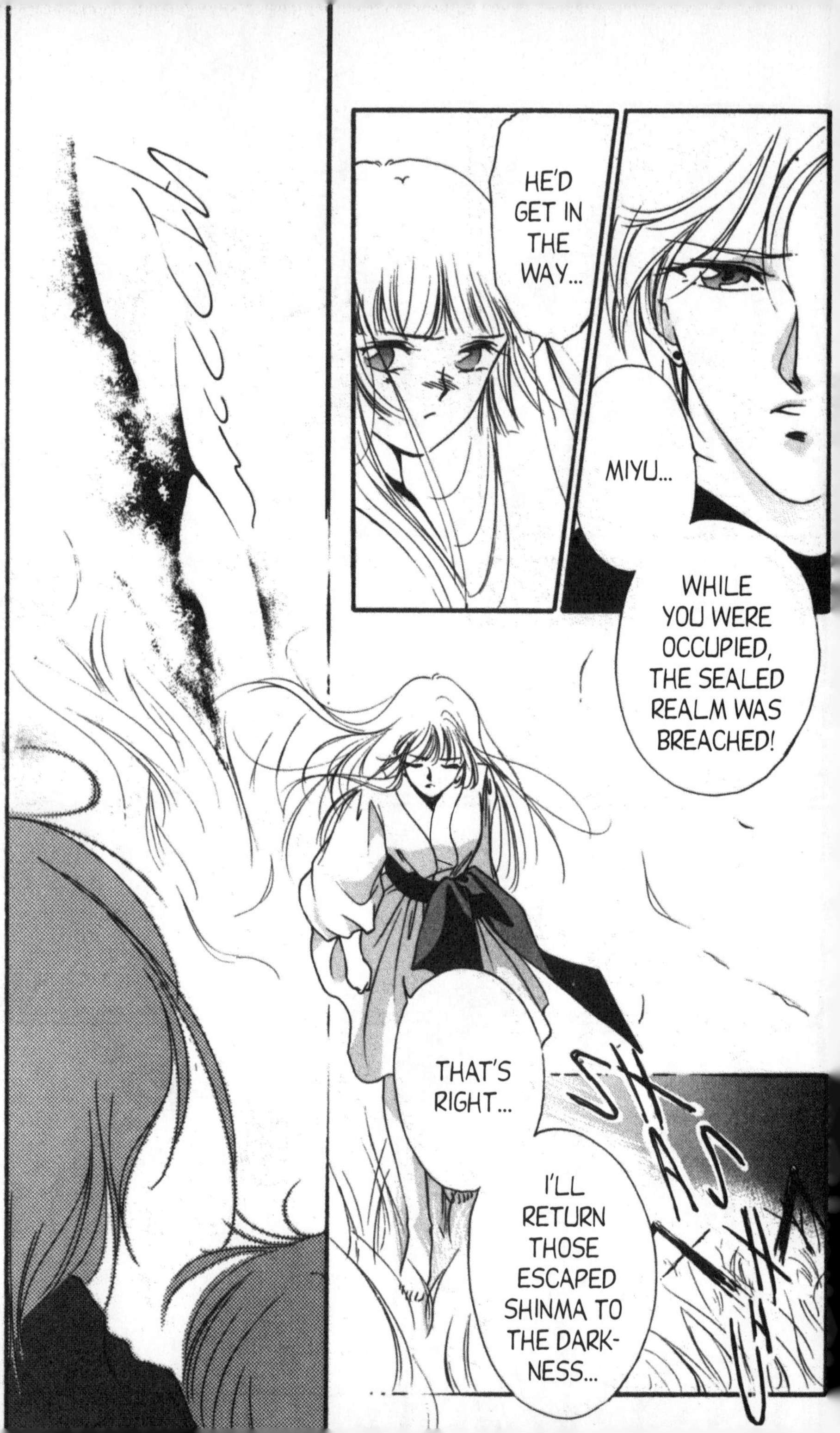
MIYU...
HE'D GET IN THE WAY...
WHILE YOU WERE OCCUPIED, THE SEALED REALM WAS BREACHED!
THAT'S RIGHT...
I'LL RETURN THOSE ESCAPED SHINMA TO THE DARK-NESS...
SHASHH

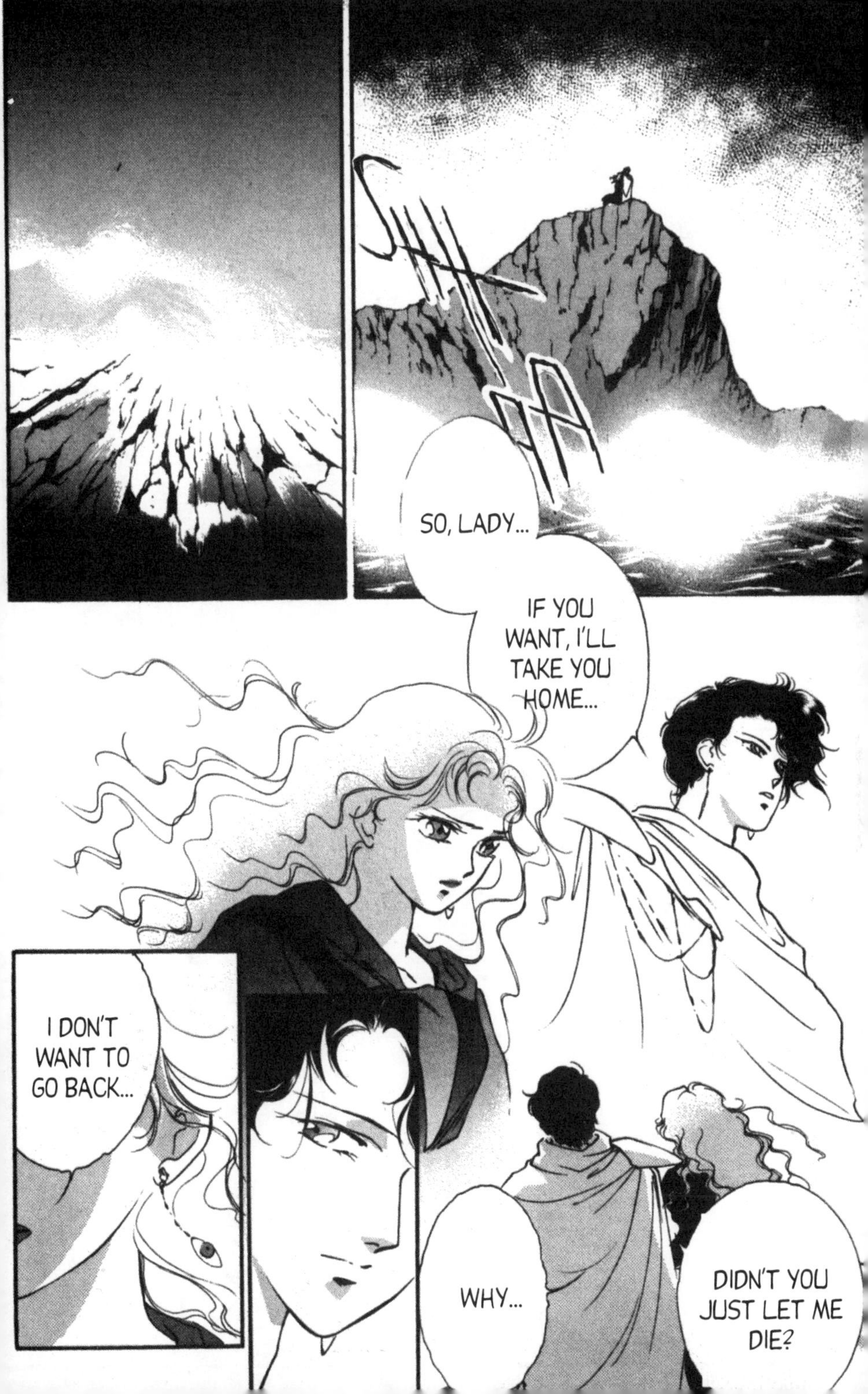
SHHAA
SO, LADY...
IF YOU WANT, I'LL TAKE YOU HOME...
I DON'T WANT TO GO BACK...
WHY...
DIDN'T YOU JUST LET ME DIE?

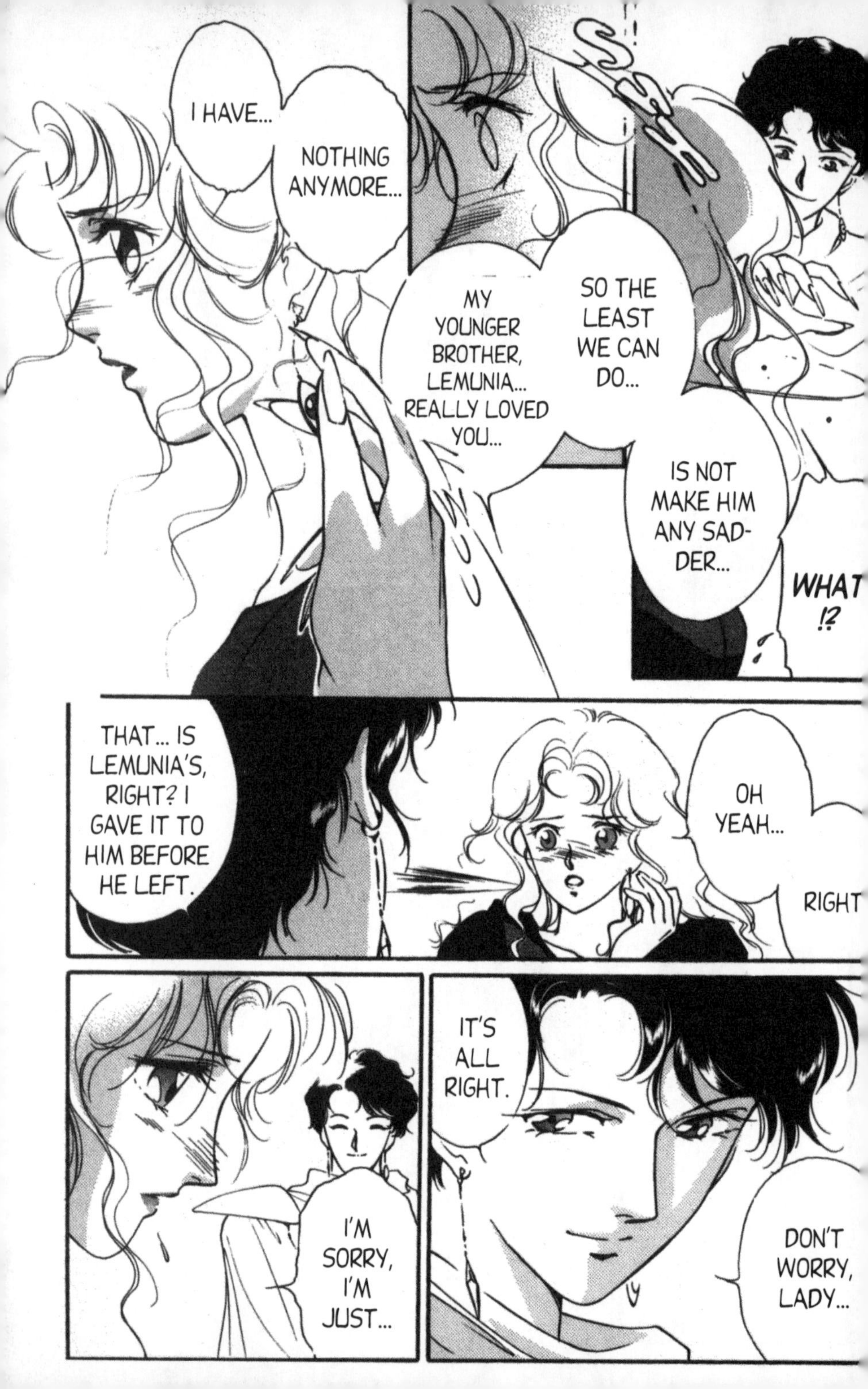
I HAVE...
NOTHING ANYMORE...
MY YOUNGER BROTHER, LEMUNIA... REALLY LOVED YOU...
SO THE LEAST WE CAN DO...
IS NOT MAKE HIM ANY SADDER...
WHAT !?
THAT... IS LEMUNIA'S, RIGHT? I GAVE IT TO HIM BEFORE HE LEFT.
OH YEAH...
RIGHT
I'M SORRY, I'M JUST...
IT'S ALL RIGHT.
DON'T WORRY, LADY...

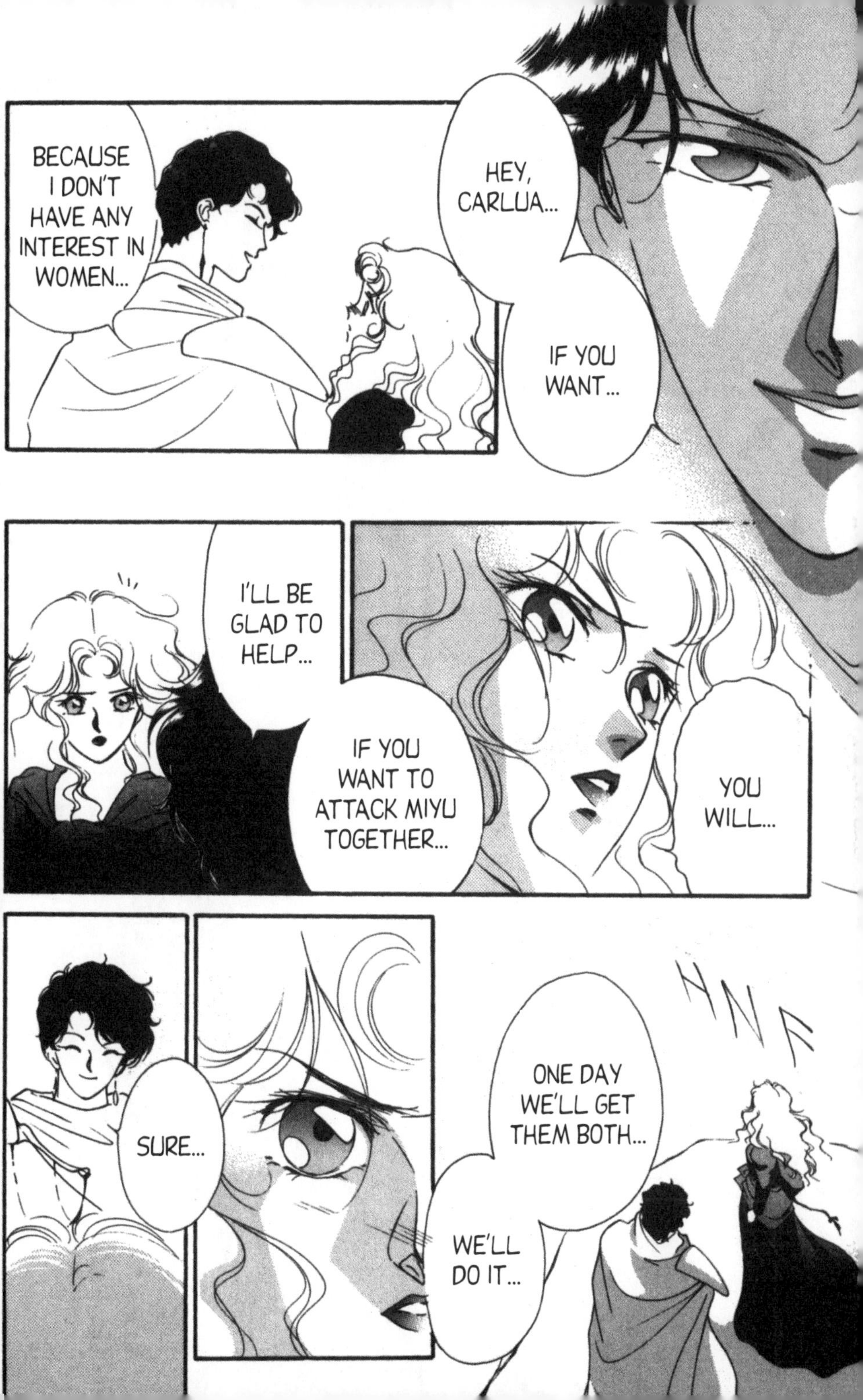
BECAUSE I DON'T HAVE ANY INTEREST IN WOMEN...
HEY, CARLUA...
IF YOU WANT...
I'LL BE GLAD TO HELP...
IF YOU WANT TO ATTACK MIYU TOGETHER...
YOU WILL...
SURE...
ONE DAY WE'LL GET THEM BOTH...
WE'LL DO IT...
HNF

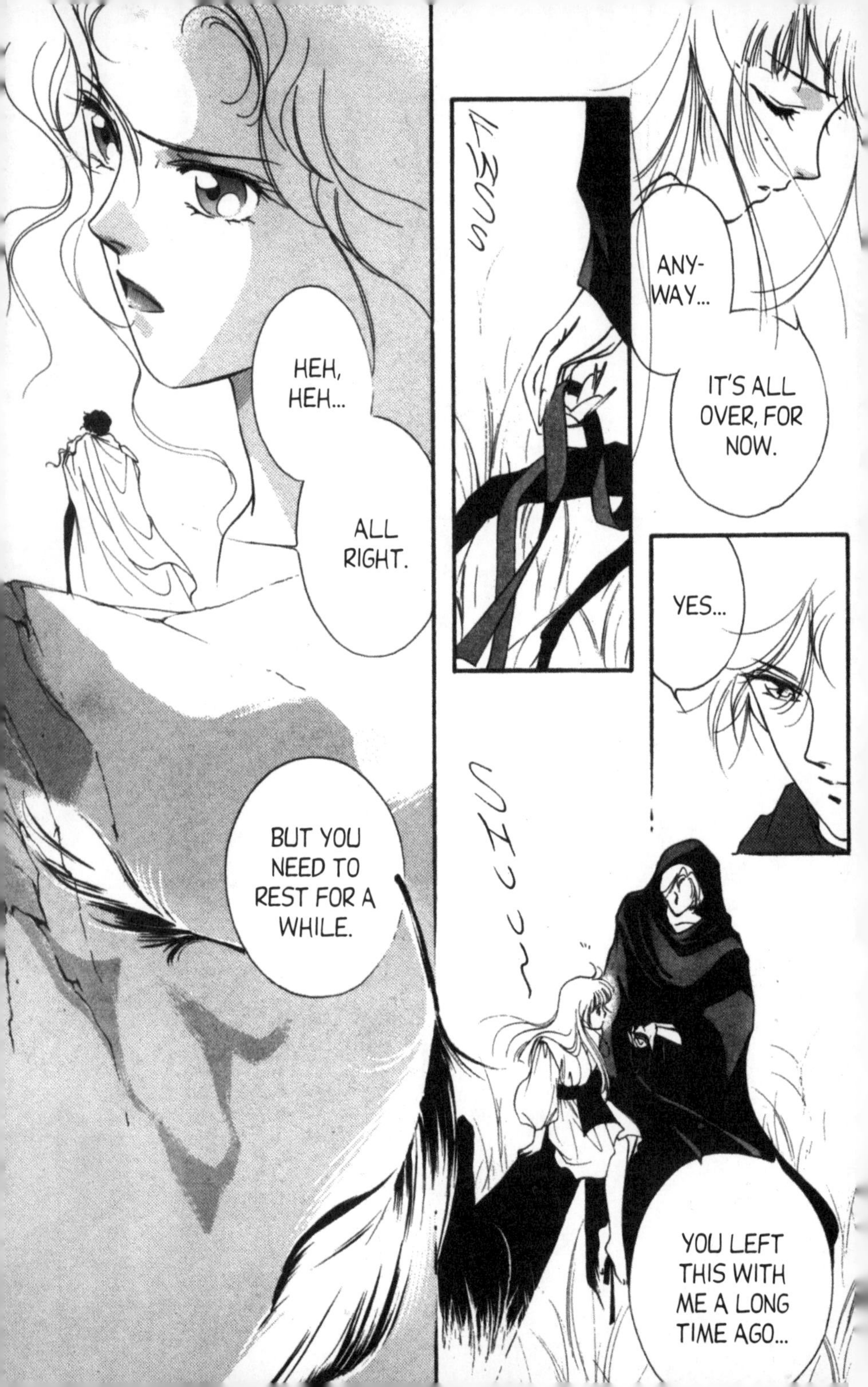
ANY-WAY...
IT'S ALL OVER, FOR NOW.
YES...
YOU LEFT THIS WITH ME A LONG TIME AGO...
HEH, HEH...
ALL RIGHT.
BUT YOU NEED TO REST FOR A WHILE.

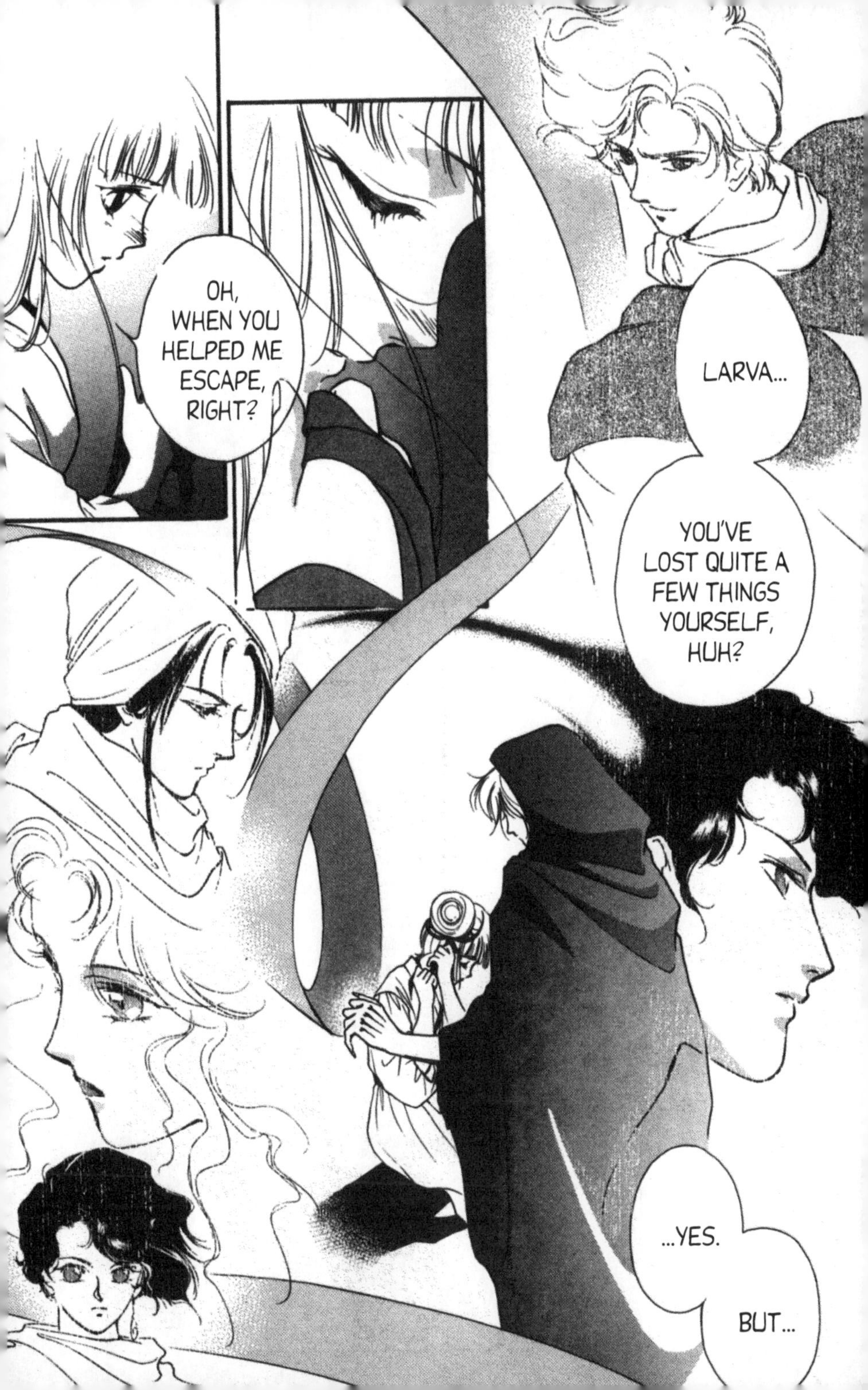
LARVA...
YOU'VE LOST QUITE A FEW THINGS YOURSELF, HUH?
OH, WHEN YOU HELPED ME ESCAPE, RIGHT?
...YES.
BUT...

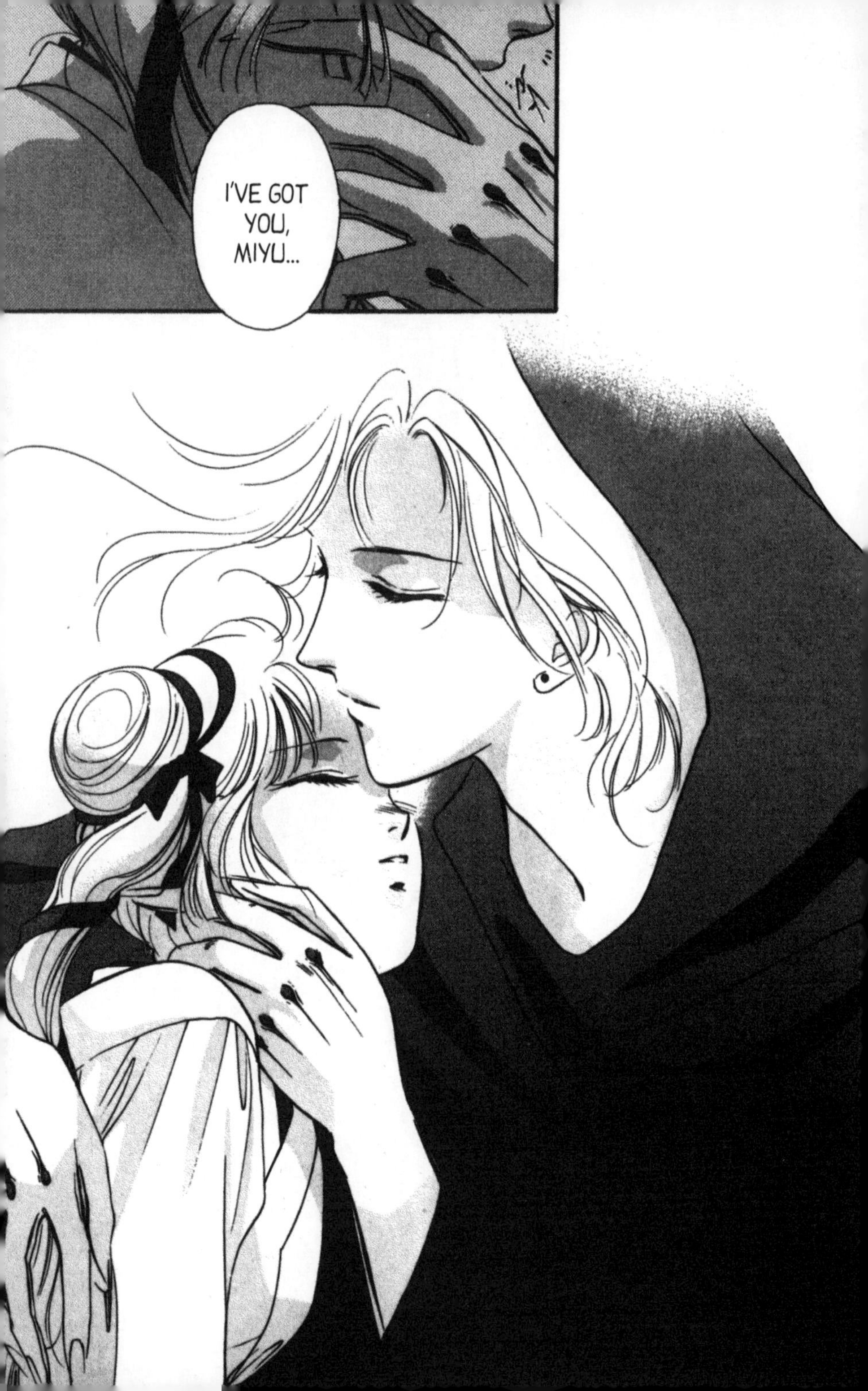
I'VE GOT YOU, MIYU...

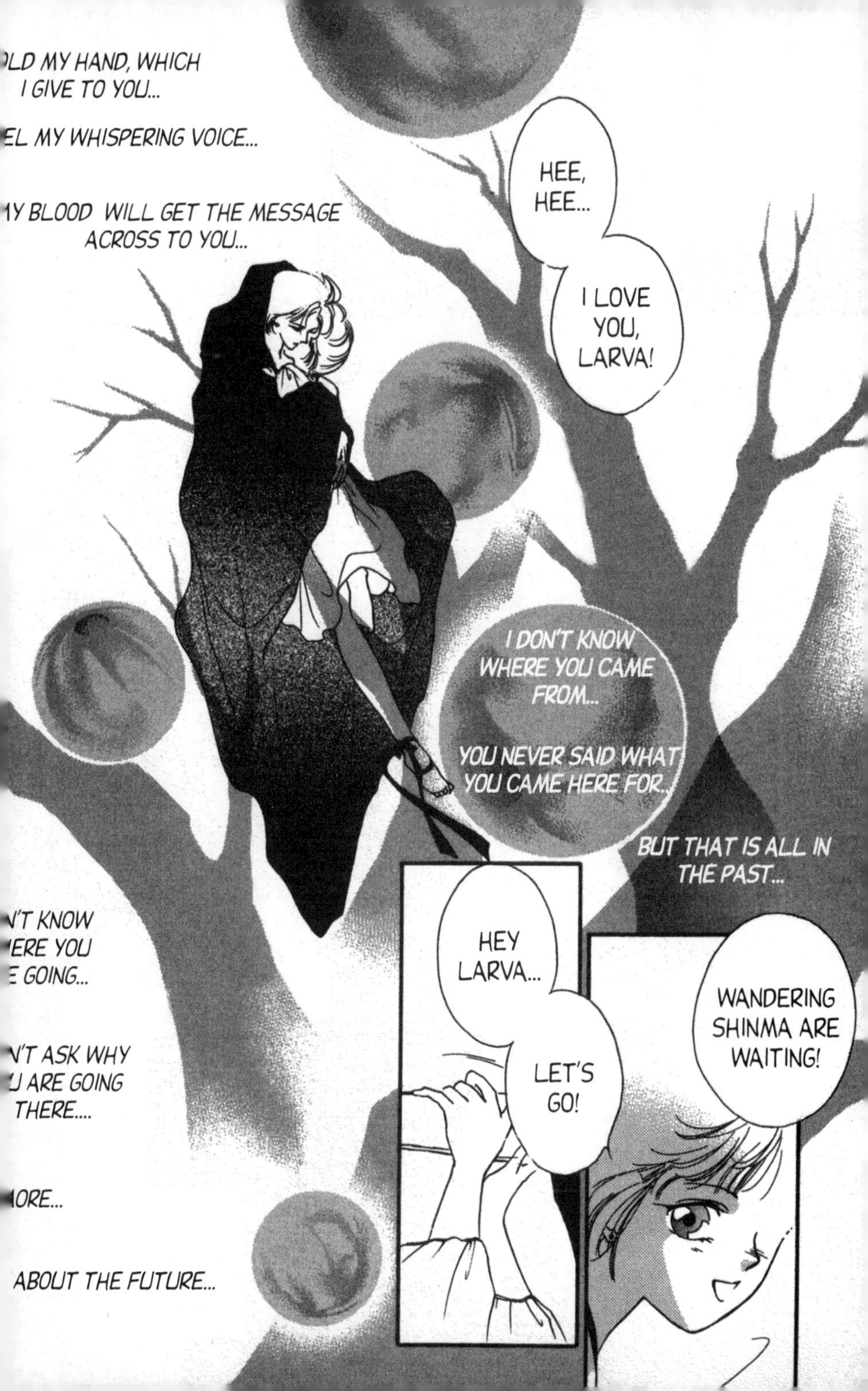
LD MY HAND, WHICH I GIVE TO YOU...
EL MY WHISPERING VOICE...
Y BLOOD WILL GET THE MESSAGE ACROSS TO YOU...
HEE, HEE...
I LOVE YOU, LARVA!
I DON'T KNOW WHERE YOU CAME FROM...
YOU NEVER SAID WHAT YOU CAME HERE FOR...
BUT THAT IS ALL IN THE PAST...
'T KNOW ERE YOU GOING...
'T ASK WHY ARE GOING THERE....
ORE...
ABOUT THE FUTURE...
HEY LARVA...
LET'S GO!
WANDERING SHINMA ARE WAITING!

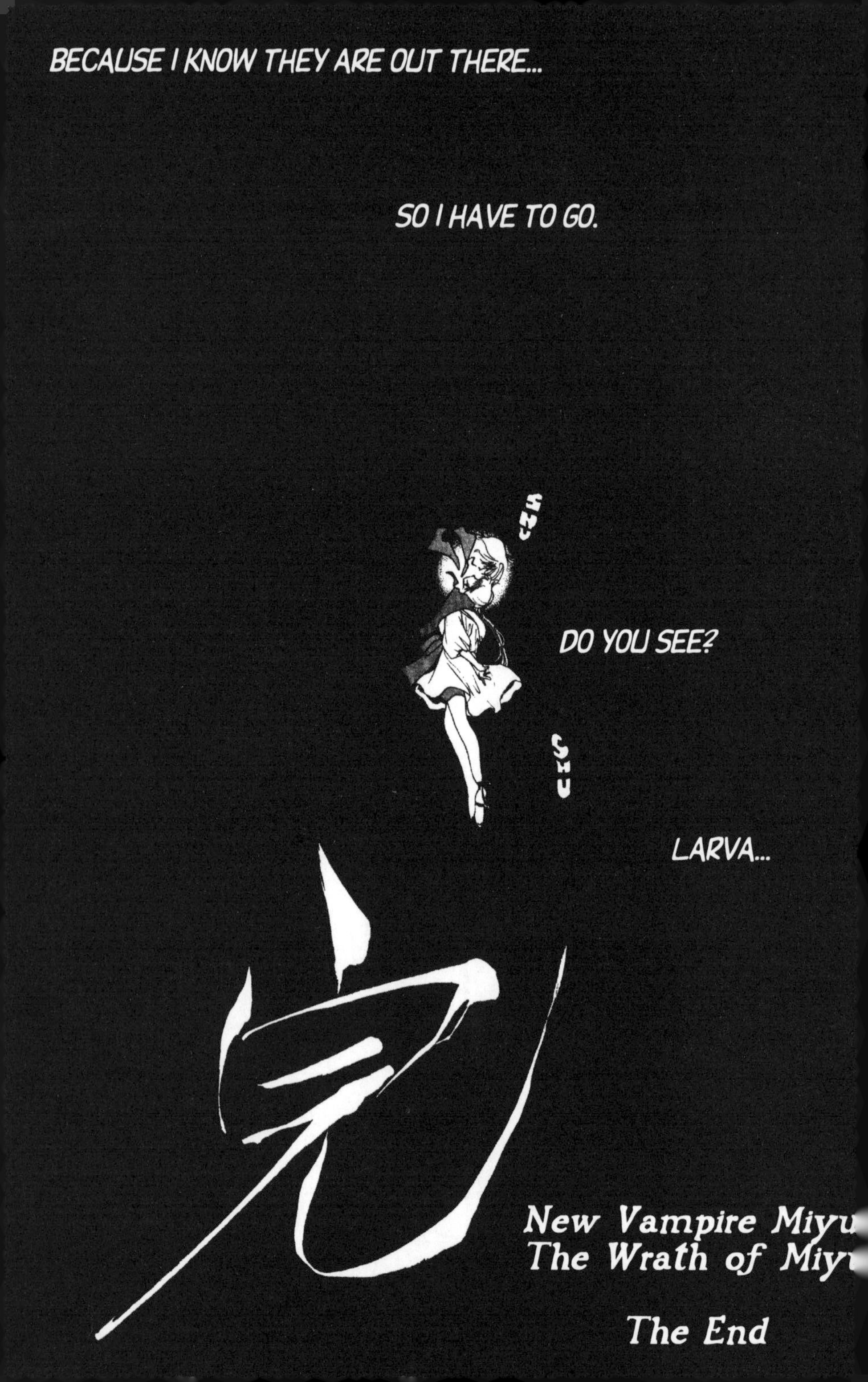
BECAUSE I KNOW THEY ARE OUT THERE...
SO I HAVE TO GO.
SHU
DO YOU SEE?
SHU
LARVA...
完
New Vampire Miyu
The Wrath of Miy
The End

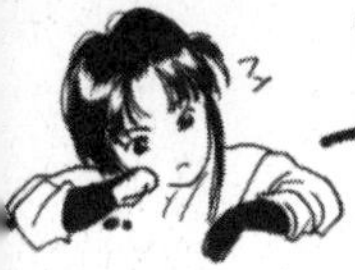

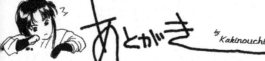

あとがき

by Kakinouchi

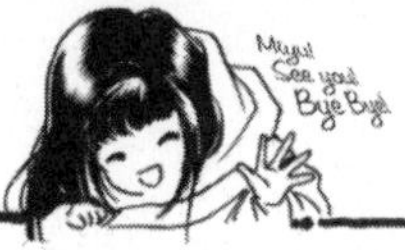
Miyu! See you! Bye Bye!

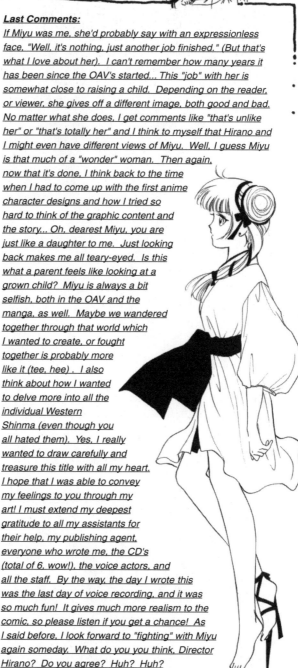

Last Comments:

If Miyu was me, she'd probably say with an expressionless face, "Well, it's nothing, just another job finished." (But that's what I love about her). I can't remember how many years it has been since the OAV's started... This "job" with her is somewhat close to raising a child. Depending on the reader, or viewer, she gives off a different image, both good and bad. No matter what she does, I get comments like "that's unlike her" or "that's totally her" and I think to myself that Hirano and I might even have different views of Miyu. Well, I guess Miyu is that much of a "wonder" woman. Then again, now that it's done, I think back to the time when I had to come up with the first anime character designs and how I tried so hard to think of the graphic content and the story... Oh, dearest Miyu, you are just like a daughter to me. Just looking back makes me all teary-eyed. Is this what a parent feels like looking at a grown child? Miyu is always a bit selfish, both in the OAV and the manga, as well. Maybe we wandered together through that world which I wanted to create, or fought together is probably more like it (tee, hee) . I also think about how I wanted to delve more into all the individual Western Shinma (even though you all hated them). Yes, I really wanted to draw carefully and treasure this title with all my heart. I hope that I was able to convey my feelings to you through my art! I must extend my deepest gratitude to all my assistants for their help, my publishing agent, everyone who wrote me, the CD's (total of 6, wow!), the voice actors, and all the staff. By the way, the day I wrote this was the last day of voice recording, and it was so much fun! It gives much more realism to the comic, so please listen if you get a chance! As I said before, I look forward to "fighting" with Miyu again someday. What do you you think, Director Hirano? Do you agree? Huh? Huh?

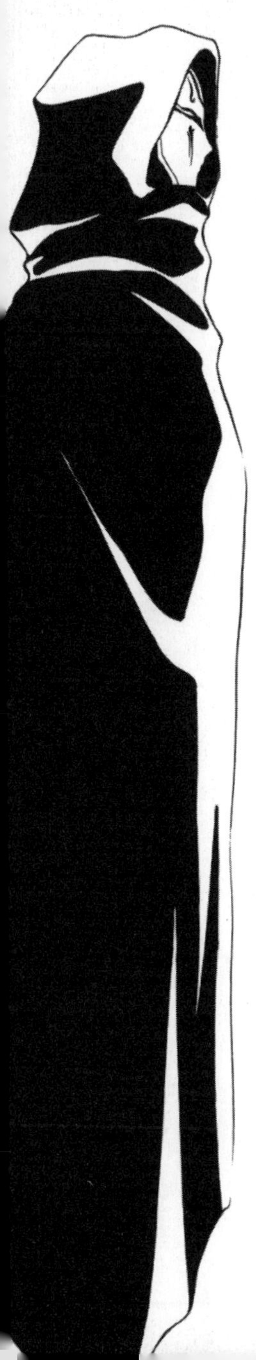

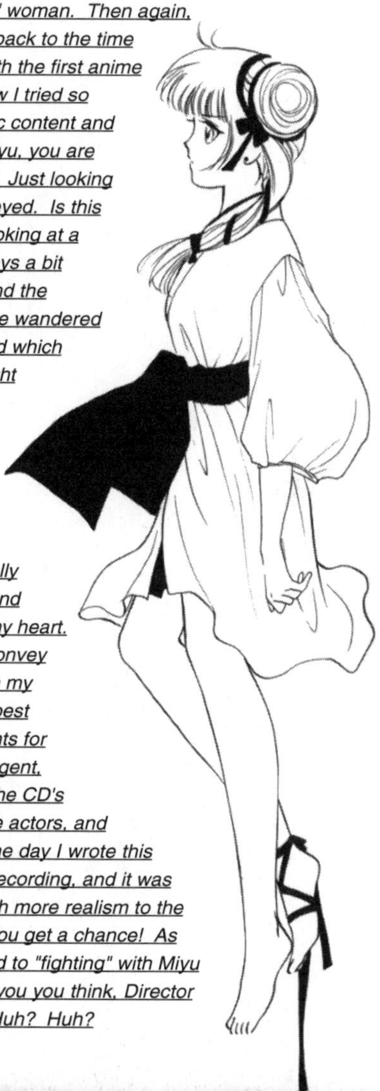

This is my sweet (sister's) section. Good job, everyone!

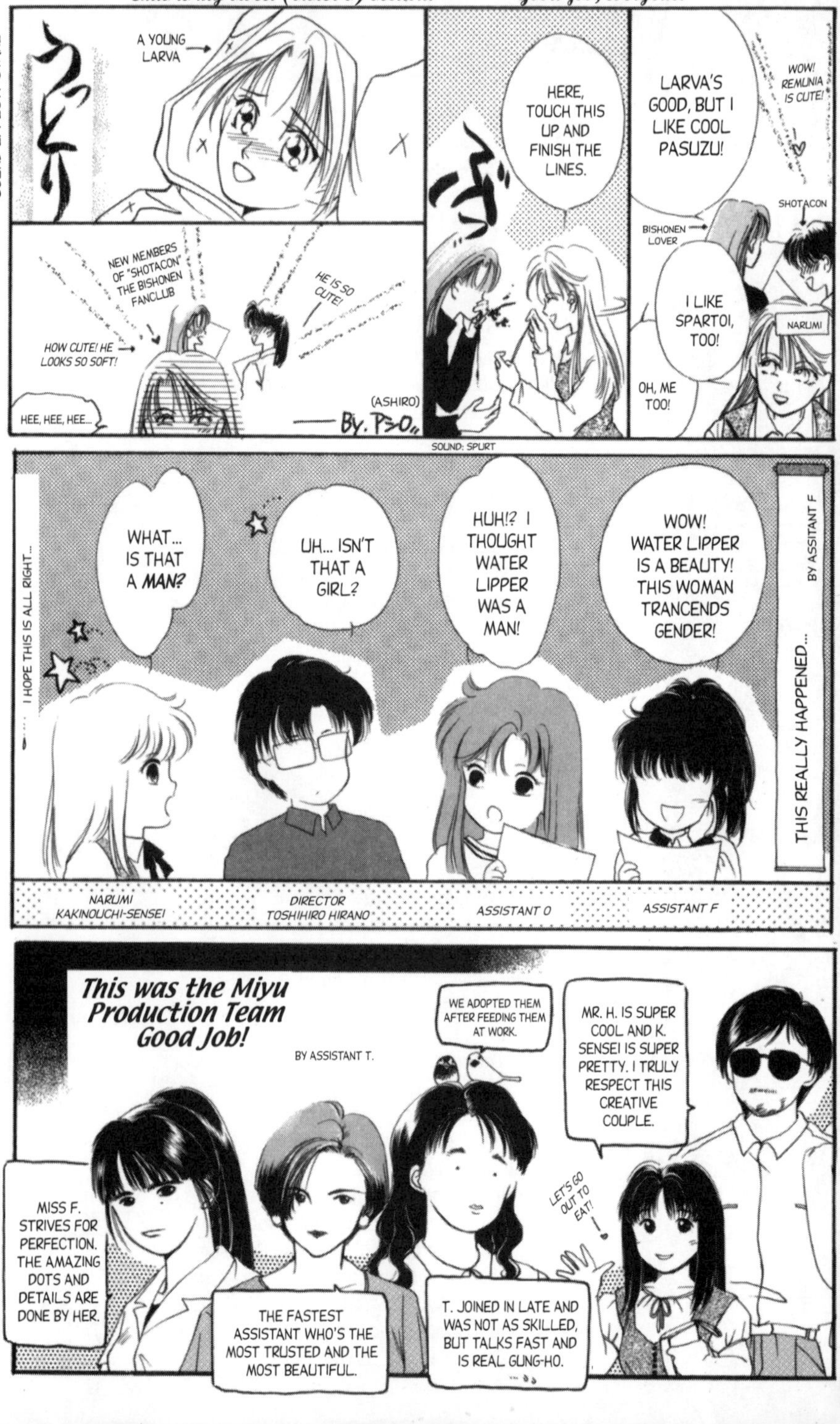

WOW! REMUNIA IS CUTE!
LARVA'S GOOD, BUT I LIKE COOL PASUZU!
SHOTACON
BISHONEN LOVER
I LIKE SPARTOI, TOO!
NARUMI
OH, ME TOO!
HERE, TOUCH THIS UP AND FINISH THE LINES.
SOUND: SPURT
SOUND EFFECT: STARE
A YOUNG LARVA
NEW MEMBERS OF "SHOTACON" THE BISHONEN FANCLUB
HE IS SO CUTE!
HOW CUTE! HE LOOKS SO SOFT!
HEE, HEE, HEE...
(ASHIRO)
By. P.O.
THIS REALLY HAPPENED...
BY ASSISTANT F
WOW! WATER LIPPER IS A BEAUTY! THIS WOMAN TRANCENDS GENDER!
HUH!? I THOUGHT WATER LIPPER WAS A MAN!
UH... ISN'T THAT A GIRL?
WHAT... IS THAT A MAN?
I HOPE THIS IS ALL RIGHT...
NARUMI KAKINOUCHI-SENSEI
DIRECTOR TOSHIHIRO HIRANO
ASSISTANT O
ASSISTANT F
This was the Miyu Production Team Good Job!
BY ASSISTANT T.
WE ADOPTED THEM AFTER FEEDING THEM AT WORK.
MR. H. IS SUPER COOL AND K. SENSEI IS SUPER PRETTY. I TRULY RESPECT THIS CREATIVE COUPLE.
LET'S GO OUT TO EAT!
MISS F. STRIVES FOR PERFECTION. THE AMAZING DOTS AND DETAILS ARE DONE BY HER.
THE FASTEST ASSISTANT WHO'S THE MOST TRUSTED AND THE MOST BEAUTIFUL.
T. JOINED IN LATE AND WAS NOT AS SKILLED, BUT TALKS FAST AND IS REAL GUNG-HO.

rting from left side and working around the bunny's face clockwise:

Left face, little text: Miyu will take a little break.
Left face, BIG text: See you again!!
Left ear: I love Quarl and Cait Sith the best (and their voices, too).
Between ears: I could never beat Miyu. Oh, no...
Right ear: Larva, are you sure you're okay like this?
Right face: I'm getting hot!!
With sweatdrops: It's hot! It's hot!
Along chin: Hopefully we can cover the rest of the story of Carlua and Remures next time...

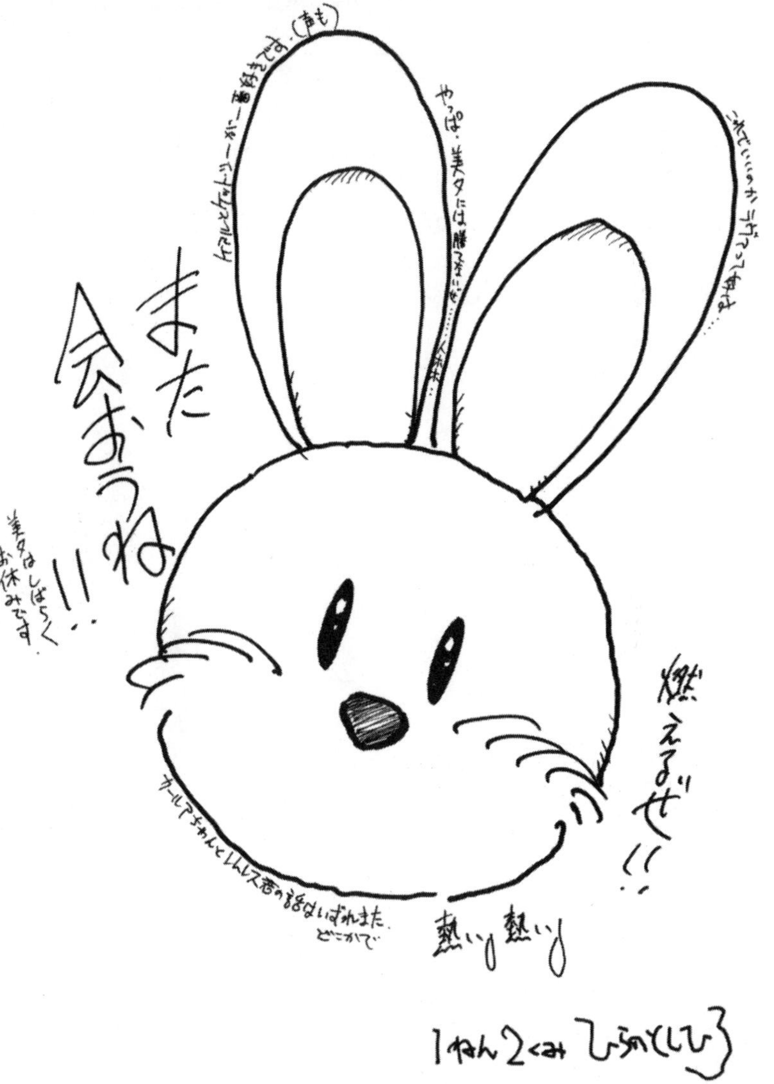

また会おうね!!
美夕はしばらくお休みです。
燃えるぜ!!
熱い熱い
1ねん2くみ ひらのとしひろ

1st Grade, 2nd class, Toshiro Hirano

d of New Vampire Princess Miyu Volume 5 《新 吸血姫 美夕五・完》

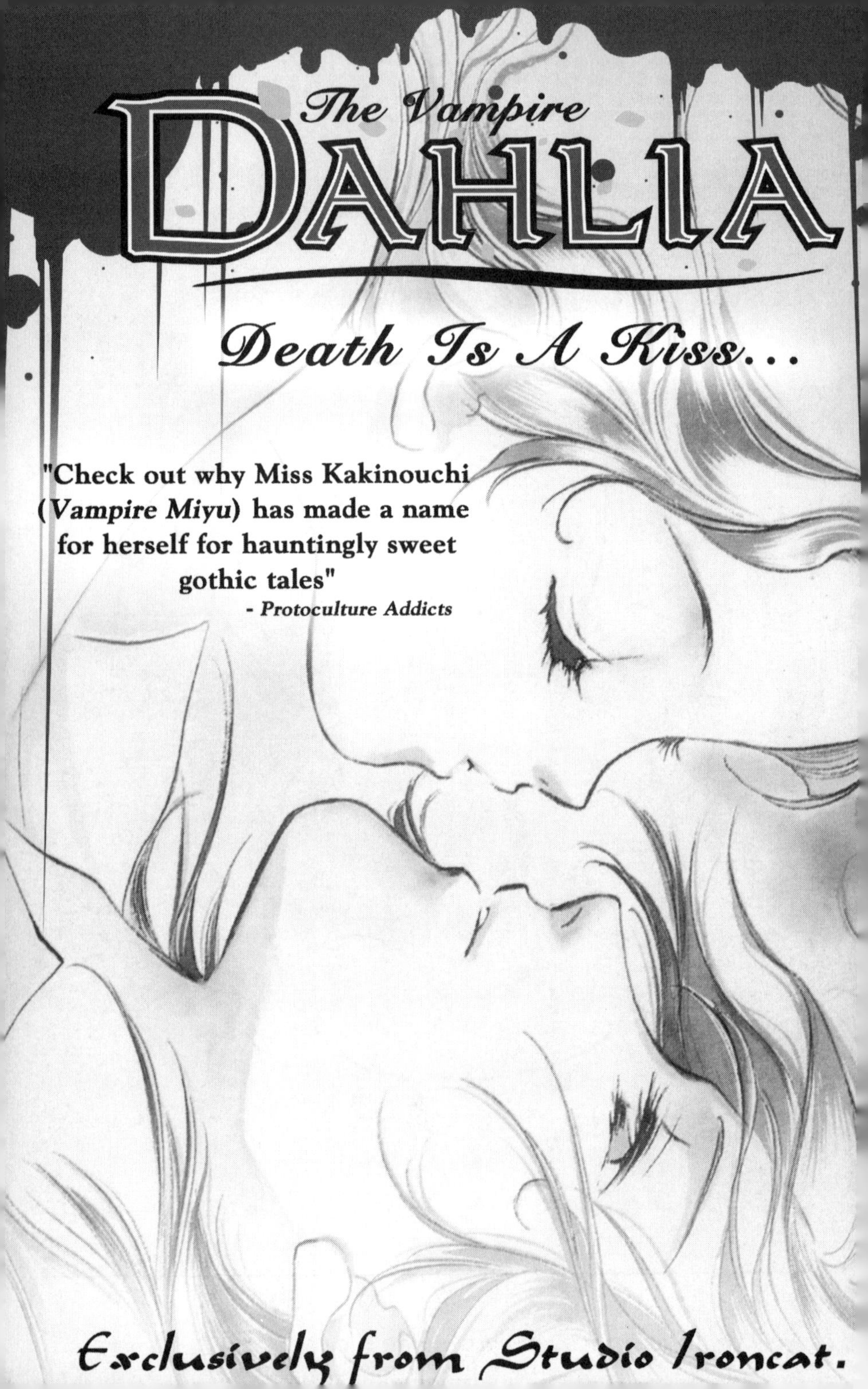
The Vampire
DAHLIA
Death Is A Kiss...
"Check out why Miss Kakinouchi (*Vampire Miyu*) has made a name for herself for hauntingly sweet gothic tales"
- *Protoculture Addicts*
Exclusively from Studio Ironcat.

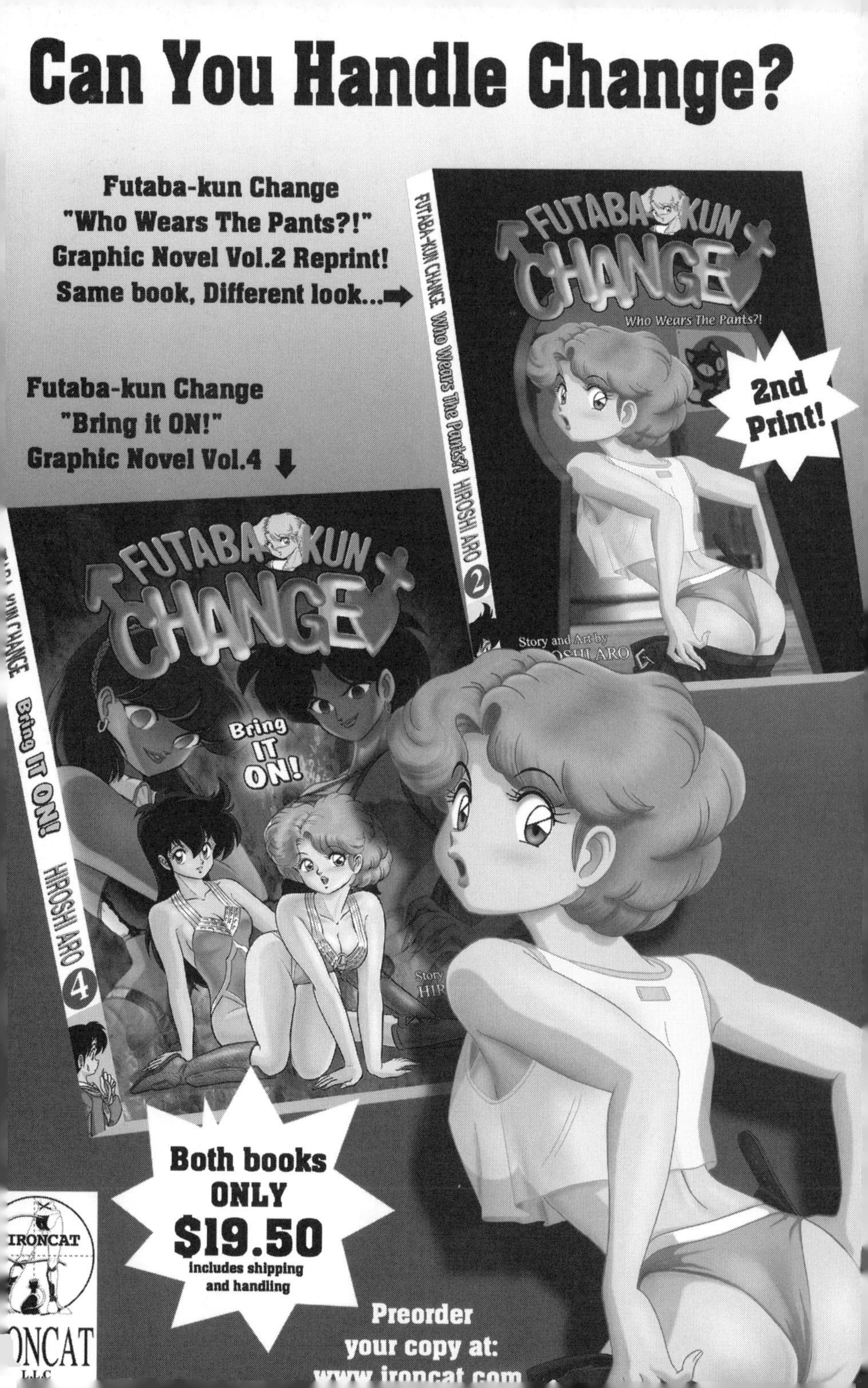
Can You Handle Change?
Futaba-kun Change
"Who Wears The Pants?!"
Graphic Novel Vol.2 Reprint!
Same book, Different look...
FUTABA-KUN CHANGE Who Wears The Pants?! HIROSHI ARO 2
FUTABA KUN CHANGE
Who Wears The Pants?!
2nd Print!
Story and Art by
Futaba-kun Change
"Bring it ON!"
Graphic Novel Vol.4
FUTABA KUN CHANGE
Bring IT ON!
Bring It ON! HIROSHI ARO 4
Both books
ONLY
$19.50
includes shipping
and handling
IRONCAT
Preorder
your copy at:
www.ironcat.com

新

美

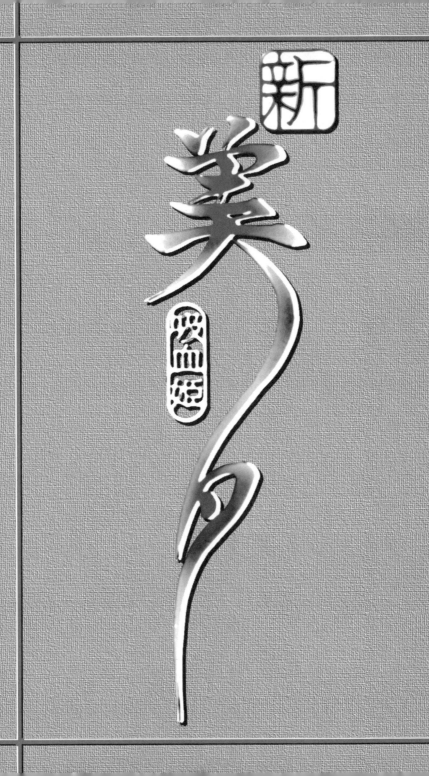